EARLY ENGLISH DRAMA

Garland Reference Library of the Humanities
(Volume 1313)

EARLY ENGLISH DRAMA

An Anthology

edited by

John C. Coldewey

Garland Publishing, Inc.
New York & London
1993

Library of Congress Cataloguing-in-Publication Data

Early English drama: an anthology / edited by John C. Coldewey.
     p. cm. — (Garland reference library of the humanities; vol. 1313)
     ISBN 0-8240-4699-4 (acid-free paper)
     ISBN 0-8240-5465-2 (pbk.: acid-free paper)
     1. English drama—To 1500. 2. English drama—Early modern and
Elizabethan, 1500–1600. 3. Mysteries and miracle-plays, English. 4. Moralities,
English. I. Coldewey, John C. II. Series.
PR1260.E27   1992
822'.208—dc20   92–7686
                                                      CIP

Printed on acid-free, 250-year-life paper
Manufactured in the United States of America

For Christine

Contents

Acknowledgments

Inevitably, an editor incurs many debts. Some are large and amorphous debts of influence, attitude, and example that cannot be acknowledged adequately or completely. Such are the longstanding debts I owe to Donald C. Baker and John Murphy, EETS editors of *The Digby Plays* and my mentors years ago, and the debts I owe to my students today, who continue to teach me to see with fresh eyes. Other debts are easier to locate and a pleasure to pay. I am first of all indebted to A.S.G. Edwards at the University of Victoria, who has encouraged me for some time to put together an anthology that would reflect my sense of the main theatrical tradition in late medieval England. I owe thanks to Michael Preston at the University of Colorado, who generously supplied me with versions of playtexts from the electronic text archive of medieval drama there; to Tom Ridgeway from the Humanities and Arts Computer Center at the University of Washington, and to Toni Bennett as well, who helped wrestle the electronic text files into more manageable form. To Richard Emmerson at Western Washington University, to Lawrence Clopper at the University of Indiana, to Christine Rose Coldewey at Portland State University, to Míceál Vaughan and, especially, to David Fowler at the University of Washington, I owe great thanks for checking and correcting various segments of my texts and glosses.

I owe an enormous debt to the ABC's of past anthology editors: Joseph Q. Adams, David Bevington, and Arthur C. Cawley, whose works I have used with an ever increasing appreciation for their judgment and expertise. This alphabetical listing can be extended neatly to D and E—Norman Davis and Mark Eccles—the fine and careful EETS editors of, respectively, *The Non-Cycle Plays and Fragments* and *The Macro Plays*. Farther ranging debts are owed others: to Milla Riggio of Trinity College in Hartford and John Hopper at AMS Press, who allowed me to see proofs of *Wisdom*, then being prepared for publication; to the Graduate School and to the English Department at the University of Washington, which supported my efforts on this book with a Faculty Research Grant and a research assistant; and to Paula Ladenburg from Garland Publishing, whose patience and good advice have saved me from a good many more stylistic or typographical errors than remain here, which are in any case my own responsibility.

Personal thanks are due to William Liddell of Birkbeck College at the University of London, and to Vic Gray, County Archivist of Essex, both of whom urged this collection and supported my efforts at each turn; to my two sons, Christopher and Devin, who patiently endured the countless hours of my distracted attention, and who have always taken a baffled delight in my scholarship. And finally, in the ancient tradition that the last should be first, I happily acknowledge the debt to my wife, Christine Rose Coldewey, who offered every comfort and encouragement through the course of this project, who gave unstintingly of her own great expertise in Middle English language and literature, and who acted as happy governor, guide, and spur to my many enthusiasms.

Introduction

Fewer than thirty-five vernacular English play texts and fragments survive from the late middle ages. Of them, four are long compilations of dramatized Biblical episodes that illustrate the cycle of human destiny from the creation of the world to the last judgment. These, the famous cycle plays, were vast, corporately-sponsored productions, performed by prosperous cities on special feast days like Corpus Christi Day or Whitsunday, usually with the cooperation of local craft and religious guilds. They flourished from the late fourteenth until the mid-sixteenth centuries. Manuscripts of complete Biblical cycles have survived from York, Chester, and the vicinity of Wakefield. The text of a fourth cycle, known as the N-Town Plays, derives from East Anglia, though its origins and history of performance are obscure. It may have been a travelling text, a compilation of various playtexts gathered together by a travelling company, or perhaps a flexible sequence of plays sponsored by a monastic institution. In addition, a few pageants, or individual episodes, from other cycle plays also survive, and they attest to the vigor of the cycle play tradition in a number of towns like Coventry, Newcastle, and Beverley. The list of sponsoring towns has been extended considerably with the systematic collection of documentary records of play performance undertaken by the Records of Early English Drama project at the University of Toronto. Understandably then, it has long been thought that the mainstream tradition of late medieval drama was defined by the cycles, whose scope, shape, poetic elaboration, and production difficulties have rightly attracted a good deal of attention.

But most of the early English theatrical productions were not connected with cycle plays at all. Recent scholarship on records of early English drama has shown that in number, frequency of performance, and geographical distribution, *non-cycle* plays were the rule, not the exception, for hundreds of communities in England during the late middle ages. This is particularly true for East Anglia—the region including Norfolk and Suffolk and parts of Cambridgeshire and Essex—though the activity was by no means limited to

1

that area of the country; everywhere, it seems, as performance records now show, non-cycle plays were an astonishingly popular source of entertainment, instruction, and profit. Earlier prevailing notions of the English dramatic tradition are slow to change, however, and it should come as no surprise that in our anthologies of medieval English drama few non-cycle plays appear.

One purpose of this collection, then, is to present as large a sampling of non-cycle plays as possible, in the belief that they represent a different mode of dramatic composition and theatrical experience from the cycle plays. The term "non-cycle" is here taken literally to refer to plays that have not come down to us as parts of one or another of the large cycle enterprises. Generally speaking, such plays fall into three categories: saint plays, morality plays, and Biblical or secular history plays. Saint plays dramatize the lives, the conversions, the miracles, and sometimes the grisly deaths of saints; they are represented in this collection by the Digby plays of *Mary Magdalene* and *The Conversion of St. Paul*. Morality plays use allegorical figures to promote the path of righteousness and to demonize the morally wrong paths a typical human being might take in the familiar journey through life; they are represented here by *Mankind*, *Everyman*, *Wisdom*, and the fragmentary *Pride of Life*. Biblical or secular history plays, which reenact strange, violent, or otherwise compelling plots on the stage, are represented here by the Croxton *Play of the Sacrament*, the Digby *Killing of the Children*, the Brome *Abraham and Isaac*, and the fragmentary *Dux Moraud*.

Although documentary evidence indicates that a wide variety of non-cycle plays were performed in many places around the country, few complete texts survived the purifying efforts of the Reformation. Even fragments of these plays are valuable, then, for they offer unique examples of what were once far more extensive traditions, with characteristic forms, subject matter, and dramatic conventions that can now only be inferred. A number of fragments are thus included here as well. *The Pride of Life* and *Dux Moraud* have already been mentioned, but there are others, equally important. The first of these, the Durham Prologue, provides a glimpse of how audience and players interacted very early in the history of this theatre. Another, the Reynes Extracts, consists of two fragments that illustrate the poetic grace, beauty, and exuberance that could attend a play's composition; they also testify to the profit motive apparent in many non-cycle play productions. The two surviving versions of the Norwich Grocers' Play demonstrate, in turn, how shifting ideologies tempered the impulse to tell the same story.

In addition to the above plays and fragments, four of the liveliest pageants from Wakefield, Chester, and York have been included in this collection for purposes of contrast. These pageants appear outside of their cycle frameworks, and thus lack some crucial part of their original resonance. Still, they provide instructive examples of how cycle and non-cycle plays could differ in aim and accomplishment. The first of these pageants, the Wakefield

Noah, dramatizes the well-known *contretemps* between old Noah and his shrewish wife. The arguments, threats, name calling, and physical beatings are no doubt less amusing when played realistically than when played in a broad, comic-book manner, but the verbal interchanges are brilliant examples of the playwright's gift for dialogue and staging. The Chester *Abraham and Isaac,* an otherwise quite ordinary cycle pageant, offers a useful counterpoint to the non-cycle Brome *Abraham and Isaac,* with which it shares hundreds of lines. A comparison of the two readily shows how non-cycle plays stretch the limits of theatrical decorum. The Wakefield *Second Shepherds' Play,* perhaps the most famous of all cycle pageants, and certainly best-known work of the playwright known as the Wakefield Master, provides an excellent example of how a powerful imagination might reshape the audience's understanding of a Biblical event—in this case the Incarnation—by incorporating extra-Biblical material. Last of all, the York *Crucifixion,* performed by the pinners (or nailmakers) illustrates how affective piety and a sponsoring guild's occupation could be brought together in a famous Biblical episode for mutual reflection.

None of the plays, dramatic fragments, or pageants brought together here should be construed as simple, rudimentary, or primitive texts that merely share pretenses to dramatic representation. They are far more than simple, historically interesting attempts to do what the Elizabethan theatre would accomplish more fully later on. A far more useful—and more accurate—way to characterize them is as remarkable celebrations of late medieval English theatricality, which reached its climax in the fifteenth and sixteenth centuries. Even Shakespeare's stage, which excelled verbally but was constrained by limited space, costumes, and machinery, could not surpass the sumptuous and spirited productions of the earlier popular theatre. In fact, not until the extravaganzas of the nineteenth and twentieth centuries would dramatic spectacle be exploited so freely and effectively as it was in the late medieval theatre. Indeed, it is hard to say which of the plays here is the most spectacular: the Digby *Mary Magdalene,* for example, with its elaborately balanced deployment of scaffold stages and devices, its portable "ship" pageant sailing in and out of the playing place, its exotic mix of Kings from the mysterious East, abstractions from the land of allegory, Biblical figures and local English sailors; or the Croxton *Play of the Sacrament,* with its exploding oven, detachable human hand, and parodic folk routines; or the Brome *Abraham and Isaac,* with its emphasis on pathos and repeated milking of the audience for sympathy; or the Digby *Conversion of St. Paul,* with its fantastic pyrotechnic displays, its lightning and fire and billowing smoke that accompanies Belial and Mercury's howled devilling, its uniquely mobile audience that apparently shifts from one playing place to another; or *Mankind* or *Wisdom,* with their brilliant and rich and suggestive costuming, their clever

Vice figures, their astonishing mix of mystical enterprise and obscene scatological dialogue; or the Digby *Killing of the Children,* with its macabre and gruesome onstage slaughter of innocent babes, bizarrely counterpointed by the farcical soldier, Watkin, who is comically thrashed by outraged mothers; or *Dux Moraud,* with its bizarre and unique exploration of societal taboos—incest, infanticide, matricide. All the non-cycle plays found here are visually spectacular, and many employ music as part of the show; all abound in special effects and wild figures, and all go well beyond the pat Horatian formula to delight and instruct. In the past, this theatricality has seldom been explored by literary critics or theatre historians, in part because the play texts were not familiar, but also because more serious questions about how theatrical elements enhance verbal meaning and how texts signify in performance have only recently been posed. One way or another the plays here promise to challenge all our interpretive skills.

Technically speaking, these plays are all comedies that amply demonstrate Christianity's salvific vision in highly accomplished theatrical ways. Yet we must also be wary of construing them simply as examples of late medieval high-jinx or circus-like chambers of horror, to fasten *only* on possibilities for spirited performance. Darker visions and more serious voices in late medieval culture find expression here as well, and many of the main conflicts in the plays still trouble humanity. The tension between human love and higher love, and the difficulty of squaring common sense and ethical behavior, for example, are not issues limited to the fifteenth or sixteenth centuries. Likewise, psychological themes worked out in the morality plays, like the consequences of guilt and retribution, or the puzzle and pathos of a good life gone bad, along with the specter of death's certain oblivion—individual and shared— are issues that are still conjured with today. And even when distanced by humor, scenes of torture remain viscerally affecting, perpetually hateful, perpetually familiar. Ugly psychological or physical cruelties portrayed in detail can be rendered more palatable, but not less appalling, simply because they happen to be planned and executed by gloating villains who are ultimately defeated, as in the Digby *Killing of the Children.* There, the horror and brutality may be mitigated by the black comedy involving Watkin, but both are finally overmatched by the contagious grief of the bereft mothers and the horror of the event itself.

Thus, when the bogeymen and spooks of the medieval imagination show up in these plays, displaying their stage antics and routines, it should be recognized that their theatrical power, often broadly comic, is regularly countered by a thematic and equally dramatic emphasis on human sorrow and loss, on the ugly power of personal rancor, on the baffling banality of evil, on the individual character's place in the somber earthbound scheme of Christian suffering. The unexpected reversals of fortune catapulting representative figures like those in *Everyman* and *Mankind* into salvific history remain simply that: the final movement in a complex orchestration of justice and mercy. In these plays, hope shrinks before the certainty of dark justice, and all of them point toward the end of the human pilgrimage through a vale of tears.

In the meantime, if we need to beware the extravagant outpourings of evil characters in these plays—the famous rantings of Herod, the shrieks and private calculations of devils and vices, the pompings and boastings of Kings—we should be equally suspicious of excesses emanating from idealized and sometimes allegorized characters aligned on the side of good. Their blatantly pious speeches and often tedious explanations of doctrinal niceties offer something of a tip-off. The pure goodness of otherwise human figures in these plays, along with the extempore moralizing of interpreters in prologues, epilogues, and running commentaries, have all too often been taken at face value in modern criticism. They should not be. What we are faced with in these plays is not the use of the profane to *prove* the sacred, like the titillating exemplum embedded in a sermon; nor do we find its opposite, the systematic subversion of sacred truths, of moral or ethical themes, by the sheer power of theatrical representation. In the poetic experience peculiar to the late-medieval theatre, primal elements of good and evil seem oddly and yet inextricably bound together by their own overstated theatricality: the plays horrify and amuse and comfort all at the same time. They pander to extreme tastes for violence and grotesque action onstage, while offering rationalizations—which once seemed true—all in the same texts. Theatrical exuberance forces an amalgam of ancient text and popular cultural forms so that these plays might reach forward to a timeless present. Ultimately, in the non-cycle plays especially, however far back their original stories may stretch, what is underscored by use of costume, accent and gesture must be held in mind: that actions of the distant past permeate the present, just as present actions determine the future. By all accounts these dramatic texts resonated in their original theatrical space much as they resonate today, and in them can be found touching explorations of recurrent conflicts and universal themes, surprising strategies, ideological face-offs, and fictive, simplified, affecting examples of men and women caught at the extremities of Christian life.

A word should perhaps be said at this point about two traditions of early English drama which are not represented here, but nevertheless existed alongside the cycle and non-cycle plays. The first is the liturgical drama— Latin drama that apparently began much earlier than most vernacular forms, ordinarily performed under monastic or other ecclesiastical auspices throughout much of Europe. The influence and significance of liturgical drama is still unclear, given its limited audience, pious intent, and ritual mode of production. The second theatrical tradition, that of the folk play and related festival celebration, was popular everywhere in the English countryside. Like liturgical drama, folk drama developed earlier than the cycle or non-cycle plays; unlike liturgical drama, it outlasted them all the way down to the present, where it is still widely practiced. This tradition includes mummers' plays, Robin Hood plays, morris dances, ritual animal disguises, plough plays, May celebrations and other such examples of seasonal ceremony. Unfortunately, apart from a sixteenth-century Robin Hood play, virtually no texts for any folk plays have survived intact from before the eighteenth century, and we must be content with the occasional folk episodes or characters smuggled into more orthodox texts from this fascinating edge of popular culture. As alternative theatrical forms, both liturgical drama and folk drama invite further study; their connections to the plays printed here can only be surmised at present. The same is true for the Cornish plays—the *Cornish Ordinalia* and *St. Mariasek,* medieval cousins of the English plays, but written in Cornish.

The plays in this collection date from the late fourteenth century to the third quarter of the sixteenth century, easily spanning a hundred and fifty years. By the end of the sixteenth century the dramatic forms they represent had passed away, but they left their mark on the mainstream tradition of English drama. Earlier critical attempts to rescue medieval plays from the dreaded characterization as "pre-Shakespearean drama," indicating a kind of warm-up for the real thing, have often emphasized unique "medieval" qualities of the texts while ignoring their remarkable theatrical legacies, particularly the contribution of non-cycle plays to the long continuum of the English dramatic tradition. It is certainly true that by the 1590s the native tradition of guild sponsorship and performance was viewed as outmoded—not simply old-fashioned and passé, but completely obsolete in doctrine, dogma, ritual echo, and satiric possibility. The rude mechanicals of *A Midsummer Night's Dream*—such clear parodies of apparent theatrical innocence, now cast in the harsher light and expectations of professional productions in London—appear on the public stage without a trace of nostalgia. The break seems complete, and the mode of theatrical experience that the cycle plays represented is for all practical purposes dead until Brecht's and Pirandello's experiments in the twentieth century.

But theatrical traditions represented by the non-cycle plays provide obvious bridges from the early English stages to Elizabethan and Jacobean theatres and beyond. As the careers of these late medieval plays came to a close—and they had, after all, flourished for a very long time—their dramatic energy was subsumed into some forms and appropriated by others, fragmented into locally sponsored disguisings, for example, or, in the court, into masques. Their stagecraft now informed royal entries and civic processions. Their outward interest in historical and Biblical matter fed into the more realistic traditions of history plays and chronicle plays; the broad strokes that depicted internal conflicts and tensions, and that allegorical map of spiritual and psychological struggle, the *psychomachia,* found representation in more realistically-oriented figures, characters who in later guise would display conflicted selves in political, social, or polemically-charged arenas, and in high renaissance tragedies.

As the morality plays, for example, shaded into interludes, they provided characters and character types, thematic resonance, and an emphasis on internal moral struggles, all of which show up in the next generation of Elizabethan theatre. It is instructive to compare the indulgent and dismissive treatment of the rude mechanicals in *A Midsummer Night's Dream*—obvious figures of communal craft productions—with the roles that the Good and Bad Angels in *Dr. Faustus* are allowed to play. These figures, clearly deriving from an earlier tradition, are here taken as serious agents and integrated into Marlowe's play without losing a shred of their original power. In the late Elizabethan and Jacobean age, the theatrical experience of conversions and inner struggle so artfully set out in the non-cycle plays, along with the dramaturgical expertise that had developed over the course of repeated productions, became part of a more verbally-textured and visually focused professional tradition. Other streams of the late medieval theatrical tradition joined this same river—folk plays, classical plays, learned neo-Latin plays from the universities, Italian *commedia dell arte* and *commedia erudite* characters and routines. Each brought unique opportunities for theatrical expansion; each added further important dimensions to the popular theatre in the great golden age of English drama.

In editing these plays I have striven to provide readable and accurate versions of the texts, basing them on the electronic archive of medieval drama texts at the University of Colorado. I have retained most of their Middle English characteristics, adding glosses and notes as seemed appropriate for ready understanding. In the brief introductions to individual plays I have tried to indicate a few of their more salient aspects, including basic manuscript information, references to standard scholarly editions and manuscript facsimiles, and useful critical sources. The more curious reader may want to consult these as well as the sources referred to in the footnotes and listed in the Suggestions for Further Reading at the back of the book.

As might be expected, editorial requirements shifted radically from play to play according to the demands of the surviving text. Generally speaking, I have respected scribal orthographic conventions, but I have regularly and silently made some emendations: *th* is substituted for thorn where it occurs, and *g* for yogh. Where necessary I modernize the usage of *u* and *v* and, less frequently, *i* and *j*; changed the characteristic East Anglian scribal *x* to *sh* and *qu* to *wh* wherever it appears; transformed pronominal "the" to "the[e]" when necessary for sense; rationalized the use of upper and lower case letters, and added light modern punctuation. I have provided a full cast list for each play, incorporating partial lists that sometimes appear in the play texts, and I have regularized speech prefixes throughout.

The Reynes Extracts

The Reynes Extracts derive their name from the manuscript in which they were preserved, a commonplace book originally belonging to Robert Reynes of Acle, a village in Norfolk. The book, which dates from the last half of the fifteenth century, contains two dramatic fragments, one from the beginning and one from the ending of a play or plays. Reynes was churchwarden in Acle in 1474, but little else is known of him. The dialect of the fragments is mainly East Anglian with a few Northerly forms.

The first speech, by the character Delight, offers a charming catalogue of worldly pleasures—of nature untamed and tamed, of outdoor landscapes and activities, and of courtly sights and sounds. The last line of the first stanza is problematic, since it seems to be spoken by a female, perhaps another character, or perhaps a spectator. The character Delight, however, is male—as he tells us, a "ladde," and the list of delights ends with a special appreciation for courtly women's "whyte pappys poppyd vp prately." These and the other pleasures described in this speech provide a rare and poetic look at ordinary joys the world held during the later fifteenth century. Whether Delight was planned as a Prologue, a vice figure, or some other kind of character in a morality play cannot be known, since the play itself has not survived. Any estimation of Delight's importance to the play would of course depend on what kind of character was originally intended. The speech is written in ten six-line tail-rhyme stanzas, rhyming *aabaab*. The meter of the lines varies from two to four stresses.

The second speech, an Epilogue, offers congratulations to the audience for their proper behavior, followed by an apology for any faults in the performance, and an invitation to a church ale to be held after the play. Church ales, sometimes called "drinkings," were one means a parish church had to make money during the late middle ages, and they acted as a popular way to bring the community together in a festive mood. The humble and apologetic demeanor of the Epilogue acts as an enticement to the ale, while the linkage between the play and the ale itself testifies to a profit motive behind the performance of some early English non-cycle plays. The speech is written in two thirteen-line stanzas, rhyming *ababbcbcbdddb* and *ababbcbcdeeed*. Most of the lines have four stresses, but the meter varies, particularly in the shorter lines.

The text of the Reynes extracts survives in Bodleian Library MS. Tanner 407, ff. 43v-44v. It was first printed by Iris Calderhead in "Morality Fragments from Norfolk," *Modern Philology,* xiv (1916), 1-9. The standard scholarly edition, by Norman Davis, appears in the EETS *Non-Cycle Plays and Fragments*; a facsimile of the manuscript, also edited by Davis, appears in *Non-Cycle Plays and the Winchester Dialogues* (see Suggestions for Further Reading).

THE REYNES EXTRACTS

A.   *A SPEECH OF DELIGHT*

Lo, here is a ladde lyght,   *cheerful lad*
Al fresch I you plyght,   *assure you*
 Galant and joly.
Wyl ye knowe what I hyght?   *am called*
5 My name, serys, is Delyght.
 [I hope not ful holy.]*

Holy, quod sche? Nay, let be!
Be Crist, it acordyth not with me,   *does not suit*
 But sporte, myrthe, and play
10 Me reioyceth for to see;
The worldys wunderys and vanyté,
 Therinne delyght I ay.   *ever*

For me semet it is to delyght   *it seems to me a delight*
To behelde the firmament lyght,   *heavens*
15 The cours of sterrys to kenne,   *to know*
The sunne with his bemys bryght,
The mone how he refulsyth the nyght,   *moon/makes radiant*
 The planetys in her circumferens renne.   *their orbits*

The skyes in her coloures rake,   *their/shift quickly*
20 The therke sladdes of clowdes blake—   *dark billows/pale clouds*
 This reioyceth me above.   *on high*
Than of the erthe delyght I take   *Then*
To see the florent wodys ther leves shake,   *flowering woods*
 The ryverys rennyng by therinne dyvers fysshes move.   *running by, where*

---

6. "Hope" is used here in its Northerly sense, "think, believe." This line may be spoken by a female member of the audience, or perhaps by a female vice character, or even by Delight himself (in a higher voice?). In any case the next line (7) responds to a female figure ("sche").

11

25 I se thes hey hyllys wher is holsom ayer;
    Benethe, the redolent medowes with ther flowres fayer,
      The therke mystes how it ascendys.   *dark fog*
    In the valeys of the cornys ylke ayer   *Through the grain-filled valley's air itself*
    I se dyvers fowlys to the wodes repayer—   *return to the woods*
30   Ther swetly syngang me mekyl amendys.   *sweet singing greatly cheers me*

    I se in these gay gardeynes wher holsum erbys spryng   *herbs*
    These pererys, the pomerys, the venys,   *pear-trees/orchards/vines*
      that swete frutys bryng
    The reed rosys and the lelyes whyte.
    I se in the gret see ther shyppys ever seylyng,   *see/sea*
35 Also how it ebbyt and flowit and fysshes therin swymmyng,   *ebbs/flows*
    The whavys how they waltyr, and se the qwall fyght.   *waves/surge/whales*

    In the hore hethys I se the hare sterte,   *bare heath*
    The forant dere huntyd, the bukke and the harte,   *fallow*
    And the swyfte grefoundes renne;   *greyhounds*
40 The foxe huntyd with howndes in the gret coverte,   *thickets*
    The swyfte flyght of hawkes, the fowlys reverte,   *turning back*
    The fawkonerys rennyng throw thykke and throwe thynne.   *running*

    Also I am gretly delyghtand   *delighting*
    In fayer courses swyftly renand,   *charges/running*
45   In harneys gledryng bryght;   *glittering*
    Stately howsys beheldand   *beholding*
    Glased with storys glasand,   *windowed with stories in glass*
      Pynnakelys ful of fanys gloriously dyght.   *Turrets/flags (or vanes)/displayed*

    Precyos aray, that plesyth me gretly,   *clothing*
50 The swet musy[ci]auns in dyvers melody,
    The cumlynesse of iche creature;   *beauty*
    And the bewté of women specyaly,
    With ther whyte pappys poppyd up prately—   *breasts/pertly*
    That passeth al other, as me semet in sure.   *surpasses/seems certain to me*

55 Me seyng now these solacious sythys,   *pleasing sights*
    Therfor in hem al my delyght is   *them*
      So sovereynlyche aboven alle.   *supremely*
    This warlde so preciously pyght is,   *arrayed*
    Therinne delyght I with alle myn mythis,   *might*
60   As for wele most speciall.   *good fortune*

B.   *AN EPILOGUE*

Now, wursheppful sovereyns that syttyn here in syth,   *sight*
   Lordys and ladyes and frankelens in fay,   *gentlemen/faith*
With alle maner of abesyans we recomaunde us ryght   *deference/commend ourselves*
   Plesantly to your persones that present ben in play;
5 And for your soferyng sylens that ye han kept this day
   In pleyng of oure play withowte ony resystens
Derely we thank yow with myght as we may,
   And for your laudabyl lystenyng in good audiens
That we have had this day.
10   And if we have passyd ony poynt in oure pleyng,
   Or moved ony materys in oure seyng
   That schuld be to youre personys displesyng,
We beseche you reporte it not away.   *not speak ill of us*

For trewly oure entent was wel to do,
15 And if ony fawte be ther fowndyn it is oure neglygensy;   *due to our negligence*
And short tyme avysement causet also,   *short notice*
   For lytell tyme of lernyng we have had sekerly,   *learning [our parts]/indeed*
   And ever man is not expert in eloquensy   *every*
     To utteryn his mater gayly onto your audiens.
20 Wherfor we beseche you of youre gret gentry   *kindness*
   The best to reporte of us in oure absens
     In every ilke a place.   *everywhere*
   Sovereyns alle insame,   *Masters all together*
   Ye that arn come to sen oure game,
25 We pray you alle in Goddys name
     To drynke ar ye pas;   *ere/go*

For an ale is here ordeyned be a comely assent*   *is hereby ordered by happy agreement*
   For alle maner of people that apperyn here this day,   *For everyone in attendance*
Unto holy chirche to ben incressement   *will go the profit*
30 Alle that excedith the costys of our play.

---

27. An ale: Church ales, sometimes called drinkings, were a popular means of bringing the parish or community together in a festive mood. Sometimes enormous quantities of drink were consumed.

The Durham Prologue

As its name would suggest, the play fragment known as The Durham Prologue survives in Durham. It consists of a single speech, written on a piece of parchment preserved at Durham Cathedral Library (Durham Dean and Chapter MS. I.2. Archidiac. Dunelm. 60, dorse), on the opposite side of a list dated 1359. The handwriting is from the late fourteenth or early fifteenth century, and both the manuscript and the dialect argue for North-easterly origins. The speech is written in six six-line stanzas, rhyming *aaabab,* the *a* lines having four stresses and the *b* lines three.

The Prologue calls on the audience to quiet down, and then summarizes the play that is to follow—apparently a version of the Theophilus legend. A rich knight loses all and despairs; he is tempted by the devil, but in the end resists through the intercession of the Blessed Virgin Mary. All details of the miraculous event in the play are of course lost with the play itself (assuming that it did exist in the first place), so it is difficult to say just how spectacular a show was being introduced. It is worth noticing, though, that the brief quotations from the Devil and from Mary, as well as the teasing allusions to action in the last stanza, are all clearly calculated as encouragement for the audience to stay.

The fragment did not appear in print until 1959, when it was published by June Cooling in "An Unpublished Middle English Prologue," *The Review of English Studies,* N.S. x (1959), 172-3. The standard scholarly edition of the Durham Prologue, by Norman Davis, appears in the EETS *Non-Cycle Plays and Fragments*; a facsimile of the manuscript, also edited by Davis, appears in *Non-Cycle Plays and the Winchester Dialogues* (see Suggestions for Further Reading).

THE DURHAM PROLOGUE

Pes, lordinges, I prai yow pes,		*Peace*
And of your noys ye stynt and ses,		*stop and cease*
Oure gamen to lett ne cry in pres		*play/hinder/together*
For your courtasy.		
5 That we yow play it is no les,		*What we play before you/lie*
Godmen, sikirly.		*certainly*
Oure myrth we make of a knyght		*entertainment*
That in his tyme was bold and wyght,		*noble*
Rich of rent, man mekill of myght,		*wealthy and mighty*
10 Proper and aupert.		*handsome/accomplished*
Swilk hap gan fall that on him light		*Such events occurred*
That put him to povert.		*into poverty*
Than he sight full wondre sore,		*sighed very painfully*
That so rich had ben before,		*Who*
15 And had nothyng to leve on more;		*more to live on*
His hert was full of grefe.		
The fende apierd untill him thor		*unto him there*
As man at his myschiefe.		*man in ruin*
He saide, "Man, lat be thi drede,		*worries*
20 Thou leve on me and my lede		*believe in/people*
And thou sall have all that the[e] nede		*shall*
Untill thi lyves ende."		
Bot sikirly, als we cone rede,		*certainly, as we might read*
Of Mary milde than was his mende.		*his remembrance*
25 Mary had of him pité,		
And till hir son scho knelid on kne,		*unto/she*
Sayd, "Son, yon body gif me.		*that person*
I chalange be right."		
Thus fro the fendes pousté		*power*
30 Boured scho the knyght.		*She fought for*

15

Me nedis yow no more to tell
O this thing how it befell;
Bot ye sall her, and ye will dwell,   *shall hear, if/stay*
   How that it sall be plaied.   *shall*
35 He kep yow all that herid hell,   *May he/who harrowed hell*
   And sithen up staied.   *and afterwards ascended*

Dux Moraud

The text of the fragment *Dux Moraud* survives in Bodleian Library MS. Eng. Poet. f.2 (R), on the opposite side of an early fourteenth-century Assize Roll for Norfolk and Suffolk. The roll records cases heard by the eminent judge William de Ormesby (d. 1317), who lived in Caister, Norfolk. The handwriting of the play fragment dates from the second quarter of the fifteenth century at the latest.

Dux Moraud is one of the strangest dramatic fragments to come down to us from the Middle Ages. Its lurid subject matter of incest, matricide and infanticide, guilt, self-recrimination and repentance seems almost Jacobean in sensibility, and nothing else like it is recorded in the drama of the era. All that survives of the play are the speeches of its principal character, Dux Moraud, though variations of its plot are echoed by poems in Latin and English. In the fragment, Dux Moraud bids farewell to his wife as she leaves on a journey; he makes amorous advances towards his daughter, who eventually murders her mother, bears a child to Dux Moraud and then murders it at his bidding. Reminded of his guilt and mortality by the sound of church bells, he finally turns away from his vicious life and repents. In this actor's part the verse form varies considerably, no doubt because it sometimes depends upon lines spoken by other characters. The most common stanza pattern is the six-line *aabccb,* with most lines having three stresses. Much of the rest of the stanzas are arranged in thirteen-line forms, rhyming *ababababcdddc.*

Dux Moraud was first edited by Wilhelm Heuser in "Dux Moraud, Einzelrolle aus einem verlorenen Drama des 14. Jahrhunderts," *Anglia,* xxx (1907), 180-208. Heuser also printed the poem that offers the closest version of the story dramatized by *Dux Moraud.* The standard scholarly edition, by Norman Davis, appears in the EETS *Non-Cycle Plays and Fragments*; a facsimile of the manuscript, also edited by Davis, appears in *Non-Cycle Plays and the Winchester Dialogues* (see Suggestions for Further Reading).

DUX MORAUD

[*Dramatis Personae:*

DUX MORAUD]
[HIS WIFE]
[HIS DAUGHTER]
[A PRIEST]

I.

[DUKE MORAUD.] Emperourys and kyngys be kende,		*lineage*
Erlys and barunnys bold		*Earls and barons*
Bachelerys and knytys to mende,		*Knight-bachelors/to remember*
Sueyerys and yemen to holde,		*Squires and yeomen to hold*
5 Knavys and pagys to sende,		
So parfyt that aryn to be solde,		*So fine/paid*
[*To the audience*]		
I prey yow, lordyngys so hende,		*courteous*
No yangelyngys ye mak in this folde		*jangling/gathering*
To-day;		
10 Als ye are louely in fas,		*As/face*
Set yow alle semly in plas,		*politely*
And I shal withoutyn falas		*deceit*
Schewe resounus here to youre pay.*		*to reward you*
Welthys I welde at my wylle,		*Riches I control*
15 In wor[l]d I am knowyn ful wyde,		
I [h]ave hert and hynd upon hille,		*have hart and hind*
I am gay on grounde for to glyde;		*handsome walking*
Semly ther I syt upon sille,		*Nobly/in state*
My wyf and my mené be my syde.		*minions*
20 I [commaund] yow tende me tylle,		*pay attention*

---

13. *i.e.*, I will reward your good behavior with a good show.

18

Or ellys I shal bate yowre pride — *abate, subdue*
  Wyt dynt, — *With force*
And therfor I warne yow onfere — *together*
That ye mak neyther criyng ne bere. — *outcry nor clamor*
25 If ye do, withoutyn duere, — *doubt*
    Strokys at yow shal I mynt. — *aim*

Duk Morawd I hot be name, — *I am called*
  Korteyser lord may be none, — *A more courteous*
Wol fer than rengnyt my fame, — *Far indeed ranges*
30 To be comly korownyt from one.* — *fittingly crowned*
I geve gode gyftys with game — *good/pleasure*
And save iche lordyng fro fone, — *every/from their foes*
Me bowyn bothe wylde and tame, — *To me bow*
Whethire so thei rydyn er gone — *ride or walk*
35   Ore scheppe. — *sail*
  I am dowty in dede,
  I am worly in wede, — *handsome in costume*
  I am semly on stede, — *noble on horseback*
    No weleny to me wyl I kyppe. — *treachery against/tolerate*

[His wife tells him she is going on a journey; he replies]
  II.
40 [MORAUD]. Dam, do now thi wylle
Thi wyage to fulfylle, — *voyage*
  To the wyl I be beyne. — *thy will/obedient*
For love I the[e] pray:
Rap the[e] faste in thi way, — *Hurry*
45 And cum hom sone ageyne. — *soon*

[His wife speaks to him; he replies]
  III.
[MORAUD]. Thorow the grace of that ich Kyngk — *same King*
That formyt us alle with wenne, — *Who/joy*
I shal me kepyn from fondyng — *temptation*
And als from blame and synne — *also*
50   With gras. — *[God's] grace*
Jhesu, als thou me wrowtys, — *as/created*
And with woundys sore me bowtys, — *sorely redeemed*
Save me fro wykyt thowtys,
    Jhesu, fayr in fas! — *face*

  IV.
55 Fare wel, my worlych wyf, — *worthy*

---

30. *i.e.*, However far my fame ranges there is no one more fittingly crowned.

Fare wel, love in lond,   *my love in this land*
Fare thou, semlyest lyf,   *most gracious creature*
  Fare thou happy in hond!   *in whatever you touch*

[Moraud addresses his daughter]
  V.
[MORAUD]. Maydyn so lovely and komly of syte,
60 I prey the[e] for love thou wyl lystyn to me;
    To here my resun I prey the[e] wel tythe,   *hear my proposal/at once*
    Love so deryn me most schewe to the[e];   *secret/must declare*
  My love to thi body is castyn so bryth,   *is inclined to thy body so beautiful*
  My wyl me most [h]ave of the[e].   *I must have*
65 Thou art lovely to leykyn and brythest with ryth,   *to sport with/right, goodness*
    I love the[e] in thowt, thou semly of ble,   *pretty/face*
      Be name.   *above all*
    Thou maydyn that moryst thi merthis with myth, *   *who increases/strongly*
    Derne dedys me most do be day and nyth   *Secret*
70   Be the worthiest woundyn, wyttyhest wyt   *By the best shaped, liveliest creature*
    The sothe tale I telle withoutyn ony blame.   *This true tale*

[His Daughter speaks; he replies]
  VI.
[MORAUD]. My fere so graciouse in gras,   *companion*
  Thanc thou shalt [h]aven of me,   *Thanks*
For thou art lovely in fas   *face*
75 And therto bryth berende of ble.   *endowed with fair complexion*
Now wyl I makyn solas,   *will I make for enjoyment*
  For my deryn love shalt thou be.   *secret*
Kys me now par amour in plas,   *as a lover here*
  Als thou art worly to se   *As/beautiful*
80   In syte.   *In appearance*
    Damysel, fayrest to fonde,   *fairest known*
    Als thou art semly to stonde,   *lovely to stand*
    Rap we us to wendyn in honde   *Let us hurry hand in hand*
    To thi chambyr that is so lovely of lythe.   *lovely to see*

[His wife has returned and Moraud is threatened]
[To his daughter]
  VII.
85 [MORAUD]. I am wondyn in gret dolour,   *wrapped in*
    With danger and tene I am bownde.   *hostility and anger/threatened*
To me thou geve tent [p]ar amowr,   *Heed me, lover*
  And lystne what I sey this stounde!   *hear/time*
Yon traytowr shal bewrey us this oure,   *betray/hour*

---

68. *i.e.*, Thou maiden whose pleasures are always increasing.

90	I telle the[e], semly on grownde;
	Than shul we [h]ave no socowr,
	But carys to us shal be fownde,
	Iwys.
	I ne may never be fawe
95	Tyl yon traytowr be slaw
	That is so rebel in sawe;
	Sorows mot ay to her kys.

90   I telle the[e], semly on grownde;   *gorgeous on earth*
     Than shul we [h]ave no socowr,   *help*
     But carys to us shal be fownde,   *troubles/brought*
     Iwys.   *Indeed*
     I ne may never be fawe   *glad*
95   Tyl yon traytowr be slaw   *slain*
     That is so rebel in sawe;   *rebellious in speech*
     Sorows mot ay to her kys.   *May sorrows ever embrace her*

[His Daughter kills his wife]
VIII.
[MORAUD]. [A]ves[to]w now slayne, be thi fay,   *Have you/faith*
the fol that dede us that tene?   *fool/harm*

IX.
100 A! Now am I mery this stound,   *time*
     That che is browt to that ded,   *she/death*
     For che suld a wreyd us on grownd,   *she would have betrayed*
     That ilke old schrewed qued,   *same old cursed villain*
     To sorowe che shuld us a found   *have brought*
105   That [h]adde ben to us ewyl red;   *an evil outcome*
     In care forsothe is che wownd,   *wrapped*
     And therfor I am mery to led   *go with*
     And gay.
     [D]amysel, lo[ve]ly of chere,   *face*
110   Mak we mary here,
     For care, withoutyn duere,   *doubt*
     Is went awey for ay.   *forever*

[His Daughter presents him with their child]
X.
[MORAUD]. A! [H]ave I begotyn this stownd   *time*
     A schyld so lovely of the[e],   *child*
115 I am in sorows wownd,   *wrapped*
     For care me most fle.   *I must*
     I prey the[e] in weltys now wownd   *with wounds now covered*
     That fot in syt myth I se.*   *That child*

[His daughter speaks; he replies]
XI.
[MORAUD]. Aa, byrd fayr and bryt,   *lady*
120 Do it out of my syt,
     For thowt I am ny sclawe!   *anxiety/nearly slain*
     [S]clo it in present   *Slay/at once*

117-118. *i.e.*, Now might I see that child covered in wounds (murdered).

That is my cowmaundement
Fast bry[n]g it of dawe!   *Take its life*

125 For al this lond I wold nowt
That lordys of this lond ad yt thowt,   *had*
That I ad synd be the[e].   *had sinned*
For serow and care that we shuld drywe   *endure*
We shuld led ever lyf ful rywe   *rueful*
130   And theron ay to be.   *forever*

Therfor I prey the[e],
For [thi] love of me,
Slo yt with thin hond!
Tha[n] shul we ben in pes,
135 Withoutyn ony lees,   *lies*
And avyn merth in lond.   *have*

[His Daughter kills the child and tells Moraud]
     XII.
[MORAUD]. [In es... al...] syng
Ther I sytte lovely in thowr,   *Where/a tower*
I thang the[e], lovely th[i]ng,
140 For thi w[e]rkyngys this oure.
For that parfyt tydyng
I geve the[e] [h]allys and bowr,   *halls and bower*
For thou, withoutyn lesyng,   *lying*
Pottyst me fro scham and dolowr.   *Saved me from*

     XIII.
145 In to kontre I wyl wend,   *country/go*
Ther to plete bothe fer and hend,   *plead (at law) both far and near*
With god d[edys] boun,   *ready, prepared*
Ther as it comyt in my mend   *Where(ever)/mind*
For to mete with lordys kynd   *gracious lords*
150   Bothe in fylde and toun.

     XIV.
Betyd me god [   ],   *Good...may happen to me*
Into contre [   ],
[   ]
But I prey the[e] this oure,
155 My der [   ] paramowre,
[   ]
I shal no more that [   ]
But sertys I shal fond
Withoutyn [   ]

160 [Ha god]day, worlych wyth! — *worthy creature*
Ha godday, lovely in lyth! — *Have a good day*
Par[ ] semly in syth,
    [ ] comly [ ].

XV.

I am my[r]thful and mery ma[r]kyd in mynd,
165 I am flour fayrest be fryt[h] for to fare, — *fairest flower seen walking by the wood*
I am fayrest in fas, ferly to fynd, — *face, wondrous to behold*
I am loveliche in lond, lyttest in lare, — *loveliest/quickest in wit*
I am comly and curteys and crafty of kynd,
  I am comly castyn fro knottys of care, — *happily released from bonds of sorrow*
170 I am lordly to leykyn lyt undyr lynd, — *to sport nimbly under a linden tree*
  I am semly to syttun syttys so sare, — *well able to sit in a seat so sorry*
    I wyl pres me in pride! — *thrust myself (forward)*
    Whan alle the lordys of this lond are gadered infere, — *together*
    I am flour of hem alle withoutyn duere, — *doubt*
175   And ellys I were woxyn of blamys ryt here — *otherwise I would be to blame*
    But I be ryal in rayis forto ryde. — *If I did not ride royally in costume*

[A church bell rings]
XVI.

[MORAUD]. A! now I here — *hear*
A belle ryngant ful nere,
    Yendyr in the kyrk. — *church*
180 Thether I wyl fare, — *go*
For I am in gret care — *very anxious*
    Ther sum god ded to werk. — *to do some good deed*

XVII

A synful katyf I am, — *wretch*
Synfully I [h]ave wrowt blam — *done wrong*
185   Be gret tyme of my lyfe.
Now, Cryst, ast thou me bowt; — *you have redeemed*
Forgeve me that blam that I [h]ave wrowt, — *have done*
    And mak me sumwhat blythe! — *happier*

For in this werd may be none, — *world*
190 That ever tok lyf with flesch and bone, — *ever was born of human kind*
    That avyt so gret blam. — *has such guilt*
But I [h]ave gras and help of the[e], — *Unless/grace*
I am lost fro the[e] so fre, — *noble*
    In helle to be be nam. — *In hell to be taken*

195 A prest now me most [h]ave, — *A priest/I must have*
If [I] shal be save

Ageynus Cryst of myth,   *Before Christ almighty*
To telle hym my blam
That I [h]ave wrowt be nam,   *done/particularly*
200   That is my thowt now tyth   *intention/quickly*
         To-day!
Jhesu, hevene-flowr,
Pot me from dolour,
And geve me gras this o[u]re   *grace this hour*
205   A prest to [h]avyn, I say!   *have*

    [The priest ministers to Moraud; he thanks him]
         XVIII.
[MORAUD]. A! Blyssyd be thou ay,   *always*
That thou com to-day
         To here my dedly syn!   *hear*
Whylys we are infere,   *together*
210 I wyl schrywe me here,   *shrive*
         For now wil I begyn.

I [h]ave led my lyf
In sorow and in stryf,
         With cursydnessys and care;
215 Yet is more in my th[o]wt,
     Synnus I [h]ave wrowt   *Sins/committed*
         Be my douter in lare.   *daughter at my instigation*

And chyld che bar be me,   *she bore of mine*
Whyk was fayr and fre   *Which/noble*
220   Bothe in body and fas,   *face*
And I myt never be fawe   *joyful*
Tyl we had hym sclawe—   *slain*
         I sey the[e] sothe cas!   *tell you the truth*

Yet more I wyl telle now.
225 Thy wyf ther che sclow,   *she slew*
         Thowr egment of me.   *my encouragement*
And thus is my lyf spend
Lord omnipotent,
         Grant me my synnus to fle.   *to leave my sins*

    [The Priest speaks to Moraud; he replies]
         XIX.
230 [MORAUD]. I wyl blely, my leve frend,   *gladly/dear*
Do penawns bothe fer and hend,   *far and near*
         To save my sowle fro wrat[h].

[Moraud meets with his daughter]
XX.
[MORAUD]. Heyl douter, lovely of syt.
 Heyl, lovely levende to-day,   *creature*
235 Cryst that is mytty in myt   *mighty*
 Save the[e] ermor and ay!   *evermore*

[His Daughter speaks; he replies]
XXI.
[MORAUD]. Lat be, my douter dere,
 Lat be, lovely in lere,   *face*
 I [h]ave forsakyn here
240 My blam and my syn.   *guilt*
 My syn I [h]ave forsake,
 And to penawns I [h]ave me take,   *betaken*
 For that wykkyd wrake   *crime*
  Now is time to blyn.   *cease*

245 And therfor I prey the[e],
 Sertys with herte fre,   *Surely/generous*
 That thou mak not me
  To falle in nomor blam!
 Now wyl I don away   *let go of*
250 My tresorys rych and gay,
 And traueylyn I wyl ay   *undertake hardship*
  For my wykyt fam.   *because of my ill repute*

  XXII.
 Now my lyf wyl passe
 Fro me this i[l]k stonde,   *very hour*
255 I am smetyn in the fas   *beaten/face*
  With carful strokys and rownde.
 Jhesu ful of gras   *(May) Jesus*
 Forgeve [the(e)] this trespas   *Forgive you this trespass*
  That thou ast don to me,   *That you have done to*
260 And geve the gras to blyn   *cease*
 Of that wykyd syn
  Whylk thou ast don so fre. *Which you have done so willingly*

 My tyme comyt faste to   *quickly to an end*
 That I shal pas yow fro,
265 In othir plas to duelle.
 In manus tuas, domine!   *Into your hands, O Lord!*
 Jhesu haue mercy on me,
  And save my sowle fro helle.
 [End of Text]

The Pride of Life

The manuscript containing *The Pride of Life* was destroyed in a fire and explosion at the Public Record Office in the Four Courts building in Dublin during a political disturbance in 1922. Fortunately, the long play fragment had already been edited and published as early as 1891, and a partial facsimile made. Originally the play was preserved on the back of a parchment account roll, covering the years 1337-1346, from the Holy Trinity Priory in Dublin. The handwriting of the play indicates that it was copied onto the account roll early in the fifteenth century, but the language of the play indicates a date of composition much earlier, perhaps in the mid-fourteenth century. Thus, the fragment provides us with one of the first and most interesting examples of a morality play. It should be noticed that the play is clearly of Irish origin, and that it was written by an author who was fully conversant with widely shared features and conventions of Middle English. Indeed, the two identifiable place names in the play are English—Berwick-upon-Tweed and the county of Kent. The Anglo-Irish nature of the play, that is to say, does not exclude it from the theatrical traditions to which all the other plays in this collection belong.

The plot of *The Pride of Life* is a straightforward example of allegorical drama, featuring a main character, the King of Life, who must learn the limits of his power on this earth, and who does so through the muscular intervention of Death. The King of Life's wife and a bishop she calls in to counsel him offer justifications for leading life in a more pious and longsighted manner, but the prideful King will not be deterred from his exultant displays of power, in which he has been encouraged by his soldiers Health and Strength. Foolishly, the King of Life challenges Death to a battle, and just as Death is about to respond the play text breaks off. The long prologue, however, makes it clear that Death accepts the challenge, enters the country to wreak havoc, and kills the King. Then, according to the prologue, in the judgment after death, the King's soul seems to be weighed in the scales of good and evil, finally being saved through the intercession of Our Lady.

A similar story appears in *The Golden Legend*, associated with the feast of the Assumption (August 15). In it, a sinner has a vision of his soul brought to be weighed in the balance before the judgment seat of God. On the advice of his defenders, Truth and Justice, he appeals to the Blessed Virgin, who lays her hand on the side of the balance containing the few good deeds, tipping the scales in his favor. When the sinner returns to himself he afterwards leads a better life. Since the last part of *The Pride of Life* has not survived, its ending can only be guessed at; but the symmetry of Truth and Justice taking the place of Health and Strength makes for a very satisfying, if fanciful, balance within the play itself.

To judge from the surviving stanzas, the *The Pride of Life* was written entirely in quatrains rhyming *abab,* with the lines alternating between three and four stresses. The play was first edited by James Mills and published in the *Account Roll of the Priory of the Holy Trinity, Dublin, 1337-1346, with the Middle English Moral Play "The Pride of Life"* (Dublin: The Royal Society of Antiquaries of Ireland, 1891). The standard scholarly edition, by Norman Davis, appears in the EETS *Non-Cycle Plays and Fragments,* where a manuscript facsimile of the first membrane containing the play is reproduced as well (see Suggestions for Further Reading).

THE PRIDE OF LIFE

[*DRAMATIS PERSONAE:*

PROLOCUTOR
REX (The King of Life)
REGINA (His Queen)
MILES 1 OR FORTITUDO (The First Soldier, Strength)
MILES 2 OR SANITAS (The Second Soldier, Health)
NUNCIUS (King's Messenger, Mirth or Solace)
EPISCOPUS (A Bishop)]

[PROLOCUTOR.] Pees, and herkynt hal ifer,	*Quiet/hearken all together*
[Ric] and por, yong and hold,	*Rich/old*
Men and wemen that bet her,	*are here*
Bot lerit and leut, stout and bold.	*Both learned/lewd (unlearned)/strong*

5 Lordinge[s] and ladiis that beth hende,	*who are at hand, courteous*
Herkenith al with mylde mode	*kind attention*
[How ou]re gam schal gyn and ende.	*play shall begin*
Lorde us wel spede that sched his blode!	*bring us success*

Now stondith stil and beth hende,	*keep quiet/be gracious*
10 [And ter]yith al for the weder,	*stay put whatever the weather*
[And] ye schal or ye hennis wende	*ere you go hence*
Be glad that ye come hidir.	*hither*

Here ye schullin here spelle	*shall hear a tale*
Of mirth and eke of kare;	*also of sorrow*
15 Herkenith and I wol you telle	*I will*
[How this oure gam] schal fare.	

[Of the Kyng of] Lif I wol you telle;	
[He stondith] first biffore	*He stands above*

28

[All men that beth] of flessch and fel   *who are made/skin*
20   [And of women i]bore.*   *of women born*

[He is, forsoth, ful] stronge to stond,   *in truth, very powerful in his life*
[And is] bycomin of kinge,   *descended*
[Yiveth] lawis in eche a londe,   *He decrees the law/many a*
[And nis] dradd of no thinge.   *is not afraid*

25   [In] pride and likinge his lif he ledith,   *and pleasure/leads*
Lordlich he lokith with eye;   *masterfully/casts his eye*
[Prin]ce and dukis, he seith, him dredith,   *fear him when he speaks*
[He] dredith no deth for to deye.   *He dreads no manner of death*

[He] hath a lady lovelich al at likinge,   *as gorgeous as he would wish*
30   Ne may he of no mirth mene ne misse;   *Nor does he stint in matters of delight*
He seith in swetnisse he wol set his likinge   *says in ease/enjoyment*
And bringe his bale boun into blisse.   *turn his sorrow quickly to joy*

Knytis he hat cumlic   *Comely knights he has*
In bred and in leint;   *in every feature*
35   Not I nevir non suc[h]   *I never knew any*
Of stotey ne off strynt.   *of such boldness or strength*

Wat helpit to yilp mucil of his mit   *What good does it do to boast so/might*
Or bost to mucil of his blys?   *so much*
[For] sorou may sit on is sit   *Though/on his throne*
40   [And] myrt[h m]ay he not miss.   *Yet he will not lack joy*

[Her ek is the] ladi of lond,   *Here also will appear*
[The fa]inist a lord for to led;   *The most glorious a lord might lead*
[Glad] may he be fort to stond   *to step forward*
[And b]ehold that blisful bled.   *handsome creature*

45   [Tha]t ladi is lettrit in lor   *learned in wisdom*
As cumli becomit for a quen,   *as is beautifully becoming*
And munit hir mac evirmor,   *And always admonishes her husband*
As a dar for dred him to ten.   *Even when she risks angering him*

Ho bid him bewar or he smert,   *She/ere he might be hurt*
50   [F]or in his lond Det wol alend,   *Death will come*
[As] ho lovit him goslic in hert   *she/deeply in her heart*
[Ho b]it him bewar of his hend.   *She bids/of his end*

18-20. See Job 41: 33-34: "Upon earth there is not his like, a creature without fear. He beholds everything that is high; he is king over all the sons of pride."

[Ho] begynit to charp of char   *She/to speak out of care for him*
Thes wordis wytout lesing: *without lying*
55   "Det dot not spar   *Death does not spare*
Knytis, cayser, ne kyng.   *Knights, emperor, nor King*

Nou lord, lev thi likynd   *Now/leave your delights*
Wyc bringit the soul gret bal."   *which/trouble*
This answer ho had of the kyng;   *she had*
60   "Ye, this a womanis tal."   *an old wives' tale*

The kyng hit ne toke not to hert   *took it not*
For hit was a womanis spec,   *Because/speech*
[And y]et hit mad him to smert   *so Death hurt him*
[W]an him mit help no lec.   *When no physician might help*

65   [The] quen yit can hir undirstond   *yet understood*
Wat help thar mit be,   *might*
And sent aftir the bicop of the lond   *bishop*
For he chout mor than he.   *knew more than she*

He cham and precit al that he couthe,   *came/preached/knew*
70   And warnit him hal of his hind;   *completely about his end*
[H]it savrit not in the kyngis mout,   *The king did not savor it*
Bot hom he bad him wynd.   *But/commanded/to go*

Wan the bicop is than wend   *bishop/is gone*
Fram that k[e]ne stryf   *bitter struggle*
75   [To Det a me]ssenger than send   *To Death a messenger then sent*
[Hat] the King of Lif.*   *Has the King of Life*

[For he] him wold do undirston[d]   *would have him understand*
[That al] he may del and dit   *That for all he might govern and master*
[He] wold cum into his ouin lond   *(Death) should come into his land*
80   On him to kyt his mit.   *To show him his might*

Deth comith, he dremith a dredfful dreme—   *brought an awesome dream*
Welle ayte al carye;   *ought all to be anxious*
And slow fader and moder and then heme: *he slew/uncle*
He ne wold none sparye.

85   Sone affter hit befel that Deth and Life   *Soon afterward it happened*
Beth togeder itaken;   *clash*
And ginnith and strivith a sterne strife   *a cruel battle begins and is fought*
[The] King of Life to wrake.   *To ruin the King of Life*

75-76. i.e., The King of Life then has a messenger sent to Death.

With him drivith adoun to grounde,   *(Death) thrusts him*
90   He dredith nothing his kniytis;   *feared nothing from*
And delith him depe dethis wounde   *dealt him a deep mortal wound*
And kith on him his miytis.   *showed him his might*

Qwhen the body is doun ibrogt   *brought down*
The soule sorow awakith;   *sorrow of the soul*
95   The bodyis pride is dere abogt,   *dearly paid for*
The soule the fendis takith.   *fiends*

And throgh priere of Oure Lady mylde   *the prayers*
Al godenisse scho wol qwyte.   *goodness she will repay*
Scho wol prey her son so mylde,   *She/pray to*
100   The soule and body schul dispyte;   *will contend*

The cors that nere knewe of care,   *body/never experienced pain*
No more then stone in weye,   *a stone in the road (or on a scale)*
Schal wit of sorow and sore care   *Shall find out about sorrow and pain*
And thrawe betwene ham tweye.   *And suffer between the two*

105   The soule theron schal be weye*   *thus/weighed*
That the fendis have ikayte;   *have caught*
And Oure Lady schal therfor preye
So that with her he schal be lafte.   *(the soul) shall be left*

Nou beith in pes and beith hende,   *peace/courteous*
110   And distourbith nogt oure place,   *not/playing place*
For this oure game schal gin and ende   *begin*
Throgh Jhesu Cristis swete grace.

Rex vivus incipiet sic dicendum: *Thus the King of Life begins speaking:*

REX. Pes, now, ye princis of powere so prowde,
Ye kingis, ye kempis, ye kniytis ikorne,   *warriors/excellent knights*
115   Ye barons bolde, that beith me obowte;   *are around me*
[Sem] schal yu my sawe,   *My speech shall please you,*
swaynis i[s]worne.   *sworn retainers*

Sqwieris stoute, stondit now stille,   *now stand at attention*
And lestenith to my hestis, I hote yu now her,   *orders, I command you/here*

---

105. Psychostasis, or the weighing of a soul, was a popular theme in medieval iconography. See Tancred Borenius and E.W. Tristram, *English Medieval Painting* (New York: Harcourt Brace & Co. [n.d.]), p. 38; Mary Phillip Perry, "On the Psychostasis in Christian Art," I and II, *The Burlington Magazine*, 22, Nov. 1912: 94-105 (of particular interest is illustration D, p. 100); and Jan. 1913: 208-218. Lines 93-108, like the rest of the Prolocutor's speech, appear to summarize the end of the play, which appears to have included a psychostasis. Unfortunately, this section of the text has not survived.

Or [I] schal wirch yu wo with werkis of wil *bring you woe with deeds*
120   And doun schal ye drive, be ye never so dere. *fall/fierce*

King ic am, kinde of kingis ikorre, *I am King, descended of famous kings*
   Al the worlde wide to welde at my wil;
Nas ther never no man of woman iborre *There was never a man born to woman*
   Oyein me withstonde that I nold him spille. *Who can stand against me/destroy*

125 Lordis of lond beith at my ledinge, *Overlords/bidding*
   Al men schal abow in hal and in bowr; *bow down/hall and home*

. . . .

[REGINA.] Baldli thou art mi bot, *Assuredly/my protector*
   Tristili and ful treu; *Trusty*
Of al mi rast thou art rot, *comfort/the root*
130   I nil chong fer no new. *will never change*

REX. Al in wel ic am biwent, *good fortune/encompassed*
   May no grisful thing me grou; *dreadful/frighten*
Likyng is wyt me bilent, *Pleasure/come to me*
   Alyng is it mi behou. *Altogether/portion*

135 Strent and Hel, knytis kete, *Strength and Health, brave knights*
   [Douti], derrist in ded, *Doughty, truest*
Lok that for no thing ye let *nothing keep you from*
   Smartli to me sped. *quickly attending to me*

Bringit wyt you brit brondis, *bright swords*
140   Helmis brit and schen; *Helmets bright/shiny*
For ic am lord ofir al londis *I am lord over*
   And that is wel isen. *easily apparent*

MILES 1. Lord, in truthe thou mit trist *might trust*
   Fethfuli to stond,
145 Thou mit liv as the[e] list, *might live as you want*
   For wonschildis thu fond. *home guards you have found*

Ic am Strent, stif and strong, *Strength, hard*
   Nevar is suc[h] non, *Like no other*
In al this world brod and long,
150   Imad of blod and bon. *Made/bone*

Hav no dout of no thing
   That evir may befal;
Ic am Streynt thi derling
   Flour of knitis al.

155 MILES 2. King of Lif, that berist the croun,   *who bears*
    As hit is skil and riyte,   *reasonable and right*
    I am Hele icom to toun,   *Health come to town*
    Thi kinde curteyse kniyte.   *courteous*

    Thou art lord of lim and life,   *limb*
160   And king withouten ende;
    Stif and strong and sterne in strif,   *Hard/cruel in battle*
    In londe qwher thou wende.   *where/go*

    Thou nast no nede to sike sore   *have/sigh sadly*
    For no thing on lyve;   *anything in life*
165 Thou schal lyve evermore: *always*
    Qwho dar with the[e] strive?   *Who would dare/contend*

    REX. Strive? Nay, to me qwho is so gode?   *who is as good as I*
    Hit were bot folye;   *It/foolishness*
    Ther is no man that me dur bode   *dare threaten*
170   Any vileynye.

    Qwherof schuld I drede   *What*
    Qwhen I am King of Life?   *When*
    Ful evil schuld he spede   *would befall whoever*
    To me that wrogt strive.   *made opposition to me*

175 I schal lyve evermo   *always*
    And croun ber as kinge;   *bear the kingly crown*
    I ne may never wit of wo,   *will never know any woe*
    I lyve at my likinge.   *for my pleasure*

    REGINA. Sire, thou saist as the liste,   *say all you want*
180   Thou livist at thi wille;   *as you wish*
    Bot somthing thou miste,   *lack*
    And therfor hold the[e] stille.   *keep quiet for a minute*

    Thinke, thou haddist beginninge
    Qwhen thou were ibore;   *When/born*
185 And bot thou mak god endinge   *Unless you*
    Thi sowle is forlore.   *lost*

    Love God and Holy Chirche,
    And have of him som eye;   *some fear*
    Fonde his werkis for to wirch   *Attempt to do his works*
190   And thinke that thou schal deye.   *contemplate*

REX. Douce dam, qwhi seistou so?   *Sweet lady, why do you say this?*
  Thou spekis nogt as the sleye.   *like the wise*
  I schal lyve evermo   *live forever*
  For bothe two thin eye.   *Before your very eyes*

195 Woldistou that I were dede   *Do you want me dead?*
  That thou miyt have a new?   *So that/a new (husband)?*
  Hore, the devil gird of thi hede   *Whore!/strike off your head*
  Bot that worde schal the[e] rewe!   *If you don't rue those words*

REGINA. Dede, sire? Nay, God wote my wil,   *Dead/knows*
200   That ne kepte I nogte;   *I would not wish that*
  Hit wolde like me full ille   *I would be ill pleased*
  Were hit thareto brogte.   *If it came to that*

[Yet] thogh thou be kinge
  Nede schalt have ende;   *you must die*
205 Deth overcomith al thinge
  Hou-so-ever we wende.   *Whichever way we turn*

REX. Ye, dam, thou hast wordis fale,   *many words*
  Hit comith the[e] of kinde;   *by nature*
  This nis bot women tale,   *is nothing but an old wives' tale*
210   And that I wol the[e] finde.   *I will show you*

I ne schal never deye
  For I am King of Life;
  Deth is undir myne eye   *in awe of me*
  And therfor leve thi strife.   *give up*

215 Thou dost bot mak myn hert sore,   *You only*
  For hit nel nogt helpe;   *will help nothing*
  I prey the spek of him no more.
  Qwhat wolte of him yelpe?   *Why brag about him?*

REGINA. Yilpe, sire? Ney, so mot I the;   *Brag/so may I thrive*
220   I sigge hit nogt therfore,   *I do not say it for that reason*
  Bot kinde techith bothe the[e] and me,   *nature*
  First qwhen we were bore,   *born*

For dowte of Dethis maistri,   *For fear of Death's power*
  To wepe and make sorowe;
225 Holy writ and prophecye
  Therof I take to borowe.   *call to witness*

Therfor, qwhile ye have migte
And the worlde at wille,   *under your control*
I rede ye serve God Almigte   *advise*
230   Bothe loude and stille.   *in all circumstances*

This world is bot fantasye
And ful of trechurye;
Gode sire, for youre curteysye
Take this for no folye.   *foolishness*

235   For, God wot the sothe,   *knows the truth*
I ne sey hit for no fabil;   *This is no fable*
Deth wol smyte to the[e],   *strike you*
In feith loke thou be stabil.   *steadfast*

REX. Qwhat prechistou of Dethis migt   *Why do you preach*
240   And of his maistrye?   *power*
He ne durst onis with me fiyt   *would not dare once/to fight*
For his bothe eye.   *For (the sake of keeping) both his eyes*

[To his knights]

Streinth and Hele, qwhat say ye,   *Strength/Health*
My kinde korin knigtis?   *excellent knights*
245 Schal Deth be lord over me
And reve me of migtis?   *rob/might*

MILES 1. Mi lord, so brouke I my bronde,   *as I may wield sword*
God that me forbede
That Deth schold do the[e] wronge
250   Qwhile I am in thi thede.   *country*

I wol withstonde him with strife   *stand against*
And make his sidis blede,
And tel him that thou art King of Life
And lorde of londe and lede.   *people*

255 MILES 2. May I him onis mete   *once*
With this longe launce,
In felde other in strete,   *or in street*
I wol him give mischaunce.   *defeat him*

REX. Ye, thes be knigtis of curteisye
260   And doghti men of dede;   *doughty*
Of Deth ne of his maistrie   *Of Death nor of his power*
Ne have I no drede.   *I have no fear*

Qwher is Mirth my messager,
  Swifte so lefe on lynde?   *Swift as the linden leaf*
265 He is a nobil bachelere
  That rennis bi the wynde.   *runs faster than*

Mirth and solas he can make
  And ren so the ro;   *And (can) run like the roe*
Liytly lepe ovre the lake
270   Qwher-so-ever he go.

Com and her me talente   *hear my wish*
  Anone and hy the[e] blyve;   *Quickly, and hasten at once*
Qwher any man, as thou hast wente,*   *Is there/as you have gone*
  Dorst with me to strive?   *Who would dare/contest*

275 NUNCIUS. King of Lif and lord of londe,
  As thou sittis on thi se   *thy throne*
And florresschist with thi brigt bronde,   *bright sword*
  To the[e] I sit on kne.   *kneel*

I am Mirth, wel thou wost,   *as you well know*
280   Thi mery messagere;
That wostou wel, withoute bost   *You know well*
  Ther nas never my pere   *There was never my equal*

Dogtely to done a dede   *Bravely to do*
  That ye have for to done,
285 Hen to Berewik opon Twede*   *From here to*
  And com oyein ful sone;   *again*

Ther is nothing the[e] iliche   *nothing like you*
  In al this worlde wide;
Of gold and silver and robis riche
290   And hei hors on to ryde.   *on high horse*

I have ben bothe fer and nere
  In bataile and in strife;

Ocke ther was never thy pere,   *But there was*
  For thou art King of Life.

295 REX. Aha! Solas, now thou seist so,   *now that you have said that*
  Thou miriest me in my mode;   *make me cheerful/heart*

---

273. i.e., Have you come across any man in all your travels.
285. Berwick-on-Tweed: the northeasternmost town in England.

Thou schal, boy, ar thou hennis go   *ere you go hence*
  Be avaunsyd, bi the rode.   *promoted/cross*

Thou schal have for thi gode wil
300   To thin avauncemente,   *for your promotion*
  The castel of Gailispire on the Hil,
  And the erldom of Kente.*

Draw the cord, Sire Streynth,
  Rest I wol now take;
305 On erth in brede ne leynth   *breadth*
  Ne was nere yet my make.   *There has never been my equal*

     Et tunc clauso tentorio dicet Regina secrete nuncio:*

REGINA. Messager, I pray the nowe
  For thi curteysye,
  Go to the bisschop, for thi prowe,   *profit*
310   And byd him hydir to hye.   *to hasten higher*

Bid him be ware before,   *advised beforehand*
  Sey him that he most preche;   *Tell him*
  My lord the King is ney lore   *nearly lost*
  Bot he wol be his leche.   *Unless/will be/physician*

315 Sey him that he wol leve nogt   *Tell him that he (the King) will not believe*
  That ever he schal deye;   *That he shall ever die*
  He is in siche errour brogte   *such/brought*
  Of God stont him non eye.   *He stands in no fear of God*

NUNCIUS. Madam, I make no tariyng
320   With softe wordis mo;
  For I am Solas, I most singe
  Overal qwher I go.   *Everywhere*

     Et cantat.   *And he sings*

Sire Bisschop, thou sittist on thi se   *throne*
  With thi mitir on thi hevede;   *mitre/head*
325 My lady the Qwen preyith the[e]   *What my lady/asks*
  Hit schold nogt be bilevyd.   *Will not be*

.   .   .   .

---

302. The earldom of Kent was vacant from the beginning of the fifteenth century.
306 s.d. And then with the tent closed the Queen says secretly to the messenger:

[EPISCOPUS.] The world is nou—so wo-lo-wo!—	*so welaway! (alas)!*
In suc[h] bal ibound	*wrapped in such evil*
That dred of God is al ago	*all gone*
330 And treut is go to ground.	*truth is laid low*
Med is mad a demisma[n],	*Reward/made/judge of all*
Streyint betit the lau;	*Strength beats (overwhelms) the law*
Geyl is mad a cepman	*Guile/made a merchant*
And truyt is don of dau.	*truth/put to death*
335 Wyt is nou al trecri,	*Intelligence/treachery*
Othis fals and gret;	*Oaths/loud*
Lov is nou al lecuri	*lechery*
And corteysi is let.	*courtesy/lost*
Play is nou vileni,	*Sport/villainy*
340 Cildrin bet onlerit,	*Children are untaught*
Halliday is glotuni—	*gluttony*
This lauis bet irerit.	*This is set up by laws*
Slet men bet bleynd	*The wise man is blind*
And lokit al amis;	*And sees all crookedly*
345 He bicomit onkynd	*has become cruel*
And that is reut, i[w]is.	*a pity indeed*
Frend may no man find	*A friend*
Of fremit ne of sib;	*stranger or relative*
The ded bet out of mind,	*The dead pass*
350 Gret soru it is to lib.	*sorrow/live*
Thes ricmen bet reuthyles,	*rich men/ruthless*
The por got to ground,	*laid low*
And fals men bet schamles,	*shameless*
The sot ic hav ifound.	*This truly I have*
355 It is wrong the ric kynyit	*the rich know it is wrong*
Al that the por dot;	*All/do (endure)*
Far that is sen day and nit	*For/seen*
Wosa wol sig sot.	*Whoever will speak the truth*
Paraventur men halt me a fol	*Perhaps/hold/to be a fool*
360 To sig that sot tal;	*say/true speech*
Thai farit as ficis in a pol—	*fare/fish/pool*
The gret eteit the smal.	*large ones eat*

Ricmen spart for no thing *The powerful hold back nothing*
   To do the por wrong;
365 Thai thingit not on hir ending *their end*
   Ne on Det that is so strong. *Nor on Death*

Nother thai lovit God ne dredit *They neither love God nor fear*
   Nother him no his lauis; *Him or His laws*
   Touart hel fast him spedit *Towards hell/they speed*
370 Ayeins har ending-daus. *before their final days*

Bot God of his godnis *Unless/out of his goodness*
   Yif ham gras to amend, *Gives them grace*
Into the delful derknys *doleful darkness*
   The got wytout hend. *without end*

375 Ther is dred and sorow *There (in hell)*
   And wo wytoutin wel; *woe without betterment*
No man may othir borou *others rescue*
   Be ther nevir so fel. *ever so many*

Ther ne fallit no maynpris, *applies no bail*
380 *Ne supersidias;** *no forebearance*
Thay he be kyng or iustis, *Though/Justice*
   He passit not the pas. *cannot pass by this event*

Lord, that for his manhed *May the Lord who/Manhood*
   And also for his god, *being God, divinity*
385 That for lov and not for dred
   Deit oppon the rod, *Died upon the cross*

Yif ou gras or lif to led *Give you grace or life*
   That be your soulis to bot; *So that/souls may be saved*
God of Hevin for his godhed *in his divine power*
390 Lev that hit so mot. Amen. *Grant that it may be so*

Tunc dicet regi: *Then he speaks to the King*

Schir Kyng, thing oppon thin end *Sir King, think upon thy death*
   And hou that thou schalt dey, *die*
Wat wey that thou schalt wend *What way/will go*
   Bot thou be bisey. *Unless/take care*

395 And eke that thou art lenust man, *also consider that/frailest*
   And haddist begyning,

---

380. *Supersedeas:* a writ suspending legal proceedings.

And evirmor hav thout opon *always/thought upon*
    Thi dredful ending.

Thou schalt thing thanne— *think too*
400 And mac the[e] evir yar— *make/always ready*
    That Det is not the man *That Death/the kind of man*
    For nothing the wil spar. *Who will spare you for anything*

Thou schalt do dedis of rit *deeds of righteousness*
    And lernen Cristis lor, *teaching*
405 And lib in hevin-lit *live/heavenly light*
    To savy thi soul fro sor. *save/pain*

REX. Wat! bissop, byssop babler,
    Schold y of Det hav dred? *Should I fear Death?*
    Thou art bot a chagler— *cackler*
410 Go hom thi wey, I red. *advise*

Wat! com thou therfor hidir *thus hither*
    Wit Deth me to afer? *With/frighten*
    That thou and he bot togidir *Oh, that you/both together*
    Into the se scot wer! *sea were thrown!*

415 Go hom, God yif the[e] sorow, *give you grief*
    Thou wreist me in my mod. *make my heart angry*
    War woltou prec tomorou? *Where would you preach*
    Thou nost ner, bi the rod! *You know not at all/cross*

Troust thou I wold be ded *Do you believe/would*
420 In mi yyng lif? *young*
    Thou lisst, screu, bolhed; *liest, you villain, stubborn fool*
    Evil mot thou t[h]riwe. *May you fare badly*

Wat schold I do at churg, wat? *church*
    Schir bisop, wostou er? *Sir Bishop, would you ever know?*
425 Nay, churc nis no wyl cat, *is no wild cat*
    Hit wol abid ther. *It will stay there*

I woll let car away, *trouble go away*
    And go on my pleying.

To hontyng and to o[th]ir play *hunting*
430 For al thi long prechyng.

I am yyng, as thou mit se, *young/you might see*
    And hau no ned to char *care*

The wyle the Quen and [mi me]ine *While/my minions*
  About me bet yar. *are at hand*

435 EPISCOPUS. Thynk, Schir Kyng, one othir trist— *on another certainty*
  That tyng misst son. *Soon this creature will fail*
  Thot thou lev nou as the[e] list, *Though you live now as you please*
  Det wol cum rit son, *Death/very soon*

And give the dethis wounde *give you*
440   For thin outrage; *your insolence*
  Within a litil stounde *short time*
  Then artou but a page. *Then you will be but a serving boy*

Qwhen thou art graven on grene, *buried under the grass*
  Ther metis fleys and molde, *Where flesh and earth meet*
445 Then helpith litil, I wene, *I think*
  Thi gay croun of golde.

Sire Kyng, have goday, *goodbye*
  Crist I you beteche. *I commend you to Christ*
  REX. Fare wel, bisschop, thi way, *go on your way*
450   And lerne bet to preche. *to preach better*

Hic adde *At this point, add:*

Nou, mafay, hit schal be sene, *on my word*
  I trow, yit to-daye, *I believe*
  Qwher Deth me durst tene *Whether Death dares anger me*
  And mete in the waye. *meets me*

455 Qwher artou, my messagere, *Where are you*
  Solas bi thi name? *named Solace*
  Loke that thou go fer and nere,
  As thou wolt have no blame,

My banis for to crye *My proclamation*
460   By dayis and bi niyte;
  And loke that thou aspye, *see what you find out*
  Ye, bi al thi migte, *might*

Of Deth and of his maistrye
  Qwher he durst com in sigte, *Whether he dares to*
465 Ogeynus me and my meyné *Against/company*
  With force and armis to figte.
  Loke that thou go both est and west
  And com ogeyne anone; *again at once*

NUNCIUS. Lorde, to wende I am prest,   *go forth/ready*
470   Lo, now I am gone.

    Et eat pla[team.]   *And he goes about the playing place*

NUNCIUS. Pes and listenith to my sawe,   *my words*
    Bothe yonge and olde;
    As ye wol nogt ben aslawe   *If/not be slain*
    Be ye never so bolde.

475 I am a messager isente
    From the King of Life;
    That ye schal fulfil his talente   *(To say) that you/desire*
    On peyne of lym and lif.

    His hestis to hold and his lawe   *commands to uphold*
480 Uche a man on honde;   *Each/firmly*
    Lest ye be henge and todraw,   *hanged/drawn*
    Or kast in hard bonde.   *fetters*

    Ye wittin wel that he is king   *You know*
    And lord of al londis,
485 Kepere and maister of al thing
    Within se and sondis.   *From coast to coast*

    I am sente for to enquer
    Oboute ferre and nere,   *Of everyone*
    Yif any man dar werre arere   *would dare start war*
490 Agein suche a bachalere.   *Against/young knight*

    To wrother hele he was ibore   *To misfortune would he be born*
    That wold with him stryve;   *Who would/fight*
    Be him sikir he is ilore   *By him surely he is ruined*
    As here in this lyve,   *life*

495 Thegh hit wer the King of Deth   *Though it were*
    And he so hardy were;
    Bot he ne hath migt ne meth   *Even he/might nor capacity*
    The King of Lif to afere;   *to frighten*

    Be he so hardy or so wode   *so bold or so foolhardy*
500 In his londe to aryve,
    He wol se his herte-blode   *see his own life-blood*
    And he with him stryve.   *If he fights with him*

                 [Here the text breaks off]

Everyman

Everyman is unlike any of the other plays included here in a number of important respects. First of all, it is the only *printed* play: that is, it has existed only in printed form from its earliest appearance, which implies a reading audience as well as a spectating one. Second, the play is a translation, an English version of the Dutch *Elckerlijc,* which it follows very closely. It thus is part of a theatrical tradition significantly different from the English one that the other plays in this collection represent. The Dutch *Elckerlijc* (1485) is one of hundreds of surviving Rederijkers' (rhetoricians') plays, which were encouraged and supported in the low countries by local Chambers of Rhetoric from the second quarter of the fifteenth century until the beginning of the seventeenth. Ordinarily, these Chambers of Rhetoric were made up of leading burgesses in their communities, bent on instilling morality and culture through the entertaining medium of drama. The translation of *Everyman* may have been made because the Dutch play was already so well-regarded in its own country. At any rate, it survives in English in four versions. Two are complete and include woodcuts; one is preserved at the Huntington Library and the other at the British Library. Both were printed by John Skot, the first around 1528-29 and the second between 1530-35. Two fragments of *Everyman* also survive; both are several pages long and both were printed by Richard Pynson. The first of these, now in the Bodleian, dates from between 1510-25, earlier than any of the others; the second fragment, now at the British Library, dates from between 1525-30. The four printed versions are unrelated to each other, though they surely derive from a common ancestor.

Despite its anomalous ancestry, *Everyman* has earned a reputation as the quintessential morality play, and indeed it represents the genre in its most distilled form. Every detail of the play contributes to its very considerable impact: its spare conception of representative allegorical character types, its insistent, unrelenting pace, its through-line of action that carries directly toward the inevitable conclusion, its unadorned language and somber tone, its unblinking depiction of the psychological and physiological processes of dying, and its religious earnestness. The poetic resonance of the play gathers as it progresses, aided by the repeated pattern of hope and disappointment, and in this regard it has a distinctively modern feel, however dated its doctrine. Despite the fact that the play is a translation—or perhaps because of that fact—it displays a verbal tightness and a sense of play with language that link it more comfortably with later Tudor interludes and early Elizabethan fare.

Missing from *Everyman* are the antics and high spirits often associated with the Vice figures common to most morality plays. Still, from the theatrical point of view *Everyman* offers ample scope for a strong performance, not the least of which might be achieved by the commanding figure of Death at the beginning and the yawning grave into which Everyman presumably descends at the end. Everyman himself changes from a naïve and desperate simpleton to a figure of gravity, grace, and courage during the course of the play, and it is the contemplation of how to die (or, the play would imply, how to live) that produces this shift. The other characters are of course more impersonal abstractions of external and internal human qualities, and the action of the play is to strip them away one by one, echoing at once the last minutes and the whole life of every human being. The Messenger who speaks the prologue and the Doctor who speaks the epilogue mediate the audience's psychological entry into and out of this long meditation—this "treatise . . . in maner of a moral play." Deceptively simple on or off the stage, *Everyman* offers one of the most memorable and powerful late-medieval parables to haunt the modern imagination.

The meter and rhyme scheme of *Everyman* is inconsistent but clearly accomplished. The Messenger who opens the play, for example, displays an elaborate rhyme scheme of seven couplets separated by seven single rhyming lines. God's first speech, which follows, begins with variations on the seven-line Rhyme Royal *(ababbcc)* and then settles down into couplets. Thereafter the play is written mainly in couplets, interspersed at no regular intervals with quatrains rhyming *abab*. The number of stresses per line varies from three to six.

Because of its popularity, *Everyman* appears in many modern editions and anthologies. The most useful, reliable, and thorough edition of the play is by G. Cooper and Christopher Wortham. The play of *Elckerlijk,* with a prose translation, can be found in John Conley and Guido deBaere, *et al., The Mirror of Everyman's Salvation: A Prose Translation of the Original Everyman;* the Rederijker plays and traditions are treated by W.M.H. Hummelen, "The Drama of the Dutch Rhetoricians," in *Everyman and Company: Essays on the Theme and Structure of the European Moral Play,* ed. by Donald Gilman; the relations between the Dutch and the English play are discussed by Elsa Strietman, "The Middle Dutch *Elckerlijc* and the English *Everyman"* in *Medium Aevum* (see Suggestions for Further Reading).

EVERYMAN

[*DRAMATIS PERSONAE:*

MESSENGER   KNOWLEDGE
DEATH   BEAUTY
EVERYMAN   STRENGTH
FELLOWSHIP   DISCRETION
KINDRED   FIVE WITS
COUSIN   ANGEL
GOODS   DOCTOR
GOOD DEEDS]

Here beginneth a treatise how the hye
Fader of heven sendeth Dethe to so-
mon every creature to Come and
gyve acounte of their lyves in
this world, and is in maner
of a morall play

MESSENGER. I pray you all gyve your audyence,
And here this mater with reverence,   *this play's matter*
By fygure a morall playe.   *In form*
The Somonynge of Everyman called it is,
5   That of our lyves and endynge shewes
How transytory we be all daye.   *always*
This mater is wonder[ou]s precyous;   *content/very important*
But the entent of it is more gracyous,   *meaning/full of grace*
And swete to bere awaye.   *take with you*
10   The story sayth: Man, in the begynnynge   *from*
Loke well, and take good heed to the endynge,   *ending (of life)*
Be you never so gay!
Ye thynke synne in the begynnynge full swete,   *sin is*

45

Whiche in the ende causeth the soule to wepe,

15　Whan the body lyeth in claye.

Here shall you se how Felawshyp and Jolyte,

Bothe Strengthe, Pleasure and Beauté,

Wyll fade from the[e] as floure in Maye;　　　　　　　*a flower*

For ye shall here how our Heven Kynge

20　Calleth Everyman to a generall rekenynge.

Gyve audyence, and here what he doth saye.

　　　God speketh

GOD. I perceyve, here in my maieste,

How that all creatures be to me unkynde,　　　　　　　*unnatural*

Lyuynge without drede in worldly prosperyte.

25　Of ghostly syght the people be so blynde,　　　　　　*spiritual*

Drowned in synne, they know me not for theyr God.

In worldely ryches is all theyr mynde;

They fere not my ryghtwysnes, the sharpe rod.　　　　*righteousness*

My lawe that I shewed, whan I for them dyed,

30　They forgete clene and shedynge of my blode rede.　　*completely*

I hanged bytwene two theves, it can not be denyed;

To gete them lyfe I suffred to be deed;　　　　　*allowed myself/dead*

I heled theyr fete, with thornes hurt was my heed.　*washed [See John 13:1-20]*

I coude do no more than I dyde, truely;

35　And nowe I se the people do clene for-sake me.

They use the seven deedly synnes dampnable,

As pryde, coveytyse, wrath, and lechery

Now in the worlde be made commendable;　　　　　　　*are acceptable*

And thus they leve of aungelles the hevenly company.　*take leave of*

40　Every man lyveth so after his owne pleasure,

And yet of theyr lyfe they be nothynge sure.　　　*by no means secure*

I se the more that I them forbere　　　　　　　　　　*spare them*

The worse they be fro yere to yere.　　　　　　　　　*become from*

All that lyveth appayreth faste;　　　　　　　　　　*grows worse*

45　Therfore I wyll, in all the haste,

Have a rekenynge of every mannes persone;

For, and I leve the people thus alone　　　　　　　　　*if*

In theyr lyfe and wycked tempestes,

Veryly they will become moche worse than beestes,　　　*Truly*

50　For now one wolde by envy another up ete;

Charyte they do all clene forgete.

I hoped well that every man

In my glory sholde make his mansyon,*　　　　　　　*take his place*

And therto I had them all electe;

---

53. See John 14:2.

55 But now I se, lyke traytours dejecte, *abject*
They thanke me not for the pleasure that I to them ment, *goodness/meant for*
Nor yet for theyr beynge that I them have lent. *their existence*
I profered the people grete multytude of mercy,
And fewe there be that asketh it hertly. *with their hearts*
60 They be so combred with worldly ryches *encumbered*
That nedes on them I must do iustyce, *I must needs do*
On every man lyvynge without fere.
Where arte thou, Deth, thou myghty messengere?

[Enter Death]
Dethe

DEATH. Almyghty God, I am here at your wyll,
65 Your commaundement to fulfyll.
GOD. Go thou to Everyman
And shewe hym, in my name,
A pylgrymage he must on hym take,
Whiche he in no wyse may escape;
70 And that he brynge with hym a sure rekenynge
Without delay or ony taryenge. *[Exit]*

DEATH. Lorde, I wyll in the worlde go renne over-all *everywhere*
And cruelly out-serche bothe grete and small. *everyone, of all degrees*
Every man wyll I beset that lyveth beestly *who/like a beast*
75 Out of Goddes lawes, and dredeth not foly.
He that loveth rychesse I wyll stryke with my darte,
His syght to blynde, and fro heven to departe— *cut off from*
Excepte that almes be his good frende—
In hell for to dwell, worlde without ende.

[Enter Everyman]

80 Loo, yonder I se Everyman walkynge.
Full lytell he thynketh on my comynge;
His mynde is on flesshely lustes and his treasure, *sensual pleasures*
And grete payne it shall cause hym to endure *suffer*
Before the Lorde, Heven Kynge.
85 Everyman, stande styll! Whyder arte thou goynge
Thus gayly? Hast thou thy Maker forgete? *forgotten*
EVERYMAN. Why askest thou?
Woldest thou wete? *(Why) would/know*
DEATH. Ye, syr. I wyll shewe you:
90 In grete hast I am sende to the[e]
Fro God out of his mageste.
EVERYMAN. What, sente to me?

DEATH. Ye, certaynly.
Thoughe thou have forgete hym here,
95 He thynketh on the[e] in the hevenly spere,   *sphere*
As, or we departe, thou shalte knowe.   *ere*
EVERYMAN. What desyreth God of me?
DEATH. That shall I shewe the[e]:
A rekenynge he wyll nedes have   *he must have*
100 Without ony lenger respyte.   *delay*
EVERYMAN. To gyve a rekenynge longer layser I crave;   *leisure*
This blynde mater troubleth my wytte.   *dark*
DEATH. On the[e] thou must take a longe journey;
Therfore thy boke of counte with the[e] thou brynge,   *accounts*
105 For tourne agayne thou can not by no waye.   *to return*
And loke thou be sure of thy rekenynge,
For before God thou shalte answere, and shewe
Thy many badde dedes, and good but a fewe;   *deeds*
How thou hast spente thy lyfe, and in what wyse,   *manner*
110 Before the chefe Lorde of paradyse.
Have ado that thou were in that waye,
For wete thou well thou shalte make none attournay.   *know well/have no*
EVERYMAN. Full unredy I am suche rekenynge to gyve.
I knowe the[e] not. What messenger arte thou?
115 DEATH. I am Dethe that no man dredeth—   *fears*
For every man I reste—and no man spareth;   *arrest/I spare*
For it is Goddes commaundement
That all to me sholde be obedyent.
EVERYMAN. O Deth, thou comest whan I had the[e] leest in mynde!
120 In thy power it lyeth me to save;   *you can save*
Yet of my good wyl I gyve the[e], yf thou wyl be kynde—
Ye, a thousande pounde shalte thou have—
And dyfferre this mater tyll an other daye.   *defer*
DEATH. Everyman, it may not be by no waye.   *not possible*
125 I set not by golde, sylver, nor rychesse,   *pay no attention to*
Ne by pope, emperour, kynge, duke, ne prynces;
For, and I wolde receyve gyftes grete,   *if*
All the worlde I myght gete;
But my custome is clene contrary.
130 I gyve the[e] no respyte. Come hens, and not tary!   *hence*
EVERYMAN. Alas, shall I have no lenger respyte?
I may saye Deth gyveth no warnynge!
To thynke on the[e], it maketh my herte seke,   *sick*
For all unredy is my boke of rekenynge.
135 But twelve yere and I myght have a-bydynge,   *If only I might have/stay*
My countynge-boke I wolde make so clere
That my rekenynge I sholde not nede to fere.   *worry*
Wherfore, Deth, I praye the[e], for Goddes mercy,

Spare me tyll I be provyded of remedy.
140 DEATH. The[e] avayleth not to crye, wepe, and praye;   *It helps you not*
   But hast[e] the[e] lyghtly that thou were gone that journaye,   *hurry quickly*
   And preve thy frendes yf thou can.   *test*
   For wete thou well the tyde abydeth no man,   *know well/waits for*
   And in the worlde eche lyvynge creature
145 For Adams synne must dye of nature.   *by natural process*
   EVERYMAN. Dethe, yf I sholde this pylgrymage take,
   And my rekenynge suerly make,   *sure*
   Shewe me, for saynt charyte,   *goodness sake*
   Sholde I not come agayne shortly?
150 DEATH. No, Everyman; and thou be ones there,   *once you are there*
   Thou mayst never more come here,
   Trust me veryly.   *truly*
   EVERYMAN. O gracyous God in the hye sete celestyall,   *high seat*
   Have mercy on me in this moost nede!
155 Shall I have no company fro this vale terestryall   *world*
   Of myne acqueyntaunce, that way me to lede?
   DEATH. Ye, yf ony be so hardy   *any*
   That wolde go with the[e] and bere the[e] company.
   Hye the[e] that thou were gone to Goddes magnyfycence,   *Hurry*
160 Thy rekenynge to gyve before his presence.
   What, wenest thou thy lyve is gyven the[e],   *do you think your life*
   And thy worldly gooddes also?
   EVERYMAN. I had wende so, veryle.   *thought/truly*
   DEATH. Nay, nay, it was but lende the[e];   *lent*
165 For as soone as thou arte go,   *gone*
   Another a whyle shall have it, and than go ther-fro,   *then go from it*
   Even as thou hast done.
   Everyman, thou arte made! Thou hast thy wyttes fyve,   *complete*
   And here on erthe wyll not amende thy lyve;   *And (yet)*
170 For sodeynly I do come.
   EVERYMAN. O wretched caytyfe, wheder shall I flee,   *villain/whither*
   That I myght scape this endles sorowe?
   Now, gentyll Deth, spare me tyll to-morowe,
   That I may amende me
175 With good aduysement.   *advice*
   DEATH. Naye, therto I wyll not consent,
   Nor no man wyll I respyte;
   But to the herte sodeynly I shall smyte
   Without ony aduysement.   *warning*
180 And now out of thy syght I wyll me hy.   *hurry*
   Se thou make the[e] redy shortely,
   For thou mayst saye this is the daye
   That no man lyvynge may scape a-waye. *[Exit]*

EVERYMAN. Alas, I may well wepe with syghes depe!
185 Now have I no maner of company
To helpe me in my journey, and me to kepe; *protect*
And also my wrytynge is full unredy. *accounting*
How shall I do now for to excuse me?
I wolde to God I had never be gete *been begotten*
190 To my soule a full grete profyte it had be,
For now I fere paynes huge and grete.
The tyme passeth. Lorde, helpe, that all wrought! *created everything*
For though I mourne, it avayleth nought.
The day passeth and is almoost ago; *gone*
195 I wote not well what for to do. *know not*
To whome were I best my complaynt to make?
What and I to Felawshyp therof spake, *What if*
And shewed hym of this sodeyne chaunce? *occurrence*
For in hym is all myne affyaunce; *trust*
200 We have in the worlde so many a daye
Be good frendes in sporte and playe. *Been*
I se hym yonder, certaynely.
I trust that he wyll bere me company;
Therfore to hym wyll I speke to ese my sorowe.
205 Well mette, good Felawshyp, and good morowe!

[Enter Fellowship]

FELLOWSHIP. Everyman, good morowe, by this daye!
Syr, why lokest thou so pyteously?
If ony thynge be a-mysse, I praye the[e] me saye, *tell*
That I may helpe to remedy.
210 EVERYMAN. Ye, good Felawshyp, ye,
I am in great jeoparde.
FELLOWSHIP. My true frende, shewe to me your mynde.
I wyll not forsake the[e] to my lyves ende,
In the waye of good company.
215 EVERYMAN. That was well spoken and lovyngly.
FELLOWSHIP. Syr, I must nedes knowe your hevynesse; *unhappiness*
I have pyte to se you in ony dystresse.
If ony have you wronged, ye shall revenged be, *If any/wronged you*
Thoughe I on the grounde be slayne for the[e],
220 Though that I knowe before that I sholde dye.
EVERYMAN. Veryly, Felawshyp, gramercy. *great thanks*
FELLOWSHIP. Tusshe! by thy thankes I set not a strawe. *care nothing*
Shewe me your grefe, and saye no more.
EVERYMAN. If I my herte sholde to you breke, *open*
225 And than you to tourne your mynde fro me *then/should turn*
And wolde not me comforte whan ye here me speke,

Than sholde I ten tymes soryer be.
FELLOWSHIP. Syr, I saye as I wyll do in dede.
EVERYMAN. Than be you a good frende at nede. *at time of need*
230 I have founde you true here-before.
FELLOWSHIP. And so ye shall evermore;
For, in fayth, and thou go to hell,
I wyll not forsake the[e] by the waye.
EVERYMAN. Ye speke lyke a good frende; I byleve you well.
235 I shall deserve it, and I maye. *repay/if I can*
FELLOWSHIP. I speke of no deservynge, by this daye!
For he that wyll saye, and nothynge do,
Is not worthy with good company to go;
Therfore shewe me the grefe of your mynde, *troubles in*
240 As to your frende moost lovynge and kynde.
EVERYMAN. I shall shewe you how it is:
Commaunded I am to go a journaye,
A longe waye harde and daungerous,
And gyve a strayte counte, without delaye, *strict account*
245 Before the hye Iuge, Adonay. *Adonais*
Wherfore, I pray you, bere me company,
As ye have promysed, in this journaye.
FELLOWSHIP. That is mater in dede! Promyse is duty; *serious matter*
But, and I sholde take suche a vyage on me, *undertake*
250 I knowe it well, it sholde be to my payne;
Also it maketh me aferde, certayne. *afraid*
But lete us take counsell here as well as we can, *deliberation*
For your wordes wolde fere a stronge man. *might frighten*
EVERYMAN. Why, ye sayd yf I had nede
255 Ye wolde me never forsake, quycke ne deed, *alive nor dead*
Thoughe it were to hell, truely.
FELLOWSHIP. So I sayd, certaynely,
But suche pleasures be set a-syde, the sothe to saye;
And also, yf we toke suche a journaye,
260 Whan sholde we agayne come?
EVERYMAN. Naye, never agayne tyll the daye of dome. *doom*
FELLOWSHIP. In fayth, than wyll not I come there!
Who hath you these tydynges brought?
EVERYMAN. In dede, Deth was with me here.
265 FELLOWSHIP. Now, by God that all hathe bought, *redeemed*
If Deth were the messenger,
For no man that is lyvynge to-daye
I wyll not go that lothe journaye— *loathsome*
Not for the fader that bygate me!
270 EVERYMAN. Ye promysed other wyse, parde. *by God*
FELLOWSHIP. I wote well I sayd so, truely; *I know*
And yet, yf thou wylte ete and drynke and make good chere,

Or haunt to women the lusty company,   *frequent*
I wolde not forsake you whyle the daye is clere,   *all day*
275 Trust me veryly.
 EVERYMAN. Ye, therto ye wolde be redy!
 To go to myrthe, solas, and playe
 Your mynde wyll soner apply,   *sooner attend*
 Than to bere me company in my longe journaye.
280 FELLOWSHIP. Now, in good fayth, I wyll not that waye; *will not go*
 But and thou wyll murder, or ony man kyll,   *If*
 In that I wyll helpe the[e] with a good wyll.
 EVERYMAN. O, that is a symple advyse in dede. *matter*
 Gentyll felawe, helpe me in my necessyte!
285 We have loved longe, and now I nede;
 And now, gentyll Felawshyp, remembre me.
 FELLOWSHIP. Wheder ye have loved me or no, *Whether*
 By Saynt Iohan I wyll not with the[e] go!
 EVERYMAN. Yet, I pray the[e], take the labour and do so moche for me *trouble*
290 To brynge me forwarde, for saynt charyte,   *escort me*
 And comforte me tyll I come without the towne. *outside of*
 FELLOWSHIP. Nay, and thou wolde gyve me a newe gowne,
 I wyll not a fote with the[e] go;   *foot*
 But, and thou had taryed, I wolde not have lefte the[e] so. *stayed*
295 And as now God spede the[e] in thy journaye,
 For from the[e] I wyll departe as fast as I maye.
 EVERYMAN. Wheder a-waye, Felawshyp? Wyll thou forsake me? *Whither*
 FELLOWSHIP. Ye, by my faye! To God I be-take the[e]. *faith/commend*
 EVERYMAN. Farewell, good Felawshyp! For the[e] my herte is sore.
300 A-dewe for ever! I shall se the[e] no more.
 FELLOWSHIP. In fayth, Everyman, fare well now at the endynge!
 For you I wyll remembre that partynge is mournynge. *[Exit]*

 EVERYMAN. A-lacke, shall we thus departe in dede— *part*
 Lady, helpe!—without ony more comforte? *(Blessed) Lady*
305 Lo, Felawshyp forsaketh me in my moost nede.
 For helpe in this worlde wheder shall I resorte? *whither*
 Felawshyp here-before with me wolde mery make,
 And now lytell sorowe for me dooth he take.
 It is sayd, "In prosperyte men frendes may fynde,
310 Whiche in adversyte be full unkynde."
 Now wheder for socoure shall I flee, *whither/comfort*
 Syth that Felawshyp hath forsaken me? *Since*
 To my kynnesmen I wyll, truely,
 Prayenge them to helpe me in my necessyte.
315 I byleve that they wyll do so,
 For "kynde wyll crepe where it may not go." *kinship/creep/walk*

I wyll go saye, for yonder I se them.   *try*
Where be ye now, my frendes and kynnesmen?

[Enter Kindred and Cousin]

KINDRED. Here be we now at your commaundement.
320   Cosyn, I praye you shewe us your entent   *needs*
In ony wyse, and not spare.   *in everything/do not hesitate*
COUSIN. Ye, Everyman, and to us declare
If ye be dysposed to go ony-whyder;   *anywhere*
For, wete you well, we wyll lyve and dye to-gyder.   *know/together*
325   KINDRED. In welth and wo we wyll with you holde,   *stay*
For over his kynne a man may be bolde.   *with/straightforward*
EVERYMAN. Gramercy, my frendes and kynnesmen kynde.   *Great thanks*
Now shall I shewe you the grefe of my mynde: *trouble*
I was commaunded by a messenger,
330   That is a hye kynges chefe offycer.
He bad me go a pylgrymage, to my payne,   *bade/on a*
And I knowe well I shall never come agayne.
Also I must gyve a rekenynge strayte,   *strict accounting*
For I have a grete enemy that hath me in wayte,   *lying in wait for me*
335   Whiche entendeth me for to hynder.   *Who intends/hold back*
KINDRED. What a-counte is that whiche ye must render?
That wolde I knowe.
EVERYMAN. Of all my workes I must shewe
How I have lyved and my dayes spent;
340   Also of yll dedes that I have used   *done*
In my tyme, syth lyfe was me lent;   *since*
And of all vertues that I have refused.
Therfore, I praye you, go thyder with me
To helpe to make myn accounte, for saynt charyte.
345   COUSIN. What, to go thyder? Is that the mater?
Nay, Everyman, I had lever fast brede and water   *would rather*
All this fyve yere and more.
EVERYMAN. Alas, that ever I was bore!   *born*
For now shall I never be mery,
350   If that you forsake me.
KINDRED. A, syr, what ye be a mery man!   *such a merry man*
Take good herte to you, and make no mone.   *moan*
But one thynge I warne you, by Saynt Anne—
As for me, ye shall go alone.
355   EVERYMAN. My Cosyn, wyll you not with me go?
COUSIN. No, by our Lady! I have the crampe in my to.   *toe*
Trust not to me; for, so God me spede,   *may God help me*
I wyll deceyve you in your moost nede.   *greatest*
KINDRED. It avayleth not us to tyse.   *entice*

360 Ye shall have my mayde with all my herte;   *woman*
       She loveth to go to feestes, there to be nyse,   *wanton*
       And to daunce, and a-brode to sterte.   *go around*
       I wyll gyve her leve to helpe you in that journey,
       If that you and she may a-gree.
365 EVERYMAN. Now shewe me the very effecte of your mynde:
       Wyll you go with me, or abyde be-hynde?   *stay*
       KINDRED. Abyde behynde? Ye[a], that wyll I, and I maye!
       Therfore farewell tyll another daye. *[Exit]*

       EVERYMAN. Howe sholde I be mery or gladde?
370 For fayre promyses men to me make,
       But whan I have moost nede they me forsake.
       I am deceyved; that maketh me sadde.
       COUSIN. Cosyn Everyman, farewell now,
       For veryly I wyll not go with you.
375 Also of myne owne an unredy rekenynge
       I have to accounte; therfore I make taryenge.   *must stay behind*
       Now God kepe the[e], for now I go. *[Exit]*

       EVERYMAN. A, Jesus, is all come here-to?   *has it come to this*
       Lo, fayre wordes maketh fooles fayne;   *glad*
380 They promyse, and nothynge wyll do, certayne.
       My kynnesmen promysed me faythfully
       For to a-byde with me stedfastly,
       And now fast a-waye do they flee.
       Even so Felawshyp promysed me.   *Just as*
385 What frende were best me of to provyde?   *to provide me with*
       I lose my tyme here longer to abyde.
       Yet in my mynde a thynge there is:
       All my lyfe I have loved ryches;
       If that my Good now helpe me myght,   *Goods*
390 He wolde make my herte full lyght.
       I wyll speke to hym in this dystresse.
       Where arte thou, my Gooddes and ryches?

           [Goods speaks]

       GOODS. Who calleth me? Everyman? What, hast thou haste?
       I lye here in corners, trussed and pyled so hye,
395 And in chestes I am locked so fast,
       Also sacked in bagges. Thou mayst se with thyn eye
       I can not styre; in packes, lowe I lye.
       What wolde ye have? Lyghtly me saye.   *Quickly tell me*
       EVERYMAN. Come hyder, Good, in al the hast thou may,   *hither/Goods*
400 For of counseyll I must desyre the[e].   *advice/asks*

GOODS. Syr, and ye in the worlde have sorowe or adversyte,   *if*
That can I helpe you to remedy shortly.
EVERYMAN. It is another dysease that greveth me;   *problem/troubles*
In this worlde it is not, I tell the[e] so.   *of*
405 I am sent for, an other way to go,
To gyve a strayte counte generall   *strict accounting*
Before thy hyest Jupyter of all.   *God*
And all my lyfe I have had ioye and pleasure in the[e],
Therfore, I pray the[e], go with me;
410 For, parauenture, thou mayst before God Almyghty   *perhaps*
My rekenynge helpe to clene and puryfye,
For it is sayd ever amonge   *always*
That "money maketh all ryght that is wronge."
GOODS. Nay, Everyman, I synge an other songe.
415 I folowe no man in suche vyages;
For, and I wente with the[e],   *if*
Thou sholdest fare moche the worse for me.
For bycause on me thou dyd set thy mynde,
Thy rekenynge I have made blotted and blynde,   *uncertain and dark*
420 That thyne accounte thou can not make truly—
And that hast thou for the love of me!   *That's what you get*
EVERYMAN. That wolde greve me full sore,   *trouble*
Whan I sholde come to that ferefull answere.   *final reckoning*
Up, let us go thyder to-gyder.   *thither*
425 GOODS. Nay, not so! I am to[o] brytell, I may not endure.
I wyll folowe no man one fote, be ye sure.
EVERYMAN. Alas, I have the[e] loved, and had grete pleasure
All my lyfe-dayes on good and treasure.   *goods*
GOODS. That is to thy dampnacyon, without lesynge,   *lying*
430 For my love is contrary to the love everlastynge.
But yf thou had me loved moderately durynge,   *during life*
As to the poore gyve parte of me,
Than sholdest thou not in this dolour be,
Nor in this grete sorowe and care.
435 EVERYMAN. Lo, now was I deceyued or I was ware;   *ere/aware*
And all I may wyte my-spendynge of tyme.   *know from misspending*
GOODS. What, wenest thou that I am thyne?   *do you think*
EVERYMAN. I had went so.   *thought*
GOODS. Naye, Everyman, I saye no.
440 As for a whyle I was lente the[e];
A season thou hast had me in prosperyte.   *For a time*
My condycyon is mannes soule to kyll;   *nature*
If I save one, a thousande I do spyll.   *destroy*
Wenest thou that I wyll folowe the[e]?   *Do you think*
445 Nay, fro this worlde not, veryle.   *truly*
EVERYMAN. I had wende otherwyse.   *thought*

GOODS. Therfore to thy soule Good is a thefe; *Goods*
For whan thou arte deed, this is my gyse— *my practice*
Another to deceyve in this same wyse
450 As I have done the[e], and all to his soules reprefe. *reproof*
EVERYMAN. O false Good, cursed thou be, *Goods*
Thou traytour to God, that hast deceyved me *who has*
And caught me in thy snare!
GOODS. Mary, thou brought thy selfe in care, *got yourself into trouble*
455 Wherof I am gladde. *For which*
I must nedes laugh; I can not be sadde. *have to*
EVERYMAN. A, Good, thou hast had longe my hertely love; *Goods/heartfelt*
I gave the[e] that whiche sholde be the Lordes above.
But wylte thou not go with me in dede?
460 I praye the[e] trouth to saye.
GOODS. No, so God me spede! *God help me*
Therfore fare well, and have good daye.   *[Exit]*

EVERYMAN. O, to whome shall I make my mone *moan*
For to go with me in that hevy journaye?
465 Fyrst Felawshyp sayd he wolde with me gone;
His wordes were very plesaunt and gaye,
But afterwarde he lefte me alone.
Than spake I to my kynnesmen, all in dyspayre,
And also they gave me wordes fayre;
470 They lacked no fayre spekynge,
But all forsake me in the endynge.
Than wente I to my Goodes that I loved best,
In hope to have comforte; but there had I leest,
For my Goodes sharpely dyd me tell
475 That he bryngeth many in to hell.
Than of my selfe I was ashamed, *Then*
And so I am worthy to be blamed;
Thus may I well my selfe hate.
Of whome shall I now counseyll take?
480 I thynke that I shall never spede
Tyll that I go to my Good Dede.
But, alas, she is so weke
That she can nother go nor speke; *neither walk*
Yet wyll I venter on her now. *take a chance on*
485 My Good Dedes, where be you?

[Enter Good Deeds]

GOOD DEEDS. Here I lye, colde in the grounde.
Thy synnes hath me sore bounde,
That I can not stere. *stir*

EVERYMAN. O Good Dedes, I stande in fere!

490 I must you pray of counseyll, *advice*
For helpe now sholde come ryght well. *would be welcome*
GOOD DEEDS. Everyman, I have understandynge
That ye be somoned a-counte to make *an accounting*
Before Myssyas, of Iherusalem kynge; *Messiah*

495 And you do by me, that journay with you wyll I take. *If you do as I say*
EVERYMAN. Therfore I come to you my moone to make. *moan*
I praye you that ye wyll go with me.
GOOD DEEDS. I wolde full fayne, but I can not stande, veryly. *very gladly/truly*
EVERYMAN. Why, is there ony thynge on you fall? *anything befall you*

500 GOOD DEEDS. Ye, syr, I may thanke you of all.
If ye had parfytely chered me, *treated me better*
Your boke of counte full redy had be. *would have been*

[Shows book]

Loke, the bokes of your workes and dedes eke *also*
Ase how they lye under the fete, *See how/underfoot*

505 To your soules hevynes.
EVERYMAN. Our Lorde Jesus helpe me!
For one letter here I can not se. *not a single*
GOOD DEEDS. There is a blynde rekenynge in tyme of dystres. *dark*
EVERYMAN. Good Dedes, I praye you helpe me in this nede,

510 Or elles I am for ever dampned in dede;
Therfore helpe me to make rekenynge
Before the Redemer of all thynge,
That Kynge is, and was, and ever shall. *shall be*
GOOD DEEDS. Everyman, I am sory of your fall,

515 And fayne wolde I helpe you, and I were able. *gladly/if*
EVERYMAN. Good Dedes, your counseyll I pray you gyve me. *advice*
GOOD DEEDS. That shall I do veryly.
Thoughe that on my fete I may not go,
I have a syster that shall with you also, *shall go*

520 Called Knowlege, whiche shall with you abyde, *Acknowledgment*
To helpe you to make that dredefull rekenynge.

[Enter Knowledge]

KNOWLEDGE. Everyman, I wyll go with the[e] and be thy gyde,
In thy moost nede to go by thy syde.
EVERYMAN. In good condycyon I am now in every thynge,

525 And am holy content with this good thynge, *wholly*
Thanked be God my creature. *creator*
GOOD DEEDS. And whan she hath brought you there
Where thou shalte hele the[e] of thy smarte, *pain*

Than go you with your rekenynge and your Good Dedes togyder,
530 For to make you joyfull at herte
Before the Blessyd Trynyte.
EVERYMAN. My Good Dedes, gramercy!   *great thanks*
I am well content, certaynly,
With your wordes swete.
535 KNOWLEDGE. Now go we togyder lovyngly
To Confessyon, that clensynge ryvere.
EVERYMAN. For joy I wepe; I wolde we were there!
But, I pray you, gyve me cognycyon   *let me know*
Where dwelleth that holy man, Confessyon.
540 KNOWLEDGE. In the hous of salvacyon;   *the Church*
We shall fynde hym in that place,
That shall us comforte, by Goddes grace.

[Knowledge leads to Confession]

Lo, this is Confessyon. Knele downe and aske mercy,
For he is in good conceyte with God Almyghty.   *good grace*
545 EVERYMAN. O gloryous fountayne, that all unclennes doth claryfy,   *purify*
Wasshe fro me the spottes of vyce unclene,
That on me no synne may be sene.   *So that*
I come with Knowlege for my redempcyon,
Redempte with herte and full contrycyon;   *Redeemed*
550 For I am commaunded a pylgrymage to take,
And grete accountes before God to make.
Now I praye you, Shryfte, moder of salvacyon,   *Confession*
Helpe my Good Dedes for my pyteous exclamacyon.   *in response to*
CONFESSION. I knowe your sorowe well, Everyman.
555 Bycause with Knowlege ye come to me,
I wyll you comforte as well as I can.
And a precyous jewell I wyll gyve the[e],
Called penaunce, voyder of adversyte;   *canceller*
Therwith shall your body chastysed be,
560 With abstynence and perseveraunce in Goddes servyture.   *service*
Here shall you receyve that scourge of me,   *whip*
Whiche is penaunce stronge that ye must endure,
To remembre thy Savyour was scourged for the[e]
With sharpe scourges, and suffred it pacyently;
565 So must thou or thou scape that paynful pylgrymage.
Knowlege, kepe hym in this vyage,
And by that tyme Good Dedes wyll be with the[e].
But in ony wyse be seker of mercy,   *certain of*
For your tyme draweth fast; and ye wyll saved be,   *time is running out*
570 Aske God mercy, and he wyll graunte truely.
Whan with the scourge of penaunce man doth hym bynde,   *himself punish*

The oyle of forgyvenes than shall he fynde. *balm*
EVERYMAN. Thanked be God for his gracyous werke!
For now I wyll my penaunce begyn.
575 This hath rejoysed and lyghted my herte, *enlightened*
Though the knottes be paynful and harde, within.
KNOWLEDGE. Everyman, loke your penaunce that ye fulfyll, *see to it*
What payne that ever it to you be; *however painful*
And Knowlege shall gyve you counseyll at wyll *when you wish*
580 How your accounte ye shall make clerely.
EVERYMAN. O eternall God, O hevenly fygure,
O way of ryghtwysnes, O goodly vysyon, *righteousness*
Whiche dyscended downe in a vyrgyn pure
Bycause he wolde every man redeme,
585 Whiche Adam forfayted by his dysobedyence: *which redemption*
O blessyd God-heed, electe and hye devyne, *Godhead/divinity*
Forgyve me my greuous offence!
Here I crye the[e] mercy in this presence. *company*
O ghostly treasure, O raunsomer and redemer, *spiritual*
590 Of all the worlde hope and conduyter, *guide*
Myrrour of joye, foundatour of mercy, *founder*
Whiche enlumyneth heven and erth therby, *illumines*
Here my clamorous complaynt, though it late be,
Receyue my prayers unworthy in this hevy lyfe!
595 Though I be a synner moost abhomynable,
Yet let my name be wryten in Moyses table. *of the elect*
O Mary, praye to the Maker of all thynge,
Me for to helpe at my endynge;
And save me fro the power of my enemy,
600 For Deth assayleth me strongly.
And, Lady, that I may by meane of thy prayer *may I, by intercession*
Of your Sones glory to be partynere,
By the meanes of his passyon, I it crave; *through the mechanism*
I beseche you helpe my soule to save.
605 Knowlege, gyve me the scourge of penaunce;
My flesshe therwith shall gyve acqueyntaunce. *be acquainted*
I wyll now begyn yf God gyve me grace.
KNOWLEDGE. Everyman, God gyve you tyme and space! *opportunity*
Thus I bequeth you in the handes of our Savyour;
610 Now may you make your rekenynge sure.
EVERYMAN. In the name of the Holy Trynyte,
My body sore punysshed shall be:

[Flogs himself]

Take this, body, for the synne of the flesshe!
Also thou delytest to go gay and fresshe, *are delighted*

615   And in the way of dampnacyon thou dyd me brynge;
      Therfore suffre now strokes of punysshynge.
      Now of penaunce I wyll wade the water clere,
      To save me from Purgatory, that sharpe fyre.
      GOOD DEEDS. *[Rising]* I thanke God, now I can walke and go,
620   And am delyvered of my sykenesse and wo.   *woe*
      Therfore with Everyman I wyll go, and not spare;   *hold back*
      His good workes I wyll helpe hym to declare.
      KNOWLEDGE. Now, Everyman, be mery and glad!
      Your Good Dedes cometh now; ye may not be sad.
625   Now is your Good Dedes hole and sounde,
      Goynge upryght upon the grounde.
      EVERYMAN. My herte is lyght, and shal be evermore;
      Now wyll I smyte faster than I dyde before.   *strike myself*
      GOOD DEEDS. Everyman, pylgryme, my specyall frende,
630   Blessyd be thou without ende!
      For the[e] is preparate the eternall glory.
      Ye have me made hole and sounde,
      Therfore I wyll byde by the[e] in every stounde.   *time of need*
      EVERYMAN. Welcome, my Good Dedes! Now I here thy voyce
635   I wepe for very swetenes of love.
      KNOWLEDGE. Be no more sad, but ever reioyce;
      God seeth thy lyvynge in his trone above.   *throne*
      Put on this garment to thy behove,   *behalf*
      Whiche is wette with your teres,
640   Or elles before God you may it mysse,
      Whan ye to your journeys ende come shall.
      EVERYMAN. Gentyll Knowlege, what do ye it call?
      KNOWLEDGE. It is a garment of sorowe;
      Fro payne it wyll you borowe   *protect*
645   Contrycyon it is
      That getteth forgyvenes;
      He pleaseth God passynge well.   *exceedingly*
      GOOD DEEDS. Everyman, wyll you were it for your hele?   *wear/spiritual health*
      EVERYMAN. Now blessyd be Jesu, Maryes sone,
650   For now have I on true contrycyon;
      And lette us go now without taryenge.
      Good Dedes, have we clere our rekenynge?
      GOOD DEEDS. Ye, in dede, I have it here.
      EVERYMAN. Than I trust we nede not fere.
655   Now, frendes, let us not parte in twayne.
      KNOWLEDGE. Nay, Everyman, that wyll we not, certayne.
      GOOD DEEDS. Yet must thou lede with the[e]
      Thre persones of grete myght.
      EVERYMAN. Who sholde they be?
660   GOOD DEEDS. Dyscrecyon and Strength they hyght,   *are called*

And thy Beaute may not abyde behynde.
KNOWLEDGE. Also ye must call to mynde
Your Fyve Wyttes as for your counseylours.
GOOD DEEDS. You must have them redy at all houres.
665 EVERYMAN. Howe shall I gette them hyder   *hither?*
KNOWLEDGE. You must call them all togyder,
And they wyll here you in-contynent.   *hear/immediately*
EVERYMAN. My frendes, come hyder and be present,   *hither*
Dyscrecyon, Strengthe, my Fyve Wyttes, and Beaute.

[Enter Discretion, Strength, Five Wits, Beauty]

670 BEAUTY. Here at your wyll we be all redy.
What wolde ye that we sholde do?
GOOD DEEDS. That ye wolde with Everyman go,
And helpe hym in his pylgrymage.
Advyse you, wyll ye with him or not in that vyage?   *Consider*
675 STRENGTH. We wyll brynge hym all thyder,   *thither*
To his helpe and comforte, ye may byleve me.
DISCRETION. So wyll we go with hym all togyder.
EVERYMAN. Almyghty God, loved may thou be!
I gyve the[e] laude that I have hyder brought
680 Strength, Dyscrecyon, Beaute, and Fyue Wyttes. Lacke I nought.   *nothing*
And my Good Dedes, with Knowlege clere,
All be in company at my wyll here.   *together as I wish*
I desyre no more to my besynes.   *for my purpose*
STRENGTH. And I, Strength, wyll by you stande in dystres,
685 Though thou wolde in batayle fyght on the grounde.   *battle fall*
FIVE WITS. And though it were thrugh the worlde rounde,   *anywhere*
We wyll not departe for swete ne soure.   *however easy or hard*
BEAUTY. No more wyll I unto dethes houre,   *until*
What so ever therof befall.
690 DISCRETION. Everyman, advyse you fyrst of all;   *be advised*
Go with a good advysement and delyberacyon.
We all gyve you vertuous monycyon   *such virtuous preparation*
That all shall be well.
EVERYMAN. My frendes, harken what I wyll tell:
695 I praye God rewarde you in his hevenly spere.   *sphere*
Now herken, all that be here,
For I wyll make my testament
Here before you all present:
In almes, halfe my good I wyll gyve with my handes twayne
700 In the way of charyte with good entent,
And the other halfe styll shall remayne
In queth, to be retourned there it ought to be.   *In a bequest/where*
This I do in despyte of the fende of hell,

To go quyte out of his perell   *free from peril*
705 Ever after and this daye.   *today and always*
KNOWLEDGE. Everyman, herken what I saye:
Go to Presthode, I you advyse,
And receyue of hym in ony wyse   *however possible*
The holy sacrament and oyntement togyder.   *Extreme Unction*
710 Than shortly se ye tourne agayne hyder;   *turn*
We wyll all abyde you here.   *wait for*
FIVE WITS. Ye, Everyman, hye you that ye redy were.   *hurry so that*
There is no Emperour, Kynge, Duke, ne Baron,
That of God hath commycyon   *authority*
715 As hath the leest preest in the worlde beynge;   *living*
For of the blessyd sacramentes pure and benygne
He bereth the keyes, and therof hath the cure
For mannes redempcyon—it is ever sure—
Whiche God for our soules medycyne
720 Gave us out of his herte with grete pyne.   *pain*
Here in this transytory lyfe, for the[e] and me,
The blessyd sacramentes seven there be:
Baptym, confyrmacyon, with preesthode good,   *Holy Orders*
And the sacrament of Goddes precyous flesshe and blod,
725 Maryage, the holy extreme unccyon, and penaunce.
These seven be good to have in remembraunce.
Gracyous sacramentes of hye devynyte.
EVERYMAN. Fayne wolde I receyue that holy body,   *Gladly/communion*
And mekely to my ghostly fader I wyll go.   *spiritual*
730 FIVE WITS. Everyman, that is the best that ye can do.
God wyll you to salvacyon brynge,
For preesthode excedeth all other thynge: *a priest's power*
To us holy scrypture they do teche,
And converteth man fro synne, heven to reche;   *reach*
735 God hath to them more power gyven
Than to ony aungell that is in heven.
With fyue wordes he may consecrate,*
Goddes body in flesshe and blode to make,
And handeleth his Maker bytwene his handes.
740 The preest byndeth and unbyndeth all bandes,   *bonds [of sin]*
Bothe in erthe and in heven.
Thou mynystres all the sacramentes seven;   *You administer*
Though we kysse thy fete, thou were worthy.
Thou arte surgyon that cureth synne deedly;
745 No remedy we fynde under God
But all onely preesthode.   *only through the priesthood*
Everyman, God gave preest that dygnyte,

---

737. Five words: "Hoc est enim corpus meum" ("This is my body."). [See Matthew 26:26]

And setteth them in his stede amonge us to be;   *in place of him*
Thus be they above aungelles in degree.

[Everyman goes to receive communion and extreme unction]

750   KNOWLEDGE. If preestes be good, it is so, suerly.
      But whan Jesu hanged on the crosse with grete smarte,   *pain*
      There he gave out of his blessyd herte
      The seven sacramentes in grete tourment;
      He solde them not to us, that Lorde omnypotent.
755   Therfore Saynt Peter the apostell dothe saye
      That Jesus curse hath all they   *all of those priests*
      Whiche God theyr Savyour do by or sell,   *Who/buy*
      Or they for ony money do take or tell.*
      Synfull preestes gyveth the synners example bad:
760   Theyr chyldren sytteth by other mennes fyres, I have harde; *heard*
      And some haunteth womens company
      With unclene lyfe, as lustes of lechery.
      These be with synne made blynde.
      FIVE WITS. I trust to God no suche may we fynde;
765   Therfore let us preesthode honour,
      And folowe theyr doctryne for our soules socoure.   *comfort*
      We be theyr shepe, and they shepeherdes be
      By whome we all be kepte in suerte.   *safety*
      Peas! For yonder I se Everyman come,   *Quiet!*
770   Whiche hath made true satysfaccyon.
      GOOD DEEDS. Me thynke it is he in dede.

      [Everyman returns]

      EVERYMAN. Now Jesu be your alder spede!   *great helper*
      I have receyued the sacrament for my redempycon,
      And than myne extreme unccyon.
775   Blessyd be all they that counseyled me to take it!
      And now, frendes, let us go with-out longer respyte.
      I thanke God that ye have taryed so longe.
      Now set eche of you on this rodde your honde,   *cross*
      And shortely folowe me.
780   I go before there I wolde be. God be our gyde!   *where I wish to be*
      STRENGTH. Everyman, we wyll not fro you go
      Tyll ye have done this vyage longe.
      DISCRETION. I, Dyscrecyon, wyll byde by you also.
      KNOWLEDGE. And though this pylgrymage be never so stronge,
785   I wyll never parte you fro.

---

758. *i.e.,* Those priests who commit simony by stealing a host or consecrating it for money.

Everyman, I wyll be as sure by the[e]
As ever I dyde by Iudas Machabee.
EVERYMAN. Alas, I am so faynt I may not stande;
My lymmes under me do folde.
790 Frendes, let us not tourne agayne to this lande,
Not for all the worldes golde;
For in to this cave must I crepe   *grave*
And tourne to erth, and there to slepe.
BEAUTY. What, in to this grave? Alas!
795 EVERYMAN. Ye, there shall ye consume, more and lesse.   *be consumed*
BEAUTY. And what, sholde I smoder here?   *smother*
EVERYMAN. Ye, by my fayth, and nevere more appere.
In this worlde lyve no more we shall,
But in heven before the hyest Lorde of all.
800 BEAUTY. I crosse out all this! Adewe, by Saynt Iohan!   *Count me out of*
I take my tappe in my lappe and am gone.   *spinning gear*
EVERYMAN. What, Beaute, whyder wyll ye?   *Whither/go*
BEAUTY. Peas! I am defe. I loke not behynde me,   *Quiet!*
Not and thou wolde gyve me all the golde in thy chest. *[Exit]*   *Not if*

805 EVERYMAN. Alas, wherto may I truste?
Beaute gothe fast awaye fro me.
She promysed with me to lyve and dye.
STRENGTH. Everyman, I wyll the[e] also forsake and denye;
Thy game lyketh me not at all.   *pleases me*
810 EVERYMAN. Why, than, ye wyll forsake me all?
Swete Strength, tary a lytell space.   *while*
STRENGTH. Nay, syr, by the rode of grace!   *cross*
I wyll hye me from the[e] fast,   *hasten away*
Though thou wepe to thy herte to-brast.   *until your heart breaks*
815 EVERYMAN. Ye wolde ever byde by me, ye sayd.
STRENGTH. Ye, I have you ferre ynoughe conveyde.   *far/escorted*
Ye be olde ynoughe, I understande,
Your pylgrymage to take on hande.
I repent me that I hyder came.   *hither*
820 EVERYMAN. Strength, you to dysplease I am to blame.
Wyll ye breke promyse that is dette?   *owed*
STRENGTH. In fayth, I care not.
Thou arte but a foole to complayne;
You spende your speche and wast your brayne.   *waste*
825 Go thryst the[e] in to the grounde. *[Exit]*   *jump in*

EVERYMAN. I had wende suer I sholde you have founde.   *thought you surer*
He that trusteth in his Strength,
She hym deceyueth at the length.   *in the end*
Bothe Strength and Beaute forsaketh me;

830   Yet they promysed me fayre and lovyngly.   *Although*
       DISCRETION. Everyman, I wyll after Strength be gone.
       As for me, I wyll leve you alone.
       EVERYMAN. Why, Dyscrecyon, wyll ye forsake me?
       DISCRETION. Ye, in fayth, I wyll go fro the[e],
835   For whan Strength goth before
       I folowe after ever more.   *always*
       EVERYMAN. Yet, I pray the[e], for the love of the Trynyte,
       Loke in my graue ones pyteously.   *once*
       DISCRETION. Nay, so nye wyll I not come.   *near*
840   Fare well, everychone!   *[Exit]*   *everyone*

       EVERYMAN. O, all thynge fayleth, save God alone—
       Beaute, Strength, and Dyscrecyon;
       For whan Deth bloweth his blast,
       They all renne fro me full fast.
845   FIVE WITS. Everyman, my leve now of the[e] I take.
       I wyll folowe the other, for here I the[e] forsake.   *others*
       EVERYMAN. Alas, than may I wayle and wepe,
       For I toke you for my best frende.
       FIVE WITS. I wyll no lenger the[e] kepe.   *protect*
850   Now fare well, and there an ende.   *[Exit]*

       EVERYMAN. O Jesu, helpe! All hath forsaken me.
       GOOD DEEDS. Nay, Everyman, I wyll byde with the[e].
       I wyll not forsake the[e] in dede;
       Thou shalte fynde me a good frende at nede.
855   EVERYMAN. Gramercy, Good Dedes! Now may I true frendes se.   *Great thanks*
       They have forsaken me, everychone;
       I loved them better than my Good Dedes alone.
       Knowlege, wyll ye forsake me also?
       KNOWLEDGE. Ye, Everyman, whan ye to Deth shall go;
860   But not yet, for no maner of daunger.
       EVERYMAN. Gramercy, Knowlege, with all my herte,   *Great thanks*
       KNOWLEDGE. Nay, yet I wyll not from hens departe   *hence*
       Tyll I se where ye shall be-come.
       EVERYMAN. Me thynke, alas, that I must be gone
865   To make my rekenynge and my dettes paye,
       For I se my tyme is nye spent awaye.   *nearly gone*
       Take example, all ye that this do here or se,   *hear*
       How they that I loved best do forsake me,
       Excepte my Good Dedes that bydeth truely.
870   GOOD DEEDS. All erthly thynges is but vanyte:*
       Beaute, Strength and Dyscrecyon do man forsake,

---

870. See Ecclesiastes 12:8.

Folysshe frendes and kynnesmen that fayre spake—
All fleeth save Good Dedes, and that am I.
EVERYMAN. Have mercy on me, God moost myghty,
875 And stande by me, thou moder and mayde, Holy Mary!
GOOD DEEDS. Fere not; I wyll speke for the[e].
EVERYMAN. Here I crye God mercy.
GOOD DEEDS. Shorte our ende and mynysshe our payne;   *Shorten/diminish*
Let us go and never come agayne.
880 EVERYMAN. In to thy handes, Lorde, my soule I commende;
Receyve it, Lorde, that it be not lost.
As thou me boughtest, so me defende,   *redeemed*
And save me from the fendes boost,   *fiend's*
That I may appere with that blessyd hoost
885 That shall be saved at the day of dome.
In manus tuas, of myghtes moost
For ever, *commendo spiritum meum.**
KNOWLEDGE. Now hath he suffred that we all shall endure;   *that which*
The Good Dedes shall make all sure.
890 Now hath he made endynge;
Me thynketh that I here aungelles synge   *It seems to me/hear*
And make grete joy and melody
Where Everymannes soule receyved shall be.

    [Enter Angel]

ANGEL. Come, excellente electe spouse, to Jesu!   *bride*
895 Here above thou shalte go
Bycause of thy synguler vertue.
Now thy soule is taken thy body fro,
Thy rekenynge is crystall-clere.
Now shalte thou in to the hevenly spere,   *sphere*
900 Unto the whiche all ye shall come
That lyveth well before the daye of dome.

    [Enter Doctor]

DOCTOR. This morall men may have in mynde.
Ye herers, take it of worth, olde and yonge,   *seriously*
And forsake Pryde, for he deceyueth you in the ende;
905 And remembre Beaute, Fyve Wyttes, Strength, and Dyscrecyon,
They all at the last do Everyman forsake,
Save his Good Dedes there dothe he take.   *Unless*
But be-ware, for and they be small,   *if*
Before God he hath no helpe at all:

886-887. Into your hands . . . I commend my spirit. [See Luke 23:46]

910 None excuse may be there for Everyman.
　　　Alas, how shall he do than?
　　　For after dethe amendes may no man make,
　　　For than mercy and pyte doth hym forsake.
　　　If his rekenynge be not clere whan he doth come,
915 God wyll saye, *"Ite, maledicti, in ignem eternum!"* *
　　　And he that hath his accounte hole and sounde,
　　　Hye in heven he shall be crounde.
　　　Unto whiche place God brynge us all thyder,
　　　That we may lyve body and soule togyder.
920 Therto helpe the Trynyte!
　　　Amen, saye ye, for saynt charyte.　　　　　　　　　　　*holy*

FINIS
Thus endith this moral play of Every Man
Imprynted at London in Poule's
chyrche yarde by me
Johan Skot

---

915. Depart, ye cursed, into everlasting fire. [See Matthew 25:41]

Wisdom

The text of *Wisdom* is preserved in two manuscripts: the Macro manuscript at the Folger Shakespeare Library in Washington, D.C. (MS. V.a.354), and the Digby manuscript at the Bodleian Library in Oxford (MS Digby 133). The Macro version is complete while the Digby version stops at line 752. Both are copies, apparently made from the same exemplar, and both date from the late fifteenth century. The provenance and language of the two manuscripts point unmistakably to East Anglian origins. The Macro version is the less carefully made, and has to be corrected by the Digby text. It was copied by the same scribe who copied most of the Macro *Mankind;* as is detailed in the introduction to that play, Latin inscriptions appearing on *Mankind* and *Wisdom* have been traced to Thomas Hyngham, monk of Bury St. Edmunds in the fifteenth century. *Wisdom*'s date of composition, like that of *Mankind,* is perhaps as early as 1465-70.

Wisdom is one of the most theatrically interesting of the morality plays, simply in terms of stage directions and display, and one of the most mixed in tone. It quotes many Latin texts from the Vulgate and draws on a long and well-developed line of wisdom literature, including the elaborate interpretations of the Biblical *Song of Songs*, and the apocryphal books of *The Wisdom of Solomon* and *Ecclesiasticus*. The first and last scenes of the play follow English versions of *Orologium Sapientiae* by the mystic Henry Suso, *The Scale of Perfection* and the *Epistle on Mixed Life* by Walter Hilton, and use two Latin treatises attributed to St. Bernard, *Meditationes de Cognitione Humanae Conditionis* and *Tractatus de Interiori Domo,* as well as the *Soliloquium* of St. Bonaventura and the anonymous *Novem Virtutes*.

For some time, no doubt in part because of the heavy freight of mystical thought, *Wisdom* was considered a dull play in need of defense, but on stage it requires no apologies. Spectacular pageantry attends the action throughout, and the serious meditations and advice contain the lighter scenes like an envelope. The plot of the play follows an apparently simple trajectory, as Wisdom, who is richly arrayed as Christ the King, contests with Lucifer to win

Anima, the human soul. Anima's Five Wits are displayed as virgins, and the Three Mights (or powers) of the soul, Mind, Will, and Understanding, waver back and forth, thoroughly swayed by Lucifer's blandishments. Disguised as a gallant, he tempts Mind to pride, Understanding to covetousness, and Will to lechery. Each succumbs and brings in six followers and minstrels: six men with red beards, six suborned jurors with double faces in hoods, and six women with "wondyrful vysors" or masks. Anima, now hideously disfigured, drives out the devils of deadly sin with contrition. Confessing offstage, she returns with her Five Wits and cleansed three Mights to rejoice in her grace and in Christ, her "soveren Wysdam."

From an allegorical point of view, the plot can thus be divided into four scenes: Innocence, Temptation, Sinful Life and Repentance. But overlaid on this plot line is a more complex action that depends upon theatrical representations as well as text, and one of the notable features of *Wisdom* is that the "properties" of characters in the play are described quite fully. Indeed, of the thirty-eight characters appearing in the play, only seven have speaking roles; all the others achieve meaning by costume and gesture. At the center of the play, for example, lies an elaborate dumbshow demonstrating how debauchery of the soul has personal, political, and social consequences (from ll. 685 to 777). Mind has succumbed to abuses of Maintenance, or personal power in defiance of law; Understanding has taken up the currying of power, abusing the law by manipulating the courts; and Will has encouraged riot by abusing natural sexual inclination. The dancing of the traitors, the compromised jurors, the gallants and prostitutes, then, functions as a celebration of Lucifer's momentary triumph over the more contemplatively grounded life urged by Wisdom. How this state of affairs occurs in the first place, and how it might be changed to heal the individual, the social order, and the realm itself, form the central meditation of the play. Other highly theatrical moments, like the Devil's carrying off from the audience a shrieking "shrewd" or naughty boy halfway through the play (l. 550 s.d.), operate in much the same manner, registering meaning by aural, musical, visual, and gestic means rather than verbal.

It is worth noting that "women" actors are called for explicitly in the stage directions to act both male and female (non-speaking) parts in the play (l. 752 s.d.). With much doubling of roles, *Wisdom* can be staged with a minimum of five or six speaking actors and six or seven extras, which would make it, like *Mankind*, a manageable play in the repertory of a travelling company.

The predominant stanzaic form of *Wisdom* is an eight-line tail-rhymed stanza rhyming *aaabaaab* or *ababbcbc*. Wisdom's speeches ordinarily have four stresses per line, while Lucifer's are much less regular, often having three or five stresses per line. In a good use of poetic decorum, when Anima's "Mights" follow Wisdom or Lucifer, they also follow the verse pattern associated with that character.

The Digby version of *Wisdom* was first published by Thomas Sharp in *Ancient Mysteries from the Digby Manuscripts* (Edinburgh: Abbotsford Club, 1835). The Macro version was published two years later in the same series, edited by W.B.D.D. Turnbull as *Mind, Will, and Understanding: A Morality*. The standard scholarly edition of the Macro version, by Mark Eccles, was published by EETS in *The Macro Plays* (1969). The standard scholarly edition of the Digby Play version, by Donald C. Baker, John L. Murphy, and Louis B. Hall, Jr., was published by EETS in *The Late Medieval Religious Plays of Bodleian MSS. Digby 133 and E Museo 160* (1982). More recently, a Middle and Modern English facing page version of the play has been published by Milla Riggio as *The Play of Wisdom* (New York: AMS Press, 1992). Facsimiles of *Wisdom* can be found in Donald C. Baker and John L. Murphy, *The Digby Plays: Facsimiles of the Plays in Bodley MSS Digby 133 and e Museo 160* (1976), and in David Bevington, *The Macro Plays: The Castle of Perseverance, Wisdom, Mankind, A Facsimile Edition with Facing Transcriptions* (1972) (see Suggestions for Further Reading).

WISDOM

[DRAMATIS PERSONAE:]*

WISDOM
ANIMA
FIVE WITS
MIND
[WILL]
UNDERSTANDING
LUCIFER

[NON-SPEAKING CHARACTERS:
THE FIVE WITS (AS VIRGINS)
A SHREWD BOY
SIX MEN DANCERS WITH MIND
SIX WOMEN DANCERS WITH WILL
MINSTRELS: TRUMPETERS, A BAGPIPER, AND A HORNPIPER
SIX OR SEVEN SMALL BOYS, AS DEVILS]

Fyrst entreth Wysdome in a ryche purpull clothe of golde wyth a mantyll of the same ermynnyde wythin, havynge abowt hys neke a ryall hood furred wyth ermyn, upon hys hede a cheveler wyth browys, a berde of golde of sypres curlyed, a ryche imperyall crown therupon sett wyth precyus stonys and perlys, in hys leyfte honde a balle of golde wyth a cros theruppon and in hys ryght honde a regall schepter, thus seyenge: *

WISDOM. Yff ye wyll wet the propyrte	*note/accoutrements*
Ande the resun of my nayme imperyall,	*meaning*
I am clepyde of hem that in erthe be	*called by those who*
Everlastynge Wysdom, to my nobley egalle;	*equal to my nobility*
5 Wyche name acordyt best in especyall	*suits me best*

DRAMATIS PERSONAE: The following list appears at the end of the Macro Manuscript of the play. Opening stage direction: Wisdom appears here as Christ the King. *Ermynnyde:* lined with ermine; *cheveler:* wig; *browys:* bangs; *golde of sypres curlyed:* curled cypress gold.

And most to me ys convenyent,   *fitting*
Allthow eche persone of the Trinyté be wysdom eternall   *is Wisdom eternal*
And all thre on[e] everlastynge wysdome togedyr present,   *all three together are*

Nevertheles, forasmoche as wysdom ys propyrly   *since Wisdom*
10   Applyede to the Sune by resune,   *Attributed/Son/reason*
And also yt fallyt to hym specyally   *belongs*
Bycause of hys hye generacyon,   *origins*
Therfor the belovyde Sone hathe this sygnyficacyon:
Custummaly Wysdom, now Gode, now man,   *Customarily*
15   Spows of the chyrche and wery patrone,   *Spouse/true patron*
Wyffe of eche chose sowle. Thus Wysdom begane.   *chosen soul*

Here entrethe Anima as a mayde, in a wyght clothe of golde gysely
purfyled wyth menyver, a mantyll of blake theruppeon, a cheveler lyke
to Wysdom, wyth a ryche chappelet lasyde behynde hangynge down
wyth to knottys of golde and syde tasselys, knelynge down to
*Wysdom, thus seyng:**

ANIMA. *"Hanc amavi et exquisivi"*—*   *This have I loved and sought*
Fro my yougthe thys have I sowte   *From/this form*
To have to my spowse most specyally,
20   For a lover of yowr schappe am I wrowte.*   *created*
Above all hele and bewty that ever was sowght   *health*
I have lovyde Wysdom as for my lyght,
For all goodnes wyth hym ys broughte.*   *comes with him*
In wysdom I was made all bewty bryghte.

25 Off yowr name the hye felycyte   *happiness, mysterious truth*
No creature knowyt full exposycyon.   *the whole answer*
WISDOM. *Sapiencia specialior est sole.*   *wisdom is unique in form*
I am foundon lyghte wythowt comparyson,   *am created*
Off sterrys above, all the dysposicyon,*   *like the stars above*
30   Forsothe of lyght the very bryghtnes,   *Indeed like the brightness of light itself*
Merowre of the dyvyne domynacyon,   *Mirror/power*
And the image of hys goodnes.*

---

16 s.d. *gysely purfyled wyth menyver:* handsomely bordered with miniver (fur); *cheveler:* wig;
chappelet lasyde behiynde: a coronet fastened at the back.
17-65. Many of these lines derive from Henry Suso, *Orologium Sapientiae.* See Eccles, p. 203.
17-20. "Hanc amavi, et exquisivi a juventute mea, et quaesivi sponsom mihi eam assumere, et amator
factus sum formae illius" ("This one have I loved and sought from my youth, and I have wished for my
spouse in such a form, and I was created to be a lover of that beauty."). [See Wisdom of Solomon 8:2]
Wisdom is female in this Apocryphal source.
21-23. See Wisdom of Solomon, 7:10, 11.
27-29. See Wisdom of Solomon, 7:29.
30-32. See Wisdom of Solomon, 7:26.

Wysdom ys better than all worldly precyosnes,   *riches*
   And all that may dysyryde be
35 Ys not in comparyschon to my lyknes.   *Is nothing*
   The lengthe of yerys in my ryght syde be
   Ande in my lefte syde ryches, joy, and prosperyte.*
   Lo, this ys the worthynes of my name.
   ANIMA.   A, soveren Wysdom, yff yowr benygnyte   *your kindness*
40 Wolde speke of love, that wer a game.   *would be delightful*

   WISDOM.   Off my love to speke, yt ys myrable.   *miraculous*
   Beholde now, Sowll, wyth joyfull Mynde,
How lovely I am, how amyable,
   To be halsyde and kyssyde of mankynde.   *embraced/by humankind*
45 To all clene sowlys I am full hende   *ready at hand*
And ever present wer that they be;   *wherever they might be*
I love my lovers wythowtyn ende
That ther love have stedfast in me.   *Who have maintained*

The prerogatyff of my love ys so grett
50 That wo tastyt therof the lest droppe sure   *That whoever tastes/least*
All lustys and lykyngys worldly shall lett;   *desires/leave*
   They shall seme to hym fylthe and ordure.   *excrement*
   They that of the hevy burthen of synne hathe cure   *Those who/have been cured*
My love dyschargethe and puryfyethe clene,
55 It strengtheth the Mynde, the sowll makyt pure,   *makes the soul pure*
And gevyt wysdom to hem that perfyghte bene.   *to those who are pure*
Wo takyt me to spowse may veryly wene,   *Whoever/truly know*
Yff above all thynge ye love me specyall,   *especially*
   That rest and tranqwyllyte he shall sene   *expect*
60 And dey in sekyrnes of joy perpetuall.   *in certainty*

The hye worthynes of my love
   Angell nor man can tell playnly.
Yt may be felt in experyens from above
   But not spoke ne tolde as yt ys veryly.   *not expressed truly*
65 The godly love no creature can specyfye.   *The love of God/express*
What wrech is that lovyth not this love   *wretch is there who*
   That lovyt hys lovers ever so tendyrly   *Who loves his (earthly) lovers*
That hys syght from them never can remowe?   *Who cannot take his eyes from*

   ANIMA.   O worthy spowse and soveren fayer,   *fair sovereign*
70 O swet amyke, owr joy, owr blys!*   *sweet beloved*
To yowr love wo dothe repeyer,   *whoever does turn*

33-37. The royal sceptre is in Wisdom's right hand; the orb of the world in his left. [See Proverbs
3:15-16 and 8:11]
69-70. From the *Orologium.*

All felycyte yn that creature ys.
Wat may I geve yow ageyn for this,   *What may I repay you*
O Creator, lover of yowr creature?
75   Though be owr freelte we do amys,   *through our frailty*
Yowr grett mercy ever sparyth reddure.   *spares us forfeiture*

A, soveren Wysdom, *sanctus sanctorum,*   *Holy of Holies*
Wat may I geve to yowr most plesaunce?
WISDOM. *Fili, prebe michi cor tuum.* *   *My son, give me your heart.*
80   I aske not ellys of all thi substance.   *nothing else*
Thy clene hert, thi meke obeysance,   *your meek obedience*
Geve me that and I am contente.
ANIMA.   A, soveren joy, my hertys affyance,   *fiancé*
The fervowre of my love to yow I present.   *fervor*

85   That mekyt my herte, yowr love so fervent.   *You who makes/with your love*
Teche me the scolys of yowr dyvynyte.   *the practices*
WISDOM. Dysyer not to savour in cunnynge to excellent   *too precise*
But drede and conforme yowr Wyll to me.   *fear me*
For yt ys the heelfull dyscyplyne that in Wysdam may be,   *healthful*
90   The drede of God, that ys begynnynge. *
The wedys of synne yt makyt to flee,   *weeds of sin*
And swete vertuus herbys in the sowll sprynge.   *virtuous herbs*

ANIMA. O endles Wysdom, how may I have knowynge
Off thi Godhede incomprehensyble?
95   WISDOM. By knowynge of yowrsylff ye may have felynge   *have some sense*
Wat Gode ys in yowr sowle sensyble.   *Of what*
The more knowynge of yowr selff passyble,   *that is possible*
The more veryly ye shall God knowe.   *more truly*
ANIMA.   O soveren Auctoure most credyble,   *Author*
100   Yowr lessun I attende, as I owe,   *as I ought*

I that represent here the sowll of man.   *I who*
Wat ys a sowll, wyll ye declare?
WISDOM. Yt ys the ymage of Gode that all began;   *who created all things*
And not only ymage, but hys lyknes ye are.   *his image*
105   Off all creaturys the fayrest ye ware   *you were*
Into the tyme of Adamys offence.   *Until the time*
ANIMA.   Lorde, sythe we, thy sowlys, yet nowt wer ther,   *were not there*
Wy of the fyrst man bye we the vyolence?   *Why/do we pay for*

---

79. See Proverbs 23:26.
87-90. "The fear of the Lord is the beginning of his love." [See Proverbs 15:33, 9:10; Ecclesiasticus 15:12]

WISDOM. For every creature that hath ben or shall   *Because/or shall be*
110   Was in natur of the fyrst man, Adame,   *Has the nature*
Off hym takynge the fylthe of synne orygynall,   *From him inheriting*
For of hym all creaturys cam.   *Since from him*
Than by hym of reson ye have blame   *Thus he is the reason/guilt*
And be made the brondys of helle.   *And are/brands*
115   Wen ye be bore fyrst of yowr dame,   *When you are first born/mother*
Ye may in no wyse in hevyn dwell,   *You can in no way*

For ye be dysvyguryde be hys synne,   *disfigured*
Ande dammyde to derknes from Godys syghte.   *out of God's sight*
ANIMA. How dothe grace than ageyn begynne?   *does divine grace*
120   Wat reformythe the sowll to hys fyrste lyght?   *his purity*
WISDOM. Wysdam, that was Gode and man ryght,   *who was/true*
Made a full sethe to the Fadyr of hevyn   *full atonement*
By the dredfull dethe to hym was dyght,   *ordained*
Off wyche dethe spronge the sacramentys sevyn,   *From which*

125 Wyche sacramentys all synne wasche awey:
Fyrst, baptem clensythe synne orygynall   *Baptism/original sin*
And reformyt the sowll in feythe verray   *transforms/true faith*
To the gloryus lyknes of Gode eternall   *Into the glorious likeness*
Ande makyt yt as fayer and as celestyall
130   As yt never dyffowlyde had be,   *As if it had never been defiled*
Ande ys Crystys own specyall,   *Now is/own intended one*
Hys restynge place, hys plesant see.   *See, spiritual site (as of a Bishop)*

ANIMA. In a sowle watt thyngys be   *may there be?*
By wyche he hathe hys very knowynge?   *Through which/true knowledge*
135 WISDOM. Tweyn partyes. The on[e] is the sensualite,   *Two parts/senses*
Wyche ys clepyde the flechly felynge.   *is called fleshly*
The fyve owtewarde wyttys to hym be serwynge.   *five outward wits*
Wan they be not rewlyde ordynatly   *When/not ruled properly*
The sensualyte than, wythowte lesynge,   *without lying*
140   Ys made the ymage of synne then of hys foly.   *by the soul's own folly*

The other parte, that ys clepyde resone,   *is called*
Ande that ys the ymage of Gode propyrly,   *proper image of God*
For by that the sowll of Gode hathe cognycyon   *For by that (reason)*
And be that hym serwyt and lovevyt duly.   *becomes one who*
145   Be the neyther parte of reson he knowyt dyscretly   *By the low/innately*
All erthely thyngys how they shall be vsyde,
Wat suffysyth to hys myghtys bodely,   *What serves/bodily needs*
Ande wat nedyt not to be refusyde.   *what should*

	Thes tweyn do sygnyfye	These two
150	Yowr dysgysynge and yowr aray,	appearance/costume
	Blake and wyght, fowll and fayer vereyly,	foul and fair, truly
	Every sowll here, this ys no nay,	Is every soul/the truth
	Blake by sterynge of synne that cummyth all-day,	the stirring
	Wyche felynge cummythe of sensualyte,	from sensuality
155	Ande wyght by knowenge of reson veray	right reason
	Off the blyssyde infenyt Deyte.	blessed infinite Deity

	Thus a sowle ys bothe fowlle and fayer:	
	Fowll as a best be felynge of synne,	beast, by feeling of sin
	Fayer as a angell, of hevyn the ayer,	heir
160	By knowynge of Gode by hys reson wythin.	through his reason

ANIMA.   Than may I sey thus and begynne
    Wyth fyve prudent vyrgyns of my reme—*   *realm*
    Thow be the fyve wyttys of my sowll wythinne: *Those are*
    *"Nigra sum sed formosa, filia Jerusalem."**

*Her entreth fyve vyrgynes in white kertyllys and mantelys, wyth
chevelers and chappelettys, and synge "Nigra sum sed formosa, filia
Jerusalem, sicut tabernacula cedar et sicut pelles Salamonis."**

165	ANIMA. The doughters of Jerusalem me not lake	find no lack in me
	For this dyrke schadow I bere of humanyte,	dark shadow
	That as the tabernacull of cedar wythowt yt ys blake	That, like
	Ande wythine as the skyn of Salamone full of bewty.	within, like
	"Quod fusca sum, nolite considerare me,	
170	Quia decoloravit me sol Jovis."*	

WISDOM.   Thus all the sowlys that in this lyff be
    Stondynge in grace be lyke to thys.   *are like this*

	A, *quinque prudentes*, yowr wyttys fyve	A, you five prudent ones
	Kepe yow clene and ye shall never deface,	disfigure
175	Ye Godys ymage never shall ryve,	tear apart
	For the clene sowll ys Godys restynge place.	
	Thre myghtys every Cresten sowll has,	Three faculties/Christian soul
	Wyche bethe applyede to the Trinyte.*	are (also) attached

MIND.   All thre here, lo, byfor yowr face—

---

162. See Matthew 25:2.
164. See 164 s.d. below.
164 s.d. "I am black, but comely, O daughter of Jerusalem, as the tents of Cedar, as the curtains of Solomon." [See Song of Songs 1:5]
169-70. "Because I am dark, look not upon me, because the sun of Jove has discolored me." [See Song of Songs 1:6]
177-78. Eccles (pp. 205-6) notes that the three faculties of the soul—Mind, Understanding, and Will—are also associated with the Father, the Son, and the Holy Ghost respectively, as *memoria, intelligentia, and voluntas (amor)*. See Augustine, *De Trinitate*, xv. 23.

Mynde.
WILL.   Wyll.
180   UNDERSTANDING.   Ande Undyrstongynge, we thre.

WISDOM. Ye thre, declare than thys,   *Each of you three*
　　Yowr syngnyfycacyon and yowr propyrte.   *meaning and your nature*
MIND. I am Mynde, that in the sowle ys
　　The veray fygure of the Deyte.   *true/Deity*
185   Wen in myselff I have Mynde and se   *When/see*
　　The benefyttys of Gode and hys worthynes,
　　How holl I was mayde, how fayere, how fre,   *whole/noble*
　　How gloryus, how jentyll to hys lyknes,   *in his likeness*

　　Thys insyght bryngyt to my Mynde
190   Wat grates I ough to God ageyn   *What gratitude/owe*
　　That thus hathe ordenyde wythowt ende   *Who/forever*
　　Me in hys blys ever for to regne.   *reign*
　　Than myn insuffycyens ys to me peyn   *Then/inadequacy*
　　That I have not werof to yelde my dett,   *nought whereof*
195   Thynkynge myselff creature most veyn;
　　Than for sorow my bren I knett.   *my brows*

　　Wen in my Mynde I brynge togedyr
　　The yerys and dayes of my synfullnes,   *years*
　　The unstabullnes of my Mynde hedyr and thedyr,   *vacillation*
200   My oreble fallynge and freellnes,   *horrible failing/frailness*
　　Myselff ryght nought than I confes,   *Myself completely worthless*
　　For by myselff I may not ryse
　　Wythowt specyall grace of Godys goodnes.
　　Thus Mynde makyt me myselff to dyspyse.

205   I seke and fynde nowere comforte
　　But only in Gode, my Creator.
　　Than onto hym I do resorte   *unto*
　　Ande say, "Have Mynde of me, my Savowr."   *Be mindful of me*
　　Thus Mynde to Mynde bryngyth that favowre;
210   Thus, by Mynde of me, Gode I kan know.   *by my own mind*
　　Goode Mynde, of Gode yt ys the fygure;   *The good Mind/type*
　　Ande thys Mynde to have all Crysten ow.   *ought to have*

WILL. And I of the soull am the Wyll,
　　Off the Godhede, lyknes and fygure.   *Of/a likeness and a type*
215   Wyth goode Wyll no man may spyll   *be lost*
　　Nor wythowt goode Wyll, of blys be sure.   *Or without*
　　Wat soule wyll gret mede recure,   *That soul which will procure/reward*
　　He must grett Wyll have, in thought or dede,

Vertuusly sett wyth consyens pure, — *a clean conscience*
220 For in Wyll stondyt only mannys dede.* — *in will only stands man's deed*

Wyll for dede oft ys take; — *deed/often taken*
Therfor the Wyll must weell be dysposyde. — *be well-disposed*
Than ther begynnyt all grace to wake, — *Then/waken*
Yff wyth synne yt be not anosyde. — *harmed*
225 Therfor the Wyll must be wele apposyde — *examined*
Or that yt to the mevynge geve consent: — *Before it/prompting*
The lybrary of reson must be wnclosyde — *collected learning*
Ande aftyr hys domys to take entent. — *its judgments*

Owr Wyll in Gode must be only sett — *in God only*
230 And for Gode to do wylfully. — *to act willfully*
Wan gode wyll resythe, Gode ys in us knett, — *resides/knit*
Ande he performyt the dede veryly. — *truly*
Off hym cummyth all wyll sett perfyghtly, — *From him*
For of owrselff we have ryght nought — *absolutely nothing*
235 But syne, wrechydnes, and foly. — *Except*
He ys begynner and gronde of Wyll and thought. — *the beginning/basis*

Than this goode Wyll seyde before — *Thus*
Ys behoveable to yche creature — *Is necessary*
Iff he cast hym to restore — *casts himself forth*
240 The soule that he hath take of cure, — *taken to cure*
Wyche of God ys the fygure,
As longe as the fygure ys kept fayer,
Ande ordenyde ever for to endure — *to live forever*
In blys, of wyche ys he the veray hayer. — *true heir*

245 UNDERSTANDING. The thyrde parte of the soule ys Undyrstondynge,
For by Undyrstondyng I beholde wat Gode ys,
In hymselff, begynnyng wythowt begynnynge,
Ande ende wythowt ende that shall never mys. — *never be lacking*
Incomprehensyble in hymselff he ys;
250 Hys werkys in me I kan not comprehende. — *His workings*
How shulde I holly hym than that wrought all this? — *hallow him then, who*
Thus by knowynge of me to knowynge of Gode I assende.

I know in angelys he ys desyderable, — *by angels/desired*
For hym to beholde thei dysyer soverenly; — *they want above all*
255 In hys seyntys most dylectable,

213-20. On the importance of the will as articulated here, see Augustine, "Cum bona voluntate omnino perire non potes, et sine bona voluntate salvari non potes" ("With good will you cannot perish altogether, and without good will you cannot be saved"), quoted by Eccles, p. 206.

For in hymm thei joy assyduly; *they take joy assiduously*
In creaturys hys werkys ben most wondyrly, *his workings are wonderful*
For all ys made by hys myght, *all this/through his power*
By hys wysdom governyde most soverenly, *all is governed*
260 And hys benygnyte inspyryt all soullys wyth lyght. *inspires*

Off all creaturys he ys lovyde sovereyn, *By all creatures/the beloved sovereign*
For he ys Gode of yche creature,
And they be his peple that ever shall reynge, *reign*
In wom he dwellyt as in hys tempull sure. *in whom he dwells*
265 Wan I of thys knowynge make reporture *declare*
Ande se the love he hathe for me wrought,
Yt bryngyt me to love that Prynce most pure,
For, for love, that Lorde made man of nought. *from nothing*

Thys ys that love wyche ys clepyde charyte, *is called*
270 For Gode ys charyte, as awtors tellys,* *as authors tell us*
Ande woo ys in charyte, in Gode dwellyt he, *whoever*
Ande Gode, that ys charyte, in hym dwellys. *Who is charity*
Thus Undyrstondynge of Gode compellys
To cum to charyte; than have hys lyknes, lo! *and then to have God in him*
275 Blyssyde ys that sowll that this speche spellys: *who utters this speech*
"*Et qui creavit me requievit in tabernaculo meo.*"*

WISDOM. Lo, thes thre myghtys in on[e] Soule be: *three powers*
Mynde, Wyll, and Undyrstondynge.
By Mynde, of Gode the Fadyr knowyng have ye; *knowledge of*
280 By Undyrstondynge, of Gode the Sone ye have knowynge;
By Wyll, wyche turnyt into love brennynge, *burning love*
Gode the Holy Gost, that clepyde ys love: *who is called love*
Not thre Godys but on[e] Gode in beynge. *being*
Thus eche clene soule ys symylytude of Gode above. *is a similitude*

285 By Mynde feythe in the Father have we,
Hoppe in owr Lorde Jhesu, by Undyrstondynge, *Hope*
Ande be Wyll, in the Holy Gost, charyte: *by Will*
Lo, thes thre pryncypall vertus of yow thre sprynge. *virtues from you three*
Thus the clene soule standyth as a kynge;
290 Ande above all this ye have free Wyll;
Off that be ware befor all thynge, *beware*
For yff that perverte, all this dothe spyll. *turns astray, all else is destroyed*

270-72. See I John 4:15, 16.
276. "And he who created me rested in my tabernacle." [See Ecclesiasticus 24:11, 12]

Ye have thre enmyes; of hem be ware: *beware of them*
   The Worlde, the Flesche, and the Fende.   *Fiend*
295 Yowr fyve wyttys from hem ye spare,   *keep from them*
   That the sensualyte they brynge not to Mynde.
   Nothynge shulde offende Gode in no kynde;   *no manner*
   Ande yff ther do, se that the nether parte of resone   *lower part of reason*
   In no wys therto lende;   *give consent*
300 Than the over parte shall have fre domynacyon.   *higher part/free reign*

Wan suggestyon to the Mynde doth apere,   *When*
   Undyrstondynge, delyght not ye therin;
   Consent not, Wyll, yll lessons to lere,   *to learn*
   Ande than suche steryngys be no syn.   *then such promptings are*
305 Thei do but purge the soule wer ys suche contraversye.   *such conflict*
   Thus in me, Wysdom, yowr werkys begynne.   *begin your work*
   Fyght and ye shall have the crown of glory
   That ys everlastynge joy, to be parteners therinne.

ANIMA. Soveren Lorde, I am bownde to the[e]!
310 Wan I was nought thou made me thus gloryus;   *When I was nothing*
   Wan I perysschede thorow synne thou savyde me;
   Wen I was in grett perell thou kept me, Cristus;   *protected*
   Wen I erryde thou reducyde me, Jhesus;   *erred/led me back*
   Wen I was ignorant thou tawt me truthe;
315 Wen I synnyde thou corecte me thus;   *corrected me thus*
   Wen I was hevy thou comfortede me by ruthe;   *sad/pity*

Wan I stonde in grace thou holdyste me that tyde;   *you support me*
   Wen I fall thou reysyst me myghtyly;   *raise me*
   Wen I go Wyll thou art my gyde;   *When I go, Will*
320 Wen I cum thou reseyvyste me most lovynly.   *When I come back*
   Thou hast anoyntyde me with the oyll of mercy;
   Thy benefyttys, Lorde, be innumerable;
   Werfor lawde endeles to the[e] I crye,   *Thus endless praise*
   Recomendynge me to thin endles powre durable.

Here in the goynge owt the Fyve Wyttys synge "Tota pulcra es" et
cetera, * *they goyng befor, Anima next, and her folowynge Wysdom,*
and aftyr hym Mynde, Wyll, and Undyrstondynge, all thre in wyght
cloth of golde, cheveleryde and crestyde in sute.
   And aftyr the songe entreth Lucyfer in a dewyllys aray wythowt and
wythin as a prowde galonte, seynge thus on thys wyse:

---

324 s.d. "Tota pulchra es, amica mea, et macula non est in te" ("You are completely beautiful, my
love, and there is no spot in thee."). [Song of Songs 4:7] Eccles points out (p. 207) that this passage
is sung as an antiphon for the procession on Trinity Sunday.

325 LUCIFER. Owt, harow, I rore!   *(Cries of distress) I bellow*
        For envy I lore.   *lour, scowl*
        My place to restore   *My (lost) place in heaven*
            God hath mad a man.   *made*
        All cum they not thore,   *If they do not all come there*
330   Woode and they wore,   *They would be crazy*
        I shall tempte hem so sorre,   *them so strongly*
            For I am he that syn begane.   *who instituted sin*

        I was a angell of lyghte;
        Lucyfeer I hyght,   *I was called*
335   Presumynge in Godys syght,
            Werfor I am lowest in hell.   *For which I am*
        In reformynge of my place ys dyght   *changing/is put*
        Man, whom I have in most dyspyght,   *contempt*
        Ever castynge me wyth hem to fyght   *devoting myself to fight*
340   In that hevynly place that he shulde not dwell.   *So that in heaven*

        I am as wyly now as than;   *wily*
        The knowynge that I hade, yet I can;   *I still know*
        I know all compleccyons of a man   *the psychological aspects*
            Werto he ys most dysposyde;   *How/tempted*
345   Ande therin I tempte hym ay-whan;   *him ever*
        I marre hys myndys to ther wan,   *perplex his mind/weakening*
        That whoo ys hym that God hym began;   *So that woe is him/created*
            Many a holy man wyth me ys mosyde.   *confounded*

        Of Gode, man ys the fygure,   *the image*
350   Hys symylytude, hys pyctowre,   *likeness/picture*
        Gloryosest of ony creature
            That ever was wrought;
        Wyche I wyll dysvygure
        Be my fals conjecture;   *By my*
355   Yff he tende my reporture   *attends my declarations*
            I shall brynge hym to nought.

        In the soule ben thre partyes iwys: *are three parts indeed*
        Mynde, Wyll, Undyrstondynge of blys.
        Fygure of the Godhede, I know well thys;
360   And the flesche of man that ys so changeable
        That wyll I tempte, as I gees;   *as I reckon*
        Thow that I pervert, synne non ys   *Though if I pervert that, it is not sin*
        But yff the Soule consent to mys,   *Unless/do amiss*
            For in the Wyll of the Soule the dedys ben damnable.

365 To the Mynde of the Soule I shall mak suggestyun,
    Ande brynge hys Undyrstondynge to dylectacyon,
    So that hys Wyll make confyrmacyon;
       Than am I sekyr inowe   *Then I am certain enough*
    That dethe shall sew of damnacyon;   *That death will result in*
370 Than of the Sowll the Dewll hath dominacyon.   *Then*
    I wyll go make hys examynacyon,   *test him*
       To all the dewllys of helle I make avow.   *a vow*

    But, for to tempte man in my lyknes,   *with my appearance*
    Yt wolde brynge hym to grett feerfullnes,
375 I wyll change me into bryghtnes,
       And so hym to-begyle,   *beguile him*
    Sen I shall schew hym perfyghtnes,   *Since/perfection*
    And vertu prove yt wykkydnes;   *prove to be*
    Thus undyr colors all thynge perverse;   *under different colors show*
380   I shall never rest tyll the Soule I defyle.

Her[e] Lucyfer devoydyth and cummyth in ageyn as a goodly galont.   *exits*

    MIND. My Mynde ys ever on Jhesu
    That enduyde us wyth vertu.   *endowed*
    Hys doctrine to sue   *to pursue*
       Ever I purpos.   *I intend*
385 UNDERSTANDING. My Undyrstondynge ys in trew   *the true God*
    That wyth feyth us dyd renew.   *Who/did us renew*
    Hys laws to pursew
       Ys swetter to me than savowre of the rose.   *It is sweeter/fragrance*

    WILL. And my Wyll ys hys Wyll veraly   *truly*
390 That made us hys creaturys so specyally,   *He who*
    Yeldynge onto hym laude and glory
       For hys goodnes.
    LUCIFER. Ye fonnyde fathers, founders of foly,   *silly old men*
    Vt quid hic statis tota die ociosi? *
395 Ye wyll perysche or ye yt aspye.   *before you see it (glory)*
       The Dewyll hath acumberyde yow expres.   *overcome you for certain*

    Mynde, Mynde, ser, have in Mynde thys!   *be mindful of this*
    MIND. He ys not ydyll that wyth Gode ys.   *who is with God*
    LUCIFER. No, ser! I prove well yis.   *(he) is*
400   Thys ys my suggestyun.
    All thynge hat dew tymes   *have due times*

---

394. The question posed in the Parable of the Laborers in the Vineyard: "Why do you stand the whole day here in idleness?" [See Matthew 20:6]

Prayer, fastynge, labour, all thes.
Wan tyme ys not kept, that dede ys amys, *When/wrong*
   The more pleynerly to yowr informacyon. *Obviously, for your information*

405 Here ys a man that lyvyt wordly, *who lives a worldly life*
Hathe wyffe, chylderne, and serwantys besy, *Has a wife*
And other chargys that I not specyfye.
   Ys yt leeffull to this man *lawful for this man*
To lewe hys labour wsyde truly, *leave his labor used truly*
410 Hys chargys perysche that Gode gaff duly, *(To let) his/gave*
Ande geve hym to preyer and es of body? *give himself over/ease of body*
   Woso do thus wyth God ys not than. *Whoso does this is not then with God*

Mertha plesyde Gode grettly thore.* *Martha pleased greatly there*
MIND. Ye, but Maria plesyde hymm moche more.
415 LUCIFER. Yet the lest hade blys for evermore. *Yet the least had eternal bliss*
   Ys not this anow? *Is this not enough?*
MIND. Contemplatyff lyff ys sett befor. *The contemplative life/higher*
LUCIFER. I may not belewe that in my lore, *my own learning*
For God hymselff, wan he was man borre, *when/born a man*
420   Wat lyff lede he? answer thou now. *What kind of life*

Was he ever in contemplacyon? *a contemplative?*
MIND. I suppos not, by my relacyon. *from what I can say*
LUCIFER. And all hys lyff was informacyon *instruction*
   Ande example to man.
425 Sumtyme wyth synners he had conversacyon;
Sumtyme wyth holy also comunycacyon; *holy men*
Sumtyme he laboryde, preyde; sumtyme tribulacyon; *had troubles*
   Thys was *vita mixta* that Gode here began; *mixed life*

Ande that lyff shulde ye here sewe. *pursue*
430 MIND. I kan not belewe thys ys trew.
LUCIFER. Contemplatyff lyff for to sewe *pursue*
   Yt ys grett drede, and se cause why: *is terrible/see the cause*
They must fast, wake, and prey, ever new,
Wse harde lyvynge and goynge wyth dyscyplyne dew, *follow due discipline*
435 Kepe sylence, wepe, and surphettys eschewe, *eschew surfeit*
   Ande yff they fayll of thys they offende Gode hyghly.

Wan they have wastyde by feyntnes, *When/wasted away*
Than febyll ther wyttys and fallyn to fondnes, *Then feeble are their wits/foolishness*
Sum into dyspeyer and sum into madnes.

413-14. Martha busied herself about the house while Mary sat and listened to Jesus. [See Luke 10:38-42]

440   Wet yt well, God ys not plesyde wyth thys.   *Note it*
        Lewe, lewe, suche syngler besynes.   *Leave, leave/strange business*
        Be in the worlde, vse thyngys nesesse.   *necessary things*
        The comyn ys best expres.   *ordinary/for certain*
        Who clymyt hye, hys fall gret ys.   *Whoever climbs*

445   MIND. Truly, me seme ye have reson.   *It seems to me that*
        LUCIFER. Aplye yow then to this conclusyun.   *Attend*
        MIND. I kan make no replicacyon.   *counter-argument*
        Your resons be grete.
        I kan not forgett this informacyon.
450   LUCIFER. Thynke theruppon, yt ys yowr saluacyon.
        Now and Undyrstondynge wolde have delectacyon,   *if Understanding/delight*
        All syngler deuocyons he wolde lett.   *unusual devotions/leave*

        Yowr fyve wyttys abrode lett sprede.   *let wander*
        Se how comly to man ys precyus wede;   *precious clothing*
455   Wat worschype yt ys to be manfull in dede;   *What honor*
        That bryngyt in dominacyon.   *brings power*
        Off the symple what profyght yt to tak hede?   *what profits it*
        Beholde how ryches dystroyt nede;
        It makyt man fayer, hym wele for to fede;   *himself to feed well*
460   And of lust and lykynge commyth generacyon.

        Undyrstondynge, tender ye this informacyon?   *do you value*
        UNDERSTANDING. In thys I fele in manere of dylectacyon.   *of delight*
        LUCIFER. A, ha, ser, then ther make a pawsacyon.   *pause*
        Se and beholde the worlde abowte.   *Look/around you*
465   Lytyll thynge suffysyt to salvacyon;   *Little things suffice for*
        All maner synnys dystroyt contryscyon;   *Every kind of sin/contrition*
        They that dyspeyer mercy have grett compunccyon;   *Those who/dis-ease*
        Gode plesyde best wyth goode Wyll, no dowte.   *God is pleased*

        Therfor, Wyll, I rede yow inclyne;   *counsel you to submit*
470   Lewe yowr stodyes, thow ben dyvyn;   *Leave/studies//though they are divine*
        Yowr prayers, yowr penance, of ipocryttys the syne,   *the sign of hypocrites*
        Ande lede a comun lyff.
        What synne ys in met, in ale, in wyn?   *is there in meat*
        Wat synne ys in ryches, in clothynge fyne?
475   All thynge Gode ordenyde to man to inclyne.   *accept*
        Lewe yowr nyse chastyte and take a wyff.   *precise chastity/marry*

        Better ys fayer frut than fowll pollucyon.
        What seyth Sensualite to this conclusyon?
        WILL. As the fyve wyttys gyff informacyon,   *five senses report*
480   Yt semyth yowr resons be goode.

LUCIFER. The Wyll of the Soule hathe fre dominacyon;
Dyspute not to moche in this wyth reson;   *too much*
Yet the nethyr parte to this taketh sum instruccyon,   *the lower part*
And so shulde the over parte but he were woode.   *higher/unless he were mad*

485   WILL. Me seme, as ye sey, in body and soule,   *It seems to me*
         Man may be in the worlde and be ryght goode.   *may live*
      LUCIFER. Ya, ser, by Sent Powle!
         But trust not thes prechors, for they be not goode,
         For they flatter and lye as they wore woode;   *as if they were mad*
490   Ther ys a wolffe in a lombys skyn.*
      WILL. Ya, I woll no more row ageyn the floode.   *row against the flood*
         I woll sett my soule on a mery pynne.   *in a joyful frame of mind*

      LUCIFER. Be my trowthe, than do ye wyslye.   *then you act wisely*
         Gode lovyt a clene sowll and a mery.   *God loves*
495   Acorde yow thre togedyr by   *If you three together agree*
         And ye may not mysfare.   *Then you should not fare badly*
      MIND. To this suggestyon agre we.
      UNDERSTANDING. Delyght therin I have truly.
      WILL. And I consent therto frelye.
500   LUCIFER.   A, ha, ser, all mery than! and awey care!

      Go in the worlde, se that abowte;   *look around*
      Geet goode frely, cast no dowte;   *Get goods freely*
      To the ryche ye se men lowly lought.   *bow lowly*
         Geve to yowr body that ys nede,   *that which it needs*
505   Ande ever be mery; let revell rowte!   *run riot*
      MIND. Ya, ellys I beschrew my snowte!   *curse*
      UNDERSTANDING. And yff I care, cache me the gowte!   *may I catch*
      WILL.   And yff I spare, the Dewyll me spede!

      LUCIFER. Go yowr wey than and do wysly.
510   Change that syde aray.   *long gown*
      MIND.   I yt dyfye.
      UNDERSTANDING. We woll be fresche, and it happe, *la plu joly* !   *all the better*
         Farwell penance!
      MIND. To worschyppys I wyll my Mynde aplye.   *To powerful men*
515   UNDERSTANDING. My Undyrstondynge in   *I'll apply my talents to*
                        worschyppys and glory.   *powerful men and fame*

      WILL. And I in lustys of lechery,
         As was sumtyme gyse of Frawnce.   *was once the fashion*

---

490. See Matthew 7:15.

Wyth "wy wyppe!"   *"Why, quick!"*
Farwell, quod I, the Dewyll ys uppe!

    Exient   *Let them exit*

520 LUCIFER. Off my dysyere now have I summe   *desire*
     Wer onys brought into custume,   *Were it once brought*
     Then farwell consyens, he wer clumme,   *conscience/silent*
       I shulde have all my Wyll.
     Resone I have made both deff and dumme;
525 Grace ys owt and put arome;   *to roam*
     Wethyr I wyll have, he shall cum.   *Whither I would want him*
       So at the last I shall hym spyll.   *destroy*

     I shall now stere hys Mynde   *stir his mind*
     To that syne made me a fende,   *Towards/that made me a fiend*
     Pryde, wyche ys ageyn kynde   *against nature*
530   And of all synnys hede.   *chief of all sins*
     So to covetyse he shall wende,   *Then/turn*
     For that enduryth to the last ende,   *that (sin) endures*
     And onto lechery, and I may hymm rende,   *unto/bend him*
       Than am I seker the Soule ys dede.   *am I certain*

535 That Soule Gode made incomparable,
     To hys lyknes most amyable,
     I shall make yt most reprouable,   *most reprehensible*
       Ewyn lyke to a fende of hell.   *Even like a fiend*
     At hys deth I shall apere informable,   *with information*
540 Schewynge hym all hys synnys abhomynable,
     Prewynge hys Soule damnable,   *Proving*
       So wyth dyspeyer I shall hym qwell.   *despair/conquer*

     Wyll in clennes ys mankyn,   *While mankind is pure*
     Verely, the soule God ys wythin;   *God is within the soul*
545 Ande wen yt ys in dedly synne,
       Yt ys werely the Develys place.   *truly*
     Thus by colours and false gynne   *pretense/cunning*
     Many a soule to hell I wyn.
     Wyde to go I may not blyne   *Far to go/cease*
550   Wyth this fals boy, God gyff hym evell grace!

Her[e] he takyt a schrewde boy wyth hym and goth hys wey cryenge.   *naughty*

MIND. Lo, me here in a new aray!   *here I am/new clothes*
     Wyppe, wyrre, care awey!   *Quick! Hurry!*
       Farwell perfeccyon!

Me semyt myselff most lyghly ay.   *I look most handsome, aye!*
555 It ys but honest, no pryde, no nay.   *I am merely being honest, indeed*
I wyll be freshest, by my fay,   *faith*
For that acordyt wyth my complexccyon.   *agrees with*

UNDERSTANDING. Ande have here one as fresche as yow!   *here is*
All mery, mery, and glade now.
560 I have get goode, Gode wott how.   *got goods, God knows how*
    For joy I sprynge, I sckyppe.   *skip*
Goode makyt on[e] mery, to Gode avowe.   *Goods make one/I swear*
Farewell consyens, I know not yow!
I am at eas, hade I inow.   *I have had enough*
565   Truthe on syde I lett hym slyppe.   *I let truth slip aside*

WILL. Lo, here on[e] as jolye as ye!   *here is one*
I am so lykynge, me seme I fle.   *filled with pleasure it seems I fly*
I have atastyde lust: farwell chastyté!   *tasted*
My hert ys evermore lyght.   *merry*
570 I am full of felycyte.   *happiness*
My delyght ys all in bewte.
Ther ys no joy but that in me.
    A woman me semyth a hevynly syght.   *seems to me*

MIND. Ande thes ben my syngler solace: *are my only pleasures*
575 Kynde, fortune, and grace.   *Nature*
Kynde nobley of kynrede me gevyn hase,   *Nature has given me nobility of birth*
Ande that makyt me soleyn.   *aloof*
Fortune in worldys worschyppe me doth lace.   *entwines me*
Grace gevyt curryus eloquens, and that mase   *gives curious eloquence that amazes*
580   That all oncunnynge I dysdeyn.   *All the ignorant I disdain*

UNDERSTANDING. And my joy ys especyall
To hurde uppe ryches, for fer to fall,   *hoard/fear of a fall*
To se yt, to handyll yt, to tell yt all,   *to count it all*
    And streightly to spare!   *to spare little*
585 To be holde ryche and reyall   *to be esteemed*
I bost, I avawnt wer I shall.   *I brag wherever I want*
Ryches makyt a man equall   *equal to all*
    To hem sumtyme hys sovereyngys wer.   *To those who once were his lords*

WILL. To me ys joy most laudable   *the best joy is*
590 Fresche dysgysynge to seme amyable,   *fresh clothing*
Spekynge wordys delectable   *sweet words*
    Perteynynge onto love.
It ys joy of joys inestymable
To halse, to kys the affyable.   *to embrace/the pliant*

595 A lover ys son perceyvable   *can easily be told*
      Be the smylynge on me, wan yt doth remove.   *by my smiling/when I undress*

MIND. To avaunte thus me semyth no schame,   *To boast seems to me*
For galontys now be in most fame.   *gallants/are most famous*
Curtely personys men hem proclame.   *Courtly/men proclaim them*
600   Moche we be sett bye.   *we esteem it*
UNDERSTANDING. The ryche covetouse wo dare blame,   *Who dares blame*
Off govell and symony thow he bere the name?   *usury and simony*
To be fals, men report yt game;   *to lie/a sport*
     Yt ys clepyde wysdom, "Ware that" quod Ser Wyly.   *Beware/Sir Guile*

605 WILL. Ande of lechory to make avawnte   *to boast of lechery*
Men fors yt no more than drynke atawnt.   *regard it/drinking too much*
Thes thyngys be now so conversant,   *so familiar*
     We seme yt no schame.   *It seems to us*
MIND. Curyous aray I wyll ever hante.   *make a habit of wearing*
610 UNDERSTANDING. Ande I falsnes, to be passante.   *surpassing*
WILL. Ande I in lust my flesche to daunte.   *to tame*
     No man dyspyes thes; they be but game.   *but sport*

MIND. In rejoys of thes; now let us synge!   *To celebrate this*
UNDERSTANDING. Ande yff I spar, evell joy me wrynge!   *slack off, ill joy to me*
615 WILL. Have at, quod I, lo, howe I sprynge!   *Here goes/leap*
     Lust makyth me wondyr wylde.   *wonderfully*
MIND. A tenowr to yow bothe I brynge.   *tenor*
UNDERSTANDING. And I a mene for ony kynge.   *middle part suitable*
WILL. And but a trebull I owtwrynge,   *if only a treble/squeak out*
620   The Devell hym spede that myrthe exyled!   *Devil take him who*

     Et cantent.   *And they sing*

MIND. How be this, trow ye nowe?   *do you think*
UNDERSTANDING. At the best, to God avowe.   *to God I vow*
WILL. As mery as the byrde on bow,   *bird on a branch*
     I take no thought.
625 MIND. The welfare of this worlde ys yn us, I a vowe!   *way of the world*
UNDERSTANDING. Lett eche man tell hys condycyons howe.   *his reasons*
WILL. Begynne ye, ande have at yow,   *you have a go*
     For I am aschamyde of ryght nought.   *nothing at all*

MIND. Thys ys cause of my worshyppe: *the reason for*
630 I serve myghty lordeschyppe
Ande am in grett tenderschyppe;   *stewardship*
     Therfor moche folke me dredys.
Men sew to my frendeschyppe   *pursue my*

For meyntnance of her schendeschyppe.   *shameful conduct*
635 I support hem by lordeschyppe.   *before my Lordship*
    For to get goode this a grett spede ys.   *goods, this is the best way*

UNDERSTANDING. And I use jorowry,   *bribe the jury*
Enbrace questys of perjury,   *Set up panels of perjury*
Choppe and chonge wyth symonye,   *change course for simony (graft)*
640   And take large yeftys.   *large gifts*
Be the cause never so try,   *Even if the opposite case is good*
I preve yt fals, I swere, I lye,
Wyth a quest of myn affye.   *bought jury panel*
    The redy wey this now to thryfte ys.   *The easy way to prosperity*

645 WILL. And wat trow ye be me?   *what do you believe of me?*
More than I take spende I threys thre.
Sumtyme I yeff, sumtyme they me,   *give to others*
    Ande am ever fresche and gay.
Few placys now ther be
650 But onclennes we shall ther see;
    It ys holde but a nysyte.   *held to be a detail*
    Lust ys now comun as the way.   *so familiar*

MIND. Law procedyth not for meyntnance.
UndERSTANDING. Trowthe recurythe not for habundance.   *appears not abundant*
655 WILL. And lust ys in so grett usance,
    We fors yt nought.   *We come to it easily*
MIND. In us the worlde hathe most affyance.   *reliance*
UNDERSTANDING. Non thre be in so grett aqweynttance.   *No other three/such*
WILL. Few ther be outhe of owr allyance.   *uncommitted to us*
660   Wyll the worlde ys thus, take we no thought!   *While/no heed*

MIND. Thought! nay, therageyn stryve I.   *against that I strive*
UNDERSTANDING. We have that nedyt us, so thryve I.   *what we need*
WILL. And yff that I care, never wyve I.   *For all I care I will never marry*
    Let them care that hathe for to sewe!   *who have to pursue it*
665 MIND. Wo lordschyppe shall sew must yt bye.   *Who wants Lordship must buy it*
UNDERSTANDING. Wo wyll have law must have monye.   *Who wants justice*
WILL. Ther povert ys the malewrye,   *Where poverty is, is misfortune*
    Thow ryght be, he shall never renewe.   *Though (a poor man) is right/win*

MIND. Wronge ys born upe boldly,   *upheld brazenly*
670 Thow all the worlde know yt opynly,
Mayntnance ys now so myghty,   *Unjust support*
    Ande all is for mede.   *for sale*
UNDERSTANDING. The law ys so coloryde falsly
By sleyttys and by perjury,   *slights*

675 Brybys be so gredy,
     That to the pore trowth ys take ryght nought a hede.   *For the poor/not heeded*

    WILL. Wo gett or loose, ye be ay wynnande.   *Who gains/you are always winning*
    Mayntnance and perjury now stande.   *Unjust support*
    Thei wer never so moche reynande   *was never/litigation*
680   Seth Gode was bore.   *Since/born*
    MIND. Ande lechery was never more vsande
    Off lernyde and lewyde in this lande.   *by both the learned and simple*
    UNDERSTANDING. So we thre be now in hande.   *hand in hand*
     WILL. Ya, and most vsyde everywere.

685 MIND. Now wyll we thre do make a dance   *we three dance*
    Off thow that longe to owr retenance,   *For you who belong/retinue*
    Cummynge in by contenance.   *Hiding behind masks*
     This were a dysporte.   *a sport*
    UNDERSTANDING. Therto I geve acordance   *offer good accord*
690   Off thow that ben of myn affyance.   *From my kind*
    WILL. Let se bytyme Ye, Meyntnance.   *Let us see in good time/Unjust support*
     Clepe in fyrst yowr resorte.   *Call in your first resort*

    Here entur six dysgysyde in the sute of Mynde, wyth rede berdys,
  and lyouns rampaunt on here crestys, and yche a warder in hys honde;
  *her mynstrallys, trumpes. Eche answere for hys name.**

    MIND. Let se cum in Indignacyon and Sturdynes,   *Disdain and Stubbornness*
    Males also and Hastynes,   *Malice and Rash Anger*
695 Wreche and Dyscorde expres,   *Vengeance and Discord*
     And the sevente am I, Mayntennance.   *Unjust Support*
    Seven ys a numbyr of dyscorde and inperfyghtnes.
    Lo, here ys a yomandrye wyth loveday to dres!*   *yeomanry/loveday*
    Ande the Devle hade swore yt, they wolde ber up falsnes*   *If the Devil/testify to*
700   Ande maynten yt at the best. This ys the Devllys dance.*   *Devil's*

    Ande here menstrellys be convenyent,   *their minstrels/nearby*
    For trumpys shulde blow to the jugemente;   *should accompany*
    Off batell also yt ys on[e] instrumente,   *Of battle*

---

692 s.d. Mind's six retainers wear his livery and have red beards (like Judas in the cycle plays). The crest with lions rampant has been associated with the badges of the Dukes of Suffolk and Norfolk (see Eccles, p. 211). Each of the vices has a staff in his hand, and the accompanying minstrels have trumpets. The vices answer to their names as Mind plays the role of Maintenance.

698. Loveday: a day for settling disputes. See J. W. Bennett, "The Medieval Loveday," *Speculum*, xxxiii (1958), 351-70, cited by Eccles, p. 211.

699-700. Even if the Devil had sworn it true, they would testify it to be a lie, and maintain it effectively.

700. The Devil's dance, associated with the folk practice involving the Lord of Misrule, with pipers and drummers dancing through the church. See Eccles, p. 211.

Gevynge comfort to fyght.
705 Therfor they be expedyente   *useful*
To thes meny of meyntement.   *these minions of Maintenance*
Blow! lett see Madam Regent,*   *a dance*
Ande daunce, ye laddys! yowr hertys be lyght.   *let your hearts*

Lo, that other spare, thes meny wyll spende.   *what the others spare, this troupe*
710 UNDERSTANDING. Ya, wo ys hym shall hem offende! *Woe to whoever offends them*
WILL. Wo wyll not to hem condescende,   *Whoever/accede to them*
He shall have threttys.   *intimidation*
MIND. They spyll that law wolde amende.   *They destroy whoever*
UNDERSTANDING. Yit Mayntnance no man dare reprehende.
715 WILL. Thes meny thre synnys comprehende: *This retinue understands*
Pryde, Invy, and Wrathe in hys hestys.   *in his commands*

UNDERSTANDING. Now wyll I than begyn my traces.   *my dance steps*
Jorowrs in on[e] hoode beer to facys.   *bear two faces*
Fayer speche and falsehede in on[e] space ys.
720 Is it not ruthe?   *a pity?*
The quest of Holborn cum into this placys.*   *jury panel (inquest)*
Ageyn the ryght ever ther rechase ys.   *Against rightful pleas/their review*
Off wom they holde not, harde hys grace ys.   *Whomever they rule against*
Many a tyme have dammyde truthe.   *have they stopped up truth*

Here entrethe six jorours in a sute, gownyde, wyth hodys abowt her
nekys, hattys of Meyntenance therupon, vyseryde dyversly; here
*mynstrell, a bagpype.**

725 UNDERSTANDING. Let se fyrst Wronge and Sleyght;   *Let's see*
Dobullnes and Falsnes, schew yowr myght;   *Duplicity and Falsehood*
Now Raveyn and Dyscheyit;   *Plunder and Deceit*
Now holde yow here togydyr.   *Now link hands*
Thys menys consyens ys so streytt   *This troupe's/s/stretched*
730 That they report as mede gevyt beyght.*   *That "reward" means being bought*
Here ys the quest of Holborn, an evyll entyrecte.   *jury panel/an evil salve*
They daunce all this londe hydyr and thedyr!

---

707. Madame Regent: apparently the name of a dance; see Eccles, p. 211.
721. The quest of Holborn: probably the jury, or inquest, presided over by the the the Sheriff and justices
of Middlesex, meeting in High Holborn; see Eccles, pp. 211-12.
724 s.d. Six jurors in livery enter, with gowns, with hoods around their necks, and wearing hats like
that of Maintenance. They are masked "diversly," perhaps with two faces pointing in opposite
directions, as in Understanding's description above; their minstrel, a bagpipe. The role of Perjury is
played by Understanding.
729-30. i.e., Their conscience is so stretched out of shape that what they call just reward means being
bought.

And I, Perjury, yowr fownder.
Now dance on, us all! The worlde doth on us wondyr!   *all of us*

735   Lo, here ys a menye love wellfare!   *a troupe that loves*
MIND. Ye, they spende that tru men spare.   *what true men give*
WILL. Have they a brybe, they have no care   *If they have a bribe*
     Wo hath wronge or ryght.   *Who is*
MIND. They fors not to swere and starre.   *They think nothing of*
740   WILL. Though all be false, les and mare.
UNDERSTANDING. Wyche wey to the woode wyll the hare   *Whichever/goes*
     They knowe, and they at rest sett als tyghte.*   *can sit tight*

     Some seme hem wyse   *Some seem to them wise*
     For the fadyr of us, Covetyse.   *To our mutual father, Covetousness*

745   WILL. Now Meyntnance and Perjury   *Now that*
Hathe schewyde the trace of ther cumpeny,   *dance steps*
Ye shall se a sprynge of Lechery,   *lively dance*
     That to me attende.   *For that*
Here forme ys of the stewys clene rebaldry.   *Their form/brothel's bare ribaldry*
750   They wene sey sothe wen that they lye.   *They seem to tell the truth*
Off the comyn they synge eche wyke by and by.*   *Commonly they sing*
     They may sey wyth tenker, I trow, "Lat amende."*   *with the tinker/"Let it amend."*

*Here entreth six women in sut, thre dysgysyde as galontys and thre as matrones, wyth wondyrfull vysurs conregent; here mynstrell, a hornepype.**

WILL. Cum slepers, Rekleshede and Idyllnes,   *Heedlessness and Idleness*
     All in all, Surfet and Gredynes,   *With each other, Surfeit and Greediness*
755   For the flesche, Spousebreche and Mastres,   *Spousebreach (adultery) and Mistress*
     Wyth jentyll Fornycacyon.   *(I dance) with refined Fornication*
Yowr mynstrell a hornepype mete   *plays a hornpipe measure*
That fowll ys in hymselff but to the erys swete.   *He is foul, but plays sweetly*
Thre fortherers of love; "Hem schrew I" quod Bete.*   *Three furtherers of love*
760   Thys dance of this damesellys ys thorow this regyn.   *of these damsels/everywhere*

741-42. *i.e.*, Whichever way the hare takes to the woods, they know where he will end up, and they can simply sit tight.

751. *i.e.*, weekly they sing in the brothels, commonly—rudely, and of (or for) the common sort.

752. *i.e.*, crying like a tinker to mend metalware, perhaps "Latten mending."

752 s.d. Will evidently plays the role of Lechery, or Fornication, while six women enter in similar livery, three dressed as gallants and three as matrons. They wear "wondyrfull" masks, perhaps close fitting—"congruent," as Eccles suggests (p. 212) or, more likely, two-faced like those of the jurors above, and as indicated by their paired names below. Their minstrel attends with a hornpipe, appropriate to cuckolds.

759. Furtherers of love: whores. "I curse them," says Betty.

MIND. Ye may not endure wythowt my Meyntenance.   *support*
UNDERSTANDING. That ys bought wyth a brybe of owr substance.
WILL. Whow, breydest thou us of thin aqueyntance?   *Whoa! Would you presume on*
   I sett the[e] at nought!   *set your value at nothing*
765 MIND. On that worde I woll tak vengeaunce.
   Wer vycys be gederyde, ever ys sum myschance.   *wherever vices are gathered*
   Hurle hens thes harlottys! Here gyse ys of France.   *Throw out/Their guise is from*
     They shall abey bytterly, by hym that all wrought!   *buy it bitterly*

UNDERSTANDING. Ill spede the[e], ande thou spare!   *if you wait around*
770 Thi longe body bare
   To bett I not spare.   *I'll not fail to beat*
     Have the[e] ageyn!   *Have at*
WILL. Holde me not! let me go! ware!   *Beware!*
   I dynge, I dasche! ther, go ther!
775 Dompe deuys, can ye not dare?   *Dumb show/not keep quiet?*
     I tell yow, owtwarde, on[e] and tweyn!   *march! One, and Two...*

  Exient   *Let them [the dancers] leave*

MIND. Now I schrew yow thus dansaunde!   *Now I curse you/dancing*
UNDERSTANDING. Ye, and ewyll be thou thryvande!   *May evil thrive in you*
WILL. No more let us be stryvande.   *quarrelling*
780   Nowe all at on[e]!   *Now all as one!*
MIND. Here was a meny onthryvande.   *an unthrifty troupe*
UNDERSTANDING. To the Devll be they dryvande.   *To the Devil may/be going*
WILL. He that ys yll wyvande,   *who is badly married*
   Wo hys hym, by the bon!   *Woe to him/bone*

785 MIND. Leve then this dalyance   *dalliance*
   Ande set we a ordenance   *make up a plan*
   Off better chevesaunce   *for a better money-making scheme*
     How we may thryve.
UNDERSTANDING. At Westmyster, wythowt varyance,
790 The nex terme shall me sore avawnce,   *Next law term/greatly advance*
   For retornys, for enbraces, for recordaunce.   *writ returns, encumbrances, recordings*
     Lyghtlyer to get goode kan no man on lyve.   *An easier way/knows no man*

MIND. Ande at the parvyse I wyll be   *church front*
   A Powlys betwyn to ande thre,   *At St. Paul's/two*
795 Wyth a menye folowynge me,   *a troupe*
     Entret, juge-partynge, and to-supporte.   *bribery, judge-sharing/secret backing*
WILL. Ande ever the latter, the lever me.   *Always last/the better for*
   Wen I com lat to the cyte   *late at night*
   I walke all lanys and weys to myn affynyte;   *after my kind*
800   And I spede not ther, to the stews I resort.   *If I don't fare well there*

MIND. Ther gettys thou nouhte, but spendys.   *get nothing, though you spend*
WILL. Yis, sumtyme I take amendys   *exact a fine*
Off hem that nought offendys,   *From those who*
    I engrose upe here purs.   *corner their purses*
805 MIND. And I arest ther no drede ys,   *no fear*
Preve forfett ther no mede ys,   *Secure a forfeit/no reward*
Ande take to me that nede ys;   *take from the needy*
    I reke not thow they curs.   *I care not if*

UNDERSTANDING. Thow they curs, never the wers I fare.
810 Thys day I endyght them I herde of never are;   *Today I indict those/never heard of*
To-morow I wyll aqwyt them, yff nede were.
    Thus lede I my lyff.
WILL. Ye, but of us thre I have lest care.
Met and drynke and ease, I aske no mare,   *no more*
815 Ande a praty wenche, to se here bare;   *pretty*
    I reke but lytyll be sche mayde or wyffe.   *care little whether*

MIND. Thys on a soper   *(I'll put) this towards*
I wyll be seen rycher,   *So that I*
Set a noble wyth goode chere   *Put forth a noble*
820   Redyly to spende.
UNDERSTANDING. And I tweyn, be this feer,   *I offer two/this company*
To moque at a goode dyner.   *To make sport*
I hoope of a goode yer,
    For ever I trost Gode wyll send.   *Which I always trust that*

825 WILL. And best we have wyne,   *With the best wine*
Ande a cosyn of myn
Wyth us for to dyne.
    Thre nobles wyll I spende frely.   *readily spend*
MIND. We shall acorde well and fyne.   *shall agree here*
830 UNDERSTANDING. Nay, I wyll not passe schylyngys nyne.   *spend more than*
WILL. No, thou was never but a swyn.   *never anything but*
    I woll be holdyn jentyll, by Sent Audre of Ely.*   *considered gentle/St. Ethelreda*

Ande now in my Mynde I have
My cosyn Jenet N.,* so Gode me save;   *Jenny N____*
835 Sche mornyth wyth a chorle, a very knave,   *suffers/churl*
    And never kan be mery.
I pley me ther wen I lyst rawe;   *when I want to sport*
    Than the chorle wyll here dysprawe.   *slander her*

---

832. Saint Audre of Ely: also known as St. Ethelreda, she established a monastery at Ely in 673.
834. Jenny N.: *"Nomen"*—any name, presumably a name of someone local or in the audience.

Who myght make hym thys to lawe, *Whoever might take him to court*
840   I wolde onys have hym in the wyrry. *then have him by the throat*

MIND. For thys I kan a remedye: *know a remedy*
I shall rebuk hym thus so dyspytuusly *harass/pitilessly*
That of hys lyff he shall wery
And qwak for very fere. *quake*
845   Ande yff he wyll not leve therby,
On hys bodye he shall abye *he shall pay for it physically*
Tyll he leve that jelousy.
Nay, suche chorlys I kan lere. *I can teach*

UNDERSTANDING. Nay, I kan better hym qwytte: *repay him*
850   Arest hym fyrst to pes for fyght, *to keep the peace for fighting*
Than in another schere hym endyght, *indict him in another shire*
He ne shall wete by wom ne howe. *know by whom or how*
Have hym in the Marschalsi seyn aryght, *before the Knight-Marshall's court*
Than to the Amralte, for they wyll byght, *Court of Admiralty/bite*
855   *A prevenire facias* than have as tyght,* *then will have him tightly*
Ande thou shalt hurle hym so that he shall have inow. *harass/enough*

WILL. Wat and thes wrongys be espyede? *What if*
UNDERSTANDING. Wyth the crose and the pyll I shall wrye yt* *conceal it*
That ther shall never man dyscrey yt *never discern*
860   That may me appeyere. *So that I might have to appear*
MIND. Ther ys no craft but we may trye yt.
UNDERSTANDING. Mede stoppyt, be yt never so allyede. *Bribery stops the law*
WILL. Wyth yow tweyn wo ys replyede, *He to whom you have replied*
He may sey he hathe a schrewde seyer. *clever manipulator*

865   MIND. Thow woldyst have wondyr of sleyghtys that be.
UNDERSTANDING. Thys make sume ryche and summe never the. *never thrive*
WILL. They must nedys grett goodys gett the[e].
Now go we to the wyne!
MIND. In trewthe I grante; have at wyth the[e]! *have at it*
870   UNDERSTANDING. Ande for a peny or to, I wyll not fle.
WILL. Mery, mery, all mery than be we!
Who that us tarythe, curs have he and myn! *Whoever delays us/my curse*

WISDOM. O thou Mynde, remembyr the[e]!
Turne thi weys, thou gost amyse. *Turn from*
875   Se what thi ende ys, thou myght not fle:
Dethe to every creature certen ys.

---

855. *A prevenire facias:* a summons for an English crime in a foreign country.
858. *the crose and the pyll:* heads and tails of a coin, i.e., with money.

They that lyve well, they shall have blys;
Thay that endyn yll, they goo to hell.
I am Wysdom, sent to tell yow thys:
880   Se in what stat thou doyst indwell.   *what state/dost now dwell*

MIND.   To my Mynde yt cummyth from farre
That dowtles man shall dey.
Ande thes weys we go, we erre.   *And if we follow these paths*
Undyrstondynge, wat do ye sey?
885   UNDERSTANDING.   I sey, man, holde forthe thi wey!   *keep on your path*
The lyff we lede ys sekyr ynowe.   *secure enough*
I wyll no Undyrstondynge shall lett my pley.   *let no/hinder*
Wyll, frende, how seyst thowe?
WILL.   I wyll not thynke theron, to Gode avowe!   *I vow*
890   We be yit but tender of age.   *still young*
Schulde we leve this lyve? Ya, whowe!   *leave this life/Yet, whoa!*
We may amende wen we be sage.   *can change when/old*

WISDOM.   Thus many on[e] unabylythe hym to grace.   *many a one disables*
They wyll not loke, but slumber and wynke.
895   They take not drede before ther face,   *no fear*
Howe horryble ther synnys stynke.
Wen they be on the pyttys brynke,   *When/hellpit's brink*
Than shall they trymbull and qwake for drede.
Yit Mynde, I sey, yow bethynke   *consider*
900   In what perell ye be now! Take hede!

Se howe ye have dysvyguryde yowr soule!   *disfigured*
Beholde yowrselff; loke veryly in Mynde!   *look truly into yourself*

Here Anima apperythe in the most horrybull wyse, fowlere than a fende. *

MIND.   Out! I tremble for drede, by Sent Powle!   *Away!*
Thys ys fowler than ony fende.
905   WISDOM.   Wy art thou creature so onkynde,   *unnatural*
Thus to defoule Godys own place,
That was made so gloryus wythowt ende?
Thou hast made the Devllys rechace.   *called back the Devil*
As many dedly synnys as ye have vsyde,
910   So many devllys in yowr soule be.
Beholde wat ys therin reclusyde!   *See what/hidden*
Alas, man, of thi Soule have pyte!

---

902 s.d. *most horrybull wyse:* a costume even more horrible than a devil.

Here rennyt owt from undyr the horrybyll mantyll of the Soull vi[i]
small boys in the lyknes of dewyllys and so retorne ageyn. *

WISDOM. What have I do? why lovyste thou not me?   *done*
 Why cherysyste thi enmye? why hatyst thou thi frende?   *do you cherish*
915 Myght I have don ony more for the[e]?
 But love may brynge drede to Mynde.

 Thou hast made the[e] a bronde of hell   *firebrand*
  Whom I made the[e] ymage of lyght.
 Yff the Devll myght, he wolde the[e] qwell,   *Devil/destroy*
920 But that mercy expellyt hys myght.   *Except that Mercy repels*
 Wy doyst thou, Soule, me all dyspyght?   *spite me*
 Why gevyst thou myn enmy that I have wrought?   *Why do you give/that which*
 Why werkyst thou hys consell? by myn settys lyght?   *little weight*
 Why hatyst thou vertu? why lovyst that ys nought?   *that which is nothing*

925 MIND. A, lorde! now I brynge to Mynde
 My horryble synnys and myn offens,
 I se how I have defowlyde the noble kynde   *noble nature*
  That was lyke to the[e] by intellygens.
 Undyrstondynge, I schew to your presens   *show to*
930 Owr lyff wyche that ys most synfull.
 Sek yow remedye, do yowr dylygens   *Seek*
 To clense the Soull wyche ys this fowll.

 UNDERSTANDING. Be yow, Mynde, I have very knowenge   *By/true knowing*
  That grettly Gode we have offendyde,
935 Endles peyn worthyi be owr dysyrvynge,   *what we deserve*
  Wyche be owrselff never may be amendyde.   *by ourselves*
  Wythowt Gode, in whom all ys comprehendyde.
 Therfor to hym let us resort.
 He lefte up them that be descendyde.   *lifts up those who*
940 He ys resurreccyon and lyve; to hem, Wyll, resort.   *life/to him*

 WILL. My Wyll was full gowe to syne,   *fully given*
  By wyche the Soule ys so abhomynable.
 I wyll retorne to Gode and new begynne   *newly begin*
 Ande in hym gronde my Wyll stable,   *solidly ground*
945 That of hys mercy he wyll me able   *Who by his mercy will make*
 To have the yiffte of hys specyall grace,   *gift*
 How hys seke Soule may be recurable   *curable*
 At the jugment before hys face.

---

912 s.d. *vi[i] small boys:* the manuscript gives *vj* small boys, but seven seem to be called for, since
they represent the seven deadly sins. [see Luke 8:2]

ANIMA. Than wyth yow thre the Soule dothe crye,
950   "Mercy, Gode" Why change I nowte,
I that thus horryble in synne lye,
    Sythe Mynde, Wyll, and Undyrstondynge be brought   *Since*
    To have knowynge they ill wrought?   *they did wrong*
    What ys that shall make me clene?   *What is it*
955   Put yt, Lorde, into my thowte!   *Put the words*
Thi olde mercy let me remene.   *By thy ancient/remain*

WISDOM. Thow the Soule Mynde take
    Ande Undyrstondynge of hys synnys allwey,   *in every way*
Beynge in Wyll, yt forsake,   *forsake sin*
960   Yit thes do not only synnys awey,   *these alone/put sins away*
    But very contrycyon, who that have may,   *true contrition*
That ys purger and clenser of synne.
    A tere of the ey, wyth sorow veray,   *with true sorrow*
That rubbyt and waschyt the Soule wythin.   *scrubs and cleanses*

965 All the penance that may be wrought,   *Not all the penance*
    Ne all the preyer that seyde be kan,   *Nor all*
Wythowt sorowe of hert relesyt nought;   *can release anything*
    That in especyall reformyth man   *That in particular reforms*
Ande makyt hym as clene as when he begane.
970   Go seke this medsyne, Soull, that beseke   *medicine*
    Wyth veray feythe, and be ye sekyr than   *true faith/if you are certain, then*
The vengeaunce of Gode ys made full meke.   *full light*

By Undyrstondynge have very contrycyon,   *true contrition*
    Wyth Mynde of your synne confessyon make,
975 Wyth Wyll yeldynge du satysfaccyon;   *full satisfaction*
    Than yowr soule be clene, I undyrtake.
    ANIMA. I wepe for sorow, Lorde! I begyn awake,
I that this longe hath slumberyde in syne.

Hic recedunt demones.   *Here the demons depart*

WISDOM.   Lo, how contrycyon avoydyth the devllys blake!   *drives out*
980   Dedly synne ys non yow wythin.   *not within you*

For Gode ye have offendyde hyghly
    Ande yowr modyr, Holy Chyrche so mylde,
Therfor Gode ye must aske mercy,
    By Holy Chyrch to be reconsylyde,   *reconciled*
985   Trustynge verely ye shall never be revylyde   *truly*
Yff ye have yowr charter of pardon by confessyon.

Now have ye foryeffnes that were fylyde.   *forgiveness who were defiled*
Go prey yowr modyr Chyrche of her proteccyon.   *pray to/for her*

ANIMA. O Fadyr of mercy ande of comfort,
990   Wyth wepynge ey and hert contryte
To owr modyr, Holy Chyrche, I wyll resort,
    My lyff pleyn schewenge to here syght.   *life plainly showing to her*
Wyth Mynde, Undyrstondynge, and Wyll ryght,
    Wyche of my Sowll the partyes be,   *Which are now parts*
995   To the domys of the Chyrche we shall us dyght,   *judgments/put forward*
    Wyth veray contricyon thus compleynnyng we.   *true contrition*

Here they go owt, and in the goynge the Soule syngyth in the most
*lamentabull wyse, wyth drawte notys as yt ys songyn in the passyon wyke:**
ANIMA. *Magna velud mare contricio, contricio tua: quis consoletur*
*tui? Plorans plorauit in nocte, et lacrime ejus in maxillis ejus.**

WISDOM. Thus seth Gode mankynde tyll   *to mankind that*
    Thes nyne poyntys ples hym all other before.*   *nine virtues/above all others*
"Gyff a peny in thy lyve wyth goode wyll   *in your life*
1000   To the pore, and that plesythe Gode more
Than mowyntenys into golde tramposyde wore   *mountains/transformed into gold*
Ande aftyr thy dethe for the[e] dysposyde."   *given away*
    Ande all the goodys thou hast in store
Shulde not profyght so moche wan thi body ys closyde.   *enclosed*

1005 The secunde poynt, Gode sethe thus:
    "Wepe on[e] tere for my love hertyly,   *Weep one tear*
Or for the passyon of me, Jhesus,
    Ande that plesyt me more specyally
Than yff thou wepte for thi frendys or goodys worldly
1010 As moche water as the se conteynys."
    Lo, contrycyon ys a soveren remedy   *the chief remedy*
That dystroythe synnys, that relessyt peynys.   *reduces penance (pains)*

The thyrde, Gode sethe: "Suffyr pacyenly for my love
    Off thi neybure a worde of repreve,   *From thy/reproof*
1015 Ande that to mercy mor dothe me move
Than thou dyscyplynyde thi body wyth peynys greve   *grievous pain*
    Wyth as many roddys as myght grow or thryve   *rods/or appear*

---

996 s.d. *drawte notys:* drawn-out, soulful notes.
996 s.d. "Greater than the sea is your breach, your contrition; what can comfort you? She weeps sore in the night, and her tears are on her cheeks." [See Lamentations 2:13 and 1:2] The verses are sung on Holy Thursday.
998-1065. The following 66 lines derive from *Novem Virtutes,* attributed to Richard Rolle. See Eccles, p. 215.

In the space of a days jornye."
Lo, who suffyryth most for Gode ys most lewe, *safest from*
1020 Slandyr, repreve, ony aduersyte. *reproof and any adversity*

The fourte, Gode sethe: "Wake on[e] owyr for the love of me, *Keep a vigil/hour*
And that to me ys more plesaunce *more pleasing*
Than yff thou sent twelve knyghtys free
To my sepulkyr wyth grett puysschaunce *great forces*
1025 For my dethe to take vengeaunce."
Lo, wakynge ys a holy thynge.
Ther yt ys hade wyth goode vsance, *When it is held*
Many gracys of yt doth sprynge. *from it*

The fyfte, Gode sethe: "Have pyte and compassyon
1030 Off thi neybur wyche ys seke and nedy, *On thy neighbor who*
And that to me ys more dylectacyon *delightful*
Than thou fastyde forty yer by and by, *Than if*
Thre days in the weke, as streytly *as strictly*
As thou cowdys in water and brede." *as you could on*
1035 Lo, pyte Gode plesyth grettly, *pleases God*
Ande yt ys a vertu soveren, as clerkys rede. *a principal virtue*

The sixte, Gode seth on this wyse: *says in this way*
"Refreyn thy speche for my reverens, *Restrain*
Lett not thy tonge thy evyn-Crysten dyspyse, *fellow Christian*
1040 Ande than plesyst thou more myn excellens
Than yff thou laberyde wyth grett dylygens
Wpon thy nakyde feet and bare
Tyll the blode folwude for peyn and vyolens *blood flowed*
Ande aftyr eche stepe yt sene were."

1045 The sevente, Cryst seth in this maner:
"Thy neybur to ewyll ne sterre not thou, *never stir*
But all thynge torne into vertu chere, *turn into virtuous behavior*
And than more plesyst thou me now
Then yf a thowsende tymys thou renne thorow *were to run through*
1050 A busche of thornys that scharpe were
Tyll thi nakyde body were all rough *all tattered*
Ande evyn rent to the bonys bare." *shredded to the bones*

The eyghte, Gode sethe this man tyll: *to this man that*
"Oftyn pray and aske of me,
1055 Ande that plesythe me more onto my wyll
Than yf my modyr and all sentys preyde for the[e]."

The nynte, Gode sethe: "Love me soverenly,   *above all things*
    Ande that to me more plesant ys
    Than yf thou went upon a pyler of tre   *a wooden pillar*
1060   That wer sett full of scharpe prykkys
    So that thou cut thi flesche into the smale partys."   *tiny pieces*
    Lo, Gode ys plesyde more wyth the dedys of charyte
    Than all the peynys man may suffer iwys.   *certainly*
    Remembyr thes poyntys, man, in thi felycité!

Here entrethe Anima, wyth the Fyve Wyttys goynge before, Mynde on the on[e] syde and Undyrstondynge on the other syde and Wyll folowyng, all in here fyrst clothynge, her chapplettys and crestys, and all hauyng on crownys, syngynge in here commynge in: "Quid retribuam Domino pro omnibus que retribuit mihi? Calicem salutaris accipiam et nomen Domini inuocabo."*

1065   ANIMA. O meke Jhesu, to the[e] I crye!
    O swet Jhesu, my delectacyon!
    O Jhesu, the sune of Vyrgyne Marye,
    Full of mercy and compassyon!
    My soule ys waschede be thy passyon   *cleansed by*
1070   Fro the synnys cummynge by sensualyte.   *From sins of the flesh*
    A, be the[e] I have a new resurreccyon.   *by thee*
    The lyght of grace I fele in me.

In tweyn myghtys of my soule I the[e] offendyde: *two powers*
    The on[e] by my inwarde wyttys, thow ben gostly;   *those that are spiritual*
1075   The other by my outwarde wyttys comprehendyde,
    Tho be the fyve wyttys bodyly;   *Those*
    Wyth the wyche tweyn myghtys mercy I crye.   *two powers*
    My modyr, Holy Chyrche, hath gowe me grace,   *has given me grace*
    Whom ye fyrst toke to yowr mercy,
1080   Yet of myselff I may not satysfye my trespas.   *by myself alone*

Magna est misericordia tue!*   *Great is your mercy*
    Wyth full feyth of forgevenes, to the[e], Lorde, I come.
    WISDOM. *Vulnerasti cor meum, soror mea, sponsa,*
    In vno ictu oculorum tuorum.*

1085   Ye have wondyde my hert, syster, spowse dere,
    In the tweyn syghtys of yowr ey: *With the twin glances/eyes*

1064 s.d. "What can I render to the Lord for all that he has given me? I will take the cup of salvation and call upon the name of the Lord." [See Psalm 115 (Hebr. 116):12, 13]

1031. See Psalms 107 (Hebr. 108):5 and 135 (Hebr. 136):13.

1083-84. "You have ravished my heart, my sister, my spouse, with one glance of your eyes." [See Song of Songs 4:9] See the next two lines (1085-86) for a translation.

By the recognycyon ye have clere,   *acknowledgment/clearly*
   Ande by the hye love ye have godly.
   It perrysschyt my hert to here yow crye,   *destroys*
1090   Now ye have forsake synne and be contryte.   *and are contrite*
   Ye were never so leve to me verelye.   *so dear/truly*
   Now be ye reformyde to yowr bewtys bryght.   *are you returned/beauty*

Ande ther yowr fyve wyttys offendyde has,   *And where each of*
   Ande to mak asythe be impotent,   *So as to make atonement powerless*
1095   My fyve wyttys, that never dyde trespas,
   Hathe made asythe to the Father suffycyent.   *sufficient atonement*
   Wyth my syght I se the people vyolent,
   I herde hem vengeaunce onto me call,   *heard them*
   I smelte the stenche of caren here present,   *of carrion*
1100   I tastyde the drynke mengylde wyth gall,   *mingled*

By towchynge I felte peyns smerte.
   My handys sprede abrode to halse thi swyre;   *stretched out to embrace thy neck*
   My fete naylyde to abyde wyth the[e], swet herte;
   My hert clovyn for thi love most dere;
1105   Myn hede bowhede down to kys the[e] here;   *bowed down*
   My body full of holys, as a dovehows.
   In thys ye be reformyde, Soule, my plesere,   *my pleaser*
   Ande now ye be the very temple of Jhesus.

Fyrst ye were reformyde by baptyme of ygnorans   *from ignorance*
1110   And clensyde from the synnys orygynall,
Ande now ye be reformyde by the sakyrment of penance   *sacrament*
   Ande clensyde from the synnys actuall.
   Now ye be fayrest, Crystys own specyall;   *you are the fairest*
   Dysfygure yow never to the lyknes of the fende.   *Never disfigure yourself*
1115   Now ye have receyvyde the crownnys victoryall   *victorious*
   To regne in blys wythowtyn ende.

MIND. Have Mynde, Soule, wat Gode hath do,   *Keep in mind/has done*
   Reformyde yow in feyth veryly.   *in faith truly*
Nolite conformari huic seculo
1120   *Sed reformamini in nouitate spiritus sensus vestri:* *
   Conforme yow not to this pompyus glory
   But reforme in gostly felynge.
   Ye that were dammyde by synn endelesly,   *damned eternally*
   Mercy hathe reformyde yow ande crownyde as a kynge.

1119-20. "Be not conformed to this world, but be transformed by the renewing of your spiritual
senses." [See Romans 12:2] See the next two lines for a translation.

1125 UNDERSTANDING. Take Undyrstondynge, Soule, now ye   *Understand now,*
      Wyth contynuall hope in Godys behest.   *God's command*
      Renouamini spiritu mentis vestre
        *Et induite nouum hominem, qui secundum Deum creatus est:**
      Ye be reformyde in felynge, not only as a best,   *as a beast*
1130   But also in the over parte of yowr reasun,   *in the higher part*
      Be wyche ye have lyknes of Gode mest   *bear most likeness to God*
      Ande of that mercyfull very congnycyon.   *true acknowledgment*

      WILL. Now the Soule yn charyte reformyde ys,
      Wyche charyte ys Gode verely.   *is God truly*
1135 *Exspoliantem veterem hominem cum actibus suis:**
      Spoyll yow of yowr olde synnys and foly   *Get rid of*
      Ande be renuyde in Godys knowynge ageyn,
      That enduyde wyth grace so specyally,   *endowed you with*
      Conservynge in peyn, ever in blys for to reyn.   *Conserving you through*

1140 ANIMA. Then wyth yow thre I may sey this
      Of Owr Lorde, soveren person, Jhesus:
      Suavis est Dominus vniuersis,
        *Et miseraciones ejus super omnia opera ejus.**
      O thou hye soveren Wysdam, my joy, Cristus,
1145   Hewyn, erthe, and eche creature
      Yelde yow reverens, for grace pleyntuus   *plenteous grace*
      Ye yeff to man, ever to induyr.   *That you give/endure*

      Now wyth Sent Powle we may sey thus
      That be reformyde thorow feythe in Jhesum: *We who are reformed*
1150 We have peas and acorde betwyx Gode and us,
      *Justificati ex fide pacem habemus ad Deum.**
      Now to Salamonys conclusyon I com:
      *Timor Domini inicium sapiencie.**
      Vobis qui timetis Deum
1155 *Orietur sol justicie:**

1127-28. "Be renewed in the spirit of your mind, and put on the new man, created in God's likeness." [See Ephesians 4:23, 24]

1135. "I would put away the old man with his deeds." [See Colossians 3:9] See the next line for a gloss on the text.

1142-43. "The Lord is good to all, and his tender mercies are over all his works." [See Psalms 144 (Hebr. 145):9]

1151. "Being justified by faith, we have peace with God." [See Romans 5:1] The preceding three lines are a contemporary translation appearing in Walter Hilton's *Scale of Perfection.* See Eccles, p. 216.

1153. "The fear of the Lord is the beginning of wisdom." [See Proverbs 1:7]

1154-55. "To you who fear the Lord shall the sun of righteousness arise." [See Malachi 4:2] The following four lines are the version from the *Scale of Perfection.* See Eccles, p. 216.

The tru son of ryghtusnes,
   Wyche that ys Owr Lorde Jhesu,
Shall sprynge in hem that drede hys meknes.   *spring up in them that fear*
   Nowe ye mut every soule renewe   *must*
1160   In grace, and vycys to eschew,
   Ande so to ende wyth perfeccyon.
   That the doctryne of Wysdom we may sew,   *That is/sow (or pursue)*
   Sapiencia Patris, grawnt that for hys passyon!   *Wisdom of the Father*
     Amen!

Mankind

The play of *Mankind* survives in the Macro manuscript, now at the Folger Shakespeare Library in Washington, D.C. (MS. V.a.354). This manuscript takes its name from an early owner, the Reverend Cox Macro (1683-1767), a native of Bury St. Edmunds. The provenance of the manuscript and the dialect of the play are unquestionably East Anglian. Two other plays are also preserved in the Macro manuscript besides *Mankind:* one is the complete copy of *Wisdom,* the other is *The Castle of Perseverance,* the longest extant morality play (triple the length of *Mankind),* and the only one for which a drawing of the stage plan has survived. The handwriting of most of *Mankind* is that of the same scribe who copied the Macro *Wisdom.* Both are inscribed as having been owned by Thomas Hyngham, monk of the monastery of Bury St. Edmunds, and both seem to have been composed around the same time, 1465-70. As Donald Baker has shown, this date can be reasonably ascertained by the coins mentioned in *Mankind,* which circulated only for a relatively brief time when a King Edward occupied the English throne (see ll. 689-90).

By all accounts, *Mankind* is an extraordinary play, and one of extremes. It provides a highly instructive example of how serious theme and comic action can play off each other in late medieval popular theatre. The plot follows the same allegorical course as *Wisdom:* a universal figure passes through the stages of innocence, temptation, sinful life, and repentance. But also like *Wisdom, Mankind's* action boosts the play far beyond what such a formulation might suggest. Eccles, in his EETS edition of *Mankind,* divides it into three scenes, from lines 1-412, 413-733, and 734-915. The play thus breaks at points where the playing area is clear and Mercy or Mischief enter alone, delivering soliloquies that initiate new directions for the action to take. This division seems theatrically sound, though it is only one of several possible ways of dividing the plot to underline thematically important moments in the play. In this regard it should be noted that toward the end of the play Mercy himself suggests that the action has followed the temptations of the World, the Flesh, and the Devil (ll. 883-890).

Any characterization of the action of *Mankind* should make clear how its rich language, which runs the gamut from learned to lewd, is bound up with the plot. The solemn, staid cadences of Mercy's opening speeches, for example, are broken by the faster paced rhythms of Mischief, who pulls Mercy into his rhyme scheme even as he taunts him. Mercy, dressed as an old cleric, does not come off well initially; and his pompous language and moral pontifications to the audience, "ye soverens that sytt and ye brothern that stonde right uppe," (l. 29) are allowed to continue just long enough (44 lines) to establish his humorless credential before Mischief begins his subversive work. Mankind himself does not enter until line 186, by which time battle lines have been firmly drawn between the redemptive power of Mercy and the decadent power of the Vice figures brought on by Mischief: New-Guise, Nowadays, and Nought. Mankind is at first easily bamboozled by the Vices, who represent the temptations of the World, but he manages to defeat their various enticements in the first half of the play by beating them away with his spade. What the World began, the Devil Titivillus is waiting in the wings to continue, and Mischief ushers in this familiar figure with his satchel and net. Before he enters, as the dialogue makes clear (ll. 413-474), an intermission breaks the action while a collection is taken up. The audience is encouraged to give generously while being titillated with advance notice of the appearance of Titivillus and his big head. Titivillus, invisible to Mankind, uses a board buried in the earth to trick him into giving up his good labors and joining New-Guise, Nowadays and Nought in their revels. And now, starting at line 638, Mischief leads man to Flesh—his own cupidity. With his coat obscenely short, Mankind seeks a lustful companion, a tapster. Mercy, defeated at every turn, is said to have hanged himself and Mankind despairs; but Mercy drives away Mankind's evil companions with a flail and counsels him to repent his sins of the World, the Flesh, and the Devil. After further admonitory speeches on the power of Mercy, Mankind departs, saved, leaving Mercy to deliver the epilogue.

The collection, or quête, that stops the action just before the entrance of Titivillus near the middle of the play is an event worth noticing, for it offers a clear example of how *Mankind* incorporates elements from the folk play tradition. One standard feature of folk plays is precisely this kind of collection, made quite openly during a performance as is done here. Two other folk play echoes in *Mankind* are the repeated calls to "Make room"—a familiar means in folk performances to clear an acting space—and the ritual entrance of Titivillus as Big Head, a character right out of the mummers plays.

The quête in *Mankind* is also important because it shows the unmistakable commercial impulse that drove the non-cycle plays. Judging from references in the play to a hostler (innkeeper), a tapster (barmaid), and a yard (perhaps an innyard), *Mankind* clearly seems designed for performance by a travelling troupe, one that supported itself by entertaining at inns and public spaces. The small number of players necessary to mount the play (six, if the actor playing Mercy doubles as Titivillus), the flexible nature of its staging, the references to varied audiences and to apparently familiar locales in Norfolk and Cambridgeshire, even the evidence of wear on the manuscript itself, all support the conclusion that *Mankind* paid its own way as a play in the repertory of itinerant players.

Two stanzaic forms predominate in *Mankind*: the first is the formal quatrain pattern rhyming *abab,* often linked by rhyme into *ababbcbc* octavos in soliloquies. This form is first introduced by Mercy, but it is also maintained by Mankind during moments of high seriousness. The second stanzaic form, practiced by Mischief and almost everyone of his persuasion, including Mankind, is an eight-line *aaabcccb* tail rhyme. Mercy's language is excessively aureate, as Mischief points out, and he and the other lowlife characters delight in mimicking and parodying Mercy's "Englisch Laten" (l. 124). Indeed, some of the most inventive moments of the play involve macaronic language and thinking. Latin quotations are everywhere in the text, and not only in the mouth of the cleric Mercy. Pedantic language and diction thus occupies only one end of a very wide scale. The other end is occupied by the language of the Vice characters, which is not merely scatalogical, but sometimes breathtakingly coarse and obscene, as in the "Cristemes songe" (ll. 333-43; Adams refused to print it in his anthology) that ends with the repeated "Holycke" ("holy" and "hole-lick"), or as in the excrement on the shoes routine (ll. 782-96).

Mankind was first published by John M. Manly in *Specimens of the Pre-Shaksperean Drama,* Vol. 1 (1897). The standard scholarly edition of *Mankind* is by Mark Eccles, published by EETS in *The Macro Plays* (1969). A Facsimile of the play can be found in David Bevington, *The Macro Plays: The Castle of Perseverance, Wisdom, Mankind, A Facsimile Edition with Facing Transcriptions* (1972) (see Suggestions for Further Reading).

MANKIND

[*DRAMATIS PERSONAE:*

MANKIND   MISCHIEF
MERCY   NEW-GUISE
TITIVILLUS   NOWADAYS
NOUGHT]

[Enter Mercy]

MERCY. The very fownder and begynner of owr fyrst creacyon
    Amonge us synfull wrechys he oweth to be magnyfyede,   *ought/glorified*
That for owr dysobedyenc[e] he hade non indygnacyon   *was not too offended*
    To sende hys own son to be torn and crucyfyede.
5   Owr obsequyouse servyce to hym shulde be aplyede,   *dutiful/offered*
Where he was lorde of all and made all thynge of nought,
    For the synnfull synnere to have hym revyvyde
And for hys redempcyon sett hys own son at nought.   *(mankind's) redemption*

Yt may be seyde and veryfyede, mankynde was dere bought.   *redeemed*
10   By the pytuose deth of Jhesu he hade hys remedye.
He was purgyde of hys defawte that wrechydly hade wrought   *default/committed*
    By hys gloryus passyon, that blyssyde lavatorye.   *cleansing action*
O soverence, I beseche yow yowr condycyons to rectyfye   *O masters*
    Ande wyth humylite and reverence to have a remocyon   *return*
15   To this blyssyde prynce that owr nature doth gloryfye,
That ye may be partycypable of hys retribucyon.   *share/redemption*

I have be the very mene for yowr restytucyon.   *been/true means*
    Mercy ys my name, that mornyth for yowr offence.   *sorrows*
Dyverte not yowrsylffe in tyme of temtacyon,
20   That ye may be acceptable to Gode at yowr goyng hence.   *So that/death*
    The grett mercy of Gode, that ys of most preemmynence,

Be medyacyon of Owr Lady that ys ever habundante   *By generous intercession*
To the synfull creature that wyll repent hys neclygence.   *To any*
I prey Gode at yowr most nede that mercy be yowr defendawnte.   *greatest/defender*

25   In goode werkys I avyse yow, soverence, to be perseverante   *masters*
To puryfye yowr sowlys, that thei be not corupte;
For yowr gostly enmy wyll make hys avaunte,   *spiritual/his boast*
Yowr goode condycyons yf he may interrupte.   *state of grace/obstruct*

O ye soverens that sytt and ye brothern that stonde ryght uppe,   *i.e., the audience*
30   Pryke not yowr felycytes in thyngys transytorye.   *Put*
Beholde not the erth, but lyfte yowr ey uppe.
Se[e] how the hede the members dayly do magnyfye.
Who ys the hede forsoth I shall yow certyfye:
I mene Owr Sauyowr, that was lykynnyde to a lambe;
35   Ande hys sayntys be the members that dayly he doth satysfye
Wyth the precyose rever that runnyth from hys wombe.   *river/abdomen*

Ther ys non such foode, be water nor by londe,
So precyouse, so gloryouse, so nedefull to owr entent,
For yt hath dyssolvyde mankynde from the bytter bonde
40   Of the mortall enmye, that venymousse serpente,
From the wyche Gode preserve yow all at the last jugement!
For sekyrly ther shall be a streyt examynacyon,   *surely/strict examination*
The corn shall be savyde, the chaffe shall be brente.   *grain/husks/burned*
I besech yow hertyly, have this premedytacyon.   *in mind*

45   MISCHIEF. I beseche yow hertyly, leve yowr calcacyon.   *threshing*
Leve yowr chaffe, leve yowr corn, leve yowr dalyacyon.   *dallying*
Yowr wytt ys lytyll, yowr hede ys mekyll, ye are full of predycacyon.   *preaching*
But, ser, I prey this questyon to claryfye:
Mysse-masche, dryff-draff,
50   Sume was corn and sume was chaffe,
My dame seyde my name was Raffe;
Onschett yowr lokke and take an halpenye.   *Open/halfpenny*

MERCY. Why com ye hethyr, brother? Ye were not dysyryde.   *called for*
MISCHIEF. For a wynter corn-threscher, ser, I have hyryde,   *hired*
55   Ande ye sayde the corn shulde be savyde and the chaff shulde be feryde,   *burned*
Ande he provyth nay, as yt schewth be this verse: *proves nothing/is shown by*
"Corn servit bredibus, chaffe horsibus, straw fyrybusque."*
Thys ys as moche to say, to yowr leude undyrstondynge,   *simple*
As the corn shall serue to brede at the nexte bakynge.
60   "Chaff horsybus" et reliqua,   *and the rest*

---

57. Grain serves for bread, chaff for horses, and straw for fires.

The chaff to horse shall be goode provente,   *provender*
When a man ys forcolde the straw may be brent,   *burned*
And so forth, *et cetera*.

MERCY. Avoyde, goode brother! Ye ben culpable   *Get out/are blameful*
65   To interrupte thus my talkyng delectable.
MISCHIEF. Ser, I have nother horse nor sadyll,   *neither*
Therfor I may not ryde.
MERCY. Hye yow forth on fote, brother, in Godys name!   *Then go*
MISCHIEF. I say, ser, I am cumme hedyr to make yow game.   *hither/sport with*
70   Yet bade ye me not go out in the Devllys name
Ande I wyll abyde.   *So*

[A manuscript leaf is missing here; apparently Mischief departs and New-
Guise, Nowadays, and Nought arrive with minstrels. New Guise and
Nowadays are urging Nought to dance.]

NEW GYSE. Ande how, mynstrellys, pley the comyn trace!   *dance*
Ley on wyth thi ballys tyll hys bely breste!   *bellows (bagpipe?)/bursts*
NOUGHT. I putt case I breke my neke: how than?   *What if*
75   NEW GYSE. I gyff no force, by Sent Tanne!   *don't care/Anne*
NOWADAYS. Leppe about lyvely! thou art a wyght man.   *spry*
Lett us be mery w[h]yll we be here!
NOUGHT. Shall I breke my neke to schew yow sporte?   *entertainment*
NOWADAYS. Therfor ever be ware of thi reporte.   *talk*
80   NOUGHT. I beschrew ye all! Her ys a schrewde sorte.   *curse you/mischievous lot*
Have theratt then wyth a mery chere!   *Have at*

Her[e] thei daunce. Mercy seyth:

MERCY. Do wey, do wey this revll, sers! do wey!   *Stop/revel*
NOWADAYS. Do wey, goode Adam? do wey?   *old man*
Thys ys no parte of thi pley.   *no concern of yours*
85   NOUGHT. Yis, mary, I prey yow, for I love not this revelynge.
Cum forth, goode fader, I yow prey!
Be a lytyll ye may assay.   *you can try a little*
Anon of[f] wyth yowr clothes, yf ye wyll play.
Go to! for I have hade a praty scottlynge.   *pretty good caper*

90   MERCY. Nay, brother, I wyll not daunce.
NEW GYSE. Yf ye wyll, ser, my brother wyll make yow to prawnce.
NOWADAYS. Wyth all my herte, ser, yf I may yow avaunce.   *help*
Ye may assay be a lytyll trace.   *try a little dance*
NOUGHT. Ye, ser, wyll ye do well,   *if you would*
95   Trace not wyth them, be my cownsell,   *Dance*

For I have tracyed sumwhat to[o] fell;   *fully*
I tell yow [it] ys a narow space.   *cramped*

But, ser, I trow of us thre I herde yow speke.   *thought*
NEW GYSE. Crystys curse hade therfor, for I was in slepe.   *had (I), since*
100   NOWADAYS. And I hade the cuppe in my honde, redy to goo to met[e].* *eat*
Therfor, ser, curtly, grett yow well.   *[speak] briefly*
MERCY. Few wordys, few and well sett!   *said*
NEW GYSE. Ser, yt ys the new gyse and the new jett.   *fashion*
Many wordys and schortely sett,
105   Thys ys the new gyse, every-dele.   *way*

MERCY. Lady, helpe! how wrechys delyte in ther synfull weys!   *Our Lady*
NOWADAYS. Say not ageyn the new gyse nowadays!   *Speak not against*
Thou shall fynde us schrewys at all assays.   *in every test*
Be ware! ye may son lyke a bofett.   *soon get a beating*
110   MERCY. He was well occupyede that browte yow brether.   *did well who/brother*
NOUGHT. I harde yow call "New Gyse, Nowadays, Nought,"
all thes thre togethere
Yf ye say that I lye, I shall make yow to slyther.   *grovel*
Lo, take yow here a trepett! *[Trips him up]*   *tripping*

MERCY. Say me yowr namys, I know yow not.   *Tell*
NEW GYSE. New Gyse, I.
NOWADAYS.   I, Nowadays.
115   NOUGHT.   I, Nought.
MERCY. Be Jhesu Cryst that me dere bowte   *dearly redeemed*
Ye betray many men.

NEW GYSE. Betray! nay, nay, ser, nay, nay!
We make them both fresch and gay.
120   But of yowr name, ser, I yow prey,
That we may yow ken.   *know*

MERCY. Mercy ys my name by denomynacyon.
I conseyve ye have but a lytyll favour in my communycacyon.   *imagine/good will*
NEW GYSE. Ey, ey! yowr body ys full of Englysch Laten.
125   I am aferde yt wyll brest.   *burst*
"*Pravo te ,*" quod the bocher onto me   *Damn you/butcher*
When I stale a leg a motun.   *stole/mutton*
Ye are a stronge cunnyng clerke.
NOWADAYS. I prey yow hertyly, worschyppull clerke,
130   To have this Englysch mad in Laten: *translated into*

98-100. (Nought, New Gyse, and Nowadays have been interrupted by Mercy while dancing, sleeping, and eating).

"I have etun a dyschfull of curdys,
Ande I have schetun yowr mowth full of turdys."   *shitten*
Now opyn yowr sachell wyth Laten wordys
    Ande sey me this in clerycall manere!
135 Also I have a wyf, her name ys Rachell;
Betwyx her and me was a gret batell;
Ande fayn of yow I wolde here tell   *gladly hear*
    Who was the most master.

NOUGHT. Thy wyf Rachell, I dare ley twenti lyse.   *lice*
140 NOWADAYS. Who spake to the[e], foll? thou art not wyse!   *fool*
Go and do that longyth to thin offyce: *which belongs to*
    Osculare fundamentum!   *Kiss my ass*
NOUGHT. Lo, master, lo, here ys a pardon bely-mett.   *satisfying*
Yt ys grawntyde of Pope Pokett,   *by Pope Wallet*
145 Yf ye wyll putt yowr nose in hys wyffys sokett,   *vagina*
    Ye shall have forty days of pardon.

MERCY. Thys ydyll language ye shall repent.
Out of this place I wolde ye went.
NEW GYSE. Goo we hens all thre wyth on[e] assent.   *hence*
150   My fadyr ys yrke of owr eloquence.   *priest/irritated by*
Therfor I wyll no lenger tary.
Gode brynge yow, master, and blyssyde Mary
To the number of the demonycall frayry!   *friary*

NOWADAYS. Cum wynde, cum reyn,
155 Thow I cumme never ageyn!
The Devll put out both yowr eyn!   *eyes*
    Felouse, go we hens tyght.   *hence quickly*
NOUGHT. Go we hens, a devll wey!   *hence/in sin*
Here ys the dore, her[e] ys the wey.
160 Farwell, jentyll Jaffrey,
    I prey Gode gyf yow goode nyght!

    Exiant simul. Cantent.   *They leave together singing*

MERCY. Thankyde be Gode, we have a fayer dylyverance   *been saved from*
    Of thes thre onthryfty gestys.   *decadent guests*
They know full lytyll what ys ther ordynance.   *duty*
165   I prve by reson thei be wers then bestys: *will prove/beasts*

A best doth after hys naturall instytucyon;   *follows/instinct*
    Ye may conseyve by there dysporte and behavour,   *can tell/their*
Ther joy ande delyte ys in derysyon   *in derision*
Of her owyn Cryste to hys dyshonur.   *their*

170 Thys condycyon of levyng, yt ys prejudycyall; *living*
    Be ware therof, yt ys wers than ony felony or treson. *any*
    How may yt be excusyde befor the Justyce of all
    When for every ydyll worde we must yelde a reson? *give*

    They have grett ease, therfor thei wyll take no thought.
175 But how then when the angell of hevyn shall blow the trumpe *trumpet*
    Ande sey to the transgressors that wykkydly hath wrought, *sinners*
    "Cum forth onto yowr Juge and yelde yowr acownte"?

    Then shall I, Mercy, begyn sore to wepe; *sadly*
    Nother comfort nor cownsell ther shall non be hade; *Neither*
180 But such as thei have sowyn, such shall thei repe.
    Thei be wanton now, but then shall thei be sade.

    The goode new gyse nowadays I wyll not dysalow. *criticize*
    I dyscomende the vycyouse gyse; I prey have me excusyde, *fashion*
    I nede not to speke of yt, yowr reson wyll tell it yow.
185 Take that ys to be takyn and leve that ys to be refusyde.

    [Enter Mankind with a spade]

MANKIND. Of the erth and of the cley we have owr propagacyon.
    By the provydens of Gode thus be we deryvatt, *derived*
    To whos mercy I recomende this holl congrygacyon:
    I hope onto hys blysse ye be all predestynatt. *destined*

190 Every man for hys degre I trust shall be partycypatt, *to his ability/share*
    Yf we wyll mortyfye owr carnall condycyon
    Ande owr voluntarye dysyres, that ever be pervercyonatt, *perversion prone*
    To renunce them and yelde us under Godys provycyon.

    My name ys Mankynde. I have my composycyon
195 Of a body and of a soull, of condycyon contrarye. *at war with each other*
    Betwyx them tweyn ys a grett dyvisyon;
    He that shulde be subjecte, now he hath the victory.

    Thys ys to me a lamentable story
    To se my flesch of my soull to have governance. *the upper hand*
200 Wher the goodewyff ys master, the goodeman may be sory. *wife/husband*
    I may both syth and sobbe, this ys a pytuose remembrance. *sigh/piteous*

    O thou my soull, so sotyll in thy substance, *exquisite*
    Alasse, what was thi fortune and thi chaunce
    To be assocyat wyth my flesch, that stynkyng dungehyll?
205 Lady, helpe! Soverens, yt doth my soull myche yll *Our Lady/great*

To se the flesch prosperouse and the soull trodyn under fote.
I shall go to yondyr man and asay hym I wyll.   *try*
I trust of gostly solace he wyll be my bote.   *help*

All heyll, semely father! Ye be welcom to this house.   *holy*
210   Of the very wysdam ye have partycypacyon.   *true/a share*
My body wyth my soull ys ever querulose.   *quarrelling*
I prey yow, for sent charyte, of yowr supportacyon.   *holy/help*

I beseche yow hertyly of yowr gostly comforte.   *spiritual*
I am onstedfast in lyvynge; my name ys Mankynde.   *fickle*
215   My gostly enmy the Devll wyll have a grett dysporte   *game*
In synfull gydynge yf he may se me ende.   *guidance*

MERCY. Cryst sende yow goode comforte! Ye be welcum, my frende.
Stonde uppe on yowr fete, I prey yow aryse.
My name ys Mercy; ye be to me full hende.   *gracious*
220   To eschew vyce I wyll yow avyse.

MANKIND. Mercy, of all grace and vertu ye are the well,   *fountain*
I have herde tell of ryght worschyppfull clerkys.   *from*
Ye be aproxymatt to Gode and nere of hys consell.   *[That] ye*
He hat[h] instytut you above all hys werkys.   *set*

225   O, yowr lovely wordys to my soull are swetere then hony.
MERCY. The temptacyon of the flesch ye must resyst lyke a man,
For ther ys ever a batell betwyx the soull and the body:
*Vita hominis est milicia super terram.**

Oppresse yowr gostly enmy and be Crystys own knyght.
230   Be never a cowarde ageyn yowr adversary.   *against*
Yf ye wyll be crownyde, ye must nedys fyght.
Intende well and Gode wyll be yow adjutory.   *helpful to you*

Remember, my frende, the tyme of contynuance.   *your life*
So helpe me Gode, yt ys but a chery tyme.   *brief*
235   Spende yt well; serve Gode wyth hertys affyance.   *loyalty*
Dystempure not yowr brayn wyth goode ale nor wyth wyn.

Mesure ys tresure. Y forbyde yow not the use.   *Moderation*
Mesure yowrsylf ever; be ware of excesse.
The superfluouse gyse I wyll that ye refuse,   *want you to*
240   When nature ys suffysyde, anon that ye sese.   *cease*
Yf a man have an hors and kepe hym not to[o] hye,   *lavishly*

---

228. The life of man on earth is a battle. [See Job 7:1]

He may then reull hym at hys own dysyere.   *rule/will*
Yf he be fede overwell he wyll dysobey   *fed*
Ande in happe cast his master in the myre.   *perhaps*

[New Guise, Nowadays, and Nought return]

245 NEW GYSE. Ye sey trew, ser, ye are no faytour.   *liar*
    I have fede my wyff so well tyll sche ys my master.
    I have a grett wonde on my hede, lo! and theron leyth a playster,   *lies/bandage*
    Ande another ther I pysse my peson.   *where I piss on my pease*
    Ande my wyf were yowr hors, sche wolde yow all to-banne.   *If/curse*
250 Ye fede yowr hors in mesure, ye are a wyse man.
    I trow, and ye were the kyngys palfreyman,   *even if/horseman*
    A goode horse shulde be gesunne.   *scarce*

MANKIND. Wher spekys this felow? Wyll he not com nere?
MERCY. All to so[o]n, my brother, I fere me, for yow.
255 He was here ryght now, by hym that bowte me dere,   *redeemed me*
    Wyth other of hys felouse; thei kan moche sorow.   *know much of*

They wyll be here ryght so[o]n, yf I owt departe.   *should have*
    Thynke on my doctryne; yt shall be yowr defence.
    Lerne wyll I am here, sett my wordys in herte.   *Learn while*
260 Wythin a schorte space I must nedys hens.   *must go*

NOWADAYS. The sonner the lever, and yt be evyn anon!   *better, if*
    I trow yowr name ys Do Lytyll, ye be so long fro hom.
    Yf ye wolde go hens, we shall cum everychon,   *everyone*
    Mo then a goode sorte.   *More/many*
265 Ye have leve, I dare well say.   *permission*
    When ye wyll, go forth yowr wey.
    Men have lytyll deynte of yowr pley   *pleasure in*
    Because ye make no sporte.

NOUGHT. Yowr potage shall be forcolde, ser; when wyll ye go dyn?   *soup/cold*
270 I have sen a man lost twenti noblys in as lytyll tyme;
    Yet yt was not I, be Sent Qwyntyn,
    For I was never worth a pottfull a wortys sythyn I was born.   *potful of vegetables*
    My name ys Nought. I loue well to make mery.
    I have be sethen wyth the comyn tapster of Bury   *been recently with*
275 And pleyde so longe the foll that I am evyn wery.   *fool/even I*
    Yet shall I be ther ageyn to-morn.   *tomorrow*

MERCY. *[To Mankind]* I have moche care for yow, my own frende.
    Yowr enmys wyll be here anon, thei make ther avaunte.   *boast*

Thynke well in yowr hert, yowr name ys Mankynde;
280   Be not unkynde to Gode, I prey yow be hys servante.

Be stedefast in condycyon; se ye be not varyant.   *Remain true in your faith*
   Lose not thorow foly that ys bowte so dere.   *through/that which is paid for*
Gode wyll prove yow son; ande yf that ye be constant,   *test*
   Of hys blysse perpetuall ye shall be partener.

285   Ye may not have yowr intent at yowr fyrst dysyere.   *what you wish*
   Se the grett pacyence of Job in tribulacyon;
Lyke as the smyth trieth ern in the feere,   *smith who tests iron*
   So was he triede by Godys vysytacyon.   *shaped*

He was of yowr nature and of yowr fragylyte;
290   Folow the steppys of hym, my own swete son,
Ande sey as he seyde in yowr trobyll and aduersyte:
   Dominus dedit, Dominus abstulit; sicut sibi placuit, ita factum est;
   sit nomen Domini benedictum! [*]

Moreover, in specyall I gyve yow in charge,
   Be ware of New Gyse, Nowadays, and Nought.
295   Nyse in ther aray, in language thei be large;   *Foolish in dress/licentious*
   To perverte yowr condycyons all the menys shall be sowte.   *means*

Gode son, intromytt not yowrsylff in ther cumpeny.   *intermix*
   Thei harde not a masse this twelmonyth, I dare well say.   *have not heard*
Gyff them non audyence; thei wyll tell yow many a lye.
300   Do truly yowr labure and kepe yowr halyday.   *respect your holyday*

Be ware of Tytivillus, for he lesyth no wey,   *loses*
   That goth invysybull and wyll not be sen.   *[He] that*
He wyll ronde in yowr ere and cast a nett befor yowr ey.   *whisper*
   He ys worst of them all; Gode lett hym never then!   *thrive*

305   Yf ye dysples Gode, aske mercy anon,   *displease/right away*
   Ellys Myscheff wyll be redy to brace yow in hys brydyll.   *Or else/put*
Kysse me now, my dere darlynge. Gode schelde yow from yowr fon!   *foes*
   Do truly yowr labure and be never ydyll.

The blyssynge of Gode be wyth yow and wyth all thes worschypp[f]ull men!
310   MANKIND. Amen, for sent charyté, amen!
     [Exit Mercy]

292-93. The Lord gave and the Lord has taken away; as was pleasing to Him, so was it done; blessed be the name of the Lord. [See Job 1:21]

Now blyssyde be Jhesu! my soull ys well sacyatt   *satiated*
  Wyth the mellyfluose doctryne of this worschyppfull man.
The rebellyn of my flesch now yt ys superatt,   *overcome*
  Thankynge be to Gode of the connynge that I kan.   *know*

315 Her[e] wyll I sytt and tytyll in this papyr   *write down*
  The incomparable astat of my promycyon.   *nature/promise*
  [To the audience] Worschypfull soverence, I have wretyn here
  The gloryuse remembrance of my nobyll condycyon.   *reminder*

To have remo[r]s and memory of mysylff thus wretyn yt ys,
320 To defende me from all superstycyus charmys:
  *"Memento, homo, quod cinis es et in cinerem reuerteri."**
  Lo, I ber on my bryst the bagge of myn armys.   *breast/coat of arms*

NEW GYSE. The wether ys colde, Gode sende us goode ferys!   *fires*
  *"Cum sancto sanctus eris et cum peruerso peruerteris"**
325 *"Ecce quam bonum et quam jocundum,"* quod the Devll to the frerys,
  *"Habitare fratres in vnum."**
MANKIND. I her a felow speke; wyth hym I wyll not mell.   *hear/bother*
Thys erth wyth my spade I shall assay to delffe.   *try to dig*
To eschew ydullnes, I do yt myn own selffe.
330 I prey Gode sende yt hys fusyon!   *foison (fruition)*

NOWADAYS. Make rom, sers, for we have be longe!   *been away*
We wyll cum gyf yow a Crystemes songe.   *give*

NOUGHT. Now I prey all the yemandry that ys here   *yeomanry*
To synge wyth us wyth a mery chere:
335 Yt ys wretyn wyth a coll, yt ys wretyn wyth a cole,   *written/coal*
NOWADAYS and NEW GYSE. Yt ys wretyn wyth a colle,
    yt ys wretyn wyth a colle,   *coal*
NOUGHT. He that schytyth wyth hys hoyll,
    he that schytyth wyth hys hoyll,   *hole*
NOWADAYS and NEW GYSE. He that schytyth wyth hys hoyll,
    he that schytyth wyth hys hoyll,
340 NOUGHT. But he wyppe hys ars clen, but he wyppe hys ars clen,   *Unless*
NOWADAYS and NEW GYSE. But he wype hys ars clen,
    but he wype his ars clen,
NOUGHT. On hys breche yt shall be sen, on hys breche yt shall be sen.
NOWADAYS and NEW GYSE. On hys breche yt shall be sen,
    on hys breche yt shall be sen.

---

321. Remember, man, that you are dust and to dust you will return. [See Job 34:15]
324. With the holy will you be holy; with the wicked will you be wicked. [See Psalms 18:25-26]
325-26. Behold how good and jolly it is for brethren to live together as one. [See Psalms 133:1]

Cantant Omnes.   *All sing*

ALL. Hoylyke, holyke, holyke! holyke, holyke, holyke!   *holy (& hole lick)*

NEW GYSE. Ey, Mankynde, Gode spede yow wyth yowr spade!
345   I shall tell yow of a maryage:
       I wolde yowr mowth and hys ars that this made   *made this song*
           Wer maryede junctly together.   *jointly*
       MANKIND. Hey yow hens, felouse, wyth bredynge.   *Hie you hence/with reproach*
       Leve yowr derysyon and yowr japyng.   *joking*
350   I must nedys labure, yt ys my lyvynge.
       NOWADAYS. What, ser, we cam but lat[e] hethyr.   *lately hither*

       Shall all this corn grow here   *Is this all the grain*
       That ye shall have the nexte yer?
       Yf yt be so, corn hade nede be dere,   *better be expensive*
355   Ellys ye shall have a pore lyffe.
       NOUGHT. Alasse, goode fadere, this labor fretyth yow to the bon.   *frays*
       But for yowr croppe I take grett mone.   *I lament greatly*
       Ye shall never spende yt alonne;
           I shall assay to geett yow a wyffe.   *try*

360   How many acres suppose ye here by estymacyon?
       NEW GYSE. Ey, how ye turne the erth uppe and down!
       I have be in my days in many goode town   *been*
           Yett saw I never such another tyllynge.
       MANKIND. Why stonde ye ydyll? Yt ys pety that ye were born!
365   NOWADAYS. We shall bargen wyth yow and nother moke nor scorne. *neither mock*
       Take a goode carte in hervest and lode yt wyth yowr corne,
           Ande what shall we gyf yow for the levynge?   *crop*

       NOUGHT. He ys a goode starke laburrer, he wolde fayn do well. *strong/gladly*
       He hath mett wyth the goode man Mercy in a schroude sell.   *at an unlucky time*
370   For all this he may have many a hungry mele.   *slim meal*
           Yet woll ye se he ys polytyke.   *correct*
       Here shall be goode corn, he may not mysse yt;
       Yf he wyll have reyn he may ouerpysse yt;   *wants/piss over*
       Ande yf he wyll have compasse he may ouerblysse yt   *compost/bless*
375   A lytyll wyth hys ars lyke.   *similarly*

       MANKIND. Go and do yowr labur! Gode lett yow never the! *May God/never thrive*
       Or wyth my spade I shall yow dynge, by the Holy Trinyté!   *injure you*
       Have ye non other man to moke, but ever me?   *mock*
       Ye wolde have me of yowr sett?   *group*
380   Hye yow forth lyvely, for hens I wyll yow dryffe.   *hence/drive*
           [Beats them with his spade]

NEW GYSE. Alas, my jewellys! I shall be schent of my wyff! *testicles/bereft*
NOWADAYS. Alasse! and I am lyke never for to thryve, *multiply*
   I have such a buffett. *beating*

MANKIND. Hens I sey, New Gyse, Nowadays, and Nowte! *Hence*
385 Yt was seyde beforn, all the menys shuld be sought *means*
To perverte my condycyons and brynge me to nought.
   Hens, thevys! Ye have made many a lesynge. *lie*
NOUGHT. Marryde I was for colde, but now am I warme. *Marred*
Ye are evyll avysyde, ser, for ye have don harme. *ill-advised*
390 By cokkys body sakyrde, I have such a peyn in my arme *God's sacred body*
   I may not chonge a man a ferthynge. *make change for*

[Mankind kneels]

MANKIND. Now I thanke Gode, knelynge on my kne.
Blyssyde be hys name! he ys of hye degre.
By the subsyde of hys grace that he hath sente me *help*
395   Thre of myn enmys I have putt to flyght.
Yet this instrument, soverens, ys not made to defende.
Davide seyth, *"Nec in hasta nec in gladio salvat Dominus."**
NOUGHT. No, mary, I beschrew yow, yt ys *in spadibus*. *by spade*
Therfor Crystys curse cum on yowr *hedybus* *head*
400   To sende yow lesse myght!

Exiant *Let them leave*

MANKIND. I promytt yow thes felouse wyll no more cum here, *promise*
For summe of them, certenly, were summewhat to[o] nere.
My fadyr Mercy avysyde me to be of a goode chere *advised*
  Ande agayn my enmys manly for to fyght. *against*

405 I shall convycte them, I hope, everychon. *conquer*
Yet I say amysse, I do yt not alon.
Wyth the helpe of the grace of Gode I resyst my fon *foes*
  Ande ther malycyuse herte. *malicious*
Wyth my spade I wyll departe, my worschypp[f]ull soverence,
410 Ande lyve ever wyth labure to corecte my insolence. *pride*
I shall go fett corn for my londe; I prey yow of pacyence; *fetch seed*
  Ryght so[o]n I shall reverte. *return*

MISCHIEF. Alas, alasse, that ever I was wrought!
Alasse the whyll, I am wers then nought! *while/worse than*
415 Sythyn I was here, by hym that me bought, *since/redeemed*

---

397. Not by spear nor by sword does the Lord save. [See 1 Samuel 17:47]

I am utterly ondon! *undone*
Myscheff, was here at the begynnynge of the game
Ande arguyde wyth Mercy, Gode gyff hym schame!
He hath taught Mankynde, wyll I have be vane, *while/gone*
420　　To fyght manly ageyn hys fon. *against/foes*

For wyth hys spade, that was hys wepyn, *weapon*
Neu Gyse, Nowadays, Nought he hath all to-beton. *beaten*
I have grett pyté to se them wepyn. *weep*
Wyll ye lyst? I here them crye. *listen/hear*

　　Clamant *They cry out (offstage)*

425　MISCHIEF. Alasse, alasse! cum hether, I shall be yowr borow. *protector*
Alac, alac! *ven[e], ven[e]!* cum hethere wyth sorowe! *come, come*
Pesse, fayer babys, ye shall have a nappyll to-morow! *Quiet/an apple*
Why grete ye so, why? *weep*

NEW GYSE. Alasse, master, alasse, my privyte! *private parts*
430　MISCHIEF. A, wher? alake! fayer babe, ba me! *kiss me*
Abyde! to[o] so[o]n I shall yt se. *Wait/soon enough*
　　NOWADAYS. Here, here, se my hede, goode master!
MISCHIEF. Lady, helpe! sely darlynge, *ven[e], ven[e]!* *poor/come, come*
I shall helpe the[e] of thi peyn; *cure your pain*
435　I shall smytt of[f] thi hede and sett yt on agayn. *cut off your head*
　　NOUGHT. By owr Lady, ser, a fayer playster! *what a fair cure*

Wyll ye of[f] wyth hys hede! That ys a schreude charme! *an evil charm*
As for me, I have non harme. *no complaints*
I were loth to forbere myn arme. *am unwilling to give up*
440　Ye pley *in nomine patris*, choppe! *"In the name of the Father" (a last blessing)*
NEW GYSE. Ye shall not choppe my jewellys, and I may. *testicles/if I can help it*
NOWADAYS. Ye, Cristys crose, wyll ye smyght my hede awey? *head*
Ther wer on[e] and on[e]! Oute! Ye shall not assay. *another (his friends)/even try it*
I myght well be callyde a foppe. *(Then)/fool*

445　MISCHIEF. I kan choppe yt of[f] and make yt agayn. *make it whole*
NEW GYSE. I hade a schreude *recumbentibus* but I fele no peyn. *shrewd knockout*
NOWADAYS. Ande my hede ys all save and holl agayn. *safe*
Now towchynge the mater of Mankynde,
Lett us have an interleccyon, sythen ye be cum hethere. *a consultation/since/hither*
450　Yt were goode to have an ende.

MISCHIEF. How, how, a mynstrell! Know ye ony ou[gh]t? *any at all*
NOUGHT. I kan pype in a Walsyngham w[h]ystyll, I, Nought, Nought.

MISCHIEF. Blow apase, and thou shall bryng hym in wyth a flewte.   *quickly/flute*
   [Nought plays; the voice of Titivillus is heard]
   TITIVILLUS. I com wyth my leggys under me.
455   MISCHIEF. How, Neu Gyse, Nowadays, herke or I goo!   *ere*
   When owr hedys wer togethere I spake of *si dedero.* *   *If I give*
   NEW GYSE. Ye, go thi wey! We shall gather mony onto,   *money for the purpose*
   Ellys ther shall no man hym se.   *(i.e., Titivillus)*

   [To the audience]
   Now gostly to owr purpos, worschypfull soverence,   *piously/masters*
460   We intende to gather mony, yf yt plesse yowr neclygence,
   For a man wyth a hede that ys of grett omnipotens.
      NOWADAYS. Kepe yowr tayll, in goodnes I prey yow, goode brother!   *tally*
   He ys a worschypp[f]ull man, sers, savyng yowr reverens.   *begging your pardon*
   He lovyth no grotys, nor pens of t[w]o pens.   *groats/pence (coins)*
465   Gyf us rede reyallys yf ye wyll se hys abhomynabull presens.   *red royals (gold coins)*
      NEW GYSE. Not so! Ye that mow not pay the ton,   *can't pay the one*
                        pay the tother.   *the other*

   At the goodeman of this house fyrst we wyll assay.   *master*
   Gode blysse yow, master! Ye say as yll, yet ye wyll not sey nay.   *you may curse*
   Lett us go by and by and do them pay.   *make them (the audience) pay*
470   Ye pay all alyke; well mut ye fare!   *Well might you fare (good luck)*
   NOUGHT. I sey, New Gyse, Nowadays: *"Estis vos pecuniatus?"*   *Are you rich?*
   I have cryede a fayer w[h]yll, I beschrew yowr *patus!* *long enough/curse on your heads*
   NOWADAYS. *Ita vere, magister.* * Cumme forth now yowr *gatus!*   *out your door*
   He ys a goodly man, sers; make space and be ware!

   [Enter Titivillus, dressed as a devil with a net]

475   TITIVILLUS. *Ego sum dominancium dominus* * and my name ys Titivillus.
   Ye that have goode hors, to yow I sey *caveatis!*   *beware*
   Here ys an abyll felyschyppe to tryse hem out at yowr gatys.   *to snatch them/door*

   Loquitur ad New Gyse: *He speaks to New Guise*

   TITIVILLUS. *Ego probo sic:* ser New Gys, lende me a peny!   *I prove it thus*
   NEW GYSE. I have a grett purse, ser, but I have no monay.
480   By the masse, I fayll t[w]o farthyngys of an halpeny;   *am short*
   Yet hade I ten pound this nyght that was.   *last night*

---

456. If I give something (I will get something back).
473. Truly then, master.
475. I am Lord of Lords.

Tityvillus loquitur ad Nowadays.   *Titivillus speaks to Nowadays*

TITIVILLUS. What ys in thi purse? thou art a stout felow.   *sturdy*
NOWADAYS. The Devll have the qwytt! I am a clen jentyllman.   *reward/upstanding*
I prey Gode I be never wers storyde then I am.   *poorer*
485   Yt shall be otherwyse, I hope, or this nyght passe.   *ere*

Tytivillus loquitur ad Nought.   *Titivillus speaks to Nought*

TITIVILLUS. Herke now! I say thou hast many a peny.
NOUGHT. *Non nobis, domine, non nobis,* by Sent Deny!   *Not of our own, Lord*
The Devll may daunce in my purse for ony peny;   *any*
Yt ys as clen as a byrdys ars.
490   TITIVILLUS. *[To the audience]* Now I say yet ageyn, *caveatis* !   *beware*
Her ys an abyll felyschyppe to tryse hem out of yowr gatys.   *snatch/door*

Now I sey, New Gyse, Nowadays, and Nought,
Go and serche the contre, anon yt be sowyte,
Summe here, summe ther; what yf ye may cache owyte?   *what can you steal*

495   Yf ye fayll of hors, take what ye may ellys.   *find no horses*
NEW GYSE. Then speke to Mankynde for the *recumbentibus*   *knockout blow*
                    of my jewellys.
NOWADAYS. Remember my brokyn hede in the worschyppe
                    of the fyve vowellys.   *wounds (?)*
NOUGHT. Ye, goode ser, and the sytyca in my arme.   *sciatica*
TITIVILLUS. I know full well what Mankynde dyde to yow.
500   Myschyff hat informyde of all the matere thorow.   *thoroughly*
I shall venge yowr quarell, I make Gode a vow.
Forth, and espye were ye may do harme.   *where you*
Take William Fyde, yf ye wyll have ony mo.   *more (companions)*
I sey, New Gyse, wethere art thou avysyde to go?   *supposed to go*

505   NEW GYSE. Fyrst I shall begyn at Master Huntyngton of Sauston,*   *Sawston*
Fro thens I shall go to Wylliam Thurlay of Hauston,   *Hawxton*
Ande so forth to Pycharde of Trumpyngton.   *Trumpington*
I wyll kepe me to thes thre.
NOWADAYS. I shall goo to Wyllyham Baker of Waltom,   *Walton*
510   To Rycherde Bollman of Gayton;
I shall spare Master Woode of Fullburn,   *Fulbourn*
He ys a *noli me tangere.*   *A "Touch me not"—touchy fellow*

505-15. The towns named here are from Cambridgeshire and Norfolk, presumably in the region where *Mankind* was played.

NOUGHT. I shall goo to Wyllyam Patryke of Massyngham,
I shall spare Master Alyngton of Botysam   *Bottisham*
515   Ande Hamonde of Soffeham,   *Swoffeham*
For drede of *in manus tuas,* qweke.   *"into your hands" (last words), (choking sound)*
Felous, cum forth, and go we hens togethyr.
NEW GYSE. Syth we shall go, lett us be well ware wethere.   *Since/aware whither*
If we may be take, we com no more hethyr.   *taken/higher*
520   Lett us con well owr neke-verse, that we have not a cheke.*   *rehearse/disaster*

TITIVILLUS. Goo yowr wey, a devll wey, go yowr wey all!
I blysse yow wyth my lyfte honde: foull yow befall!   *bad luck (an inverted blessing)*
Com agayn, I werne, as so[o]n as I yow call,   *I command*
And brynge yowr avantage into this place.   *gatherings*
525   To speke wyth Mankynde I wyll tary here this tyde   *at this time*
Ande assay hys goode purpose for to sett asyde.   *try to change his*
The goode man Mercy shall no lenger be hys gyde.
I shall make hym to dawnce another trace.   *dancestep*

Ever I go invysybull, yt ys my jett,   *fashion*
530   Ande befor hys ey thus I wyll hange my nett
To blench hys syght; I hope to have hys fote-mett.   *blind/foot size (for snare)*
To yrke hym of hys labur I shall make a frame.   *frustrate him in/trap*
Thys borde shall be hyde under the erth prevely;   *board/secretly*
[Buries a board under Mankind's dirt]
Hys spade shall enter, I hope, onredyly;   *only with difficulty*
535   Be then he hath assayde, he shall be very angry   *By the time/tried*
Ande lose hys pacyens, peyn of schame.   *with the penalty*
I shall menge hys corne wyth drawke and wyth durnell;   *mix/seeds/weeds*
Yt shall not be lyke to sow nor to sell.   *suitable*
Yondyr he commyth; I prey of cownsell.   *keep quiet*
540   He shall wene grace were wane.   *think grace is gone*

[Enter Mankind, with seeds]

MANKIND. Now Gode of hys mercy sende us of hys sonde!   *his message*
I have brought sede here to sow wyth my londe.
Qwyll I overdylew yt, here yt shall stonde.   *[Puts seeds down]*   *While/dig*
*In nomine Patris et Filii et Spiritus Sancti,** now I wyll begyn.

[Titivillus steals Mankind's seeds]

545   Thys londe ys so harde yt makyth unlusty and yrke.   *tired and frustrated*
I shall sow my corn at aventur and lett Gode werke.   *at random*

---

520. Neck-verse: the first verse of Psalm 51. Reciting it in court gained benefit of clergy—no hanging.

[Discovers his seeds are missing]

Alasse, my corn ys lost! here ys a foull werke!
I se[e] well by tyllynge lytyll shall I wyn.
Here I gyff uppe my spade for now and for ever.

Here Titivillus goth out wyth the spade.

550　MANKIND. To occupye my body I wyll not put me in dever.   *in devoir (labor)*
　　　I wyll here my evynsonge here or I dysseuer.   *hear/ere I leave*
　　　　Thys place I assyng as for my kyrke.   *assign to be/church*
　　　　Here in my kerke I knell on my kneys.   *church/kneel*
　　　　Pater noster qui es in celis.   *Our Father who art in heaven...*

[Titivillus enters again]

555　TITIVILLUS. I promes yow I have no lede on my helys.   *lead in my heels*
　　　I am here ageyn to make this felow yrke.   *frustrated*

　　[To audience]
　　Qwyst! pesse! I shall go to hys ere and tytyll therin.   *Whist! Quiet!/whisper*
　　A schorte preyere thyrlyth hewyn; of thi preyere blyn.   *pierces heaven/cease*
　　Thou art holyer then ever was ony of thi kyn.
560　Aryse and avent the[e]! nature compellys.   *go out/nature calls*

[Mankind rises]

MANKIND. I wyll into the yerde, soverens, and cum ageyn son.
For drede of the colyke and eke of the ston   *kidney stone*
I wyll go do that nedys must be don.
　My bedys shall be here for whosummever wyll ellys.   *prayer beads/wants them*

　　Exiat   *Let him leave*

565　TITIVILLUS. Mankynde was besy in hys prayere, yet I dyde hym aryse.   *made*
　　He ys conveyde, be Cryst, from hys dyvyn servyce.   *moved*
　　Wethere ys he, trow ye? Iwysse I am wonder wyse;   *Whither/I think/wondrously*
　　　I have sent hym forth to schyte lesynges.   *little lies*
　　Yff ye have ony sylver, in happe pure brasse,   *perhaps*
570　Take a lytyll powder of Parysch and cast ouer hys face,   *the coin's*
　　Ande evyn in the howll-flyght let hym passe.   *during the night*
　　　Titivillus kan lerne yow many praty thyngys.   *teach/pretty*

---

544. In the name of the Father and of the Son and of the Holy Ghost. (Mankind is blessing himself.)

I trow Mankynde wyll cum ageyn so[o]n,
Or ellys I fere me ewynsonge wyll be don. *fear*
575 Hys bedys shall be trysyde asyde, and that anon. *thrown*
    Ye shall a goode sport yf ye wyll abyde. *have/stay*
Mankynde cummyth ageyn, well fare he!
I shall answere hym *ad omnia quare*. *at every query*
Ther shall be sett abroche a clerycall mater. *stirred up/concern*
580 I hope of hys purpose to sett hym asyde.

[Mankind enters again]

MANKIND. Evynsong hath be in the saynge, I trow, a fayer wyll. *been going on*
I am yrke of yt; yt ys t[o]o longe be on myle. *tired/by a mile*
Do wey! I wyll no more so oft over the chyrche-style. *go so often to church*
    Be as be may, I shall do another. *otherwise*
585 Of labure and preyer, I am nere yrke of both; *tired*
I wyll no more of yt, thow Mercy be wroth. *angry*
My hede ys very hevy, I tell yow forsoth. *truly*
    I shall slepe full my bely and he wore my brother. *my bellyfull even if he were*

[To the audience]
TITIVILLUS. Ande ever ye dyde, for me kepe now yowr sylence. *If*
590 Not a worde, I charge yow, peyn of forty pens. *on penalty*
A praty game shall be scheude yow or ye go hens. *crafty/showed here*
    Ye may here hym snore; he ys sade aslepe. *hear/sound*
Qwyst! pesse! the Devll ys dede! I shall goo ronde in hys ere. *Whist! Quiet!/next to*
    [Whispers in his ear]
Alasse, Mankynde, alasse! Mercy hath stown a mere! *stolen a mare*
595 He ys runn away fro hys master, ther wot no man where; *no one knows*
    Moreover, he stale both a hors and a nete. *stole/neat (ox)*

But yet I herde sey he brake hys neke as he rode in Fraunce;
But I thynke he rydyth on the galouse, to lern for to daunce, *gallows/dance*
Bycause of hys theft, that ys hys gouernance. *penalty*
600 Trust no more on hym, he ys a marryde man. *ruined*
Mekyll sorow wyth thi spade beforn thou hast wrought. *Great/before*
Aryse and aske mercy of Neu Gyse, Nowadays, and Nought.
Thei cun avyse the for the best; lett ther goode wyll be sought, *can advise*
    Ande thi own wyff brethell, and take the a lemman. *deceive/mistress*

[To the audience]
605 Farwell, everychon! for I have don my game, *everyone/completed*
For I have brought Mankynde to myscheff and to schame.
    [Waking]
MANKIND. Whope who! Mercy hath brokyn hys neke-kycher, *neckerchief*
                he avows,

Or he hangyth by the neke hye uppon the gallouse.   *gallows*
Adew, fayer masters! I wyll hast me to the ale-house   *go*
610   Ande speke wyth New Gyse, Nowadays and Nought
And geett me a lemman wyth a smattrynge face.   *darling/kissable*

[New Guise enters, noose hanging from his neck]

NEW GYSE. Make space, for cokkys body sakyrde, make space!
A ha! well overron! Gode gyff hym evyll grace!   *well outrun*
We were nere Sent Patrykes wey, by hym that me bought.   *redeemed*

615   I was twychyde by the neke; the game was begunne.
A grace was, the halter brast asonder: *ecce signum!**   *Luckily/noose broke*
The halff ys abowte my neke; we hade a nere rune!   *close call*
"Beware," quod the goodewyff when sche smot of here   *said/struck/her*
                                        husbondys hede, beware!
Myscheff ys a convicte, for he coude hys neke-verse.   *knew*
620   My body gaff a swynge when I hynge uppon the casse.   *gallows*
Alasse, he wyll hange such a lyghly man, and a fers,   *lovely/fierce*
For stelynge of an horse, I prey Gode gyf hym care!   *sorrow*

Do wey this halter! What devll doth Mankynde here, wyth sorow!   *Take off*
Alasse, how my neke ys sore, I make avowe!   *I swear*
625   MANKIND. Ye be welcom, Neu Gyse! Ser, what chere wyth yow?   *what's new*
NEW GYSE. Well ser, I have no cause to morn.   *mourn*
MANKIND. What was that abowte yowr neke, so Gode yow amende?   *help you*
NEW GYSE. In feyth, Sent Audrys holy bende.   *neck band*
I have a lytyll dyshes, as yt plesse Gode to sende,   *disease (problem)*
630   Wyth a runnynge ryngeworme.

[Enter Nowadays, with stolen church goods]

NOWADAYS. Stonde arom, I prey the, brother myn!   *Make room*
I have laburryde all this nyght; wen shall we go dyn?
A chyrche her[e] besyde shall pay for ale, brede, and wyn.
Lo, here ys stoff wyll serve.   *serve to pay*
635   NEW GYSE. Now by the holy Mary, thou art better marchande then I!
NOUGHT. Avante, knavys, lett me go by!   *Away, rogues*
I kan not geet and I shulde sterve.   *If I cannot steal*

[Enter Mischief in chains]
MISCHIEF. Here cummyth a man of armys! Why stonde ye so styll?   *soldier*
Of murder and manslawter I have my bely-fyll.
640   NOWADAYS. What, Myscheff, have ye ben in presun? And yt be yowr wyll,   *If*

---

616. Behold the evidence!

Me semyth ye have scoryde a peyr of fetters.   *stolen*
MISCHIEF. I was chenyde by the armys: lo, I have them here.
The chenys I brast asundyr and kyllyde the jaylere,
Ye, ande hys fayer wyff halsyde in a cornere;   *embraced*
645   A, how swetly I kyssyde the swete mowth of hers!

When I hade do, I was myn owyn bottler;   *done/butler*
I brought awey wyth me both dysch and dublere.   *plate*
Here ys anow for me; be of goode chere!   *enough*
Yet well fare the new chesance!   *venture*
650 MANKIND. *[Kneels]* I aske mercy of New Gyse, Nowadays, and Nought.
Onys wyth my spade I remember that I faught.   *Once*
I wyll make yow amendys yf I hurt yow ought
   Or dyde ony grevaunce.

NEW GYSE. What a devll lykyth the[e] to be of this dysposycyon?
655 MANKIND. I drempt Mercy was hange, this was my vysyon,   *hanged*
Ande that to yow thre I shulde have recors and remocyon.   *reconciliation*
   Now I prey yow hertyly of yowr goode wyll.
I crye yow mercy of all that I dyde amysse.
   [To his friends]
NOWADAYS. I sey, New Gys, Nought, Tytivillus made all this: *did*
660 As sekyr as Gode ys in hevyn, so yt ys.   *sure*
   NOUGHT. Stonde uppe on yowr feet! why stonde ye so styll?

NEW GYSE. Master Myscheff, we wyll yow exort
Mankyndys name in yowr bok for to report.   *book (of followers)*
MISCHIEF. I wyll not so; I wyll sett a corte.   *convene a court*
665 Nowadays, mak proclamacyon,
            And do yt *sub forma jurys*, dasarde!   *in legal form, fool*
NOWADAYS. Oyyt! Oyyy! Oyet! All manere of men and comun women   *Oyez*
To the cort of Myschyff othere cum or sen!   *either*
Mankynde shall retorn; he ys on[e] of owr men.
670 MISCHIEF. Nought, cum forth, thou shall be stewerde.

NEW GYSE. Master Myscheff, hys syde gown may be tolde.   *coat/taken toll of*
He may have a jakett therof, and mony tolde.   *money counted*

   Nought scribit.   *writes*

MANKIND. I wyll do for the best, so I have no colde.   *as long as*
   Holde, I prey yow, and take yt wyth yow.
675 Ande let me have yt ageyn in ony wyse.   *any case*
NEW GYSE. I promytt yow a fresch jakett after the new gyse.   *latest fashion*
MANKIND. Go and do that longyth to yowr offyce,   *what you need to*
   And spare that ye mow!   *save what you can*

NOUGHT. Holde, master Myscheff, and rede this.

680 MISCHIEF. Here ys *blottybus in blottis,*   *(Latinate gibberish)*
     Blottorum blottibus istis.
     I beschrew yowr erys, a fayer hande!   *curse your ears/good handwriting*
     NOWADAYS. Ye, yt ys a goode rennynge fyst.   *cursive fist*
     Such an hande may not be myst.   *avoided*
685 NOUGHT. I shulde have don better, hade I wyst.   *known*
     MISCHIEF. Take hede, sers, yt stoude you on hande.   *concerns you here*

     [Announces:]

     Carici tenta generalis   *The General Court being held*
     In a place ther goode ale ys   *where*
     Anno regni regitalis   *In the regnal year of king no-one*
690   *Edwardi nullateni*   *of Edward the Nothing*
     On yestern day in Feuerere—the yere passyth fully,   *February/ends*
     As Nought hath wrytyn; here ys owr Tulli,   *Cicero*
     Anno regni regis nulli !   *In the regnal year of no-one*

     NOWADAYS. What how, Neu Gyse! Thou makyst moche taryynge.   *What ho!*
695 That jakett shall not be worth a ferthynge.
     [New Guise pushes through the audience]
     NEW GYSE. Out of my wey, sers, for drede of fyghtynge!
     Lo, here ys a feet tayll, lyght to leppe abowte!   *fit tail (of the gown)*
     NOUGHT. Yt ys not schapyn worth a morsell of brede;
     Ther ys to[o] moche cloth, yt weys as ony lede.   *weighs as much*
700 I shall goo and mende yt, ellys I wyll lose my hede.
     [Pushes back through the audience]
     Make space, sers, lett me go owte.

     MISCHIEF. Mankynde, cum hethere! God sende yow the gowte!
     Ye shall goo to all the goode felouse in the cuntre aboute;
     Onto the goodewyff when the goodeman ys owte.
705 "I wyll," say ye.
     MANKIND.   I wyll, ser.
     NEW GYSE. There arn but sex dedly synnys, lechery ys non,
     As yt may be verefyede be us brethellys everychon.   *by us wretches*
     Ye shall goo robbe, stell, and kyll, as fast as ye may gon.
     "I wyll," sey ye.
     MANKIND.   I wyll, ser.

710 NOWADAYS. On Sundays on the morow erly betyme   *morning*
     Ye shall wyth us to the all-house erly to go dyn   *ale-house*
     And forbere masse and matens, owres and prime.   *leave off/canonical hours*
     "I wyll," sey ye.
     MANKIND.   I wyll, ser.

MISCHIEF. Ye must have be yowr syde a longe *da pacem*,   *give-peace (a dagger)*
715 As trew men ryde be the wey for to onbrace them,   *undo*
Take ther monay, kytt ther throtys, thus overface them.   *overpower*
"I wyll," sey ye.
MANKIND.   I wyll, ser.

[Naught returns with a much-shortened gown]

NOUGHT. Here ys a joly jakett! How sey ye?
NEW GYSE. Yt ys a goode jake of fence for a mannys body.   *jacket/defense*
720 Hay, doog, hay! whoppe whoo! Go yowr wey lyghtly!   *quickly*
Ye are well made for to ren.   *run*

[Mercy enters]

MISCHIEF. Tydyngys, tydyngys! I have aspyede on[e]!   *Alert! Alert!/seen the one*
Hens wyth yowr stuff, fast we were gon!   *Off with/quickly*
I beschrew the last shall com to hys hom.   *The last one home's cursed*

Dicant Omnes.   *All speak*

725 ALL. Amen!

MERCY. What how, Mankynde! Fle[e] that felyschyppe, I yow prey!
MANKIND. I shall speke wyth the[e] another tyme, to-morn,   *tomorrow*
                          or the next day.
We shall goo forth together to kepe my faders yer-day.   *death-anniversary*
A tapster, a tapster! Stow, statt, stow!   *A barmaid (whore)/Hold on*
730 MISCHIEF. A myscheff go wyth her! I have a foull fall.   *May harm go/I took*
Hens, awey fro me, or I shall beschyte yow all.
NEW GYSE. What how, ostlere, hostlere! Lende us a football!
Whoppe whow! A, now! A, now! A, now! A, now!

[They leave with Mankind kicking the ball]

MERCY. My mynde ys dyspersyde, my body trymmelyth   *distracted/trembles*
                          as the aspen leffe.
735 The terys shuld trekyll down by my chekys, were not   *were it not for*
                          yowr reverrence. *your (the audience)*
Yt were to me solace, the cruell vysytacyon of deth.   *would be comfort*
Wythout rude behaver I kan not expresse this inconvenyens. *swearing/misfortune*
Wepynge, sythynge, and sobbynge were my suffycyens;   *sighing/sustenance*
All naturall nutriment to me as caren ys odybull.   *carrion is odious*
740 My inwarde afflixcyon yeldyth me tedyouse unto yowr presens.   *makes me*
I kan not bere yt evynly that Mankynde ys so flexybull.   *calmly/fickle*

Man onkynde, wherever thou be! for all this world was *Man-unkind*
                    not aprehensyble, *could not see how*
   To dyscharge thin orygynall offence, thraldam and captyvyte, *bondage and*
   Tyll Godys own welbelouyde son was obedient and passyble. *ready to suffer*
745   Every droppe of hys bloode was schede to purge thin iniquite.
   I dyscomende and dysalow thin oftyn mutabylyte. *changeability*
   To every creature thou art dyspectuose and odyble. *hateful/odious*
      Why art thou so oncurtess, so inconsyderatt? Alasse, who ys me! *discourteous/woe*
   As the fane that turnyth wyth the wynde, so thou *weathervane*
                    art convertyble. *changeable*

750   In trust ys treson; thi promes ys not credyble;
      Thy perversyose ingratytude I can not rehers. *perverse/tell again*
   To God and to all the holy corte of hevyn thou art despectyble,
      As a nobyll versyfyer makyth mencyon in this verse:
   "*Lex et natura, Cristus et omnia jura*
755   *Damnant ingratum, lugent eum fore natum.*"*

   O goode Lady and Mother of mercy, have pety and compassyon *pity*
   Of the wrechydnes of Mankynde, that ys so wanton and so frayll! *On/who*
   Lett mercy excede justyce, dere Mother, amytt this supplycacyon, *grant/prayer*
   Equyte to be leyde onparty and mercy to prevayll. *Justice/set aside*

760   To sensuall lyvynge ys reprovable, that ys nowadays, *is to blame for all*
      As be the comprehence of this mater yt may be specyfyede. *this story will show*
   New Gyse, Nowadays, Nought wyth ther allectuose ways *alluring*
   They have pervertyde Mankynde, my swet sun, I have well espyede. *son/seen*

   A, wyth thes cursyde caytyfs, and I may, he shall not *wretches, if I can help it*
                 long indure.
765   I, Mercy, hys father gostly, wyll procede forth and do my propyrte. *special action*
   Lady, helpe! This maner of lyvynge ys a detestabull plesure. *Our Lady*
   Vanitas vanitatum, all ys but a vanyté. *Vanity of vanities*

   Mercy shall never be convicte of hys oncurtes condycyon. *convinced/uncourteous*
   Wyth wepynge terys be nygte and be day I wyll goo and never sesse.
770   Shall I not fynde hym? Yes, I hope. Now Gode be my protecyon!
   My predylecte son, where be ye? Mankynde, *vbi es?* *Most beloved/where are you?*

   MISCHIEF. My prepotent fader, when ye sowpe, sowpe owt *most powerful/sup*
                  yowr messe. *portion*
   Ye are all to-gloryede in yowr termys; ye make many a lesse. *lie*

754-55. "Law and nature, Christ and all justice damn the ingrate; they lament that he was born." The
"nobyll versyfyer" remains unknown.

Wyll ye here? He cryeth ever "Mankynde, *vbi es?*"   *hear/where are you?*
775 NEW GYSE. Hic hyc, hic hic, hic hic, hic hic!   *Here, here, here...*
   That ys to sey, here, here, here! ny dede in the cryke.   *near/creek*
   Yf ye wyll have hym, goo and syke, syke, syke!   *seek, seek, seek*
   Syke not overlong, for losynge of yowr mynde!

NOWADAYS. Yf ye wyll have Mankynde, how *domine, domine, dominus*!   *Lord*
780 Ye must speke to the schryve for a *cape corpus*,   *sheriff/a "take his body" (a writ)*
   Ellys ye must be fayn to retorn wyth *non est inventus*.   *he is not found (a legal phrase)*
   How sey ye, ser? My bolte ys schett.   *shot (I am pissing)*
NOUGHT. I am doynge of my nedyngys; be ware how ye schott!   *am shitting/aim*
   Fy, fy, fy! I have fowll arayde my fote.   *foully splattered/foot*
785 Be wyse for schotynge wyth yowr takyllys, for Gode wott   *weapons/knows*
   My fote ys fowly overschett.   *covered with shit*

MISCHIEF. A parlement, a parlement! Cum forth, Nought, behynde.   *Let's gather*
   A cownsell belyve! I am aferde Mercy wyll hym fynde.   *A counsel quickly/afraid that*
   How sey ye, and what sey ye? How shall we do wyth Mankynde?
790 NEW GYSE. Tysche! a flyes weyng! Wyll ye do well?   *Tush/wing*
   He wenyth Mercy were honge for stelyng of a mere.   *thinks/hanged/mare*
   Myscheff, go sey to hym that Mercy sekyth everywere.
   He wyll honge hymselff, I undyrtake, for fere.   *bet/fear*
   MISCHIEF. I assent therto; yt ys wyttyly seyde and well.

795 NOWADAYS. Qwyppe yt in thi cote; anon yt were don.   *Whip (wrap the rope)/quickly*
   Now Sent Gabryellys modyr saue the clothes of thi schon!   *covering/shoes*
   All the bokys in the worlde, yf thei hade be undon[e],   *opened*
   Kowde not a cownselde us bett.   *have/better*

   Hic exit Myscheff   *Here Mischief leaves*

MISCHIEF. How, Mankynde! Cumm and speke wyth Mercy, he is
                    here fast by.   *nearby*
800 MANKIND. A roppe, a rope, a rope! I am not worthy.
   MISCHIEF. Anon, anon, anon! I have yt here redy,
   Wyth a tre also that I have gett.   *found*

Holde the tre, Nowadays, Nought! Take hede and be wyse!
NEW GYSE. Lo, Mankynde! do as I do; this ys thi New Gyse.
805 Gyff the roppe just to thy neke; this ys myn avyse.   *Tighten/advice*
   MISCHIEF. Helpe thisylff, Nought! Lo, Mercy ys here!   *Look out!*
   He skaryth us wyth a bales; we may no lengere tary.   *a scourge*

   [New Guise slips and hangs himself]

NEW GYSE. Qweke, qweke, qweke! Alass, my thrott! I beschrew yow, mary!
Mercy, Crystys coppyde curse go wyth yow, and Sent Davy!   *heaped up*

[They rescue him]

810   Alasse, my wesant! Ye were sumwhat to[o] nere.   *throat*

         Exiant   *Let them all leave*

MERCY. Aryse, my precyose redempt son! Ye be to me full dere.
         He ys so tymerouse, me semyth hys vytall spryt doth exspyre.   *fearful, it seems*
MANKIND. Alasse, I have be so bestyally dysposyde, I dare not apere.   *been*
         To se yowr solaycyose face I am not worthy to dysyere.   *comforting*
815 MERCY. Yowr crymynose compleynt wondyth my hert   *confessions of crime*
                                           as a lance.
         Dyspose yowrsylff mekly to aske mercy, and I wyll assent.
         Yelde me nethyr golde nor tresure, but yowr humbyll obeysyance,   *yield*
         The voluntary subjeccyon of yowr hert, and I am content.

MANKIND. What, aske mercy yet onys agayn? Alas, that were
                                           a vyle petycyun.   *petition*
820   Evyr to offend and ever to aske mercy, that ys a puerilite.   *childishness*
         Yt ys so abhominabyll to rehers my iterat transgrescion,   *say again/repeated*
         I am not worthy to have mercy be no possibilite.   *by no way*

MERCY. O Mankend, my singler solas, this is a lamentabyll excuse.   *singular*
         The dolorus terys of my hert, how thei begyn to amownt!   *mount*
825 O pirssid Jhesu, help thou this synfull synner to redouce!   *pierced/come back*
         Nam hec est mutacio dextre Excelsi; vertit impios et non sunt. *

         Aryse and aske mercy, Mankend, and be associat to me.   *next*
         Thy deth schall be my hevynesse; alas, tys pety yt schwld be thus.
         Thy obstinacy wyll exclude the[e] fro the glorius perpetuite.
830   Yet for my lofe ope thy lyppys and sey *Miserere mei, Deus!**
MANKIND. The egall justyse of God wyll not permytte sych   *equitable*
                                           a synfull wrech
         To be revyvyd and restoryd ageyn; that were impossibyll.
MERCY. The justyce of God wyll as I wyll, as hymsylfe doth preche:
         Nolo mortem peccatoris, inquit,* yff he wyll be redusyble.   *recovered*

835 MANKIND. Than mercy, good Mercy! What ys a man wythowte mercy?   *Then*
         Lytyll ys our parte of paradyse were mercy ne were.   *not there*

---

826. For this is the change of the right hand of the Most High; he overthrew the wicked and they are
no more. [See Psalms 77:10, Proverbs 12:7]
830. Have mercy upon me, O God.
834. I do not want the sinner's death, he said. [See Ezekiel 33:11]

Good Mercy, excuse the inevytabyll objeccion of my gostly enmy.
The prowerbe seyth "The trewth tryith the sylfe." Alas, I have mech care.   *tests*

MERCY. God wyll not make yow prevy onto hys last jugement.
840   Justyce and Equite shall be fortyfyid, I wyll not denye.   *strengthened*
Trowthe may not so cruelly procede in hys streyt argument   *Truth/strict*
But that Mercy schall rewle the mater wythowte contraversye.*   *So/rule/no doubt*

Aryse now and go wyth me in thys deambulatorye.   *cloister*
Inclyne yowyr capacite; my doctrine ys convenient.   *Attend/befitting*
845   Synne not in hope of mercy; that ys a cryme notary.   *notorious*
To truste overmoche in a prince yt ys not expedient.   *To presume*

In hope when ye syn ye thynke to have mercy, be ware of that aventure. *possibility*
The good Lord seyd to the lecherus woman of Chanane,   *Canaan*
The holy gospell ys the awtorite, as we rede in scrypture,   *the authority*
850   *"Vade et jam amplius noli peccare."**

Cryst preservyd this synfull woman takeyn in awowtry;   *adultery*
He seyde to here theis wordys, "Go and syn no more."   *her these*
So to yow, go and syn no more. Be ware of veyn confidens of mercy; *presumption*
Offend not a prince on trust of hys favour, as I seyd before.   *in trust*

855   Yf ye fele yoursylfe trappyd in the snare of your gostly enmy,
Aske mercy anon; be ware of the contynuance.   *at once/continuing*
Whyll a wond ys fresch yt ys provyd curabyll be surgery,   *by*
That yf yt procede ovyrlong, yt ys cawse of gret grevans.   *it is the cause of*

MANKIND. To aske mercy and to have, this ys a   *have it granted*
lyberall possescion.   *precious*
860   Schall this expedycius petycion ever be alowyd,   *granted*
as ye have insyght?   *do you think?*
MERCY. In this present lyfe mercy ys plente, tyll deth makyth   *plentiful*
hys dyvysion;
But whan ye be go, *vsque ad minimum quadrantem**   *are gone*
ye schall rekyn your ryght.   *figure/reward*
Aske mercy and have, whyll the body wyth the sowle hath   *receive it*
hys annexion;   *are together*
Yf ye tary tyll your dyscesse, ye may hap of your desyre   *death/perhaps*
to mysse.   *miss your chance*
865   Be repentant here, trust not the owr of deth; thynke on this lessun:
*"Ecce nunc tempus acceptabile, ecce nunc dies salutis."**

841-42. In the final judgment, Truth will be tempered by Mercy.
850. Go and sin no more. [See John 8:11]
862. To the smallest farthing. [See Matthew 5:25]
866. Behold, now is the accepted time; behold, now is the day of salvation. [See 2 Corinthians 6:12]

All the vertu in the wor[l]d yf ye myght comprehend   *Even if you had*
   Your merytys were not premyabyll to the blys abowe,   *would not entitle you to*
   Not to the lest joy of hevyn, of your propyr efforte to ascend.   *your own*
870   Wyth mercy ye may; I tell yow no fabyll, scrypture doth prove.   *as Scripture*

MANKIND. O Mercy, my suavius solas and synguler   *sweet comfort*
                     recreatory,   *only refreshment*
   My predilecte spesyall, ye are worthy to have my love;   *specially loved one*
   For wythowte deserte and menys supplicatorie   *without deserving and wanting means*
   Ye be compacient to my inexcusabyll reprowe.   *compassionate/shame*

875 A, yt swemyth my hert to thynk how onwysely I have wroght.   *grieves/acted*
   Tytivillus, that goth invisibele, hyng hys nett before my eye
   And by hys fantasticall visionys sediciusly sowght,
   To New Gyse, Nowadayis, Nowght causyd me to obey.

MERCY. Mankend, ye were oblivyows of my doctrine monytorye.   *warning*
880 I seyd before, Titivillus wold asay yow a bronte.   *try to attack you*
   Be ware fro hensforth of hys fablys delusory.   *from*
   The prowerbe seyth, *"Jacula prestita minus ledunt."*[*]

   Ye have thre adversaryis and he ys mayster of hem all: *them*
   That ys to sey, the Devell, the World, the Flesch and the Fell.   *Skin*
885 The New Gyse, Nowadayis, Nowgth, the World we may hem call;   *them*
   And propyrly Titivillus syngnyfyth the Fend of helle;   *Fiend*

   The Flesch, that ys the unclene concupissens of your body.   *concupiscence*
   These be your thre gostly enmyis, in whom ye have put your confidens.
   Thei browt yow to Myscheffe to conclude your temporall glory,
890 As yt hath be schewyd before this worcheppyll audiens.   *been shown*

   Remembyr how redy I was to help yow; fro swheche   *from such endeavors*
                     I was not dangerus;   *distant*
   Wherfore, goode sunne, absteyne fro syn evermore after this.
   Ye may both save and spyll yowr sowle that ys so precyus.   *destroy*
   Libere velle, libere nolle[*] God may not deny iwys.   *truly*

895 Be ware of Titivillus wyth his net and of all enmys will,   *intents*
   Of your synfull delectacion that grevyth your gostly substans.   *pleasure/soul*
   Your body ys your enmy; let hym not have hys wyll.
   Take your leve whan ye wyll. God send yow good perseverans!   *Depart*

---

882. Known darts sting less.
894. Chosen or not chosen, freely,...

MANKIND. Syth I schall departe, blyse me, fader, her then I go.   *Since/ere I go*
900   God send us all plente of hys gret mercy!
MERCY. *Dominus custodit te ab omni malo!*
In nomine Patris et Filii et Spiritus Sancti. Amen.*

Hic exit Mankend.   *Here Mankind leaves*

MERCY. Wyrschepyll sofereyns, I have do my propirté: *shown my properties*
Mankynd ys deliveryd by my faverall patrocynye.   *happy intercession*
905   God preserve hym fro all wyckyd captivité
And send hym grace hys sensuall condicions to mortifye!   *disposition*

Now for hys love that for us receyvyd hys humanité,   *Jesus's/who*
Serge your condicyons wyth dew examinacion.   *Search/consciences/due*
Thynke and remembyr the world ys but a wanité,   *vanity*
910   As yt ys provyd daly by diverse transmutacyon.   *proved daily/example*

Mankend ys wrechyd, he hath sufficyent prove.   *proved enough*
Therefore God grant yow all *per suam misericordiam*   *by his mercy*
That ye may be pleyferys wyth the angellys abowe   *playfellows (companions)*
And have to your porcyon *vitam eternam*. Amen!   *eternal life as your portion*

901-2. May the Lord preserve you from all evil. In the name of the Father and of the Son and of the Holy Ghost. Amen.

The Brome *Abraham and Isaac*

The text of the Brome *Abraham and Isaac* survives in a fifteenth-century commonplace book now at Yale University Library ("The Book of Brome," ff. 15^r-22^r). Also preserved in the manuscript besides *Abraham and Isaac* is part of John Lydgate's "Pageant of Knowledge." The manuscript is named after Brome Hall in Suffolk, the home of at least one of its early owners, Sir Edward Kerrison, and probably the place where the play was copied. The provenance of the manuscript places it either at Brome Hall itself or another nearby manor originally belonging to the Cornwallis family, from whom Kerrison had purchased the property. The dialect of the play is generally East Anglian, and it was evidently copied sometime after 1454. Interestingly, the first word or two of each character's speech is underlined in red at the beginning of the line, as are a number other words within the line throughout the play. It may be that the underlining acted as cues or as mnemonic devices for actors, for an overseer of the play, or for an early reader.

Six Middle English dramatizations of the story of Abraham and Isaac have survived from the late middle ages, more than for any other Biblical episode. Each of the four cycles devotes a pageant to the subject, and in addition to the Brome play another independent version exists, the Northampton *Abraham*. The popularity of the story as a basis for drama is due in part to its importance as an Old Testament prefiguration of Christ's sacrifice on the cross, and in part to its nearly universal pathetic appeal. The story, that is to say, offers both doctrinal justification and theatrical spectacle.

The Brome play is generally considered the best of all the extant versions. More than any of the others it skillfully marshals the Biblical material to coincide with ordinary sympathies, capitalizing on familiar iconic figures and using poetic shorthand to underline the difficulty, the power, and the significance of Abraham's choice. The parallels between Abraham and God, and between Isaac and Jesus, are underlined from the start with references to Isaac as Abraham's most-loved son. And at the heart of the play, as Abraham and Isaac make their way to the sacrificial hill, the stage action and the language unmistakably echo the events of Christ's passion (ll. 211-296). There are important similarities between Abraham and Isaac, too. Like Abraham, Isaac is curious, docile and obedient, but his touching compliance receives an unusual human dimension. Unique to this play, Isaac repeatedly and pathetically invokes his mother, emphasizing the human scale of the action. Abraham's discomfort over Isaac's "passion" works of course to humanize God's decision to sacrifice Jesus. But it is left to the Doctor character, who brings the play to a close, to cap the themes of spiritual courage and obedience, and to extend the emotional urgency of the action into the world of the audience, addressing parents watching the play who have lost or might lose a child. Like the mother of Isaac, whose presence is powerfully imaged forth by Isaac's plaintive speeches, Biblical grieving here gives way to real loss as the play comes to rest in the present.

The language of the play bears out its reputation for inventiveness and excellence. The most frequent meters are four and five line stanzas rhyming *abab* and *abaab,* although longer stanzas appear occasionally. Like other good playwrights the author uses poetic form to underscore action in the play. During emotionally charged moments, for example, the dialogue is conducted at a more frantic pace, and characters often share stanzas—during Isaac's troubled questioning of Abraham (ll. 150-170), for example, or when his death seems most imminent (ll. 285-300), or when both characters express profound relief at the Angel's intervention (ll. 325-355).

One feature of the Brome *Abraham and Isaac* that needs to be remarked on further is its similarity to the Chester cycle version of the play (also included in this anthology). Parallel passages in the two plays extend over 200 lines (Brome 105-315 and Chester 229-420) and include the central dialogue between Abraham and Isaac. The nature of the relationship between the two plays has long been the subject of scholarly debate, which has focused in the main on the question of which play acted as a model for the other. Brome appears to have come off as the more original, but in these discussions important issues like the proliferation of Abraham and Isaac texts, or the differing effects the plays seem intended to produce, have often been lost from view.

The Brome *Abraham and Isaac* was first edited by Lucy Toulmin Smith in *Anglia,* vii (1884), 316-37. The standard scholarly edition, by Norman Davis, appears in the EETS *Non-Cycle Plays and Fragments*; a facsimile of the manuscript, also edited by Davis, appears in *Non-Cycle Plays and the Winchester Dialogues* (see Suggestions for Further Reading).

THE BROME *ABRAHAM AND ISAAC*

[*DRAMATIS PERSONAE:*

ABRAHAM
ISAAC
DEUS
ANGEL
A DOCTOR (of theology)]

[Enter Abraham]
ABRAHAM. Fader of Hevyn Omnipotent,
  Wyth all my hart to the[e] I call;
Thow hast goffe me both lond and rent,   *given/income*
And my lyvelod thow hast me sent;   *livelihood*
5   I thanke the[e] heyly evermore of all.   *highly*

Fyrst off the erth thou madyst Adam,
  And Eve also to be hys wyffe;
All other creaturys of them t[w]oo cam;
And now thow hast grant to me, Abraham,   *granted*
10   Her[e] in thys lond to lede my lyffe.

In my age thou hast grantyd me thys,
  That thys yowng chyld wyth me schall won;   *live*
I love no thyng so myche, iwysse,   *much/to be sure*
Excepe thin owyn selffe, der Fader of blysse,   *dear*
15   As Ysaac her[e], my owyn swete son.

I have dyverse chyldryn moo,   *more*
  The wych I love not halffe so wyll;   *well*
Thys fayer swet chyld, he schereys me soo, *sweet/cheers*
In every place wer that I goo,
20   That noo dessece her[e] may I fell.   *unease, harm/feel*

138

And ther, Fadyr of Hevyn, I the[e] prey,   *And therefore*
  For hys helth and also for hys grace;   *salvation*
Now, Lord, kepe hym both nygth and day   *night*
That never dessese nor noo fray   *unhappiness/harm*
25   Cume to my chyld in noo place.

Now cum on, Ysaac, my owyn swet chyld;
  Goo we hom and take owre rest.
ISAAC. Abraham, myn owyn fader so myld,
  To folowe yow I am full prest,   *in a hurry*
30   Bothe erly and late.
ABRAHAM. Cume on, swete chyld, I love the[e] best
  Off all the chyldryn that ever I begat.

[In Heaven]

DEUS. Myn angell, fast hey the[e] thy wey,   *hurry*
  And onto medyll-erth anon thou goo;   *down to earth*
35   Abrams hart now wyll I asay,   *test*
  Wethere that he be stedfast or noo.

Sey I commaw[n]dyd hym for to take
  Ysaac, hys yowng sonne, that he love so wyll,
And wyth hys blood sacryfyce he make,
40   Yffe ony off my frenchepe he wyll fell.   *friendship, love/feel*

Schow hym the wey onto the hylle
  Wer that hys sacryffyce schall be;
I schall asay now hys good wyll,   *test*
  Whether he lovyth better hys chyld or me.
45   All men schall take exampyll hym be   *by him*
My commaumentys how they schall fulfyll.

[On Earth]

ABRAHAM. Now, Fader of Hevyn, that formyd all thyng,
  My preyerys I make to the[e] ageyn,
For thys day my tender offryng
50   Here must I geve to the[e], certeyn.
Lord God, Allmyty Kyng,
  Wat maner best woll make the[e] most fayn?   *beast/glad*
Yff I had therof very knoyng,   *true knowledge*
  Yt schuld be don wyth all my mayn   *might*
55   Full sone anon.
  To don thy plesyng on an hyll,   *do/pleasure*

Verely yt ys my wyll,
Dere Fader, God alon.

ANGEL. Abraham, Abraham, wyll thou rest!   *rest well*
60   Owre Lord comandyth the[e] for to take
Ysaac, thy yowyng son that thow lovyst best,
And wyth hys blod sacryfyce that thow make.   *make sacrifice with*

Into the Lond of V[y]syon thow goo,   *Land of Moriah*
And offer thy chyld onto thy Lord—
65   I schall the[e] lede—and schow all-soo
Unto Goddys hest, Abraham, acord,   *bidding/comply*
And folow me upon thys gren.   *grass*
ABRAHAM. Wollecom to me be my Lordys sond,   *is my Lord's messenger*
And hys hest I wyll not wythstond;   *bidding/stand/against*
70   Yyt Ysaac, my yowng sonne in lond,   *Yet/on earth*
A full dere chyld to me have byn.   *has*

I had lever, yf God had be plesyd   *would rather*
For to a forbore all the good that I have,   *to have forgone/goods*
Than Ysaac my son schuld a be desessyd,   *have been distressed*
75   So God in Hevyn my sowll mot save!   *may*

I lovyd never thyng soo mych in erde,   *never loved/on earth*
And now I must the chyld goo kyll.
Lord God, my conseons ys stron[g]ly steryd,   *conscience*
And yyt my dere Lord, I am sore aferd
80   To groche ony thyng ayens yowre wyll.   *complain at all against*

I love my chyld as my lyffe,
But yyt I love my God myche more,
For thow my hart woold make ony stryffe,   *though/might*
Yyt wyll I not spare for chyld nor wyffe,
85   But don after my Lordys lore.   *Lord's command*

Thow I love my sonne never so wyll,   *though/ever*
Yyt smyth of[f] hys hed sone I schall.   *smite*
Fader of Hevyn, to the[e] I knell,   *kneel*
An hard deth my son schall fell   *feel*
90   For to honore the[e], Lord, wythall.

ANGEL. Abraham, Abraham, thys ys wyll seyd,
And all thys comamentys loke that thou save;   *keep*
But in thy hart be nothyng dysmayd;
ABRAHAM. Nay, nay, forsoth, I hold me wyll payd,   *blessed*
95   To plesse my God wyth the best that I have;

For thow my hart be hevely sett   *though*
   To see the blood of my owyn dere son,
Yyt for all thys I wyll not lett,   *be hindered*
But Ysaac, my son, I wyll goo fett,   *fetch*
100   And cum asse fast as ever we con.   *can*

Now, Ysaac, my owyn son dere,
   Wer art thow, chyld? Speke to me.
ISAAC. My fayer swet fader, I am here,
   And make my preyrys to the Trenyté.

105   ABRAHAM. Rysse up, my chyld, and fast cum heder,
   My gentyll barn that art so wysse,   *child*
For we t[w]o, chyld, must goo to-geder,
   And onto my Lord make sacryffyce.

ISAAC. I am full redy, my fader, loo!
110   Yevyn at yowr handys I stand rygth here,   *Even*
And watsoever ye byd me doo,
   Yt schall be don with glad chere,
    Full wyll and fyne.
ABRAHAM. A! Ysaac, my owyn son soo dere,
115   Godys blyssyng I gyffe the[e], and myn.

Hold thys fagot upon thi bake,   *stick/back*
   And her[e] myselffe fyere schall bryng.
ISAAC. Fader, all thys her[e] wyll I packe;
   I am full fayn to do yowre bedyng.   *bidding*
120   ABRAHAM. A! Lord of Hevyn, my handys I wryng,
   Thys chyldys wordys all towond my harte.   *greatly wound*

Now, Ysaac, son, goo we owr wey
   Onto yon mownte, wyth all owr mayn.   *might*
ISAAC. Go we, my dere fader, as fast as I may
125   To folow yow I am full fayn,   *glad*
    Allthow I be slendyr.
ABRAHAM. A! Lord, my hart brekyth on tweyn,
   Thys chyldys wordys, they be so tender.

Ysaac, son, anon ley yt down,   *now lay*
130   No lenger upon thi backe yt hold;
For I must make me redy bon   *quickly*
   To honowre my Lord God as I schuld.

ISAAC. Loo, my dere fader, wer yt ys!   *there*
   To cher yow allwey I draw me nere;   *cheer*

135 But, fader, I mervell sore of thys,   *wonder greatly at*
    Wy that ye make thys hevy chere;   *sad face*

And also, fader, evermore dred I:
    Wer ys yowr qweke best that ye schuld kyll?   *Where/live beast*
Both fyer and wood we have redy,
140 But queke best have we non on this hyll.

A qwyke best, I wot wyll, must be ded,   *know/killed*
    Yowr sacryfyce for to make.
ABRAHAM. Dred the[e] nowgth, my chyld, I the[e] red,   *Fear not/advise*
Owre Lord wyll send me onto thys sted   *into this place*
145 Summ maner a best for to take,   *kind of beast*
    Throw his swet sond.   *messenger*
ISAAC.   Ya, fader, but my hart begynnyth to quake,
    To [see] that scharpe sword in yowre hond.

Wy bere ye yowre sword drawyn soo?
150 Off yowre contenaunce I have mych wonder.   *expression*
ABRAHAM. A! Fader of Hevyn, so I am woo!
Thys chyld her[e] brekyth my harte onsonder.

ISAAC. Tell me, my dere fader, or that ye ses,   *before you stop*
    Bere ye yowr sword draw[n] for me?
155 ABRAHAM. A! Ysaac, swet son, pes! pes!   *quiet*
    For iwys thow breke my harte on thre.   *truly/in three*

ISAAC. Now trewly, sumwat, fader, ye thynke
    That ye morne thus more and more.
ABRAHAM. A! Lord of Hevyn, thy grace let synke,   *let thy grace descend*
160 For my hart wos never halffe so sore.

ISAAC. I preye yow, fader, that ye wyll let me yt wyt,   *know*
    Wyther schall I have ony harme or noo?
ABRAHAM. Iwys, swet son, I may not tell the[e] yyt,   *Truly/yet*
    My hart ys now soo full of woo.   *woe*

165 ISAAC. Dere fader, I prey yow, hydygth not fro me,   *hide it*
    But sum of yowr thowt that ye tell on.   *thought*
ABRAHAM. A! Ysaac, Ysaac! I must kyll the[e].
ISAAC.   Kyll me, fader? alasse! wat have I don?

Yff I have trespassyd ayens yow owt,   *at all*
170 With a yard ye may make me full myld;   *rod*
And wyth yowre scharp sword kyll me nogth.
For iwys, fader, I am but a chyld.   *truly*

ABRAHAM. I am full sory, son, thy blood for to spyll,

    But truly, my chyld, I may not chese. *choose*

175 ISAAC. Now I wold to God [my] moder were her[e] on this hyll!

    Sche woold knele for me on both hyre kneys

      To save my lyffe.

    And sythyn that my moder ys not here,

    I prey yow, fader, schonge yowr chere, *change your mood*

180   And kyll me not wyth yowyre knyffe.

ABRAHAM. Forsothe, son, but yyf I the[e] kyll, *unless*

    I schuld greve God rygth sore, I drede;

    Yt ys hys commawment and also hys wyll

    That I schuld do thys same dede.

185 He commawndyd me, son, for serteyn,

    To make my sacryfyce wyth thy blood.

ISAAC. And ys yt Goddys wyll that I schuld be slayn?

ABRAHAM. Ya, truly, Ysaac, my son soo good,

    And therfor my handys I wryng.

190 ISAAC. Now, fader, ayens my Lordys wyll *against*

    I wyll never groche, lowd nor styll; *complain/loudly or quietly*

    He mygth a sent me a better desteny *might have*

    Yf yt had a be hys plecer. *had been his pleasure*

ABRAHAM. Forsothe, son, but yf I ded this dede, *unless/do*

195   Grevosly dysplessyd owre Lord wyll be.

ISAAC. Nay, nay, fader. God forbede

    That ever ye schuld greve hym for me.

Ye have other chyldryn, on[e] or too,

    The wyche ye schuld love wyll be kynd; *well, by nature*

200 I prey yow, fader, make ye no woo, *woe*

    For, be I onys ded and fro yow goo, *once I am dead/gone*

    I schall be sone owt of yowre mynd.

Therfor doo owre Lordys byddyng,

    And wan I am ded, than prey for me;

205 But, good fader, tell ye my moder nothyng,

    Sey that I am in another cuntré dwellyng.

ABRAHAM. A Ysaac, Ysaac, blyssyd mot thow be!

My hart begynnyth stronly to rysse, *strongly/beat*

    To see the blood off thy blyssyd body. *To think of*

210 ISAAC. Fadyr, syn yt may be noo other wysse, *other way*

    Let yt passe over as wyll as I.

But, fader, or I goo onto my deth,   *before*
  I prey yow blysse me wyth yowre hand.
ABRAHAM. Now, Ysaac, wyth all my breth,
215   My blyssyng I yeve the[e] upon thys lond,   *give*
    And Godys also therto, iwys.   *truly*
  A, Ysaac, Ysaac, son, up thow stond,
    Thy fayere swete mowthe that I may kys.

ISAAC. Now, forwyll, my owyn fader so fyn,   *farewell/noble*
220 And grete wyll my moder in erde.   *greet/earthly mother*
But I prey yow, fader, to hyd my eyne,   *eyes*
  That I se not the stroke of yowr scharpe swerd,
    That my fleysse schall defyle.
ABRAHAM.   Son, thy wordys make me to wepe full sore;
225 Now, my dere son Ysaac, speke no more.
 ISAAC.   A, my owyn dere fader, werefore?   *why not?*
  We schall speke togedyr her[e] but a wylle.   *little while*

And sythyn that I must nedysse be ded,   *since/must needs be*
  Yyt, my dere fader, to yow I prey,   *yet*
230 Smyth but fewe strokys at my hed,   *Smite*
  And make an end as sone as ye may,
    And tery not to longe.   *delay*
ABRAHAM.   Thy meke wordys, chyld, make me afray;
  So welawey may be my songe,   *"alas"*

235 Excepe alonly Godys wyll.   *Were it not*
  A! Ysaac, my owyn swete chyld,
  Yyt kysse me ayen upon thys hyll!   *Yet/again*
  In all thys ward ys [non] soo myld.   *world/no one*

ISAAC. Now, truly, fader, all thys teryyng   *delay*
240 Yt doth my hart but harme;   *only*
I prey yow, fader, make an enddyng.
ABRAHAM.   Cume up, swet son, onto my arme.

I must bynd thy handys too
  Allthow thow be never soo myld.
245 ISAAC. A mercy, fader! Wy schuld ye do soo?   *Have mercy*
ABRAHAM.   That thow schuldyst not let [me], my chyld.   *hinder*

ISAAC. Nay, iwysse, fader, I wyll not let yow;
  Do on for me yowre wyll,   *Have your way*
And on the purpos that ye have set yow,
250 For Godys love kepe yt forthe styll.   *always foremost*

I am full sory thys day to dey,   *die*
  But yyt I kepe not my God to greve;   *must*
Do on yowre lyst for me hardly,   *will*
  My fayer swete fader, I yeffe yow leve.   *give*

255 But, fader, I prey yow evermore,
  Tell ye my moder no dell;   *nothing*
Yffe sche wost yt, sche wold wepe full sore,   *knew*
  For iwysse, fader, sche lovyt me full wyll;   *truly/loved*
  Goddys blyssyng have mot sche!   *may*
260 Now forwyll, my moder so swete,   *farewell*
  We t[w]oo be leke no mor to mete.   *unlikely*
ABRAHAM. A, Ysaac Ysaac! Son, thou makyst me to gret,   *weep*
  And wyth thy wordys thow dystempurst me.   *upset*

ISAAC. Iwysse, swete fader, I am sory to greve yow,   *Truly*
265 I cry yow mercy of that I have donne,   *forgive*
And of all trespasse that ever I ded meve yow;
  Now, dere fader, foryyffe me that I have donne.
  God of Hevyn be wyth me!
ABRAHAM. A, dere chyld, lefe of thy monys;   *stop your moans*
270 In all thy lyffe thow grevyd me never onys,   *offended/once*
Now blyssyd be thow, body and bonys,
  That thow were bred and born to me!

Thow hast be to me chyld full good;   *have been*
  But iwysse, chyld, thow I morne never so fast,   *truly/though/ever/strongly*
275 Yyt must I nedys here at the last
In thys place sched all thy blood.

Therfor, my dere son, here schall thou lye,
  Onto my warke I must me stede,   *set myself*
Iwysse I had as leve myselffe to dey,   *Truly/rather*
280 Yffe God wyll be plecyd wyth my dede,   *would be pleased*
  And myn owyn body for to offere.
ISAAC. A, mercy, fader, morne ye no more,
  Yowr wepyng make my hart sore
  As my owyn deth that I schall suffere.

285 Yowre kerche, fader, abowt my eyn ye wynd!   *kerchief/eyes*
ABRAHAM. So I schall, my swettest chyld in erde.   *on earth*
ISAAC. Now yyt, good fader, have thys in mynd,   *yet*
  And smyth me not oftyn wyth yowr scharp swerd,   *smite*
  But hastely that yt be sped.

Here Abraham leyd a cloth over Ysaacys face, thus seyyng:

290 ABRAHAM.   Now, forewyll, my chyld, so full of grace.   *farewell*
    ISAAC.   A, fader, fader, torne downgward my face,   *turn downward*
       For of yowre scharpe sword I am ever adred.

    ABRAHAM.   To don thys dede I am full sory,
       But, Lord, thyn hest I wyll not wythstond.   *command*
295 ISAAC.   A, Fader of Hevyn, to the[e] I crye,
       Lord, reseyve me into thy hand!

    ABRAHAM.   Loo, now ys the tyme cum, ceretyn,
       That my sword in hys necke schall bite.
       A! Lord, my hart reysyth therageyn,   *throbs*
300   I may not fyndygth in my harte to smygth;   *smite*
          My hart wyll not now thertoo,   *will not assent*
       Yyt fayn I woold warke my Lordys wyll;
       But thys yowyng innosent lygth so styll,   *lies*
       I may not fyndygth in my hart hym to kyll.
305   Fader of Hevyn! what schall I doo?

    ISAAC.   A, mercy, fader, wy tery ye so,
       And let me ley thus longe on this heth?   *heath*
       Now I wold to God the stroke were doo.   *done*
       Fader, I prey yow hartely, schorte me of my woo,   *lessen my woe*
310   And let me not loke thus after my degth.   *anticipate my death*

    ABRAHAM.   Now, hart, wy wolddyst not thow breke on thre?
       Yyt schall thou [not] make me to my God onmyld.   *disobedient*
       I wyll no lenger let for the[e],   *be hindered*
       For that my God agrevyd wold be.
315   Now hoold the stroke, my owyn dere chyld.

    Her[e] Abraham drew hys stroke and the angell toke the sword in hys
    hond soddenly.

    ANGEL.   I am an angell, thow mayist be blythe,   *happy*
       That fro heuyn to the[e] ys senth;
       Owre Lord thanke the[e] an hundyrd sythe   *times*
       For the kepyng of hys commawment.

320 He knowyt[h] thi wyll and also thy harte,
       That thow dredyst hym above all thyng,
       And sum of thy hevynes for to departe
       A fayyr ram yynder I gan brynge;   *yonder/did*

    He standyth teyed, loo! among the brerys.   *tethered/briars*
325 Now, Abraham, amend thy mood,

For Ysaac, thy yowng son that her[e] ys,
　Thys day schall not sched hys blood;

Goo, make thy sacryfece wyth yon rame,
　For onto heuyn I goo now hom.
330　Now forwyll, blyssyd Abraham,　　　　　　　　*farewell*
　　The wey ys full gayn [that I mot gon].　　　　*straight*
　　Take up thy son soo free.　　　　　　　　　*noble*
　ABRAHAM.　A! Lord, I thanke the[e] of thy gret grace,
　　Now am I yethed on dyvers wysse.　　　*comforted in many ways*
335　Arysse up, Ysaac, my dere sunne, arysse,
　　Arysse up, swete chyld, and cum to me.

　ISAAC.　A, mercy, fader, wy smygth ye nowt?　　　*smite*
　　A, smygth on, fader, onys wyth yowre knyffe!　　*once*
　ABRAHAM.　Pesse, my swet sun, and take no thowt,　*Peace/thought*
340　For owre Lord of Hevyn hath grant thi lyffe,　　*granted thy*
　　Be hys angell now,

　　That thou shalt not dey this [day], sunne, truly.　　*die*
　ISAAC.　A, fader, full glad than wer I,　　　*would I be*
　　Iwys, fader, I sey iwys,　　　　　　　　*Truly*
345　Yf thys tall wer trew!　　　　　　　　*If only this tale*
　ABRAHAM.　An hundryd tymys, my son fayer of hew,
　　For joy thi mowth now wyll I kys.

　ISAAC.　A, my dere fader, Abraham,
　　Wyll not God be wroth that we do thus?
350　ABRAHAM.　Noo, noo! Harly, my swyt son,　　　*Heartily*
　　For he hath sent us yyn same rame　　　　　*yon*
　　Hethyr down to us.

　　Yyn best schall dey here in thi sted,　　　*Yon beast/thy place*
　　In the worthchup of owr Lord alon;　　　　*worship*
355　Goo, fet hym hethyre, my chyld, inded.　　　*fetch*
　ISAAC.　Fader, I wyll goo hent hym be the hed,　*seize*
　　And bryng yon best wyth me anon.　　　　*beast*

　　A, scheppe, scheppe! blyssyd mot thou be　　*sheep*
　　That ever thow were sent down heder!
360　Thow schall thys day dey for me,　　　　*die*
　　In the worchup of the Holy Trynyté.
　　　Now cum fast and goo we togeder
　　　　To my fader in hy;　　　　　　　*haste*
　　　Thow thou be never so jentyll and good,

365   Yyt had I lever thow schedyst thi blood,   *rather*
        Iwysse, scheppe, than I.   *Truly*

        Loo, fader, I have browt here full smerte   *brought/right away*
           Thys jentyll scheppe, and hym to yow I gyffe: *give*
        But, Lord God, I thanke the[e] with all my hart,
370   For I am glad that [I] schall leve,   *live*
          And kys onys my dere moder.   *once again*
        ABRAHAM. Now be rygth myry, my swete chylld,
        For thys qwyke best that ys so myld,   *live beast*
          Here I schall present before all othere.

375   ISAAC. And I wyll fast begynne to blowe,
          Thys fyere schall brene a full good spyd.   *burn/speed*
        But fader, wyll I stowppe down lowe,   *while/stoop*
        Ye wyll not kyll me with yowre sword, I trowe?
        ABRAHAM.   Noo, harly, swet son, have no dred,   *heartily*
380   My mornyng ys past.   *mourning*
        ISAAC.   Ya! but I woold that sword were in a gled,   *sheath*
          For iwys, fader, yt make me full yll agast.   *truly/very fearful*

Here Abraham mad[e] hys offryng, knelyng and seyyng thus:

        ABRAHAM. Now, Lord God of Hevyn, in Trynyté,
          Allmyty God Omnipotent,
385   Myn offeryng I make in the worchope of the[e],   *worship*
          And wyth thys qweke best I the[e] present.   *live beast*
        Lord, reseyve thow myn intent,
        As [thow] art God and grownd of owr gre.   *grace*

        DEUS. Abraham, Abraham, wyll mot thow sped,   *well may*
390   And Ysaac, thi yowng son the[e] by!
        Truly Abraham, for thys dede
        I schall multyplye yowrys botherys sede   *your descendents'*
          As thyke as sterrys be in the skye,   *stars*
            Bothe more and lesse;   *big and small*
395   And as thyke as gravell in the see,
          So thyke multyplyed yowre sede schall be;
          Thys grant I yow for yowre goodnesse.

        Off yow schall cume frewte gret [won]   *of/great fruit*
          And ever be in blysse wythowt yynd,   *end*
400   For ye drede me as God alon   *Because you*
        And kepe my commawmentys everyschon.   *everyone*
          My blyssyng I yeffe wersoever ye wend.

ABRAHAM. Loo! Ysaac, my son, how thynke ye
  Be thys warke that we have wrogth?   *Of/done*
405 Full glad and blythe we may be,
  Ayens [the] wyll of God that we grucched nott,   *Against/complained*
    Upon thys fayere hetth.   *ground*
ISAAC. A, fader, I thanke owre Lord every dell,   *completely*
That my wyt servyd me so wyll,
410   For to drede God more than my detth.

ABRAHAM. Why! derewordy son, wer thow adred?   *precious*
  Hardely, chyld, tell me thy lore.   *Heartily/thought*
ISAAC. Ya! be my feyth, fader, now have I red,   *now I believe*
  I wos never soo afrayd before
415   As I have byn at yyn hyll.   *been/yon*
  But, be my feyth, fader, I swere   *by*
  I wyll nevermore cume there
    But yt be ayens my wyll.   *Unless/against*

ABRAHAM. Ya, cum on wyth me, my owyn swet son,   *Yea*
420 And homward fast now let us goon.   *go*
ISAAC. Be my feyth, fader, therto I un,   *own up*
  I had never so good wyll to gon hom,
    And to speke wyth my dere moder.
ABRAHAM. A! Lord of Hevyn, I thanke the[e],
425   For now may I led hom wyth me
    Ysaac, my yowynge son soo fre,   *noble*
    The gentyllest chyld above all other.

Now goo we forthe, my blyssyd son.
ISAAC. I grant, fader, and let us gon,   *go*
430 For be my trowthe, wer I at home
  I wold never gon owt under that forme,   *like that*
  Thys may I wyll avoee.   *avow*
  I pray God yeffe us grace evermo,   *give/evermore*
  And all thow that we be holdyng to.   *those/beholden to*

435 DOCTOR. Lo! sovereyns and sorys, now have we schewyd, *sirs/shown*
  Thys solom story to gret and smale;   *solemn*
  It ys good lernyng to lernd and lewyd,   *learned and ignorant*
    And the wysest of us all,
    Wythowtyn ony berryng.   *any dispute*
440 For thys story schoyt yowe [here]   *shows*
  How we schuld kepe to owr po[we]re   *as best we can*
    Goddys commaumentys wythowt grochyng. *complaining*

Trowe ye, sorys, and God sent an angell   *Do you think, sirs, if*
    And commaundyd yow yowre chyld to slayn,
445 Be yowre trowthe ys ther ony of yow   *By your truth*
    That eyther wold [groche] or stryve therageyn?   *complain or work against it*

How thynke ye now, sorys, therby?   *Sirs*
    I trow ther be thre ore a fowr or moo;   *I think/more*
And thys women that wepe so sorowfully
450 Whan that hyr chyldryn dey them froo,   *their/die and leave them*
        As nater woll, and kynd;   *as happens in nature, and family*
    Yt ys but folly, I may wyll awooe,   *avow*
    To groche ayens God or to greve yow,   *complain against/grieve*
    For ye schall never se hym myschevyd, wyll I know,   *harmed/well*
455   Be lond nor watyr, have thys in mynd.   *By*

And groche not ayens owre Lord God,   *complain/against*
    In welthe or woo, wether that he yow send,   *whichever*
Thow ye be never so hard bestad,   *beset*
    For whan he wyll, he may yt amend.   *wishes*
460 Hys comawmentys treuly yf ye kepe wyth goo[d] hart,
    As thys story hath now schowyd yow befor[n]e,
And feytheffully serve hym qwyll ye be quart,   *while/alive*
    That ye may plece God bothe evyn and morne.   *please*
    Now Jhesu, that weryt[h] the crown of thorne,
465 Bryng us all hevyn-blysse!

    Finis

The Norwich Grocers' Play

No manuscript of the Norwich Grocers' Play has survived, but two versions of the text have been preserved in an eighteenth-century transcript of the Norwich Grocers' Book, a collection of important documents and accounts belonging to the Grocers' guild during the sixteenth century. The Grocers' Play dramatizes the creation of Eve, the Temptation in the Garden, and the Fall. Two alternative prologues allow the play to be mounted as part of a sequence of Biblical plays in Norwich or to stand alone. Version A dates from sometime before 1533, when it was copied into the Grocers' Book. It lacks some speeches in the middle of the play, from God's discovery of Adam's disobedience to the actual expulsion from the Garden of Eden. Version B is complete and dates from 1565—so that, strictly speaking, it is an Elizabethan play. This version shows its roots firmly embedded in reformation ideology. Taken together, the two versions of the Grocers' play reveal perhaps more clearly than any of the other plays included in this collection how the deep shifts in religious and social sensibilities during the sixteenth century are inscribed in the English theatrical tradition.

Norwich vied with York during the late middle ages as the second most powerful city in England. From the late fourteenth through the sixteenth centuries the wool trade brought tremendous prosperity to East Anglia, and Norwich, its chief city, flourished on a large scale. Its prosperity is reflected in the wide range of musical and theatrical entertainments sponsored by the town. One testimony of this range of festivities can be found in the Norwich Assembly Proceedings from 1527, which lists activities traditionally organized by St. Luke's Guild (a spiritual guild rather than a craft guild) starting on the Monday after Pentecost:

> . . . at which daye and the daye next folowyng many and diuers disgisinges and pageauntes as well of the liff and marterdams of diuers and many hooly sayntes as also many other lyght and feyned figures and pictures of other persones and bestes, the sight of which disgisinges and pageauntes, as than goyng aboute a

151

greate circuitt of the said Citie, as yerly the Tuysday in the same weke seruyng
of the lord named the Lord of Mysrule at Tomlond within the same Citie, have
ben and yet is so covetid specially by the people of the countré, by force wherof
yerly at that tyme more than any other tyme of the yere the people of the countré
haue abundauntly vsed to resorte to the said Citie, by reason of which resorte of
people as well many merchaundises as vitaille by the citezens and inhabitauntes
withyn the said Citie yerly more at that tyme than eny othe[r] tyme in the yere
arn vttered and sold, to the grette releeff, socour, aide, and comfforte of the
citezens and inhabitauns. . .

(Quoted in Davis, *Non-Cycle Plays*, p. xxvii)

Processions with images and beasts, costumed "diguisings," Saints plays, the
Lord of Misrule and other entertainments, all brought business in from the
countryside at Whitsuntide. But sponsoring such festivities year after year
was proving burdensome to St. Luke's Guild, and it proposed, in the latter
part of the 1527 entry quoted above, that the city and its craft guilds take
charge of the procession and pageants. The city agreed, and Norwich
Grocers' Play seems to have been composed as a direct result of this civic
ordinance. According to a list drawn up not long after this arrangement was
reached, the Grocers' Guild and others collaborated to sponsor pageants on
eight Old Testament and four New Testament subjects. (See Davis, *Non-Cycle
Plays*, pp. xxix-xxx) The Grocers' guild was in charge of the third pageant,
"Paradyse." Other pageants ranged in subject matter from the Creation of the
World to "Helle Carte" and "The Holy Gost." Whether these pageants were
full-scale plays put on at Whitsuntide or *tableau vivants* in procession on
Corpus Christi Day is not always clear from the accounts, nor can it be said
with any certainty whether the plays were performed singly, all together,
sequentially, or in smaller groups.

There is no doubt, however, that the Grocers' play was performed, for a cast
list survives in the Grocers' Book (with one "Frances Fygot" playing Eve)
along with inventories of props extending over several years. The most
famous prop is the "Rybbe Colleryd Redd," used for staging Eve's creation
from the side of Adam. Other entries in the Grocers' Book record wigs and
gloves, a mask for God the Father, and various pieces of costumes for other
characters. The last entry in the book concerns the sad fate of the pageant
wagon, a two-level "Howsse of Waynskott" with a "nether parte" built on a
cart or wagon. By 1570 it was so badly deteriorated from having been left
outdoors that it was scrapped.

Version A of the Grocers' Play, a relatively straightforward account of the
story told in Genesis, balances dialogue and action with the help of an organ,
which offers musical counterpoint to the story and finally accompanies the
song of "dolorous sorowe" with which the play ends. The predominant
metrical form is rhyme royal, *ababbcc*. The B version of the play seems a much
more elaborate creation, both in terms of theatre and theology. Certainly the

two alternative prologues found at the beginning of B indicate that it was written as a flexible piece able to stand on its own or to fit into a larger sequence of pageants. New to the B version are the characters of Prolocutor, who introduces and interprets the play for the audience, those of the morality figures Dolor and Misery, who pinion Adam until he despairs, and the Holy Ghost, who toward the end of the play offers to guide Man and Woman with Pauline righteousness. The play has been revised "accordynge unto the Skripture," and it might be noted that the Holy Ghost is an especially appropriate character to appear during Whitsuntide, a time of year celebrating the coming of the Holy Ghost to the disciples. Adam closes the play with a speech that justifies the "forepredestination" brought about by means of Christ's sacrifice. Thus, instead of ending on a note of sorrow, version B concludes by rejoicing in the Fortunate Fall. The rhyme schemes of the play are mixed and sometimes highly complicated; while rhyme royal occurs, no stanzaic form predominates. Tripartite "Old Musick" helps bring this play to a close.

The two texts of the Norwich Grocers' Play have been preserved in an eighteenth-century transcription made by the antiquarian John Kirkpatrick (d. 1728), now at the Norfolk Record Office in Norwich (Case 21, shelf f [box 11, file 68], fols. 1-5v). The original "Grocers' Book" he was copying has not survived. Kirkpatrick's transcription of the play and of extracts from this book were first published by Robert Fitch in "Norwich Pageants. The Grocers' Play," *Norfolk Archaeology,* v (1859), 8-31. The standard scholarly edition of the play, by Norman Davis, appears in the EETS *Non-Cycle Plays and Fragments.* A modern edition of civic and ecclesiatical records pertinent to the performance of the Grocers' play and to other entertainments in Norwich after 1540 can be found in David Galloway's *REED: Norwich 1540-1642.* Earlier extracts from the Norwich Corporation Records appear in Henry Harrod, "A Few Particulars Concerning Early Norwich Pageants," *Norfolk Archaeology,* iii (1852), 3-18, and in the introduction to the EETS edition of the play (see Suggestions for Further Reading).

THE NORWICH GROCERS' PLAY – A

DEUS (& AN ANGEL)   ADAM
EVE   LUCIFER]

THE STORY OF THE CREACION OF EVE, WITH THE EXPELLYNG OF ADAM AND EVE OUT OF PARADYCE.

DEUS. *Ego principium Alpha et Omega in altissimis habito:*[*]
   In the hevenly empery I am resydent.   *empire*
   Yt ys not semely for man, *sine adjutorio,*   *without a helpmeet*
   To be allone, nor very convenyent.
5   I have plantyd an orcheyard most congruent   *nearby*
   For hym to kepe and to tylle, by contemplacion: *out of consideration*
   Let us make an adjutory of our formacion   *helper/creation*

   To hys symylutude, lyke in plasmacion.   *likeness/formation*
   Into Paradyce I wyll nowe descende
10 With my mynysters angelicall of our creacion
   To assyst us in owr worke that we intende,
   A slepe into man be soporacion to sende.   *sleep inducement*
   A rybbe out of mannys syde I do here take;
   Bothe flesche and bone I do thys creatur blysse;
15 And a woman I fourme, to be his make,   *mate*
   Semblable to man; beholde, here she ys.   *similar*

ADAM. O my Lorde God, incomprehensyble, withowt mysse, *certainly*
   Ys thy hyghe excellent magnyficens.
   Thys creature to me ys *nunc ex ossibus meis,* *now bone of my bone*
20 And *virago* I call hyr in thy presens,   *"made from man"*
   Lyke onto me in natural preemynens.
   Laude, honor, and glory to the[e] I make.   *Praise*
   Both father and mother man shall for hyr forsake.

---

1. I am the beginning and the end, living on high. [See Revelations 1:8]

DEUS. Than my garden of plesure kepe thou suer.   *take care of /unfailingly*
25   Of all frutes and trees shall thou ete and fede,
    Except thys thre of connyng, whyle ye bothe indure;   *tree of knowledge/live*
    Ye shall not touche yt, for that I forbede.
    ADAM. Thy precept, Lorde, in will, worde, and dede
    Shall I observe, and thy request fulfyll
30   As thou hast commandyd, yt ys reason and skyll.
    DEUS. Thys tre ys callyd of connyng good and yll;   *knowledge of/evil*
    That day that ye ete therof shall ye dye,
    Morte moriemini, yf that I do you aspye.   *By death will you be struck*

    Showe thys to thy spowse nowe bye and bye.
35   I shall me absent for a tyme and space;
    A warned man may live: who can yt denye?
    I make the[e] lord therof; kepe wyll my place;   *well*
    If thou do thys, thou shall have my grace;
    Into mortalité shall thou elles falle.
40   Looke thow be obedyent whan I the[e] calle.

    ADAM. Omnipotent God and hygh Lord of all,
    I am thy servante, bownde onder thyn obedyens,
    And thou my creatour, one God eternall;
    What thou commandest, I shall do my dylygens.
45   DEUS. Here I leve the[e], to have experyens,
    To use thys place in vertuse occupacion,   *virtuous*
    For nowe I wyll retorne to myn habitacion.

    ADAM. O lovely spowse of Godes creacion,
    I leve the[e] here alone, I shall not tary longe,
50   For I wyll walk a whyle for my recreacion
    And se over Paradyce, that ys so stronge.   *vigorous*
    Nothyng may hurt us nor do us wronge;
    God ys owr protectour and soverayn guyde;
    In thys place non yll thyng may abyde.

55 LUCIFER. O gemme of felicyté and femynyne love,
    Why hathe God under precept prohybyte thys frute,   *prohibited*
    That ye shuld not ete therof to your behofe?   *benefit*
    Thys tre ys plesant withowten refute.   *undeniably*

    EVE. *Ne forte,* we shuld dye, and than be mortall;   *Not true*
60   We may not towche yt, by Godes commandement.
    LUCIFER. *Nequaquam,* ye shall not dye perpetuall,   *Never*
    But ye shuld be as godes resydent,
    Knowyng good and yll spyrytuall;
    Nothyng can dere you that ys carnall.   *harm you*

65   EVE. For us than nowe what hold you best,   *Then/do you recommend*
       That we do not owr God offende?
       LUCIFER. Eate of thys apple at my requeste.
       To the[e] Almyghty God dyd me send.
       EVE. Nowe wyll I take therof; and I entend
70   To please my spowse, therof to fede,
       To knowe good and ylle for owr mede.   *reward*

       ADAM. I have walkyd abought for my solace;
       My spowse, how do you? tell me.
       EVE. An angell cam from Godes grace
75   And gaffe me an apple of thys tre.   *gave*
       Part therof I geffe to the[e];   *give*
       Eate therof for thy pleasure,
       For thys frute ys Godes own treasure.

       DEUS. Adam, Adam, wher art thou thys tyde?   *at this hour*
80   Byfore my presens why dost thou not apere?

     [Apparently there was a gap in the play manuscript at this point.]

               Musick.

     Aftyr that Adam and Eve be drevyn owt of Paradyse they schall speke thys foloyng:

       ADAM. O with dolorows sorowe we maye wayle and weepe!
       Alas, alas, whye ware we soo bolde?
       By owr fowle presumpsyon we are cast full deepe,
       Fro pleasur to payn, with carys manyefold.   *From/numerous cares*
85   EVE. With wonderous woo, alas! it cane not be told;   *woe*
       Fro Paradyce to ponyschment and bondage full strong.   *From*
       O wretches that we are, so euer we shall be inrollyd;   *recorded*
       Therof owr handes we may wryng with most dullfull song.   *doleful*

     And so thei shall syng, walkyng together about the place, wryngyng ther handes.

       Wythe dolorous sorowe, we maye wayle and wepe
90   Both nyght and daye in sory sythys full depe.   *sorry sight*

N.B.—These last 2 lines set to musick twice over and again, for a chorus of 4 pts. *

---

90 s.d. Fitch includes this note on the music, which is presumably Kirkpatrick's. See Introduction.

THE NORWICH GROCERS' PLAY – B

[*DRAMATIS PERSONAE:*

PROLOCUTOR	LUCIFER
DEUS	DOLOR
ADAM	MYSERYE
EVE	HOLY-GHOST]

THE STORYE OF THE TEMPTACION OF MAN IN PARADYCE, BEING THERIN PLACYD, AND THE EXPELLYNGE OF MAN AND WOMAN FROM THENCE, NEWELY RENUID AND ACCORDYNGE UNTO THE SKRIPTURE, BEGON THYS YERE ANNO 1565, ANNO 7. ELIZ.

[First Alternative Prologue]

ITEM. Yt ys to be notyd that when the Grocers Pageant is played withowte eny other goenge befor yt then doth the Prolocutor say in this wise:

[PROLOCUTOR.] Lyke as yt chancyd befor this season,   *Just as has happened*
    Owte of Godes scripture revealid in playes
Was dyvers stories sett furth by reason
    Of pageantes apparellyd in Wittson dayes,*   *pageant wagons decorated*
5   And lately be fal[l]en into decayes;   *But/are fallen*
Which stories dependyd in theyr orders sett   *Such stories/in their progression*
    By severall devices, much knowledge to gett.

Begynny[n]g in Genesis,* that story repleate
    Of God his creacion of ech lyvynge thynge,
10 Of heaven and of erth, of fysh smalle and greate,

---

4. Wittson days: Whit-Sunday (Pentecost), the seventh Sunday after Easter, plus the following Monday and Tuesday. According to civic records, entertainments were often staged in Norwich during this time.
8. See Genesis 1-2.

Of fowles, herbe and tre, and of all bestes crepynge,   *going on the earth*
Of angelles, of man, which of erth hath beynge,   *who live on*
And of the fall of angelles, in the Apocalips to se;*
Which stories with the Skriptures most justly agree.   *[dramatized] stories*

15   Then followed this owr pageant, which sheweth to be   *puts forward*
     The Garden of Eden, which God dyd plante,
As in the seconde chapter of Genesis ye se;
     Wherin of frutes pleasant no kynde therof shulde wante;   *creatures*
In which God dyd putt man to cherish tre and plante,
20   To dresse and kepe the grounde, and eate what frute hym lyste,   *cultivate/desired*
Exept the tre of Knoweledge, Godes high wyll to resyste.

The story sheweth further that after man was blyste,   *blessed*
     The Lord did create woman owte of a ribbe of man;
Which woman was deceyvyd with the Serpentes darkned myste;   *dark confusions*
25   By whose synn owr nature is so weak no good we can;   *can [do]*
     Wherfor they were dejectyd, and caste from thence than
Unto dolloure and myseri and to traveyle and payne   *trouble*
Untyll Godes spright renvid; and so we ende certayne.   *spirit changed*

*Note that yf ther goeth eny other pageantes before yt, the Prolocutor
sayeth as ys on the other syde and leaveth owte this.*

[Second Alternative Prologue]

PROLOCUTOR. As in theyr former pageantes is semblably declared   *similarly*
     Of Godes mighty creacion in every lyvyng thynge,
As in the fyrst of Genesis* to such it is prepared   *first (chapter)*
     As lust they have to reade to memory to brynge   *they wanted*
5   Of pride and fawle of angells that in Hell hath beinge;   *been*
In the seconde of Genesis of mankynde hys creacion   *second (pageant)*
Unto this Garden Eden is made full preparacion.

And here begyneth owr pageant to make the declaracion,
     From the letter C. in the chapter before saide,
10   How God putt man in Paradyse to dresse yt in best fassion,   *tend*
     And that no frute therof from hym shuld be denayed,   *denied*
     Butt of the tre of lyffe that man shuld be afraide
To eate of, least that daye he eat that he shuld dye;   *lest*
And of womanes creacion appering by and bye;

---

13. See Revelations 12:7–9.
3. This reference, and the one in l. 6, are to the first two chapters in the Book of Genesis, which
concern the creation of the world and of Adam and Eve in the Garden of Eden. They may also refer to
the first and the second pageants. The third book, and the third pageant, concerns Man's disobedience.

15 And of the deavilles temptacion, diseaivinge with a lye
      The woman, beinge weakest, that cawsed man to tast.
      That God dyd so offende, that even contynentlye   *instantly*
      Owte of the place of joye was man and woman caste,
      And into so great dolloure and misery browght at last;
20 Butt that by God his spright was comforted ageyne.   *Except/(man's) spirit*
      This is of this owr pagent the some and effect playne.   *summary*

[THE CREATION OF EVE, THE TEMPTATION AND THE FALL]

DEUS. I am *Alpha et homega*, my *Apocalyps* doth testyfye,*
      That made all of nothinge for man his sustentacion;   *support*
      And of this pleasante garden that I have plant most goodlye   *planted*
      I wyll hym make the[e] dresser for his good recreacion.   *cultivator*
5   Therfor, Man, I gyve yt the[e], to have thy delectacion.   *delight*
      In eatyng thou shalt eate of every growenge tre,
      Exepte the tre of knowledge, the which I forbydd the[e];

      For in what daye soever thou eatest thou shallt be   *whatever day*
      Even as the childe of death; take hede: and thus I saye,
10 I wyll the[e] make an helper, to comforte the[e] allwaye.   *always*
      Beholde, therfore, a slepe I bryng this day on the[e],
      And oute of this thy ribbe, that here I do owte take,
      A creature for thy help behold I do the[e] make.
      Aryse, and from thy slepe I wyll the[e] nowe awake,
15 And take hyr unto the[e], that you both be as one
      To comfort one th'other when from you I am gone.   *each other*

      And, as I saide before when that thou wert alone,
      In eatyng thow mayst eate of every tre here is,
      Butt of the tre of knowledge of good and evyll eate non,   *nothing*
20 Lest that thou dye the[e] deth by doenge so amysse.
      I wyll departe now wher myne habytacion is.
      I leave you here. . . . .*
      Se that ye have my woordes in most high estymacion.

      Then Man and Woman speke bothe.

ADAM & EVE. We thanke the[e], mighty God, and gyve the[e] honoracion. *honor*

      Man spekethe.

---

1. I am the beginning and the end. [See Revelations 1:8]
22. Part of the stanza is apparently missing from the MS.

25 ADAM. Oh bone of my bones and flesh of my flesh eke,   *also*
    Thow shalte be called Woman, bycaus thow art of me.
Oh gyfte of God most goodlye, that hath us made so lyke,
    Most lovynge spowse, I muche do here rejoyce of the[e].
EVE. And I lykewyse, swete lover, do much rejoyce of the[e].
30 God therefore be praised, such comforte have us gyve   *he has given*
    That ech of us with other thus pleasantly do lyve.
ADAM. To walke abowt this garden my fantasye me meve;   *inclination/move*
    I wyll the[e] leave alone tyll that I turne ageyne;
Farewell, myn owne swete spouse, I leave the[e] to remayne.
35 EVE. And farewell, my dere lover, whom my hart doth conteyn.

    The Serpent speketh.

LUCIFER. Nowe, nowe, of my purpos I dowght nott to atteyne;   *doubt*
    I can yt nott abyde in theis joyes they shuld be.
Naye, I wyll attempt them to syn unto theyr payne;   *tempt*
    By subtyllty to catch them the waye I do well se;   *cunning*
40   Unto this, angell of lyght I shew mysylfe to be; *
With hyr for to dyscemble, I fear yt nott at all,
    Butt that unto my haight some waye I shall hyr call.   *power*
Oh lady of felicite, beholde my voyce so small!
    Why have God sayde to you, "Eate nott of every tre
45   That is within this garden?" Therin now answere me.

EVE. We eate of all the frutte that in the grounde we se,
    Exepte that in the myddest wherof we may nott taste,
For God hath yt forbydd, therfor yt may not be,
    Lest that we dye the deth and from this place be caste.
50 LUCIFER. Ye shall not dye the deth; he make you butt agaste;   *only afraid*
    Butt God doth know full well that when you eate of yt,
Your eys shall then be openyd and you shall at the last
    As godes both good and evyll to knowe ye shal be fytt.   *be able*
EVE. To be as God indede and in his place to sytt,
55   Thereto for to agre my lust conceyve somewhatt;   *agrees with my desires*
Besydes the tre is pleasante to gett wysedome and wytt,   *knowledge*
    And nothyng is to be comparyd unto that.
LUCIFER. Than take at my request, and eate, and fere yt natt.

    Here she takyth and eatyth, and Man cumyth in and sayeth unto hyr:

ADAM. My love, for my solace, I have here walkyd longe.   *comfort*
60   Howe ys yt nowe with you? I pray you do declare.
EVE. Indede, lovely lover, the Heavenly Kyng most stronge

---

40. Angel of light. [See Isaiah 14:12]

To eate of this apple his angell hath prepare;   *So that you might eat/prepared by*
Take therof at my hande th'other frutes emonge,
For yt shall make you wyse and even as God to fare.   *to be*

Then Man taketh and eatyth and sayethe:

65 [ADAM.] Alack! alacke! my spouse, now se I nakid we ar;
The presence of owr God we can yt nott abyde.
We have broke his precepte he gave us of to care;   *observe*
From God therfor in secrete in some place lett us hide.
EVE. With fygge-leavis lett us cover us, of God we be nott spyede.   *by/spied*
70 DEUS. Adam! I saye Adam! Wher art thou nowe this tyde,   *time*
That here before my presence thou dost nott nowe apere?
ADAM. I herde thy voyce, Oh Lorde, but yett I dyd me hide.
For that which I am naked I more greatly dyd feare.   *Because*

DEUS. Why art thou then nakyd? Who so hath cawsed the[e]?
75 ADAM. This woman, Lord and God, which thou hast gyven to me.
DEUS. Hast thou eat of the frute that I forbyd yt the[e]?
Thow woman, why hast thou done unto him thys trespace?   *offense*
EVE. The Serpente diseayvyd me with that his fayer face.
DEUS. Thow Serpente, why dydst thou this wise prevente my grace,   *in this way*
80 My creatures and servantes in this maner to begyle?   *trick*
LUCIFER. My kind is so, thou knowest and that in every case—   *My nature*
Clene out of this place theis persons to exile.   *Completely out*

DEUS. Cursed art for causynge my commandement to defyle,   *are you*
Above all cattell and beastes. Remayne thou in the fylde,   *More than/creatures*
85 Crepe on thy belly and eate duste for this thy subtyll wyle;   *wily craft*
The womans sede shall overcome the[e], thus that have I wylde.   *willed*
Thou, Woman, bryngyng chyldren with payne shall be dystylde,   *infused*
And be subject to thy husbonde, and thy lust shall pertayne
To hym: I hav determynyd this ever to remayne.   *always to be so*
90 And to the[e], Man, for that my voyce thou didst disdayne,   *because*
Cursed is the erth for ever for thy sake;
Thy lyvyng shall thou gett with swett unto thy payne,   *sweat*
Tyll thou departe unto the erth [wherof] I dyd the[e] make.   *back to*

Beholde, theis letherin aprons unto yourselves now take.
95 Lo! Man as one of us hath bene, good and evyll to knowe;
Therfor I wyll exempt hym from this place to aslake,   *exile/weaken*
Lest of the tre of lyfe he eate and ever growe.
Myne angell, now cum furth and kepe the waye and porte,   *guard/gate*
Unto the tre of lyffe that they do not resorte.

100 ANGEL. Departe from hence at onys from this place of comforte,
     No more to have axcesse or elles for to apere.   *access*
From this place I exile you, that you no more resorte,
     Nor even do presume ageyne for to com here.

     Then Man and Woman departyth to the nether parte of the pageant*
     and Man sayeth:

     [ADAM.] Alack! myn owne sweteharte, how am I stroke with feare,   *struck*
105   That from God am exiled, and browght to payne and woo.   *Who/woe*
Oh! what have we lost! Why dyd we no more care,
     And to what kynde of place shall we resorte and goo?
EVE.   Indede into the worlde now must we to and fro,
     And where and how to rest, I can nott say at all.
110 I am even as ye ar, what so ever me befall.

     Then cumeth Dolor and Myserye and taketh Man by both armys and
     Dolor sayeth:

     [DOLOR.] Cum furth, O Man, take hold of me!
     Through envy hast lost thy heavenly lyght
By eatinge; in bondage from hence shall be.
     Now must thou me, Dolor, have allways in sight.
115 MYSERYE.   And also of me, Myserye, thou must taste and byte,
Of hardenes and of colde and eke of infirmitie;   *also*
     Accordinge to desarte thy portion is, of right,   *by desert*
     To enjoy that in me that is withoute certentye.

ADAM. Thus troublyd, nowe I enter into dolor and miserie.
120   Nowe, Woman, must we lerne owr lyvynges to gett.   *how to make*
With labor and with travell; ther is no remedye,   *travail*
     Nor eny thyng therfrom we se that maye us lett.   *hinder*

     Then cumyth in the Holy Ghost comforting Man and sayeth:

HOLY-GHOST. Be of good cheare, Man, and sorowe no more.
     This Dolor and Miserie that thou hast taste,
125 Is nott in respect, layd up in store,   *Cannot compare to what is*
     To the joyes for the[e] that ever shall last.
     Thy God doth nott this the[e] away to cast,   *does not because of this*
     But to try the[e] as gold is tryed in the fyer;   *to test*
     In the end, premonyshed, shalt have thy desyre.   *forewarned, you*

---

103 s.d. "Pageant" here refers to a wagon with a two-level decorated stage built on it, briefly described in the *Grocers Book* as "a Howsse of Waynskott paynted & buylded on a Carte w[i]tt[h] fowre whelys." The Grocers' pageant wagon evidently depicted Paradise. See Davis, *Non-Cycle Plays*, xxix, xxxv, and Galloway, *REED: Norwich,* 52, 344.

130 Take owte of the Gospell that yt the[e] requyre,   *that which*
　　　Fayth in Chryst Jhesu, and grace shall ensewe.
　　　I wyl be thy guyde and pay the[e] thy hyer   *wages*
　　　For all thy good dylygence and doenge thy dewe.   *duty*
　　　Gyve eare unto me, Man, and than yt ys trewe,
135 Thou shalt kyll affectes that by lust in the[e] reygne   *passions*
　　　And putt Dolor and Mysery and Envy to payne.   *to defeat*

　　　Theis armors ar preparyd, yf thou wylt turn ageyne,
　　　　To fyght wyth; take to the[e], and reach Woman the same;   *hand to*
　　　The brest-plate of rightousnes Saynte Paule wyll the[e] retayne;*
140　The shylde of faythe to quench, thy fyrye dartes to tame;
　　　The hellmett of salvacion the devyles wrath shall lame;
　　　And the swrode of the Spright, which is the worde of God—   *(Holy) Spirit*
　　　All theis ar nowe the[e] offred to ease thy payne and rodd.   *punishment*

　　　ADAM.　Oh! prayse to The[e], Most Holye, that hast with me abode,   *who/stayed*
145　In mysery premonyshynge by this Thy Holy Spright.   *forewarning*
　　　Nowe fele I such great comforte, my syns they be unlode
　　　　And layde on Chrystes back, which is my joye and lyght.
　　　This Dolor and this Mysery I fele to me no wight;   *not a bit*
　　　No! Deth is overcum by forepredestinacion,   *predestination*
150 And we attayned wyth Chryst in heavenly consolacion.   *reconciled*
　　　Therfor, myne owne swett spous, withouten cavylacion,   *objection*
　　　　Together lett us synge, and lett our hartes reioyse,
　　　And gloryfye owr God wyth mynde, powre, and voyse.　　Amen.

　　　Old Musick Triplex, Tenor, Medius, Bass*

　　　With hart and voyce
155　Let us reioyce
　　　And prayse the Lord alwaye
　　　For this our joyfull daye,
　　　To se of this our God his maiestie,   *the majesty of our God*
　　　Who hath given himsellfe over us
160　To raygne and to governe us.
　　　Lett all our harte[s] reioyce together,
　　　And lett us all lifte up our voyce, on[e] of us with another.   *each with one another*

139-142. See Isaiah 59:17; Ephesians 6:10-17.
153 s.d. Fitch includes this note on the music, which is presumably Kirkpatrick's. See Introduction.

The Digby *Conversion of St. Paul*

The text of the Digby *Conversion of St. Paul* is preserved at Oxford on fols. 37^r-50^v of Bodleian MS. Digby 133, a manuscript book composed of miscellaneous and originally independent works now bound together, including three other plays found in this anthology: *Mary Magdalene, The Killing of the Children,* and a long fragment of *Wisdom.* The volume was part of the bequest of Sir Kenelm Digby's personal books to the Bodleian Library in 1634. Like the Macro manuscript—which contains *The Castle of Perseverance, Mankind,* and the full text of *Wisdom*—the Digby manuscript acts as one of the most important textual witnesses to the tradition of non-cycle plays in late medieval England. Like the Macro Plays too, the Digby Plays are all East Anglian in origin, as their various provenances and dialects attest. The copy of *The Conversion of St. Paul* in the Digby manuscript dates from the first quarter of the sixteenth century, although some additions to the play were made up to thirty or forty years later.

The earliest known owner of *The Conversion of St. Paul* was Myles Blomefylde (1525-1603), a licensed physician, a practitioner of white magic and alchemy, and an avid collector of books. His name, initials, or rebus appear not only on this play, but on the Digby *Mary Magdalene* and the *Wisdom* fragment—and, incidentally, on the only known copy of Henry Medwall's *Fulgens and Lucrece.* A native of Bury St. Edmunds in Suffolk, Blomefylde resided in Chelmsford, Essex, from the 1560s until his death in 1603. He acted as Churchwarden in Chelmsford for many years, and he may have acquired the Digby plays from the church there, which sold off its playbooks in time for Myles to buy them. It is also possible that he acquired the plays from William Blomfild, another alchemist and the author of *Blomfild's Blossoms* (the longest alchemical poem in English). William was probably a relative of Myles, and clearly older, since he had been a monk in the monastery at Bury St. Edmunds before its dissolution.

However *The Conversion of St. Paul* came into Blomefylde's hands, it already had a relatively long and elaborate stage history. The entire Belial and

Mercury episode, for example, and the directions for "Daunce" (at lines 14, 154, and 345) that punctuate the scene divisions before Poeta's moralizing, were added by a later hand, distinctly different from that of the main text, indicating that at some point in its performance history the play must have projected a more pious flavor. Still, the addition of ranting Devils and dancing simply carry further the play's embellishments of its Biblical sources. As theatre, *The Conversion of St. Paul* is unique in its explicit use of multiple "stations," or playing sites, complete with stages of some sort, between which the audience moved. Three times the spectators of this play are directed to follow in procession as the action travels from station to station (at lines 8-14, 155-61, 354-59).

Other notable theatrical effects include Paul actually riding his horse onstage, "abowt the place, owt of the pl[ace]," and the "fervent" (or flash of light) and "gret tempest" that afflict Paul on the road to Damascus. The Devils' scene itself offers the most obvious spectacle in the play, balancing the earlier enlightenment of Paul, featuring the "fyering" and the "cryeng and roryng" of Belial and Mercury. The devil's threats lead to Paul's sermon on the seven deadly sins (ll. 502-71), and then the end of the play comes rather abruptly, with a reference to Paul escaping from danger over the city walls in a basket ("or a lepe anon"). The conclusion is managed, like other significant moments in the play, by the figure Poeta, who acts as a kind of theological master of ceremonies, a mediating character both part of and apart from the action and the audience. His role brings dramatic and thematic significance to the spectacle in *The Conversion of St. Paul,* and it displays quite openly the theatrical, religious and political self-consciousness that informs the best of these late medieval non-cycle plays.

The stanzaic form of the Digby *Conversion of St. Paul,* including the interpolated Devil scene, is a very regular rhyme royal, *ababbcc,* usually with four stresses per line. The play was first edited by Thomas Sharp in *Ancient Mysteries from the Digby Manuscripts* (1835). The standard scholarly edition of the play, edited by Donald C. Baker, John L. Murphy, and Louis B. Hall, Jr., appears in the EETS *The Late Medieval Religious Plays of Bodleian MSS. Digby 133 and E Museo 160* (1982); a facsimile of the manuscript, edited by Donald C. Baker and John L. Murphy, appears in *The Digby Plays: Facsimiles of the Plays in Bodley MSS Digby 133 and e Museo 160* 1976). A discussion of the history of the text can be found in Donald C. Baker and John L. Murphy, "The Late Medieval Plays of MS Digby 133: Scribes, Dates and Early History," *RORD,* x (1967); the Digby Plays' connection with Chelmsford is explored by John C. Coldewey in "The Digby Plays and the Chelmsford Records," *RORD,* xviii (1975); some theatrical implications of the plays (including the *Conversion)*, as evidenced by their texts, appears in Donald C. Baker's "When is a Text a Play" in Briscoe and Coldewey, *Contexts for Early English Drama* (see Suggestions for Further Reading).

THE DIGBY *CONVERSION OF ST. PAUL*

[*DRAMATIS PERSONAE:*

POETA
DEUS
AN ANGEL
SAULUS, or Saul, later St. Paul
ANANIAS, a Disciple at Damascus
CAYPHA (Caiphas), a Chief Priest of the Temple in Jerusalem
ANNA, another Chief Priest
MILES 1 and MILES 2 (two soldiers with Saul
AN OFFICER of the Chief Priests
SERVUS (The Servant of Saul
STABULARIUS, a Stable-groom
BELIAL, a Devil
MERCURY, another Devil
THE HOLY GHOST]

POETA. *Rex glorie*, kyng omnipotent,   *King of glory*
 Redemer of the world by thy power divine,
And Maria, that pure vyrgy[n] quene most excellent,
 Wyche bare that blyssyd babe Jhesu that for us sufferd payne,
5 Unto whoys goodnes I do inclyne,   *whose*
Besechyng that Lord, of hys pytous influens,   *merciful*
To preserve and governe thys wyrshypfull audyens.

Honorable frendys, besechyng yow of lycens   *permission*
 To procede owur processe,* we may [show] under your correccyon,
10 The conversyon of Seynt Paule, as the Byble gyf experyens. *tells*
 Whoo lyst to rede the booke *Actum Appostolorum*,* *He who would*

---

9. To go forward with our performance (or procession).
10. See Acts of the Apostles, 9:1-25, which gives the Biblical version of this story.

Ther shall he have the very notycyon.   *actual text*
But, as we can, we shall us redres,   *as best we can/honor*
Brefly, wyth yowur favour, begynyng owur proces.

    [Jerusalem. First Station]   *Daunce*

Here entryth Saule, goodly besene in the best wyse,   *well-dressed*
lyke an aunterous knyth, thus sayyng: *bold knight*

15 SAUL. Most dowtyd man I am lyvyng upon the ground,   *Most feared man*
    Goodly besene, wyth many a ryche garlement!   *garment*
    My pere on lyve I trow ys nott found.   *peer alive/believe*
    Thorow the world, fro the oryent to the occydent,   *Throughout*
    My fame ys best knowyn undyr the fyrmament.   *I am most famous/heavens*
20 I am most drad of pepull unyuersall;   *dreaded/universally*
    They dare not dysp[l]ease me most noble.

    Saule ys my name—I wyll that ye notyfy—   *take notice, tell*
    Whych conspyreth the dyscyplys wyth thretys and menacys;   *who confounds*
    Before the pryncys of prestys most noble and hye,   *chief priests*
25 I bryng them to punnyshement for ther trespace.
    We wyll them nott suffer to rest in no place,
    For they go abouyte to preche and gyff exemplis
    To destroye oure lawes, sinagoges, and templis.

    By the god Bellyall, I schall make progresse   *travel*
30 Unto the pryncys, both Caypha and Anna,
    Where I schall aske of them in suernes   *authorization*
    To persue thorow all Dammask and Liba.   *search/Damascus and Libya*
    And thus we schall soone after than
    Bryng them that so do lyff into Jerusalem,   *that live so*
35 Both man and child that I fynd of them.

Her[e] cummyth Sa[u]le to Caypha and Anna, prestys of the tempyll.

SAUL. Nobyll prelatys and pryncys of regalyte,   *of royal authority*
    Desyryng and askyng, of your benyngne wurthynes,   *benign*
    Your letters and epystolys of most soverente,   *the highest supremacy*
    To subdue rebellyous that wyll of frawardnes   *who act with obstinance*
40 Agaynst our lawes rebell or transgresse,
    Nor wyll not inclyne, but mak objecc[y]on: *submit/resistance*
    To pursue all such, I wyll do proteccyon.   *ask for protection*

CAYPHA. To your desyer we gyf perfyth sentens,   *request/complete accord*
    Accordyng to your petycyons that ye make postulacyon,   *where you make request*
45 Bycause we know your trewe delygens

To persue all tho that do reprobacyon — *those/trespass*
Agayns owur lawes by ony redarguacyon. — *opposition*
Wherefor, shortly we gyf in commandment
To put down them that be dy[s]obedyent.

50 ANNA. And by thes letturs that be most reverrent— — *revered*
   Take them in hand, full agre therto— — *fully agreed to*
Constreyne all rebellys by owur [w]hole assent; — *complete*
   We gyf yow full power so to doo.
   Spare not hardly for frend nor foo! — *show no mercy to*
55 All thos ye fynd of that lyfe in thys realme,
Bounde, loke ye bryng them into Jerusalem — *Be bound*

Her[e] Saule resayvyth ther letters.

SAUL. Thys precept here I take in hande, — *This order*
   To fullfyll after yowur wyllys both, — *according to*
Wher I shall spare wythin this londe — *Thus*
60   Nother man nor woman—to this I make an oth— — *oath*
   But to subdue, I wyll not be loth. — *loath*
Now folow me, knytys and servauntys trewe,
Into Damaske, as fast as ye can sewe. — *Damascus/follow*

MILES 1. Unto your commaundment I do obeysaunce.
65   I wyll not gaynsay nor make delacyon, — *contradict nor delay*
But wyth good mynd and harty plesaunce — *enthusiasm*
   I shall yow succede, and make perambulacyon — *follow/the journey*
   Thorowoute Damaske wyth all delectacyon, — *with pleasure*
And all thoo rebell and make resystens, — *those who*
70 For to oppres I wyll do my delygens. — *To oppress them/best*

MILES 2. And in me shalbe no neclygens,
   But to thys precept myself I shall applye
To do your behest wyth all convenyens, — *command/speed*
   Wythowt eny frowardnes or eny obstynacy— — *bad will*
75 Non shall appere in me—but, verely,
Wyth all my mynd I yow insure, — *assure*
To resyst tho rebellys I wyll do my cure. — *those/duty*

SAUL. Truly, to me yt ys grett consolacyon
   To here thys report that ye do avauns. — *hear/put forward*
80 For your sapyencyall wyttys I gyf commendacyon; — *wise*
   Ever at my nede I have founde yow constant.
   But, knytys and seruuantys that be so plesaunt,
I pray yow anon my palfray ye bryng, — *horse*
To spede my jurney wythowt lettyng. — *hindrance*

Here goyth Sa[u]le forth a lytyll asyde for to make hym redy to ryde,
the servua[n]t thus seyng:

85 SERVUS. How, hosteler, how! A peck of otys and a botell of haye!   *oats/bundle*
Com off apase, or I wyll to another inne!   *Come quickly*
What, hosteler, why commyst not thy way?
Hye the[e] faster, I beshrew thi skynne!   *curse*
STABLE-GROOM. I am non hosteler, nor non hostelers kynne,   *kin*
90 But a jentylmanys servuant, i[f] Thou dost know!
Such crabyysh wordys do aske a blow.

SERVUS. I cry yow mercy, syr! I wyst well sumwhat ye were,   *really thought*
Owther a gentylman or a knave, me thynkyth by your physnomy!   *Either/face*
Yf on[e] loke yow in the face that never se yow ere,   *saw you before*
95 Wold thynk ye were at the next dore by.   *(One) would/next door (stall)*
In good fayth, I wenyd yow had bene an hosteler, verely!   *thought*
I sye suche another jentylman wyth yow a barowfull bare   *pushing a barrow full*
Of horsdowng and doggys tordys, and sych other gere.

And how yt happenyd a mervelous chance betyde: *event happened*
100 Your felow was not suer of foote, and yet he went very brode,   *wide*
Butt in a cow tord both dyd ye slyde!
And, as I wene, your nose therin rode;   *think*
Your face was bepayntyd wyth sowters code!   *cobbler's wax*
I sey never sych a sygt, I make God a vow!   *never saw such*
105 Ye were so begrymlyd and yt had bene a sowe.   *as filthy as a sow*

STABLE-GROOM. In fayth, thou never syest me tyll this day.   *saw*
I have dwellyd wyth my master thys seven yere and more.
Full well I have pleasyd hym, he wyll not say nay,
And mykyll he makyth of me therfore.   *makes much of me*
110 SERVUS. By my trowth, than be ye changyd to a new lore?   *new discipline*
A servand ye are, and that a good.
Ther ys no better lokyth owt of a hood.

STABLE-GROOM. Forsoth, and a hood I use for to were,   *always*
Full well yt ys lynyd wyth sylk and chamlett;   *camlet (expensive cloth)*
115 Yt kepyth me fro the cold, that the wynd doth me not dere,   *bother*
Nowther frost nor snow that I therby do sett.   *do I thus care about*
SERVUS. Yea, yt ys a dobyll hood, and that a fett.   *fit (fine one)*
He was a good man that made yt, I warant yow;
He was nother horse ne mare nor yet yokyd sow!   *yoked (tethered)*

Here commyth the fyrst knyth to the stabylgrom, saying: *stablegroom*

120 MILES 1. Now, stabyllgrom, shortly bryng forth away   *quickly*
       The best horse, for owur lorde wyll ryde.
       STABLE-GROOM. I am full redy. Here ys a palfray,   *horse*
       Ther can no man a better bestryde.
       He wyll conducte owur lorde and gyde   *guide (him)*
125 Thorow the world; he ys sure and abyll
       To bere a gentyllman, he [ys] esy and prophetabyll.   *easygoing and well-trained*

       Her[e] the knyth cummyth to Saule wyth a horse.

       MILES 1. Behold, Syr Saule, Your palfray ys comm,   *horse*
       Full goodly besene, as yt ys yowur desyer,
       To take yowur vyage thorow every regyon.   *voyage (quest)*
130 Be nott in dowt he wyll spede your mater,   *business*
       And we, as your servauntys, wyth glad chere
       Shall gyf attendance. We wyll nott gaynsay,   *oppose*
       But folow yow where ye go, be nygt or day.

       SAUL. Unto Damask I make my progressyon   *make my way*
135 To pursue all rebellyous beyng froward and obstynate   *rebellious (people)*
       Agayns our lawes be ony transgressyon.   *any*
       Wyth all my delygens myself I wyll prepar[at]e,   *prepare myself*
       Concernyng my purpose to oppres and seperate;   *To carry out my purpose/disunite*
       Non shall rejoyce that doth offend,
140 But utterly to reprove wyth mynde and intende.   *to be corrected/intent*

       Her[e] Sa[u]le rydyth forth wyth hys servantys abowt the place, owt of
       the pl[ace].

       CAYPHA. Now Saule hath takyn hys wurthy vyage   *voyage, mission*
       To pursue rebellyous, of what degre thei be,   *rebellious (people)*
       He wyll non suffer to raygne nor have passage
       Wythin all thys regyon, we be in sertayn[te].   *we may be sure*
145 Wherefor I commende hys goodly dygnyte,   *Thus*
       That he thus alway takyth in hande,   *can always*
       By hys power to governe thus all thys lande.

       ANNA. We may lyve in rest by hys consolacyon.
       He defendyth us, wherefor we be bownde
150 To love hym intyrely wyth our harttys affeccyon,
       And honour hym as champyon in every stownde.   *every place*
       Ther ys non such lyvyng upon the grounde,   *on earth*
       That may be lyke to hym, nor be hys pere,   *peer*
       Be est nor west, ferre nor nere.   *far/near*

Poeta—si placet.   *if it pleases*
Daunce
Conclusyon

155   POETA. Fynally, of this stac[y]on thus we mak a conclusyon.   *this location*
    Besechyng thys audyens to folow and succede
  Wyth all your delygens this generall processyon;
    To understande this matter, w[h]o lyst to rede   *who would like*
    The Holy Bybyll for the better spede,   *aid*
160   Ther shall he have the perfyth intellygens,   *perfect*
  And thus we comyt yow to Crystys magnyfycens.

*Finis istius stacionis et altera sequitur.**

[The Road to Damascus]
POETA. Honorable frendys, we beseche yow of audyens   *to listen to us*
    To here our intencyon, and also our prosses.   *hear/performance, procession*
  Upon our matter, be your favorable lycens,   *by your permission*
165   Another part of the story we wyll redres: *turn attention to*
    Here shalbe brefly shewyd, wyth all our besynes,   *activity*
  At thys pagent Saynt Poullys convercyon.   *stage*
  Take ye good hede, and therto gyf affeccyon.   *attention*

Here commyth Saule, rydyng in wyth hys servantys.

  SAUL. My purpose to Damask fully I intende;   *To (carry out) my purpose*
170   To pursewe the dyscypulys, my lyfe I apply.
  For to breke down the chyrchys thus I condescende.   *am resolved*
    Non I wyll suffer that shall edyfey—   *those who build (them)*
    Perchaunce owur lawes they mygte therby,
    And the pepull also, turne and converte,
175   Whych shuld be gret hevynes unto myn hart.

  Nay, that shall nott be butt layd apart!   *but shall be destroyed*
    The prynces have govyn me full potestacyon.   *given/power*
  All that I fynd, thei shall nott start,   *escape*
    But bounde to Jerusalem, wyth furyous vyolacyon,   *be sent/violent treatment*
180   Befor Cesar, Caypha, and Annas [have] presentacyon.   *to be presented*
  Thus shalbe subduyd tho wretchys of that lyfe,
  That non shall injoy, nother man, chy[l]de, nor wyfe.

Here comyth a fervent, wyth gret tempest, and Saule faulyth   *flash of light*
down of[f] hys horse; that done, Godhed spekyth in hevyn.

---

162 s.d. The end of this station, and another follows.

DEUS. Saule, Saule! Why dost thou me pursue?   *persecute*
  Yt ys hard to pryke agayns the spore!   *strike against the spur*
185 I am thi Savyour that ys so trwe,   *who is*
  Whych made hevyn and erth, and eche creature.   *who*
  Offende nott my goodnes; I wyll the[e] recure.   *save*
SAUL. O Lord, I am aferd, I trymble for fere!
  What woldyst I ded? Tell me here.   *What would you have me do?*

190 DEUS. Aryse, and goo thou wyth glad chere
  Into the cyte a lytyll besyde,   *city nearby*
  And I shall the[e] socor in every dere,   *aid/injury*
  That no maner of yll shal betyde,   *So that/shall occur*
  And I wyll ther for the[e] provyde   *let you know*
195 By my grete goodnes what thou shalt doo.
  Hy the[e] as fast thether as thou mast goo.   *Hie/as you can go*

SAUL. O mercyfull God, what aylyth me?
  I am lame, my leggys be take me fro;
  My sygth lykwyse, I may nott see—   *sight*
200 I can nott tell whether to goo.   *whither*
  My men hath forsake me also.
  Whether shall I wynde, or whether shall I pas?
  Lord, I beseche the[e], helpe me of thy grace!

MILES 1. Syr, we be here to help the[e] in thi nede—
205   Wyth all our affyance we wyll nott sesse.   *loyalty/cease*
SAUL. Than in Damask I pray yow me lede,   *lead*
  I[n] Godys name, accordyng to my promyse.
 MILES 2. To put forth yowur hand, loke ye dresse.   *address yourself*
  Cum on your way. We shall yow bryng
210 Into the cyte wythowt taryng.   *Into the city without tarrying*

Here the knyghtys lede forth Sa[u]le into a place, and Cryst apperyth to Annanie, sayng:

DEUS. Ananie, Ananie! Where art thou, Ananie?

ANANIAS. Here, Lord! I am here truly.

DEUS. Go thy way, and make thi curse   *course*
  As I shall assyng the[e] by myn advysse,   *show thee/advice*
215 Into the strete, *qui dicitur rectus*,   *which is called "Straight"*
  And in a certayn house, of warantyse,   *certainty*
  Ther shall ye fynd Saule in humble wyse,
  As a meke lambe that a wolf before was namyd.   *Meek as a lamb, who*
  Do my behest, Be nothyng ashamyd.   *bidding*

220	He wantyth hys syth, by my punyshment constrayned;	*sight*
	Prayeng unto me, I assure thou shalt hym fynd.	
	Wyth my stroke of pyte sore ys he paynyde,	*sorely*
	Wantyng hys sygth, for he ys truly blynyde.	*sight*
	ANANIAS. Lord, I am aferd, for alway in my mynd	
225	I here so myche of hys furyous cruelte,	*furious*
	That for spekyng of thi name to deth he will put me.	

	DEUS. Nay, Ananie, nay, I assure the[e],	
	He wulbe glad of thy cummyng.	
	ANANIAS. A, Lord, but I know of a certayn[té]	*certainty*
230	That thy seyntys in Jerusalem to deth he doth bryng!	*saints*
	Many yllys of hym I have bekennyng,	*have knowledge of*
	For he hath the poure of the pryncys alle,	*power*
	To save or spylle, do which he schall.	*kill/whatever*

	DEUS. Be nothyng a-drad. He ys a chosen vessell,	
235	To me assyngned by my Godly eleccyon.	*choice*
	He shall bere my name before the kyngys and chylder of Israell,	*chosen race*
	By many sharpe shourys sufferyng correccyon;	*fierce attacks*
	A gret doctor of benyngne conpleccyon,	*(He is) a learned divine*
	The trwe precher of the hye devynete,	*high*
240	A very pynacle of the fayth, I ensure the[e].	*assure*

	ANANIAS. Lorde, thy commandment I shall fullfyll;	
	Unto Saule I wyll take my waye.	
	DEUS. Be nothyng in dowte for good nor yll.	*Do not fear, come what may*
	Farewell, Ananie. Tell Saule what I do say.	

	Et exiat Deus.	*And let God go out*

245	ANANIAS. Blyssyd Lord, defende me as thou best may!	
	Gretly I fere hys cruell tyranny,	*Saul's*
	But to do thi precept, myself I shall applye.	*thy command/apply myself*

Here Ananias goth toward Saule.

	MILES 1. I marvayle gretly what yt doth mene,	
	To se[e] owur master in thys hard stounde!	*in this difficult time*
250	The wonder grett lythtys that were so shene	*wondrously/lights/bright*
	Smett hym doune of[f] hys hors to the grownde,	
	And me thowt that I hard a sounde	*heard*
	Of won spekyng wyth voyce delectable,	*one*
	Whych was to [vs] wonderfull myrable.	*amazing*

255 MILES 2. Sertenly thys lygt was ferefull to see, *light*
     The sperkys of fyer were very fervent. *brilliant*
     Yt inflamyd so grevosely about the countre, *widely*
     That, by my trowth, I went we shuld a bene brent! *I thought/have been burned*
     But now, serys, lett us relente *sirs/return*
260 Agayne to Caypha and Anna to tell this chaunce, *event*
     How yt befell to us thys grevauns.

Her[e] Saule ys in comtemplacyon.

SAUL. Lord, of thi coumfort moch I desyre,
     Thou mygty Prynce of Israell, Kyng of pyte, *pity*
     Whyche me hast punyshyd as thi presoner, *who*
265 That nother ete nor dranke thys dayes thre. *neither*
     But, gracyos Lorde, of thi vysytacyon I thanke the[e];
     Thy servant shall I be as long as I have breth,
     Thowgh I therfor shuld suffer dethe.

Here commyth Anania to Saule, sayeng:

ANANIAS. Pease be in thys place and goodly mansyon! *house*
270 Who ys wythin? Speke, in Crystys holy name!
     SAUL. I am here, Saule. Cum in, on Goddys benyson! *blessing*
     What ys your wyll? Tell, wythowten blame.
     ANANIAS. From Almyghty God sertanly to the[e] sent I am, *truly*
     And Ananie men call me wheras I dwell. *where*
275 SAUL. What wold ye have? I pray yow me tell.

ANANIAS. Gyfe me your hand for your awayle; *comfort*
     For as I was commaundyd by hys gracyos sentens, *words*
     He bad the[e] be stedfast, for thou shalt be hayle. *healed*
     For thys same cause he sent me to thi presens.
280 Also, he bad the[e] remember hys hye excellens,
     Be the same tokyn that he dyd the[e] mete *sign/meet*
     Toward the cyte, when he apperyd in the strete. *Near the city*

Ther mayst thou know hys power celestyall,
     How he dysposyth every thyng as hym lyst; *as it pleases him*
285 Nothyng may wythstand hys mygte essencyall;
     To stond upryght, or els doun to thryste— *thrust*
     Thys ys hys powur, yt may not be myste, *mistaken*
     For who that yt wantyth, lackyth a frende. *lacks it*
     Thys ys the massage that he doth the[e] sende.

290 SAUL. His marcy to me ys ryght welcom!
     I am ryght glad that yt ys thus.

Hic aparebit Spiritus Sanctus super eum. *

ANANIAS. Be of good chere and perfyte jubylacyon!   *perfect*
    Discendet super te Sprytus Sanctus, *
    Whych hath wyth hys hye grace illumynyd us.
295 Put fo[r]th thi hond, and goo wyth me—
    Agayne to thy syght here I restore the[e]!

SAUL. Blyssyd Lord, thankys to yow ever bee!
    The swame ys fallyn from my eyes twayne!   *scales are fallen*
    Where I was blynyd and cowd nott see,   *could*
300 Lord, thou hast sent me my syght agayne.
    From sobbyng and wepyng I can not refrayne
    My pensyve hart full of contryccyon;
    For my offencys, my body shal have punycyon.

    And where I have vsed so gret persecucyon
305 Of thi descyplys thorow all Jerusalem,   *through*
    I wyll [ayd] and defende ther predycacyon,   *preaching*
    That th[e]y dyd tech on all this reme.   *in/realm*
    Wherefor, Ananie, at the watery streme
    Baptyse me, hartely I the[e] praye,
310 Among your numbyr, that I electe and chosen be may!

ANANIAS. Onto this well of mych vertu   *Unto/font/great*
    We wyll us hye wyth all our delygens!   *hasten*
SAUL. Go yow before, and after I shall sewe,   *follow*
    Laudyng and praysyng our Lordys benevolens!
315 I shall never offend hys mygty magnyfycens,
    But alway observe hys preceptys, and kepe.   *keep (them)*
    For my gret unkyndnes my hart doth wepe!   *unnaturalness*

ANANIAS. Knele ye down upon thys grownde,
    Receyuyng thys crystenyng wyth good intent,
320 Whyche shall make yow [w]hole of your dedly wound
    That was infecte wyth venom nocent.   *noxious*
    Yt purgyth synne, and fendys pourys so fraudelent   *the false fiend's powers*
    It putyth asyde; where thys doth attayne,   *has effect*
    In every stede, he may not obtayne!   *place/prevail*

325 I crysten yow, wyth mynd full perfyght,
    Reseyvyng yow into owur relygyon,
    Ever to be stedfast, and never to flyt,   *stray*

---

291 s.d. Here the Holy Ghost will appear above him.
293. The Holy Ghost descends over you.

But ever constant, wythowt varyacyon.
Now ys fulfyllyd all our observacyon,   *rite*
330   Concludyng, thou mayst yt ken,   *may know it*
In nomine patris et filij et spiritus sancti, Amen. *

SAUL. I am ryght glad as foule on flyte   *bird in the air*
That I have receyvyd this blyssyd sacrement!
ANANIAS. Com on your way, Saule, for nothyng lett!   *delay*
335   Take yow sum coumforth for your bodyes noryschment.
Ye shall abyde wyth the dyscyplys verament   *truly*
Thys many dayes in Damask cyte,   *For many days*
Untyll the tyme more perfyt ye may be.

SAUL. As ye commande, holy father Ananie,
340   I full assent at yow[ur] request,   *fully assent to*
To be gydyd and rulyd as ye wyll have me,
Evyn at your pleasur, as ye thynk best;
I shall not offend, for most nor lest.   *for anything*
Go forth yowur way, I wyll succede   *follow you*
345   Into what place ye wyll me lede.

    Daunce   Conclusyo

POETA. Thus Saule ys convertyd, as ye se expres,   *plainly*
The very trw servant of our Lord Jhesu.   *true*
Non may be lyke to hys perfygt holynes,   *None*
So nobyll a doctor, constant and trwe;   *true*
350   Aftyr hys conversyon never mutable, but styll insue   *wavering/always striving*
The lawys of God to teche ever more and more,
As Holy Scrypture tellyth whoso lyst to loke therfore.   *whoever would*

Thus we comyte yow all to the Trynyte,   *commit*
Conkludyng thys stacyon as we can or may,   *location*
355   Under the correccyon of them that letteryd be;   *learned*
Howbeyt unable, as I dare speke or say,   *Although unlearned*
The compyler hereof shuld translat veray   *truly*
So holy a story, but wyth favorable correccyon   *but always*
Of my honorable masters, of ther benygne supplexion.   *and with their additions*

    Finis istius secunde stacionis et sequitur tarcia. *

360   POETA. The myght of the Fadirys potenciall Deite   *Father's potent*
Preserve thys honorable and wurshypfull congregacyon,

---

331. In the name of the Father and of the Son and of the Holy Ghost, Amen.
359 s.d. The end of the second station, and the third follows.

That here be present of hye and low degre,   *of all ranks*
To vnderstond thys pagent at thys lytyll stacyon,   *little place*
Whych we shall procede wyth all our delectac[y]on,   *go forward to with pleasure*
365   Yf yt wyll plese yow to gyf audyens favorable.
Hark wysely therto—yt ys good and profetable!

[Jerusalem. *Caypha and Anna in the temple. Enter the knights.]*

MILES 1.   Nobyll prelatys, take hede to owur sentens!   *words*
    A wundyrfull chaunce fyll and dyd betyde   *event occurred/befell*
    Vnto owur master Saull when he departyd hens,   *hence*
370   Into Damaske purposyd to ryde.
    A mervelous lygt fro th'telement dyd glyde,   *the heavens*
    Whyche smet doun hym to grunde, both horse and man,   *smote*
    Wyth the ferfulest wether that ever I in cam!   *came in from*

MILES 2.   It ravysshid hym, and his spiritys did benomme!   *numb*
375   A swete dulcet voyce spake hym unto,
    And askyd wherfor he made suche persecucyon
    Ageynst hys dyscyplys, and why he dyd soo.
    He bad hym into Damaske to Ananie goo,
    And ther he shuld reseyve baptym truly;
380   And now clene ageyns owur lawys he ys, trwly!   *completely opposed to*

CAYPHA.   I am sure thys tale ys not trw!   *true*
    What, Saule convertyd from our law?
    He went to Damask for to pursue
    All the dyscyplys that dyd wythdraw
385   Fro owur fayth—thys was hys sawe!   *saying*
    How say ye, Anna, to thys mater? This ys a mervelos chans!   *amazing event*
    I can not beleve that thys ys of assurans!   *credible*

ANNA.   No, Caypha, my mynde trwly do [I] tell,
    That he wyll not turne in no maner wyse,
390   But rather to deth put and expell
    All myscreauntys and wretchys that doth aryse
    Agaynst our lawes be ony enterpryse!   *any*
    Say the trwth, wyth[owt] ony cause frawdelent,
    Or els, for your talys, ye be lyke to be shent!   *lies/punished*

395   MILES 1.   Ellys owur bodyes may [ye] put to payn!   *Otherwise may our bodies*
    All that we declare, I sye yt wyth my nye—   *saw with my eye*
    Nothyng offendyng, but trwly do justyfye!

CAYPHA.   By the gret god, I do marvayle gretly!
    And thys be trw that ye do reherse,   *If/true/report*

400 He shall repent hys rebellyous treytory,   *treachery*
That all shalbe ware of hys falsnes!   *So that*
We wyll not suffer hym to obtayne, dowtles,   *prevail*
For meny perellys that myght betyde   *Since/might occur*
By hys subtyll meanys on every syde.

405 ANNA. The law ys commyttyd to owur advysment,   *entrusted/keeping*
Wherfor we wyll not se yt decay,
But rather uphold yt, help and agment,   *augment*
That ony reprofe to us fall may   *Lest any reproof*
Of Cesar th'emproure by nygt or day!   *From/the Emperor*
410 We shall to such maters harke and attende,
Accordyng to the lawes, our wyttys to spende!

Here to enter a dyvel wyth thunder and fyre, and to avaunce   *put himself forward*
hymsylfe, sayeng as folowyth, and hys spech spokyn, to syt
downe in a chayre:

BELIAL. Ho, ho, beholde me, the mygte prynce of the partys infernall!
Next unto Lucyfer I am in magestye!
By name I am nominate the god Belyall—   *called*
415 Non of more mygte nor of more excellencye!   *No one*
My powre ys pryncypall, and now of most soferaynte;   *highest*
In the templys and synagogys who deneyth me to honore,   *whoever refuses*
My busshopys, thorow my motyon, thei wyl hym sone devoure!   *my action/destroy*

I have movyd my prelatys, Cayphas and Anna,   *instructed*
420 To persew and put downe by powre ryall,   *royal*
Thorow the sytyes of Damaske and Liba,   *cities of Damascus and Libya*
All soch as do worship the hye God supernall.   *divine*
There deth ys conspyryd wythowt any favoure at all;   *arranged/mercy*
My busshopys hathe chosyne won most rygorus   *one (who is)*
425 Them to persew, howse name ys Saulus.   *whose*

Ho! Thus as a god most hye in magestye
I rayne and I rule over creaturys humayne.
Wyth soverayne sewte souyte to ys my deyte;   *royal petitions my deity is sued*
Mans mynd ys applicant as I lyst to ordeyne!   *directed as I choose*
430 My law styll encreasyth, wherof I am fayne!   *glad*
Yet of late I have hard of no newys, truly,
Wherfor I long tyll I speke wyth my messenger Mercurye.

Here shall entere another devyll callyd Mercury, wyth a fyeryng,
commyng in hast, cryeng and roryng, and shall say as folowyth:

MERCURY. Ho! Owyt, owyt! Alas, thys sodayne chance!   *Out! Out!/new event*
    Well may we bewayle this cursyd adventure!   *occurrence*
435   BELIAL. Marcurye, what aylyst thou? Tell me thy grevaunce!
    Ys ther any that hath wrowyte us dyspleasure?   *wrought*
    MERCURY. Dyspleasure inowgh, therof ye may be sure!
    Our law at lengthe yt wylbe clene downe layd,   *overrun*
    For yt decayth sore, and more wyl, I am afrayd!

440   BELIAL. Ho, how can that be? Yt ys not possyble!
    Co[n]syder, thou foole, the long contynuance!
    "Decaye," quod–a! Yt ys not credyble!   *says he*
    Of fals tydyngys, thou makyst here utterance!   *false news*
    Behold how the people hath no pleasaunce   *pleasure*
445   But in syn, and to folow our desyere,   *Except*
    Pryde and voluptuosyte ther hartys doth so fyre.   *inflame*

    Thowye on[e] do swaver away from our lore,   *Though one might fall*
    Yet ys our powre of suche nobylyte,   *excellence*
    To have hym agayne, and twoo therfore,   *That we get/and another*
450   That shal preferre the prayse of owre maiestye!   *Who will praise*
    What ys the tydyngys? Tell owt, lett us see!   *news*
    Why arte thou amasyd so? Declare afore us,   *so dazed*
    What fury ys fallyn that troblyth the[e] thus?

    MERCURY. Ho! Owyt, owyte! He that I most trustyd to,
455   And he that I thowyte wold have ben to us most specyall,
    Ys now of late turnyd, and our cruell foo!   *converted/foe*
    Our specyall frynd, our chosen Saull,
    Ys becomme servante to the hye God eternall!
    As he dyd ryde on our enemyes persecutyon,   *go forth to persecute*
460   He was sodenly strykyn by the hye provysyon,   *divine Providence*

    And now ys baptysyd, and promys he hath made
    Never to vary, and soch grace he hath opteynyd   *to waver/obtained*
    That ondowtyd hys fayth from hym can not fade.   *undoubtedly*
    Wherfor to complayne I am constraynyd,
465   For moch by hym shuld we have prevaylyd.
    BELIAL. Ho! Owyt, owyt! What, have we loste
    Our darlyng most dere, whom we lovyd moste?

    But ys yt of trowth that thou doyst here specyfye?   *do*
    MERCURY. Yt ys so, undowytyd! Why shuld I fayne?   *feign*
470   For thowyte, I can do non other but crye!   *Just thinking of it*

    Here thei shall rore and crye, and then Belyal shal saye:
    BELIAL. Owyte! This grevyth us worse than hell payne!

The conversyon of [a] synner certayne   *certainly*
Ys more payne to us and persecutyon,   *painful*
Than all the furyes of the infernall dongyon!

475   MERCURY.   Yt doyth not avayl us thus to lament,   *doth*
      But lett us provyd for remedy shortlye!
      Wherfor let us both, by on[e] assent,   *together*
         Go to the busshopys and move them pryvelye   *urge/privately*
         That by some sotyl meane thei may cause hym to dye.
480   Than shal he in our law make no dysturbaunce,   *Then*
      Nor hereafter cause us to have more grevaunce!

      BELIAL.   Wel sayd, Mercurye! Thy cowncel ys profytable.
         Ho, Saul, thou shalt repent thy unstablenes!
      Thou hadyst ben better to have byn confyrmable   *better to have conformed*
485   To our law—for thy deth, dowtles,   *doubtless*
         Yt ys conspyryd to reward thy falsnes!   *has been arranged*
      Thowgh on[e] hath dyssayvyd us, yet nowadays   *deceived*
      Twenti doyth gladly folow oure layes: *laws*

      Some by Pryde, some thorowgh Envye;
490   Ther rayneth thorow my myght so moch dysobedyaunce,   *reigns*
      Ther was never among Crystyans less charyte
         Than ys at this howre; and as for Concupysence,   *Lechery*
         [He] rayneth as a lord thorow my violence!   *reigns like*
      Glotony and Wrath every man doth devyse,   *employ*
495   And most now ys praysyd my cosyn Covytyce!   *Covetousness*

      Cum, Mercury, let us go and do as we have sayd;
         To delate yt any lenger, yt ys not best!   *delay*
      MERCURY.   To bryng yt abowyt, I wold be wel apayd!   *pleased*
         Tell yt be done, let us not rest!
500   BELIAL.   Go we than shortly! Let us departe,
      Hys deth to devyse, syth he wyl not revart!   *since/turn back*

      Here thei shal vanyshe away wyth a fyrye flame, and a tempest.
      Here aperyth Saul in hys dyscyplys wede, sayng: *garment*

      SAUL.   That Lord that ys shaper of see and of sonde,
         And hath wrowyt wyth hys worde al thyng at hys wyl,   *wrought*
      Save this asemly that here syttyth or stond,   *assembly*
505   For hys meke mercy, that we do not spyll.   *Because of/destroy (them)*
      Graunte me, good Lorde, thi pleasure to fulfyll,
      And send me soch spech that I the truth say,
      My ententyons profytable to meve yf I may.   *effect*

	Welbelovyd fryndys, ther be seven mortal synnys,	*deadly*
510	Whych be provyd pryncypall and pryncys of poysons.	*chief and princes*
	Pryde, that of bytternes all bale begynnys,	*sorrow*
	Wythholdyng all fayth, yt fedyth and foysonnys,	*nourishes*
	As Holy Scrypture baryth playn wytnes:	*bears full witness*
	*Initium omnium peccatorum su[per]bia est—**	
515	That often dystroyth both man and best.	*beast*

	Off all vyces and foly, pryde ys the roote;	
	Humylyte may not rayn ner yet indure.	*reign nor endure*
	Pyte, alak, that ys flower and boot,	*and remedy*
	Ys exylyd wher pryde hath socour.	*nourishment*
520	*Omnis qui se exaltat humiliabitur:**	
	Good Lord, gyf us grace to understond and persever,	
	Thys wurd, as thou bydyst, to fulfyll ever.	*you bid*

	Whoso in pryde beryth hym to hye,	*raises himself up*
	Wyth mysheff shalbe mekyd as I mak mensyon.	*trouble shall be humbled*
525	And I therfor assent and fully certyfy	
	In text, as I tell the trw entencyon	
	Of perfygt goodnes and very locucyon:	*perfect/true saying*
	*Noli tibi dico in altum sapere sed time**	
	Thys ys my consell: bere the[e] not to hye,	*too high*

530	But drede alway synne and folye	*always beware*
	Wrath, envy, covytys, and slugyshnes;	*and sloth*
	Exeunt owt of thy sygt glotony and lechery,	*Banish*
	Vanyte and vayneglory, and fals idylnes.	
	Thes be the branchys of all wyckydnes.	
535	Who that in hym thes vyces do roote,	*Whoever allows/to take root*
	He lackyth all grace, and bale ys the boote.	*blessings/sorrow/reward*

	"Lern at myself, for I am meke in hart,"	*Learn from*
	Owur Lorde to hys servantys thus he sayth,	
	"For meknes I sufferyd a spere at my hart;	*To show meekness (humility)*
540	Meknes all vycys anullyth and delayeth;	
	Rest to soulys ye shall fynd in fayth":	*for your souls/truly*
	Discite a me quia mitis sum et corde humilis,	
	*Et invenietis requiem animabus vestris.**	

---

514. Pride is the beginning of all sin. [See apocryphal book of Ecclesiaticus, 10:9-15]
520. Everyone who exalteth himself shall be humbled. [See Luke 18:14]
528. I say to you be not proud, but fear. [See Romans 11:20]
542-43. Learn from me, for I am meek and humble in heart, and you will find rest for your souls. [See Matthew 11:29]

	So owur Savyour shewyth us exampls of meknes,	
545	Thorow grace of hys goodnes mekly us groundys.	*instructs*
	Trwly yt wyll us save fro the synnes sekenes,	*sickness of sin*
	For Pryde and hys progeny mekenes confoundys.	

Quanto maior es tanto humilia te in omnibus: *
The gretter thou art, the lower loke thu be;
550   Bere the[e] never the hyer for thi degre.   *higher because of your rank*

Fro sensualyte of fleshe, thyself loke thou lede;   *From/lead yourself away*
Unlefully therin use not thy lyfe.   *Unlawfully*
Whoso therin delyteth, to deth he must nede.   *delights/must needs die*
It consumyth nature, the body sleyth wythowt knyf;
555   Also yt styntyth nott but manslawter and stryf.   *stops/but [leads to]*
Omnis fornicator aut immundus non habet hereditatem Christi: *
Non[e] shall in hevyn posses that be so vnthryfty!*   *so sinful*

Fle[e] fornycac[y]on, nor be no letchour,
But spare your speche, and spek nott theron: *But be careful in*
560   *Ex habundancia cordis os loquitur:* *
Who movyth yt oft, chastyte lovyth non;   *urges it often*
Of the hartys habundans, the tunge makyth locucyon.   *fullness/speaks*
What manys mynde ys laboryd, therof yt spekyth—   *Whatever man's/is working on*
That ys of suernes, as Holy Scryptur tretyth.   *certainty/discusses*

565   Wherfor I reherse thys wyth myn owyn mowthe:
*Caste viuentes templum Dei sunt**
Kepe clene your body from synne uncuth;   *impure*
Stabyll your syghtys, and look ye not stunt,   *Steady/cease*
For of a sertaynte I know at a brunt,   *all at once*
570   *Oculus est nuncius peccati**
That the iey ys ever the messenger of foly.   *eye*

SERVUS SAC. Whate, ys not thys Saule that toke hys vyage
Into Jerusalem, the dyscyplys to oppresse?
Bounde he wold bryng them, yf ony dyd rage   *Sworn to bring/any did preach about*
575   Upon Cryst—this was hys processe—   *story*
To the pryncys of prestys, he sayde, dowtles.   *chief priests/surely*

---

548. By how much you are great, by so much should you humble yourself in all things. [See Ecclesiaticus 3:17-20]

556. No fornicator or unclean person has any inheritance in [the kingdom] of Christ. [See Ephesians 5:5]

557. i.e., No one who is so unchaste will achieve heaven.

560. From the fullness of the heart the mouth speaks. [See Matthew 12:34, Luke 6:45]

566. Those who live purely are the temple of God. [See 1 Corinthians 6:18-19]

570. The eye is the messenger of sin. [See John 9:41]

Thorow all Damask and also Jerusalem,
Subdwe all templys that he founde of them.   *He would throw down*

SAUL. Yes, sertaynly, Saule ys my proper name,
580   That had in powr the full dominion—   *full authority*
To hyde yt fro you, yt were gret shame,   *would be*
    And mortall synne, as in my opynyon—
    Under Cesar and prystys of the relygyon,
And templys of Jues that be very hedyous,   *hateful*
585   Agayns almyghty Cryst, that Kyng so precyous.

SERVUS SAC. To Anna and Caypha ye must make your recurse.   *return*
    Com on your way, and make no delacyon!   *delay*
SAUL. I wyll yow succede, for better or wors,   *follow*
    To the pryncys of prystys wyth all delectacyon!   *chief priests/pleasure*
590   SERVUS SAC. Holy prystys of hye potestacyon,   *power*
    Here ys Saule! Lok on hym wysely—
He ys another man than he was, verely!   *different*

SAUL. I am the servant of Jhesu almyghty,
    Creator and maker of see and sonnd,   *sea/sand*
595   Whiche ys kyng conctypotent of hevyn glory,   *all powerful*
    Chef comfort and solace, both to fre and bonde,   *the free and the unfree*
    Agayns whos power nothyng may stonde!
Emperowr he ys, both of hevyn and hell,
Whoys goodnes and grace althyng doth excell!   *whose/everything*

    Recedit paulisper.   *He withdraws for a little while*

600   CAYPHA. Unto my hart thys ys gret admyracyon,   *wonder*
    That Saule ys thus mervelously changyd!
I trow he ys bewytchyd by sum conjuracyon   *I believe*
    Or els the devyll on hym ys avengyd!
    Alas, to my hart yt ys dessendyd   *heart has fallen*
605   That he ys thus takyn fro our relygyon!
How say ye, Anna, to thys convercyon?

ANNA. Full mervelously, as in my concepcyon,   *magically/understanding*
    Thys w[o]nderfull case, how yt befell;   *seems to have happened*
To se thys chaunce so sodenly don,   *event/accomplished*
610   Unto my hart yt doth grete yll!
    But for hys falsnes we shall hym spyll!   *kill*
    By myn assent to dethe we wyll hym bryng,
Lest that more myschef of hym may spryng.

CAYPHA. Ye say very trew! We mygt yt all rewe!   *might/regret*
615   But, shortly, in thys we must have advysement,   *counsel*
     For thus agayns us he may nott contynew—   *So that*
     Peraventur, than, of Cesar we may be shent!   *It could happen/disgraced*
     ANNA. Nay, I had lever in fyer he were brent,   *would rather*
     Than of Cesar we shuld have dysp[l]easure,   *should displease*
620   For sych a rebell and subtyle fals treator!   *such*

     CAYPHA. We wyll command the gatys to be kept aboute,   *guarded*
     And the wallys suerly on every stede,   *securely/place*
     That he may not eskape nowhere owyte.
     For dye he shall, I ensuer yow indede!   *assure*
625   ANNA. Thys traytour rebellyous, evyll mut he spede,   *may evil take him*
     That doth this unhappynes agayns all!   *Who*
     Now, every costodyer, kepe well hys wall!   *guard*

     SERVUS SAC. The gatys be shytt, he can note skape!   *shut*
     Every place ys kepte well and sure,
630   That in no wyse he may, tyll he be take,
     Gett owt of the cyte by ony conjecture!   *trick*
     Upon that caytyf and fals traytour   *criminal*
     Loke ye be avengyd wyth deth mortall,
     And judge hym as ye lyst to what end he shall!   *to whatever fate you want*

635   ANGEL. Holy Saule, I gyf yow monycyon!   *warning*
     The pryncys of Jues entende, sertayn,   *Jewish high priests*
     To put yow to deth! But by Goddys provysyon
     He wyll ye shall lyve lenger, and optayn!   *will you to/prosper*
     And after thy deth thou shalt rayng   *reign*
640   Above in hevyn wyth owur Lordys grace.   *blessings*
     Convay yowurself shortly into another place!

     SAUL. That Lordys pleasur ever mut be down,   *must be done*
     Both in hevyn and in hell, as hys wyll ys!
     In a beryng baskett or a lepe anon,   *carrying basket or a carrier*
645   I shall me co[n]vay wyth help of the dyscyplys
     For every gate ys shett, and kept wyth multytud of pepull[ys];   *shut/guarded by*
     But I trust in owur Lord that ys my socour,   *help*
     To resyst ther malyce and cruell furour.   *ire*

     Conclusyo[n]

     POETA. Thus leve we Saule wythin the cyte,   *leave*
650   The gatys kep by commandment of Caypha and Anna;   *guarded*
     But the dyscyplys in the nygt over the wall truly,   *night*

As the Bybull sayeth: *dim[i]serunt eum summitt[en]t es in sporta.* *
And Saule, after that, in Jerusalem vera,   *truly*
Joyned hymself and ther accompenyed
655 Wyth the dyscyplys wher thei were unfayned.   *undisguised*

Thys lytyll pagent thus conclud we
As we can, lackyng lytturall scyens,   *literary skill*
Besechyng yow all, of hye and low degré,   *rank*
Owur sympylnes to hold excusyd and lycens,   *tolerate*
660 That of retoryk have non intellygens,
Commyttyng yow all to owur Lord Jhesus,
To whoys lawd ye syng: *Exultet celum laudibus!* *   *praise*

Finis co[n]vercionis Sancti Pauli   End of the Conversion of St. Paul

---

652. They sent him forth, letting him down in a basket. [See Acts 9:25]
662. "Heaven will rejoice with praise," the opening words of a concluding hymn. Baker, in the introduction to the EETS edition of the Digby Plays (p. xxiv), quotes the following hymn used on the feast of the conversion of St. Paul:

> *Exsultet Coelum laudibus,*
> *Resultet terra gaudiis*
> *Apostolorum gloriam*
> *Sacra canunt solemnia.*

The Digby *Mary Magdalene*

The text of the Digby *Mary Magdalene* survives in Oxford at the Bodleian Library, in fols. 95^r-145^r of MS. Digby 133, the manuscript compilation briefly described in the introduction to the Digby *Conversion of St. Paul*. Like the *Conversion,* this play also bears the initials of Myles Blomefylde, its earliest known owner, on its first leaf (95^r). The handwriting of *Mary Magdalene* and other manuscript evidence point to the Digby copy being made around 1515-1525, although its language indicates a date of composition somewhat before then, probably late in the fifteenth century. The dialect suggests an East Anglian origin, perhaps in Norfolk. Myles Blomefylde's ownership of the play introduces the real possibility that its theatrical career extended into Chelmsford, Essex, during the third quarter of the sixteenth century. Further particulars regarding the provenance of the Digby manuscript and its implications for the stage history of the Digby plays are discussed in the introduction to the Digby *Conversion of St. Paul.*

It is no exaggeration to say that the Digby *Mary Magdalene* is the most extravagant play in the whole of early English drama. Over 2100 lines long— almost twice as long any other non-cycle play except *The Castle of Perseverance*—it dramatizes the life and times of Mary Magdalene as described in *The Golden Legend.* As was recognized long ago, the plot of the play falls roughly into two parts. The first (to line 924) deals with the privileged private life of Mary, tracing her family life with her sister Martha and brother Lazarus, her inheritance of Magdalen Castle, her temptation to a life of debauchery, and her conversion from it by Jesus, who brings Lazarus back from the grave. The second part (lines 925-2143) dramatizes Mary's public life of good works and its adventures, including her converting the King and Queen of Marseilles, throwing down their heathen temple, and traveling with them by ship to Jerusalem to meet St. Peter, her retirement into a wilderness bower where she is tended by angels and a priest, and finally, her death and welcome into heaven.

But this simple characterization of the plot line of *Mary Magdalene* does not begin to describe the riches found in the play or the elaborate theatrical demands it imposes on the director. It incorporates, for example, virtually every character type employed on the late medieval stage—familiar figures like the boastful Roman Emperor and ranting Herod from the Biblical cycle plays; the holy hero(ine) with the attendant priest from the saints plays; the World, the Flesh, the Devil, along with their allegorical companions, and the seven deadly sins, a Good Angel, Bad Angels and vices from the moralities; plus and exotic Kings and Queens and many, many other ordinary and extraordinary characters. There are, in fact over *fifty* speaking parts in the play, so that any production would clearly have to make great use of doubling.

The multiplicity of acting parts is nearly matched by the multiplicity of stages, or scaffolds, or playing sites. In whatever way they might be configured—whether in a circle like the stage plan of the *Castle of Perseverance,* or in facing rows with a playing ground between them, or like a rectangular tournament field—the staging has to represent a daunting array of places. These include an arbor, a desert, a sea, a tavern, a burning temple with a giant idol named Mament (Mohammed), a boat stage that actually "sails" across the playing space, Magdalen Castle and the Castle at Marseilles, a Hell-mouth, and a Heaven stage with ascending clouds in which Angels travel. At least nineteen distinct locations are mentioned in the stage directions or text of *Mary Magdalene.* Since the second part of the play initiates a completely new wave of action after some lapse of time, and involves a whole new range of characters and sets, theatrical economy might well dictate the doubling and interchange of various stages as well as characters. In any case it should be readily apparent that this play displays enormous theatrical ambition, that it demands and will repay close scrutiny.

The stanzaic forms in *Mary Magdalene* offer as much variety as its characters and stages. The basic metrical form is a four-stress line, frequently alliterating, used in stanzas that often change to suit the character speaking. Nearly half of the play is written in double quatrains (*ababbcbc*), and nearly a quarter in single *abab* quatrains; beyond these are to be found twenty eight-line tail-rhyming stanzas (*aaabcccb*) alongside six-line, nine-line and ten-line tail-rhyming stanzas, nearly a dozen bob-and-wheel stanzas of various lengths, several other stanzaic forms, and twenty-nine unrhymed lines.

Mary Magdalene was first edited by Thomas Sharp in *Ancient Mysteries from the Digby Manuscripts* (1835). The standard scholarly edition of the play, edited by Donald C. Baker, John L. Murphy, and Louis B. Hall, Jr., appears in the EETS *The Late Medieval Religious Plays of Bodleian MSS. Digby 133 and E Museo 160* (1982); a facsimile of the manuscript, edited by Donald C. Baker and John L. Murphy, appears in *The Digby Plays: Facsimiles of the Plays in Bodley MSS Digby 133 and e Museo 160.* A discussion of the history of the text can be found in Donald C. Baker and John L. Murphy, "The Late Medieval Plays of MS Digby 133: Scribes, Dates and Early History," *RORD,* x (1967); the Digby Plays' connection with Chelmsford is explored by John C. Coldewey in "The Digby Plays and the Chelmsford Records," *RORD,* xviii (1975); the theatrical history of the plays (including *Mary Magdalene)*, as evidenced by their texts, appears in Donald C. Baker's "When is a Text a Play" in Briscoe and Coldewey, *Contexts for Early English Drama* (see Suggestions for Further Reading).

THE DIGBY *MARY MAGDALENE*

[Emperor Tiberius Caesar's Court, Rome]

IMPERATOR. I command sylyns, in the peyn of forfetur,   *penalty*
   To all myn audyeans present general!   *audience*
Of my most hyest and mytyest volunte,   *will*
   I woll it be knowyn to al the wor[l]d unyversal   *require*
5 That of heven and hell chyff rewlar am I,   *chief ruler*
   To w[h]os[e] magnyfycens non stondyt[h] egall!   *none stands equal*
For I am soveren of al soverens subjugal   *subject sovereigns*
   Onto myn empere, beyng incomparable
Tyberyus Sesar, w[h]os[e] power is potencyall!   *potent*

10 I am the blod ryall most of soverente—   *of royalest blood*
   Of all emperowers and kyngys my byrth is best,
And all regeouns obey my myty volunte!   *will*
   Lyfe and lem and goodys all be at my request!   *limb*
   So, of all soverens, my magnyfycens most mytyest
15 May nat be agaynsayd of frend nor of foo,   *denied*
   But all abydyn jugment and rewle of my lyst.   *submit to/wishes*
All grace upon erth from my goodnes commy[h]t fro,
And that bryngis all pepell in blysse so!
For the most worthyest, woll I rest in my sete!   *[Sits]*

20 SERYBYL. Syr, from your person growy[h]t moch grace!
IMPERATOR. Now, for thin[e] answer, Belyall blysse thi face!
Mykyl presporyte I gyn to porchase—   *much/amass*
   I am wonddyn in welth from all woo!   *wound, protected*

Herke thou, provost, I gyff the[e] in commandment   *order*
25   All your pepull preserve in pesabyl possessyon.   *peaceable*
Yff ony ther be to my goddys [dys]obedyent,
   Dyssevyr tho harlottys and make to me declaracyon.   *separate out, find*
     And I shall make all swych to dye,   *such*
     Thos precharsse of Crystys incarnacyon!   *preachers*
30 PROVOST. Lord of all lorddys, I shall gyff yow informacyon.   *[Exit]*
IMPERATOR. Lo, how all the wor[l]d obeyi[h]t my domynacyon!
   That person is nat born that dare me dysseobey!

Syrybbe, I warne yow, se that my lawys
   In all your partyis have dew obeysavns!   *parts, regions*
35 Inquere and aske, eche day that dawnnys
   Yf in my pepul be fovnd ony weryouns   *variance, resistance*
   Contrary to me in ony chansse,   *any way*
Or wyth my goldyn goddys grocth or grone!   *grouch, complain*
   I woll marre swych harlottys wyth mordor and myschanse!   *such/murder*

40 Yff ony swyche remayn, put hem in repreffe,   *reproof*
   And I shall yow releff!   *reward*

SERYBYL. Yt shall be don, lord, wythowtyn ony lett   *hindrance*
       or wythowt doth!   *[Exit]*
IMPERATOR. Lord and lad to my law doth lowte!   *bow down*
Is it nat so? Sey yow all wyth on[e] showte!

Here answerryt[h] all the pepul at onys: "Ya, my lord, ya!"

45   IMPERATOR. So, ye froward folkys, now am [I] plesyd!   *stubborn*
    Sett wyn and spycys to my consell full cler.   *for my council*
    Now have I told yow my hart, I am wyll plesyd.
    Now lett us sett don alle, and make good chyr!   *cheer*

[Magdalene Castle, Bethany]

Her[e] entyr Syrus, the fader of Mary Mavdleyn.

SYRUS. Emperor and ky[n]ggys and conquerors kene,
50   Erlys and barons and knytys that byn bold,   *Earls/Knights/be*
    Berdys in my bower so semely to senne,   *Maidens/see*
    I commav[n]d yow at onys my hestys to hold!   *orders/uphold*
    Behold my person, glysteryng in gold,
    Semely besyn of all other men!
55   Cyrus is my name, be cleffys so cold!   *cliffs*
    I command yow all obedyent to beyn!   *be*

W[h]oso woll nat, in bale I hem bryng,   *into unhappiness*
    And knett swyche caytyfys in knottys of care!   *tie such villains into*
Thys castell of Mavdleyn is at my wylddyng,   *wielding, rule*
60   Wyth all the contre, bothe lesse and more,
    And lord of Jherusalem! Who agens me don dare?   *dare act*
Alle Beteny at my beddyng be;   *Bethany/bidding*
    I am sett in solas from al syyng sore,   *safe in solace/sighing*
And so shall all my posteryte
65   Thus for to leven in rest and ryalte.   *live/royalty*

I have her[e] a sone that is ful trew to me—
    No comlyar creatur of Goddys creacyon;
T[w]o amyabyll douctors full brygth of ble;   *daughters/fair of face*
    Ful gloryos to my syth, an[d] ful of delectacyon;   *sight*
70   Lazarus my son, in my resspeccyon,   *regard*
       Here is Mary, ful fayur and ful of femynyte,
    And Martha, ful [of] beute and of delycyte,   *beauty/delicacy*
    Ful of womanly merrorys and of benygnyte.   *graces*
    They have fulfyllyd my hart wyth consolacyon.

75   Here is a coleccyon of cyrcumstance—
        To my cognysshon nevyr swych anothyr,   *knowledge/such*
        As be demonstracyon knett in contynens,   *shows constancy*
        Save alonly my lady that was ther mother!
        Now, Lazarus my sonne, whech art ther brothyr,   *who is*
80   The lordshep of Jherusalem I gyff the[e] aftyr my dysses,   *decease*
        And Mary, thys castell alonly, an non othyr;
        And Martha shall have Beteny, I sey exprese.   *outright*
        Thes gyftys I graunt yow wythowtyn les,   *lies*

        Whyll that I am in good mynd!   *sound mind*

85   LAZARUS. Most reverent father, I thank yow hartely
        Of yower grett kyndnes shuyd onto me!   *shown*
        Ye have grauntyd swych a lyfelod worthy   *livelihood*
        Me to restreyn from all nessesyte.   *keep from need*
        Now, good Lord, and hys wyll it be,
90   Graunt me grace to lyue to thy plesawans,   *by your wishes*
        And ayens hem so to rewle me,   *according to them/rule*
        Thatt we may have joye wythowtyn weryauns.   *variance*

        MARY. Thou God of pes and pryncypall counsell,   *peace*
        More swetter is thi name than hony be kynd!   *by its nature*
95   We thank yow, fathyr, for your gyftys ryall,   *royal*
        Owt of peynys of poverte us to onbynd.   *pains/unbind*
        Thys is a preservatyff from streytnes we fynd,   *hardship*
        From wordly labors to my coumfortyng,   *to comfort me*
        For thys lyfflod is abyll for the dowtter of a kyng,   *livelihood/fit/daughter*

100   Thys place of plesavns, the soth to seye!   *pleasant place (castle)*
        MARTHA. O, ye good fathyr of grete degre,   *high estate*
        Thus to departe wyth your ryches,   *part with*
        Consederyng ower lowlynes and humylyte,   *humble deservings*
        Vs to save from wordly dessetres!   *distress*
105   Ye shew us poyntys of grete jentylnes,   *examples*
        So mekly to meyntyn us to your grace.   *support*
        Hey in heven avansyd mot yow be   *high/advanced might you*
        In blysse, to se that Lordys face
        Whan ye shal hens passe!   *hence*
110   SYRUS. Now I rejoyse wyth all my mygthtys!
        To enhanse my chyldryn, it was my delyte!   *provide for*
        Now, wyn and spycys, ye jentyll knyttys,
        Onto thes ladys of jentylnes.

Here shal they be servyd wyth wyn and spycys.

[The Emperor's Court]

IMPERATOR. Syr provost, and skrybe, juggys of my rem,	*scribe/judges/realm*
115 My massengyr I woll send into ferre cuntre,	
Onto my sete of Jherusalem	*unto/city*
Onto Herowdes, that regent ther ondyr me,	
And onto Pylat, juggys of the covntre—	
Myn entent I woll hem teche.	
120 Take he[e]d, thou provost, my precept wretyn be,	
And sey, I cummaund hem as they woll be [wyth]owt wrech,	*unharmed*
Yf ther be ony in the cuntre ageyn my law doth prech,	*who/against*

Or ageyn my goddys ony trobyll tellys,	*speaks troublingly against*
That thus agens my lawys rebellys,	*who thus*
125 As he is regent and in that reme dwellys,	*since/realm*
And holdyth hys croun of me be ryth,	*right*
Yff ther be ony harlettys that agens me make replycacyon	*villains/speak against*
Or ony moteryng ayens me make wyth malynacyon.	*muttering/made/malice*
PROVOST. Syr, of all thys they shall have informacyon,	
130 So to uphold yower renoun and ryte!	

IMPERATOR. Now, massengyr, wythowtyn taryyng,	
Have here gold onto thi fe.	
So bere thes lettyrs to Herowdes the kyng,	
And byd hem make inquyrans in every cuntre,	*inquiry*
135 As he is jugge in that cuntre beyng!	
NUNCIUS. Soveren, your arend it shall be don ful redy	*errand*
In alle the hast that I may.	*haste*
For to fullfyll your byddyng	
I woll nat spare, nother be nyth nor be day! *[Exit]*	*neither by night*

Here goth the masengyr toward Herowdes.

[Herod's Court, Jerusalem]

140 HEROD. In the wyld, wanyng world, pes all at onys!	*quiet now*
No noyse, I warne yow, for greveyng of me!	*offending*
Yff yow do, I shal hourle of yower hedys,	*hew off*
be Mahondys bonys,	*Mohammed's*
As I am trew kyng to Mahond so fre!	
Help! Help, that I had a swerd!	
145 Fall don, ye faytours, flatt to the ground!	*scoundrels*
Heve of your hodys and hattys, I cummaund yow alle!	*Heave off/hoods*
Stond bare hed, ye beggars! Wo made yow so bold?	
I shal make yow know your kyng ryall!	*royal*
Thus woll I be obeyyd thorow al the world,	

150   And whoso wol nat, he shal be had in hold,
     And so to be cast in carys cold,   *cold comfort*
     That werkyn ony wondyr ayens my magnyfycens!   *trick*
     Behold these ryche rubyys, red as ony fyr,   *any fire*
     Wyth the goodly grene perle full sett abowgth!   *set in pearl*
155   What kyng is worthy, or egall to my power?   *equal*
     Or in thys world who is more had in dowt   *fear*
     Than is the hey name of Herowdes, Kyng of Jherusalem,   *high*
     Lord of Alapye, Assye, and Tyr,   *Aleppo, Asia, Tyre*
     Of Abyron, Beryaby, and Bedlem?   *Hebron, Beersheba, Bethlehem*
160   All thes byn ondyr my governouns!
     Lo, all thes I hold wythowtyn reprobacyon!   *reproof*
     No man is to me egall, save alonly the emperower   *equal*
     Tyberyus, as I have in provostycacyon!   *governorship*
     How sey the[e] phylyssoverys be my ryche reyne?
165   Am nat I the grettest governowur?
     Lett me ondyrstond whatt can ye seyn!

PHILOSOPHER. Soueren, and it plece yow, I woll expresse!   *please*
     Ye be the rewlar of this regyon,
     And most worthy sovereyn of nobylnes
170   That evyr in Jude barre domynacyon!   *Judaea held*
     Bott, syr, skreptour gevytt[h] informacyon,   *Scripture*
     And doth rehersse it verely,
     That chyld shal remayn of grete renovn,   *a child/be born*
     And all the world of hem shold magnyfy: *make him great*

175   *"Et ambulabunt gentes in lumine [tuo], et reges*
     *In splendore ortus tui."**

HEROD. And whatt seyst thow?
PHILOSOPHER 2. The same veryfyit[h] my bok as how,

     As the skryptour doth me tell   *Scripture*
180   Of a myty duke shal rese and reyn,   *rise*
     Whych shall reyn and rewle all Israell.   *who/rule*
     No kyng ayens hys worthynes shall opteyn,   *against/prevail*
     The whech in profesy hath grett eloquence:

185   *"Non avferetur s[c]eptrum [de] Juda, et dux de*
     *Femore eius, donec veniet [qui] mitendus est."**

175-76. And the nations will walk in your light, and kings in the brightness of your rising. [See Isaiah 60:3, a text for the Epiphany (January 6)]

184-85. The sceptre will not be withdrawn from Judaea, nor a leader from her loins, until he comes who is to be sent. [See Genesis 49:10]

HEROD. A! Owt! Owt! Now am [I] grevyd all wyth the worst!
　Ye dastardys! Ye doggys! The dylfe mote yow draw!   *may the devil tear you apart*
　Wyth fleyyng flappys I byd yow to a fest!   *a flogging*
　A swerd! A swerd! Thes lordeynnys wer slaw!   *That these louts were slain*
190　Ye langbaynnys! Losellys! Forsake ye that word!   *longbones/scoundrels*
　　That caytyff shall be cawth, and suer I shall hem flaw!   *wretch/caught/flay*
　For hym many mo shal be marry[d] wyth mordor!   *more/marred/murder*

MILES 1. My sovereyn lord, dyssemay yow ryth nowt!   *do not dismay yourself*
　They ar but folys, ther eloquens wantyng;
195　For in sorow and care sone they shall be cawt.
　Ayens us they can mak no dysstonddyng!   *withstanding*

MILES 2. My lord, all swych shall be browte before your audyens   *such/presence*
　And levyn ondyr your domynacyon,   *live*
　Or ellys dammyd to deth wyth mortal sentense,   *doomed/deadly*
200　Yf we hem gett ondyr ower gubernacyon!   *them/governance*

HEROD. Now thys is to me a gracyows exsortacyon,   *exhortation*
　And grettly reioysyth to my sprytys indede!
　Thow[gh] thes sottys ayens me make replycacyon,   *reply*
　I woll suffer non to spryng of that kenred;   *their kind, tribe*
205　Some voys in my lond shall sprede,   *voice*
　Prevely or pertely in my lond abouth.   *privately or openly/all about*
　Whyle I have swych men, I nede nat to drede   *such*
　But that he shal be browt ondyr, wythowtyn do[u]th!   *doubt*

Her[e] commyt[h] the emperowers masengyr, thus sayyng to Herowdes:

MESSENGER. Heyll, prynse of bovntyowsnesse!
210　Heyll, myty lord of to magnyfy!   *praiseworthy*
　Heyll, most of worchep of to expresse!   *worthy of honor*
　Heyll, reytyus rewlar in thi regensy!   *righteous ruler*
　My sofereyn Tyberyus, chyff of chyfalry,   *chief/chivalry*
　Hys soveren sond hath sent to yow here: *sound (message)*
215　He desyrth yow and preyit[h] on eche party   *desires/prays in every particular*
　To fulfyll hys commaundment and desyre.

Here he shall take the lettyrs onto the kyng.

HEROD. Be he sekyr I woll natt spare   *sure/refrain*
　For [to] complyshe hys cummaunddment,
　Wyth sharp swerddys to perce the [m] bare   *pierce*
220　In all covntres wythin thys regent,   *region*
　For hys love to fulfyll hys intentt.
　Non swych shall from ower handys stertt,   *such/shrink away*

For we woll fulfyll hys ryall juggement   *royal*
Wyth swerd and spere to perce [them] thorow the hartt!

225 But, masengyr, reseyve thys lettyr wyth,   *now*
  And ber ytt onto Pylattys syth!   *bear/sight*
  MESSENGER. My lord, it shall be don ful wygth.
   In hast I woll me spede! *[Exit]*

  [Pilate's Court, Jerusalem]

  PILATE. Now ryally I reyne in robys of rych[e]sse,   *royally*
230 Kyd and knowyn both ny and ferre   *understood/nigh*
  For juge of Jherusalem, the trewth to expresse,
   Ondyr the Emperower Tyberius Cesar!
   Therfor I rede yow all bewarre   *warn*
  Ye do no pregedyse ayen the law!   *prejudice against*
235 For and ye do, I wyll yow natt spare   *If*
  Tyl ye have jugment to be hangyd and draw!   *torn apart*

  For I am Pylat, pr[o]mmyssary and pres[e]dent!   *appointed head and governor*
  Alle renogat robber inperrowpent,   *All renegade robbers*
   To put hem to peyn, I spare for no pete!   *them/torture/pity*
240 My serjauntys semle, qwat s[e]ye ye?   *seemly/what*
  Of this rehersyd I wyll natt spare!   *aforesaid/make exceptions*
   Plesauntly, syrrys, aunswer to me,   *sirs*
   For in my herte I shall have the lesse care.   *worry*

  SARGEANT 1. As ye have seyd, I hold it for the best,
245 Yf ony swych among us may we know!   *such*
  SARGEANT 2. For to gyff hem jugment I holdd yt best,   *give them*
   And so shall ye be dred of hye and low!   *dreaded by*

  PILATE. A, now I am restoryd to felycyte!

  Her[e] comyt[h] the Emprorys masengyr to Pylat.

  MESSENGER. Heyll, ryall in rem, in robis of rychesse!   *royal in realm*
250 Heyl, present thou prynsys pere!   *now present*
  Heyl, jugge of Jherusalem, the trewth to expresse!
   Tyberyus the Emprower sendyt[h] wrytyng herre,
   And prayyt yow, as yow be hys lovyr dere,   *friend*
  Of this wrytyng to take avysement
255 In strenthyng of hys lawys cleyr,
  As he hath set yow in the state of jugment.

Her[e] Pylat takyt[h] the lettyrs wyth grete reverens.

    PILATE. Now, be Martys so mythy, I shal sett many a snare,   *mighty*
    Hys lawys to strenth in al that I may.   *strengthen*
    I rejoyse of hys renown and of hys wylfare,   *rejoice in*
260   And for thi tydynggys I geyff the[e] this gold today.
    MESSENGER. A largeys, ye, lord, I crye this day,   *largesse*
    For this is a yeft of grete degre!   *gift*
    PILATE. Masengyr, onto my sovereyn thou sey,
    On the most specyall wyse recummend me!   *speak well of me*

Her[e] avoydyt[h] the masengyr, and Syrus takyt[h] hys deth.

[Magdalen Castle, Bethany]

265 SYRUS. A, help, help! I stond in drede!
    Syknes is sett ondyr my syde!
    A, help! Deth wyll aquyte me my mede!   *give me my deserts*
    A, gret God, thou be my gyde!
    How I am trobyllyd, both bak and syde!
270 Now, wythly help me to my bede.   *quickly/bed*
    A! This rendyt[h] my rybbys! I shall nevyr goo nor ryde!   *tears apart*
    The dent of deth is hevyar than led!   *dint, blow/lead*
    A, lord, lord, what shal I doo this tyde?   *time*
    A, gracyows God, have ruth on me,   *pity*
275 In thys word no lengar to abyde!
    I blys yow, my chyldyrn, God mot wyth us be!   *may God be with us*

Her[e] avoydyt[h] Syrus sodenly, and than sayyng Lazarus: *exit*

    LAZARUS. Alas! I am sett in grete hevynesse!   *put*
    Ther is no tong my sorow may tell,   *tongue*
    So sore I am browth in dystresse!   *brought into*
280 In feyntnes I falter for [th]is fray fell!   *this painful distress*
    Thys dewresse wyl lett me no longar dwelle,   *duress/live*
    But God of grace sone me redresse!   *Unless/helps me*
    A, how my peynys don me repelle!   *attack me*
    Lord, wythstond this duresse!   *stand with [me] in*

285 MARY. The inwyttyssymus God that evyr shal reyne,   *all-knowing*
    Be hys help and sowlys sokor!   *soul's succour*
    To whom it is most nedfull to cumplayn,
    He to bry[n]g us owt of ower dolor;   *that He may lead us*
    He is most mytyest governowre,
290 From soroyng us to restryne.   *to assuage our grief*

MARTHA. A, how I am sett in sorowys sad,
   That long my lyf Y may nat indevre!   *endure*
Thes grawous peynys make me ner mad!   *grievous/nearly*
   Vnder clovyr is now my fathyris cure,   *clover*
295 That sumtyme was here ful mery and glad   *who once was*
   Ower Lordys mercy be hys mesure,   *reward*
And defeynd hym from peynys sad.

LAZARUS. Now, systyrs, ower fatherys wyll we woll exprese;   *can say openly*
   Thys castell is owerys wyth all the fee!   *income*
300 MARTHA. As hed and governower, as reson is,
   And on this wyse abydyn wyth yow wyll wee.   *in this way*
We wyll natt desevyr, whattso befalle!   *separate, disagree*
MARY. Now, brothyr and systyr, welcum ye be,
And therof specyally I pray yow all!

[World's Stage]

Her[e] shal entyr the Kyng of the Wor[l]d, the Flesch, and the Dylfe,   *Devil*
wyth the Seven Dedly Synnys, a Bad Angyll, an[d] an Good Angyl,
thus seyyng the Wor[l]d:

305 WORLD. I am the World, worthyest that evyr God wrowth,   *wrought*
   And also I am the prymatt portature   *strongest support (of life)*
Next heveyn, yf the trewth be sowth,   *sought*
   And that I jugge me to skryptur;   *appeal to Scripture*
And I am he that lengest shal induere,   *endure*
310 And also most of domynacyon!
   Yf I be hys foo, w[h]oo is abyll to recure?   *foe/recover, prosper*
For the whele of fortune wyth me hath sett hys senture.   *set me at the center*

In me restyt[h] the ordor of the metellys sevyn,   *seven metals*
The whych to the seven planyttys ar knett ful sure: *knit, connected*
315 Gold perteynyng to the sonne, as astronemere nevyn;   *affirm*
   Sylvyr to the mone, whyte and pure;
Iryn onto the Maris that long may endure;
The fegetyff mercury onto Mercuryus;   *fugitive*
   Copyr onto Venus, red in hys merrour;
320 The frangabyll tyn to Jubyter, yf ye can dyscus;   *breakable*
On this planyt Saturne, ful of rancure,   *rancor*
   This soft metell led, nat of so gret puernesse;
Lo, alle this rych tresor wyth the Wor[l]d doth indure—
   The seuyn prynsys of hell, of gret bowntosnesse!   *bounteousness*
325 Now, who may presume to com to my honour?   *rival*
PRIDE. Ye, worthy Wor[l]d, ye be gronddar of gladnesse   *grounder, founder*

To them that dwellyn ondyr yower domynacyon!
COVETYSE. And whoso wol nat, he is sone set asyde
Wheras I, Couetyse, take mynystracyon! *Where I have power*
330 WORLD. Of that I pray yow, make no declareracyon!
    Make swych to know my soverreynte, *Let all such know*
    And than they shal be fayn to make supplycacyon, *glad*
    Yf that they stond in ony nesessyte.

[Flesh's Stage]

Her[e] shal entyr the Kynge of Flesch, wyth Slowth, Gloteny, Lechery.

FLESH. I, Kyng of Flesch, florychyd in my flowers *adorned*
335 Of deyntys delycyows I have grett domynacyon! *delicious*
So ryal a kyng was neuyr borne in bowrys, *royal/bowers, common places*
    Nor hath more delyth, ne more delectacyon! *delight, nor more*
    For I have comfortatywys to my comfortacyon: *comforts/ease*
    Dya galonga, ambra, and also margaretton— *galingale (root), amber, pearls*
340 Alle this is at my lyst, ayens alle vexacyon! *pleasure/against all vexation*

All wykkyt thyngys I woll sett asyde. *unpleasant*
    Clary, pepur long, wyth granorum paradysy, *Cleary (plant)/paradise (spice)*
Zenzybyr and synamom ateverytyde— *Ginger and cinnamon*
    Lo, alle swych deyntyys delycyus use I! *such dainties*

345 Wyth swyche deyntyys I have my blysse!
    Who woll covett more game and gle, *sport*
My fayere spowse Lechery to halse and kysse? *embrace*
Here ys my knyth Gloteny, as good reson is, *knight*
    Wyth this plesavnt lady to rest be my syde.
350 Here is Slowth, anothyr goodly of to expresse! *worthy to tell*
    A more plesavnt compeny doth nowher abyde!

LECHERY. O ye prynse, how I am ful of ardent love,
    Wyth sparkyllys ful of amerowsnesse! *glittering with*
Wyth yow to rest fayn wold I aprowe, *gladly/apply*
355 To shew plesavns to your jentylnesse! *pleasure*
FLESH. O ye bewtews byrd, I must yow kysse!
    I am ful of lost to halse yow this tyde! *lust/embrace/time*

[Devil's Stage]

Here shal entyr the prynse of dyllys in a stage, and *devils*
helle ondyrneth that stage, thus seyyng the Dylfe:

SATAN. Now I, prynse pyrles, prykkyd in pryde, *peerless*
　　Satan, [y]ower sovereyn, set wyth every cyrcumstanse,
360　For I am atyred in my towyr to tempt yow this tyde! *dressed/time*
　　As a kyng ryall I sette at my plesavns, *sit/pleasure*
　　Wyth Wroth [and] Invy at my ryall retynawns! *royal retinue*
　　The bolddest in bowyr I bryng to abaye, *to bay*
　　Mannis sowle to besegyn and bryng to obeysavns! *besiege/submission*
365　Ya, [wyth] tyde and tyme I do that I may! *what I can*
　　For at hem I have dysspyte that he shold have the joye *him/resentment*
　　　That Lycyfer wyth many a legyown lost for ther pryde.
　　The snarys that I shal set wher nevyr set at Troye! *were*
　　　So I thynk to besegyn hem be every waye wyde— *in every way*
370　　I shal getyn hem from grace whersoeuyr he abyde— *bring*
　　That body and sowle shal com to my hold, *within my grasp*
　　　　Hym for to take!
　　　Now, my knythtys so stowth, *knights/stout*
　　　Wyth me ye shall ron in rowte, *run riot*
375　　My consell to take for a skowte, *plan*
　　　　Whytly that we were went for my sake! *Quickly/on our way*
WRATH. Wyth wrath or wyhyllys we shal hyrre wynne! *wiles*
ENVY. Or wyth sum sotyllte sett hur in synne! *subtlety/her (Mary)*
SATAN. Com of, than, let us begynne *let's go*
380　　　To werkyn hure sum wrake! *to do her some harm*

[World's Stage]

Her shal the Deywl go to the Wor[l]d wyth hys compeny.

SATAN. Heyle, Wor[l]d, worthyest of abowndans! *wealth*
　　In hast we must a conseyll take! *haste/confer*
　　Ye must aply yow wyth all your afyavns, *followers*
　　A woman of whorshep ower servant to make. *worship*

385　WORLD. Satan, wyth my consell I wyll the[e] awansse! *advance, help*
　　I pray the, cum up onto my tent. *[Satan ascends]*
　　Were the Kyng of Flesch her[e] wyth hys asemlaunvs! *If only/assemblage*
　　　Masengyr! Anon, that thou werre went
　　　　Thys tyde! *At once*
390　　Sey the Kyng of Flesch wyth grete renown, *Tell*
　　　Wyth hys consell that to hym be bown, *Council (companions)*
　　　In alle the hast that evyr they mown, *can muster*
　　　　Com as fast as he may ryde!

MESSENGER. My lord, I am your servant, Sensualyte!
395　　Your masege to don, I am of glad chyr! *do/cheer*

Ryth sone in presens ye shal hym se, *Right*
Your wyl for to fulfylle her[e]!

[Flesh's Stage]

Her[e] he goth to the Flesch, thus seyyng:

MESSENGER. Heyl, lord in lond, led wyth lykyng! *by pleasure*
Heyl, Flesch in lust, fayyrest to behold!
400 Heyl, lord and ledar of emprore and kyng!
The worthy Wor[l]d, be wey and wold, *by highway and field*
Hath sent for yow and your consell! *Council*
Satan is sembled wyth hys howshold, *assembled*
Your cov[n]seyl to have, most fo[r] aweyle. *help*

405 FLESH. Hens in hast, that we ther wh[e]re! *haste/were*
Lett us make no lengar delay.
MESSENGER. Gret myrth to ther hertys shold yow arere, *raise up*
Be my trowth I dare safly saye!

[World's Stage]

Her[e] comyt the Kyng of Flesch to the Wor[l]d, thus seyyng:

FLESH. Heyl be yow, soverens lefe and dere! *beloved*
410 Why so hastely do ye for me send?
WORLD. A! We are ryth glad we have yow here, *right*
Ower counsell togethyr to comprehend! *[They sit]*
Now, Satan, sey your devyse! *tell us your plan*
SATAN. Serys, now ye be set, I shal yow say:
415 Syrus dyyd this odyr day— *died/other*
Now Mary, hys dowctor, that may, *daughter/maid*
Of that castel beryt[h] the pryse. *owns it*

WORLD. Sertenly, serys, I yow telle,
Yf she in vertu stylle may dwelle,
420 She shal byn abyll to dystroye helle, *be able*
But yf your cov[n]seyll may othyrwyse devyse! *Unless*
FLESH. Now ye, Lady Lechery, yow must don your attendans, *attend to this*
For yow be flowyr fayrest of femynyte!
Yow shal go desyyr servyse, and byn at hure atendavns, *be at her attendance*
425 For ye shal sonest entyr, ye beral of bewte! *beryl of beauty*

LECHERY. Serys, I abey your covnsell in eche degre— *every way*
Stryttwaye thethyr woll I passe! *Straightaway thither*
SATAN. Spiritus malyngny shal com to the[e], *Malign Spirit (Bad Angel)*

Hyre to tempt in every plase.   *place*
430 Now alle the six that here be,

Wysely to werke, hyr fawor to wynne,
To entyr hyr person be the labor of lechery,   *is the job of*
That she at the last may com to helle.   *So that*
How, how, spiritus malyng—thou wottyst what I mene?   *malign spirit/you know*
435 Cum owt, I sey! Heryst nat what I seye?   *Appear/hear you not*
BAD ANGEL. Syrrys, I obey your covnsell in eche degree;   *every way*
Stryttwaye thethyr woll I passe!   *Straightaway thither*
Speke soft, speke soft, I trotte hyr to tene!   *I hurry to harm her*
I prey the[e] pertly, make no more noyse!   *openly*

[Magdalene Castle, Bethany]

*Her[e] shal alle the Seuyn Dedly Synnys besege the castell tyll
[Mary] agre to go to Jherusalem. Lechery shall entyr the
castell wyth the Bad Angyl, Thus seyyng Lechery:*

440 LECHERY. Heyl, lady most laudabyll of alyauvns!   *alliance*
Heyl, oryent as the sonne in hys reflexite!   *brilliant/sun/shining*
Myche pepul be comfortyd be your benyng afyavuns.   *Many /benign radiance*
Bryter than the bornyd is your bemys of bewte,   *burnished*
Most debonarius wyth your aungelly delycyte!   *gracious/angelic delight*
445 MARY. Qwat personne be ye, that thus me comende?   *What*
LECHERY. Your servant to be, I wold comprehende!   *aspire*

MARY. Your debonarius obedyauns ravyssyt[h] me to   *gracious*
          trankquelyte!
Now, syth ye desyre in eche degree,   *since/in every way*
To receyve yow I have grett delectacyon!   *pleasure*
450 Ye be hartely welcum onto me—
Your tong is so amyabyll, devydyd wyth reson.

LECHERY. Now, good lady, wyll ye me expresse
Why may ther no gladdnes to yow resort?   *come to you*
MARY. For my father I have had grett hevynesse—
455 Whan I remembyr, my mynd waxit[h] mort.   *dead, grief stricken*
LECHERY. Ya, lady, for all that, be of good comfort,
For swych obusyouns may brede myche dysese.   *such abuses/unease*
Swych desepcyouns potyt[h] peynys to exsport;   *to put aside*
Prynt yow in sportys whych best doth yow plese!   *Put yourself in delights*

460 MARY. Forsothe, ye be welcum to myn hawdyens!   *presence*
Ye be my hartys leche!   *healer*
Brother Lazarus, and it be yower plesauns,   *if/pleasure*

And ye, systyr Martha, also, in substawns   *commit*
Thys place I commend onto your governons,
465   And onto God I yow beteche!

LAZARUS. Now, systyr, we shal do your intente,
In thys place to be resydent,
Whyle that ye be absent,
    To kepe this place from wreche!   *ruin*

[Tavern Stage, Jerusalem]

Here takyt[h] Mary hur wey to Jherusalem wyth Luxsurya,
and they shal resort to a tavernere. Thus seyy[n]g the tavernere:

470 TAVERNER. I am a taverner, wytty and wyse,
    That wynys have to sell gret plente!   *wines*
Of all the taverners, I bere the pryse,   *win the prize*
    That be dwellyng wythinne the cete!
Of wynys I have grete plente,
475   Both whyte wynne and red that [is] so cleyre.

Here ys wynne of Mawt and malmeseyn,   *Malt/malmsey*
    Clary wynne, and claret, and other moo;
Wyn of Gyldyr, and of Gallys, that made at the Groine,*
    Wyn of Wyan and Vernage, I seye also—
480   Ther be no bettyr as ferre as ye can goo!

LECHERY. Lo, lady, the[e] comfort and the[e] sokower   *succour*
    Go we ner and take a tast—
Thys shal bryng your sprytys to favor!   *ease your spirits*
    Tavernere, bryng us of the fynnest thou hast!
485 TAVERNER. Here, lady, is wyn, a repast,
To man and woman a good restoratyff.
    Ye shall nat thynk your mony spent in wast—
From stodyys and hevynes it woll yow relyff!   *studies/care/relieve*

MARY. Ywys, ye seye soth, ye grom of blysse!   *Truly/bringer*
490 To me ye be courtes and kynde.   *courteous*

Her[e] shal entyr a galaunt, thus seyyng:

CURIOSITY. Hof, hof, hof! A frysch new galavnt!
    Ware of thryst, ley that adoune!   *Beware*
What? Wene ye, syrrys, that I were a marchant,   *Did you think*

---

478. Guelder: in the Netherlands; Galles: in France; Groine: in Spain; Guyenne/Vernage: in Italy.

Because that I am new com to town?
495 Wyth sum praty tasppysstere wold I fayne rownd! *pretty barmaid/gladly whisper*
I have a shert of reynnys wyth slevys peneawnt, *shirt of Raines/pendant*
A lase of sylke for my lady constant! *lace*
A, how she is bewtefull and ressplendant!

Whan I am from hyre presens, Lord, how I syhe! *sigh*
500 I wol awye sovereyns, and soiettys I dysdeyne! *follow/subjects*
In wyntyr a stomachyr, in somyr non att al; *waistcoat*
My dobelet and my hossys evyr together abyde. *jacket/hose*
I woll, or even, be shavyn for to seme thyng! *before evening/young*
Wyth here ayen the her I love mych pleyyng— *hair against the hair*
505 That makyt[h] me ileyant and lusty in lykyng. *elegant/pleasure*
Thus I lefe in this wor[l]d, I do it for no pryde! *live*

LECHERY. Lady, this man is for yow, as I se can, *can see*
To sett yow [i]n sporttys and talkyng this tyde! *now*
MARY. Cal hym in, tavernere, as ye my love wyll han, *if*
510 And we shall make ful mery yf he wolle abyde!
TAVERNER. How, how, my mastyre Coryossyte!
CURIOSITY. What is your wyll, syr? What wyl ye wyth me?
TAVERNER. Here ar jentyll women dysyore your presens to se, *desiring*
And for to drynk wyth yow thys tyde. *now*

515 CURIOSITY. A, dere dewchesse, my daysyys iee! *duchess/daisy's eye*
Splendaunt of colour, most of femynyte, *Resplendant*
Your sofreyn colourrys set wyth synseryte! *courtly*
Consedere my love into yower alye, *alliance*
Or ellys I am smet wyth peynnys of perplexite! *smitten/pains*

520 MARY. Why, syr, wene ye that I were a kelle? *did you think/where*
CURIOSITY. Nay, prensses, parde, ye be my hertys hele, *princess/heart's healer*
So wold to God ye wold my love fele!

MARY. Qwat cause that ye love me so sodenly? *What*
CURIOSITY. O nedys I must, myn own lady!
525 Your person, itt is so womanly,
I can not refreyn me, swete lelly!

MARY. Syr, curtesy doth it yow lere! *teach*
CURIOSITY. Now, gracyus gost wythowtyn pere, *spirit/equal*
Mych nortur is that ye conne. *Great breeding/you know*
530 But wol yow dawns, my own dere? *dance*
MARY. Syr, I asent in good maner.
Go ye before, I sue yow nere, *follow*
For a man at alle tymys beryt reverens. *needs respect*

CURIOSITY. Now, be my trowth, ye be wyth other ten.   *grieved by something else*
535   Felle a pese, tavernere, let us sen—   *Fill a cup/see*
    Soppys in wynne, how love ye [thos]?
    MARY. As ye don, so doth me.   *do*
    I am ryth glad that met be we—   *right*
    My love in yow gynnyt[h] to close!   *come together*

540   CURIOSITY. Now, derlyng dere, wol yow do be my rede?   *heed my advice*
    We have dronkyn and ete lytyl brede—   *little*
    Wyll we walk to another stede?   *place*
    MARY. Ewyn at your wyl, my dere derlyng!
    Thowe ye wyl go to the wor[l]dys eynd,
545   I wol nevyr from yow wynd,   *wend, go*
    To dye for your sake!   *[Exeunt]*

[World's Stage]

Here shal Mary and the galont avoyd, and the Bad
Angyll goth to the Wor[l]d, the Flych, and the Dylfe,
hus sayyng the Bad Angyl:

BAD ANGEL. A lorges, a lorges, lorddys alle at onys!   *largess/all together*
    Ye have a servant fayur and afyabylle,
    For she is fallyn in ower grogly gromys!   *drunken grasp*
550   Ya, Pryde, callyd Corioste, to hure is ful laudabyll,   *dear*
    And to hure he is most preysseabyll,   *precious*
    For she hath graunttyd hym al hys bonys!   *requests*
    She thynkyt hys person so amyabyll,
    To here syte, he is semelyare than ony kyng in tronys!   *sight/seemlier/thrones*

555   SATAN. A, how I tremyl and trott for these tydyngys!   *tremble and shake*
    She is a soveryn servant that hath hure fet in synne!   *fetched, feet set*
    Go thow agayn and evyr be hur gyde!
    The lavdabyll lyfe of lecherry let hur nevyr lynne,   *give up*
    For of hure al helle shall make reioysseyng!   *rejoicing*

Here goth the bad angyl to Mari agayn.

560   SATAN. Farewell, farewell, ye t[w]o nobyl kyngys this tyde,   *time*
    For hom in hast I wol me dresse!   *go*
    WORLD. Farewell, Satan, prynsse of pryde!
    FLESH. Farewell, sem[l]yest alle sorowys to sesse! *[Exeunt]*   *fair ceaser of sorrow*

[Central Playing Place]

Here shal Satan go hom to hys stage, and Mari shal entyr into
the place alone, save the Bad Angyl, and al the Seven Dedly Synnys
shal be conveyyd into the howse of Symont Leprovs, they shal be   *devils*
arayyd lyke seven dylf, thus kept closse; Mari shal be in   *arbor*
an erbyr,thus seyyng:

MARY. A, God be wyth my valentynys,   *lovers*
565   My byrd swetyng, my lovys so dere!
        For they be bote for a blossum of blysse!   *bought*
        Me mervellyt sore they be nat here,   *I wonder*
        But I woll restyn in this erbyre,   *rest*
        Amons thes bamys precyus of prysse,   *Among/balms/price*
570   Tyll som lovyr wol apere
        That me is wont to halse and kysse.   *inclined/embrace*

        Her[e] shal Mary lye doun and slepe in the erbyre.   *arbor*

        [Simon's Stage]

SIMON. Thys day holly I pot in rememberowns,   *put*
        To solas my gestys to my power;
        I have ordeynnyd a dynere of substawns,   *ordered/feast*
575   My chyff freyndys therwyth to chyre.   *cheer*
        Into the sete I woll apere,   *city/go*
        For my gestys to make porvyawns,   *get provisions*
        For tyme drayt[h] ny to go to dyner,   *draws nigh*
        And my offycyrs be redy wyth ther ordynowns.   *arrangements*

580   So wold to God I myte have aqueyntowns   *I wish I could/acquaintance*
        Of the Profyth of trew perfytnesse,   *perfection*
        To com to my place and porvyowns;   *feast*
        It wold rejoyse my hert in gret gladnesse,
        For the report of hys hye nobyllnesse
585   Rennyt[h] in contreys fer and nere—   *Runs/countries*
        Hys precheyng is of gret perfythnes,   *perfection*
        Of rythwysnesse, and mercy cleyre.   *righteousness*

        [Central Playing Place]

        Here entyr Symont into the place, the Good Angyll thus seyyng to Mary
        [in her Arbor]:

GOOD ANGEL. Woman, woman, why art thou so onstabyll?   *fickle*
        Ful bytterly thys blysse it wol be bowth!   *pleasure/bought*
590   Why art thou ayens God so veryabyll?   *against/inconstant*
        W[h]y, thynkys thou nat God made the[e] of nowth?   *nought*

In syn and sorow thou art browth,　　　　　　　　　*brought*
Fleschly lust is to the[e] full delectabyll;
Salve for thi sowle must be sowth,　　　　　　　　　*sought*
595　And leve thi werkys vayn and veryabyll!

Remembyr, woman, for thi pore pryde,
How thi sowle shal lyyn in helle fyre!
A, remembyr how sorowful itt is to abyde,
Wythowtyn eynd in angure and ir[e]!　　　　*(God's) anger and ire*
600　Remembyr the[e] on mercy, make thi sowle clyre!　　　　*pure*
I am the gost of goodnesse that so wold the[e] gydde.　　　*spirit/guide*

MARY. A, how the speryt of goodnesse hat[h] promtyt me this tyde,　　*now*
And temtyd me wyth tytyll of trew perfythnesse!　　*name/perfection*
Alas, how betternesse in my hert doth abyde!　　　　*bitterness*
605　I am wonddyd wyth werkys of gret dystresse.　　　　*wounded*
A, how pynsynesse potyt[h] me to oppresse,　　*pensiveness/oppresses*
That I have synnyd on every syde!
O Lord, w[h]o shall put me from this peynfulnesse?
A, w[h]oo shal to mercy be my gostly gyde?

610　I shal porsue the Prophett wherso he be,
For he is the welle of perfyth charyte.　　　　　　　*fount*
Be the oyle of mercy he shal me relyff.
Wyth swete bawmys, I wyl sekyn hym this syth,　　*balms/seek/moment*
And sadly folow hys lordshep in eche degre.　　　　　*soberly*

[Central Playing Place: Simon's Stage]

Here shal entyr the Prophet wyth hys desyplys,
thus seyyng Symont Leprus:

615　SIMON. Now ye be welcom, mastyr, most of magnyfycens!
I beseche yow benyngly ye wol be so gracyows　　　　*benignly*
Yf that it be lekyng onto yower hye presens,　　　　*If it please*
Thys daye to com dyne at my hows!

JESUS. Godamercy, Symont, that thou wylt me knowe!　　*recognize me so*
620　I woll entyr thi hows wyth pes and unyte.　　　　*wholeness*
I am glad for to rest ther grace gynnyt[h] grow.　　　*where*
For wythinne thi hows shal rest charyte,
And the bemys of grace shal byn illumynows.
But syth thou wytystsaff a dynere on me,　　　　*since/vouchsafe*
625　Wyth pes and grace I entyr thi hows.

SIMON. I thank yow, mastyr most benyng and gracyus,   *benign*
    That yow wol, of your hye soverente.
To me itt is a joye most speceows,   *special*
    Wythinne my hows that I may yow se.
630 Now syt to the bord, mastyrs alle!   *table*

Her[e] shal Mary folow alonge, wyth this lamentacyon:

MARY. O I, cursyd cayftyff, that myche w[h]o hath wrowth   *woe/wrought*
    Ayens my makar, of mytys most!   *almighty*
I have offendyd hym wyth dede and thowth,   *thought*
    But in hys grace is all my trost,
635   Or ellys I know well I am but lost,

Body and sowle damdpnyd perpetuall!   *damned*
Yet, good Lord of lorddys, my hope [is] perhenuall   *perennial*
    Wyth the[e] to stond in grace and favour to se;
Thow knowyst my hart and thowt in especyal—
640   Therfor, good Lord, aftyr my hart reward me!   *conscience*

Her[e] shal Mary wasche the fett of the prophet wyth
the terrys of hur yys, whypyng hem wyth hur herre,   *wiping/hair*
and than anoynt hym wyth a precyus noyttment.   *ointment*
Jhesus dicit: *speaks*

JESUS. Symond, I thank the[e] speceally
    For this grett r[e]past that here hath be.
But Symond, I telle the[e] fectually,   *earnestly*
    I have thyngys to seyn to the[e].
645 SIMON. Mastyr, qwat your wyll be,   *what*
And it plese yow, I well yow here;   *If*
    Seyth your lykyng onto me,   *what you want*
And al the plesawnt of your mynd and desyyr.   *pleasure*

JESUS. Symond, ther was a man in this present lyf,
650   The wyche had t[w]o dectours well suere,   *debtors surely*
The whych wher pore, and myth make no restoratyf,   *might/repayment*
    But stylle in ther dett ded induour.   *remain*
The on[e] owt hym an hondyrd pense ful suere,   *owed*
    And the other, fefty, so befell the chanse;
655   And becawse he coud nat hys mony recure,   *recover*
They askyd hym foryewnesse, and he foryaf in substans.   *forgiveness*

But, Symont, I pray the, answer me to this sentens:
    Whych of thes t[w]o personnys was most beholddyn to that man?
SIMON. Mastyr, and it plese your hey presens,

660 He that most owt hym, as my reson yef can.	*understand*
JESUS. *Recte iudicasti!* Thou art a wyse man,	*Rightly judged*
And this quessyon hast dempte trewly.	*ruled*
Yff thou in thi concyens remembyr can,	
Ye t[w]o be the dectours that I of specefy.	*You two are*
665 But, Symond, behold this woman in all wyse,	*every way*
How she wyth terys of hyr bettyr wepyng	
She wassheth my fete and dothe me servyse,	*service to*
And anoy[n]tyt[h] hem wyth onymentys, lowly knelyng	
And wyth hur her, fayur and brygth shynnyng,	*her hair/brightly*
670 She wypeth hem agayn wyth good entent.	
But, Symont, syth that I entyrd thi hows,	*since*
To wasshe my fete thou dedyst nat aplye,	
Nor to wype my fete thou were nat so favorus;	*gracious*
Wherfor, in thi conscyens, thou outtyst nat to replye!	*ought*
675 But, woman, I sey to the[e], verely,	
I forgeyffe the[e] thi wrecchednesse,	
And [w]hol in sowle be thou made therby!	
MARY. O, blessyd be thou, Lord of evyrlastyng lyfe,	
And blyssyd be thi berth of that puer vergynne!	*from*
680 Blyssyd be thou, repast contemplatyf,	*holy feast*
Ayens my seknes, helth and medsyn!	*Against*
And for that I have synnyd in the synne of pryde,	*because*
I wol en[h]abyte me wyth humelyte.	*dress myself*
Ayens wrath and envy, I wyll devyde	*Against*
685 Thes[e] fayur vertuys, pacyens and charyte.	
JESUS. Woman, in contryssyon thou art expert,	
And in thi sowle hast inward mythe,	*powers*
That sumtyme were in desert,	*once/dried up*
And from therknesse hast porchasyd lyth.	*darkness/light*
690 Thy feyth hath savyt the[e], and made the[e] bryth!	*bright*
Wherfor I sey to the[e], *"Vade in pace."*	*Depart in peace*
Wyth this word sevyn dyllys shall devoyde from	*devils/go out of*
the woman, and the Bad Angyll entyr into hell wyth thondyr.	
MARY. O thou, gloryus Lord, this rehersyd for my sped,	*undertook/betterment*
Sowle helth at t[h]ys tyme for to recure.	*Soul's/recover*
Lord, for that I was in whanhope, now stond I in dred,	*despair*
695 But that thi gret mercy wyth me may endure.	*Unless*
My thowth thou knewyst wythowttyn ony dowth.	*thought/doubt*

Now may I trost the techeyng of Isaye in scryptur,
W[h]os report of thi nobyllnesse rennyt[h] fere abowt!*   *runs, is widely known*

JESUS. Blyssyd be they at alle tyme
700   That sen me nat, and have me in credens.   *see, belief*
Wyth contryssyon thou hast mad[e] a recumpens   *recompense*
Thi sowle to save from all dystresse.
Beware, and kepe the[e] from alle neclygens,
And aftyr, thou shal be partenyr of my blysse!   *afterwards*

Here devodyt Jhesus wyth hys desipyllys, the Good
Angyll reioysyng of Mawdleyn: *about*

705   GOOD ANGEL. Holy God, hyest of omnipotency,
The astat of good governouns to the[e] I recummend,   *state, upkeep/entrust*
Humbylly besecheyng thyn inper[i]all glorye
In thi devyn vertu us to comprehend.   *include*

And, delectabyll Jhesu, soverreyn sapyens,   *Wisdom*
710   Ower feyth we recummend onto your pur pete,   *entrust/pity*
Most mekely prayyng to your holy aparens,   *appearance*
Illumyn ower ygnorans wyth your devynyte!

Ye be clepyd Redempcyon of sowlys defens,   *called*
Whyche shal ben obscuryd be thi blessyd mortalyte.
715   O *Lux Vera*, gravnt us yower lucense,   *True Light*
That wyth the spryte of errour I nat sedu[c]et be!   *seduced*

And, *Sperytus Alme*, to yow most benyne,   *Bounteous Spirit*
Thre persons in Trenyte, and on[e] God eterne,
Most lowly ower feyth we consyngne,   *humbly/submit*
720   That we may com to your blysse gloryfyed from malyngne,   *malice*
And wyth your gostely bred to fede vs, we desyern.   *spiritual/desire*

[Devil's Stage]

SATAN. A! Owt, owt, and harrow! I am hampord wyth hate!   *crazed*
In hast wyl I set our jugment to se!
Wyth thes[e] betyll-browyd bycheys I am at debate!
725   How, Belfagour and Belzabub! Com up here to me!

Here aperytt[h] t[w]o dyvllys before the mastyr.

697-98. See Isaiah 11:2-4; also perhaps Luke 11:17 and John 4:29. Mary is sometimes identified with
the Samaritan woman in medieval commentaries.

BELZABUB. Here, lord, here! Qwat wol ye?   *What do you want?*
SATAN. The jugment of harlottys here to se,   *knaves*
Settyng in judycyal-lyke astate.

How, thow bad angyll! Apere before my grace!
730 BAD ANGEL. As flat as fox, I falle before your face!
SATAN. Thow theffe! W[h]y hast thou don alle this trespas,   *vagabond/wrong*
To lett yen woman thi bondys breke?
BAD ANGEL. The speryt of grace sore ded hyr smyth,   *did smite her*
And temptyd so sore that ipocryte!
735 SATAN. Ya, thys hard balys on thi bottokkys shall byte!   *bales, torments*
In hast, on the[e] I wol be wreke!   *avenged*

Cum up, ye horsons, and skore awey the yche,   *whip*
And wyth thys panne, ye do hym pycche!   *smear him with*
Cum of, ye harlottys, that yt wer don!   *Come on*

Here shall they serve all the sevyn as they do the frest   *Seven Deadly Sins/first*

740 SATAN. Now have I a part of my desyere!
Goo into this howsse, ye lordeynnys here,   *louts*
And loke ye set yt on afeyere—   *see that/on fire*
And that shall hem awake!

*Here shall the tother deyllys sett the howse on afyere, and make
a sowth, and Mari shall go to Lazar and to Martha.*   *a soot (smoke)*

SATAN. So! Now have we well afrayyd these felons fals!   *fried*
745 They be blasyd, both body and hals!   *burned/neck*
Now to hell lett us synkyn als,
To ower felaws blake!

[Magdalene Castle, Bethany]

MARY. O brother, my hartys consolacyown!
O blessyd in lyff, and solytary!
750 The blyssyd Prophet, my comfortacyown,   *comfort*
He hathe made me clene and delectary,   *sweat*
The wyche was to synne a subiectary.*   *who/subject to sin*
Thys Kyng, Cryste, consedyryd hys creacyown;   *remembered*
I was drynchyn in synne deversarye   *drowned/diverse*
755 Tyll that Lord relevyd me be hys domynacyon.   *power*

752-53. Perhaps an adaptation of Job 10:9.

Grace to me he wold nevyr denye;
Thowe I were nevyr so synful, he seyd, "*Revertere*"!*   *"Turn again"*
I, synful creature, to grace I woll aplye;
The oyle of mercy hath helyd myn infyrmyte.

760   MARTHA. Now worchepyd be that hey name Jhesu,   *high*
      The wyche in Latyn is callyd Savyower!
      Fulfyllyng that word evyn of dewe,   *due, just honor*
         To alle synfull and seke, he is sokour.   *sick/succour*
      LAZARUS. Systyr, ye be welcum onto yower towyre!   *tower*
765   Glad in hart of yower obessyawnse,   *(I am) glad/ obedience*
         Wheyl that I leffe, I wyl serve hym wyth honour,   *While*
      That ye have forsakyn synne and varyawns.   *changeableness*

      MARY. Cryst, that is the lyth and the cler daye,   *light*
         He hath oncuryd the therknesse of the clowdy nyth, *uncovered/darkness/night*
770   Of lyth the lucens and lyth veray,   *light/luminescence/true light*
         W[h]os prechyng to us is a gracyows lyth,   *light*
      Lord, we beseche the[e], as thou art most of myth,   *might*
      Owt of the ded slep of therknesse, defend us aye!   *darkness/ever*
      Gyff us grace evyr to rest in lyth,   *light*
775   In quyet and in pes to serve the[e], nyth and day.   *night*

      Here shall Lazar take hys deth, thus seyyng:

      LAZARUS. A! Help, help, systyrs, for charyte!
         Alas! Dethe is sett at my hart!
      A! Ley on handys! Wher are ye?
         A, I faltyr and falle! I wax alle onquarte!   *unhealthy*
780   A, I bome above, I wax alle swertt!   *buzz in my head/dark*
      A, good Jhesu, thow be my gyde!
         A, no lengar now I reverte!   *return*
      I yeld up the gost, I may natt abyde!

      MARY. O, good brother! Take coumforth and myth,   *strength*
785   And lett non hevynes in yower hart abyde!
      Lett away alle this feyntnesse and fretth,   *fretting*
         And we shal gete yow leches, yower peynys to devyde. *doctors/cut down*

      MARTHA. A, I syth and sorow, and sey, "Alas"!   *sigh*
         Thys sorow ys apoynt to be my confusyon!   *meant*
790   Jentyl systyr, hye we from this place,
      For the Prophe[t] to hym hatt[h] grett delectacyon.   *delight*

---

757. See Canticles 6:13 (and perhaps Ezekiel 33:11).

Good brothere, take somme comfortacyon   *comfort*
For we woll go to seke yow[er] cure.

    [Central Playing Place]

    Here goth Mary and Martha, and mett wyth Jhesus, thus seyyng:

MARY AND MARTHA. O, Lord Jhesu, ower melleflueus swettnesse,
795   Thowe art grettest Lord in glorie!
    Lovyr to the[e], Lord, in all lowlynesse,   *(As a) lover of thee, Lord*
        Comfort thi creatur that to the[e] crye!   *Give comfort to*
        Behold yower lovyr, good Lord, specyally,
    How Lazare lyth seke in grett dystresse.   *is sick*
800   He ys thi lovyr, Lord, suerly!   *surely*
    Onbynd hym, good Lord, of hys hevynesse!   *sorrow*

JESUS. Of all infyrmyte, ther is non[e] to deth.   *like*
    For of all peynnys, that is inpossyble   *(death) is incomprehensible*

    To undyrestond be reson; to know the werke,   *occupations*
805   The joye that is in Jherusallem hevenly,
    Can nevyr be compylyd be counnyng of clerke—   *understood/studying*
        To se the joyys of the Fathyr in glory,
    The joyys of the Sonne whych owth to be magnyfyed,   *ought*
    And of the Therd Person, the Holy Gost, truly,
810   And alle thre but on[e] in heven gloryfyed!

    Now, women that arn in my presens here,   *you women who are*
        Of my wordys take awysement.   *advice*
    Go hom ayen to yower brothyr Lazere—   *again*
        My grace to hym shall be sent.

815   MARY. O, thow gloryus Lord here present,
    We yeld to the[e] salutacyon!
        In ower weyys we be expedyent.   *we will hurry*
    Now, Lord, us defend from trybulacyon!

    [Magdalene Castle, Bethany]

    Here goth Mary and Martha homvard, and Jhesus devodyt.   *exits*

LAZARUS. A! In woo I waltyr as wavys in the wynd!   *woe/am tossed/waves*
820   Awey ys went all my sokour!   *All help is gone*
    Deth, Deth, thou art onkynd!
        A, now brystyt[h] myn hartt! This is a sharp showyr!   *attack*
    Farewell, my systyrs, my bodely helth!

Mortuus est.   *He dies*

MARY. Jhesu, my Lord, be yower sokowre,   *help*
825 And he mott be yower gostys welth!   *May he/spirits*

MILES 1. Goddys grace mott be hys govemour,   *may be*
     In joy evyrlastyng fore to be!
MILES 2. Amonge alle good sowlys, send hym favour,
     As thi powere ys most of dygnyte!

830 MARTHA. Now, syn the chans is fallyn soo,   *since it has happened*
     That deth hath drewyn hym don this day,   *drawn him down*
     We must nedys ower devyrs doo,   *do our duties*
     To the erth to bryng hym wythowt delay.
     MARY. As the use is now, and hath byn aye,   *custom/ever*
835 Wyth wepers to the erth yow hym bryng.   *weepers*
     Alle this must be donne as I yow saye,
     Clad in blake, wythowtyn lesyng.   *black/delay*

MILES 1. Gracyows ladyys of grett honour,
     Thys pepull is com here in yower syth,   *sight*
840 Wepyng and weylyng wyth gret dolour,
     Because of my lordys dethe.

*Here the on[e] knygth make redy the ston, and other
bryng in the wepars, arayyd in blak.*   *weepers*

MILES 1. Now, good fryndys that here be,
     Take up thys body wyth good wyll,
     And ley it in hys sepoltur, semely to se;   *sepulchre, handsomely*
845 Good Lord hym save from alle manyr ille!

*Lay hym in. Here al the pepyll resort to the castell,
thus seyyng Jhesus [in the place]:*

JESUS. Tyme ys comyn of very cognyssyon.   *true knowledge*
     My dyssyplys, goth wyth me
For to fulfyll possybyll peticion;   *grant a plea*
     Go we together into Jude,   *Judaea*
850 There Lazar, my frynd, is he.
Gow we together as chyldyurn of lyth,   *Go/light*
     And, from grevos slepe, saven heym wyll we!   *grievous*

DISCIPLES. Lord, it plese yower myty volunte,   *(if) it/will*
     Thow he slepe, he may be savyd be skyll.   *by*
855 JESUS. That is trew, and be possybilyte;   *it is possible (to revive)*

Therfor, of my deth shew yow I wyll.   *as my own death will show*
My Fathyr, of nemyows charyte,   *exceeding*
Sent me, hys Son, to make redemcyon,
Wyche was conseyvyd be puer verginyte,   *Who/by pure*
860   And so in my mother had cler incarnacyon;
And therfore must I suffyre grevos passyon
Ondyre Pounse Pylat, wyth grett perplexite,
Betyn, bobbyd, skoernyd, crownnyd wyth thorne—   *Beaten, mocked*
Alle this shall be the soferons of my deite.

865   I, therfor, hastely folow me now,   *Aye*
For Lazar is ded, verely to preve;
Whe[r]for I am joyfull, I sey onto yow,
That I knowlege yow therwyth, that ye may it beleve.

[Magdalen Castle]

Here shal Jhesus com wyth hys dissipulys, and on[e]
Jew tellyt[h] Martha:

JEW. A, Martha, Martha! Be full of gladnesse!
870   For the Prophett ys comyng, I sey trewly,
Wyth hys dyssypyllys in grett lowlynesse;
He shall yow comfortt wyth hys mercy.

Here Martha shall ronne ayen Jhesus, thus seyyng: *toward*

MARTHA. A, Lord! Me, sympyl creatur, nat denye,   *do not deny me*
Thow I be wrappyd in wrecchydnesse!
875 Lord, and thou haddyst byn here, verely,   *if*
My brother had natt a byn ded—I know well thysse.   *would not be dead*

Jhesus dicit.   *Jesus speaks*

JESUS. Martha, docctor, onto the I sey,   *daughter, unto*
Thy brother shall reyse agayn!
MARTHA. Yee, Lord, at the last day,
880   That I beleve ful pleyn.

JESUS. I am the resurreccyon of lyfe, that evyr shall reynne,
And whoso belevyt verely in me
Shall have lyfe evyrlastyng, the soth to seyn.   *to speak truly*
Martha, belevyst thow this?
885 MARTHA. Ye, forsoth, the Prynsse of blysch!   *Yea/bliss*
I beleve in Cryst the Son of Sapyens,   *divine Wisdom*

Whyche wythowt eynd ryngne shall he   *will reign without end*
To redemyn us freell from ower iniquite!   *frail creatures*

Here Mary shall falle to Jhesus, thus seyyng Mary: *before*

MARY. O, thou rythewys regent, reynyng in equite,   *righteous*
890   Thou gracyows Lord, thou swete Jhesus!
And thou haddyst byn here, my brothyr alyfe had be!   *If/would be alive*
  Good Lord, myn hertt doth this dyscus!   *contemplate*
JESUS. Wher have ye put hym? Sey me thys.
MARY. In hys mo[nu]ment, Lord, is he.
895 JESUS. To that place ye me wys.   *bring me*
  Thatt grave I desyre to se.

Take of[f] the ston of this monument!

The agrement of grace here shewyn I wyll.   *covenant*

MARTHA. A, Lord, yower preseptt fulfyllyd shall be.   *command*
900   Thys ston I remeve wyth glad chyr.
Gracyows Lord, I aske the mercy!
  Thy wyll mott be fullfyllyd here!   *May your will*

Here shall Martha put of[f] the grave ston.

JESUS. Now, Father, I beseche thyn hey paternyte,   *high*
That my prayour be resowndable to thi Fathyr[h]od in glory,   *resound*
905 To opyn theyn erys to thi Son in humanyte.   *ears*
  Nat only for me, but for thi pepyll, verely,
That they may beleve, and betake to thi mercy.   *bring themselves*
Fathyr, fore them I make supplycacyon!
Gracyows Father, gravnt me my bone!   *boon, prayer*

910 Lazar, Lazer! Com hethyr to me!

Here shall Lazar aryse, trossyd wyth towellys, in a shete.   *trussed*

LAZARUS. A, my Makar, my Savyowr! Blyssyd mott thou be!   *may*
Here men may know thi werkys of wondyre!
Lord, nothy[n]g ys onpossybyll to the[e],
For my body and my sowle was departyd asondyr!   *divided*
915   I shuld a rottytt, as doth the tondyre,   *have rotted/tender*
Fleysch from the bonys a-consumyd away!
  Now is aloft that late was ondyr!   *up/lately/under*

The goodnesse of God hath don for me here,   *done this*
For he is bote of all balys to onbynd,   *boot, remedy/bales, woes*
920   That blyssyd Lord that here ded apere!

Here all the pepull and the Jewys, Mari and Martha, wyth on[e] woys sey
thes[e] wordys: "We beleve in yow, Savyowr, Jhesus, Jhesus, Jhesus!"

JESUS. Of yower good hertys I have advertacyounys,   *signs*
    Wherethorow in sowle, [w]holl made ye be.   *Whereby*
Betwyx yow and me be nevyr varyacyounys,   *divergence*
    Wherfor I sey, "*Vade in pace.*"   *"Depart in peace"*

Here devoydyt[h] Jhesus wyth hys desypyllys;   *exits*
Mary and Martha and Lazare gon hom to the castell, and here
begynnyt[h] [the Kyng of Marcylle] hys bost:

    [King of Marseilles Palace]

925   KING. Avantt! Avant the[e], onworthy wrecchesse!   *Away/wretches*
    Why lowtt ye nat low to my lawdabyll presens,   *bow*
Ye brawlyng breellys and blabyr-lyppyd bycchys,   *rascals*
    Obedyenly to obbey me wythowt offense?   *Obediently*

I am a sofereyn semely that ye se butt seyld!   *handsome sovereign/seldom*
930   Non swyche ondyr sonne, the sothe for to say!   *None such under the sun/truth*
Whanne I fare fresly and fers to the feld,   *freshly/fierce*
    My fomen fle[e] for fer of my fray!   *foes/attack*
Even as an enperower I am [h]onored ay,   *always*

W[h]anne baner gyn to blasse and bemmys gyn to blow,   *banners begin/flap/trumpets*
935   Hed am I heyest of all hethennesse holld!   *I am held Head and Highest*
Both kynggys and cayserys I woll they shall me know,   *caesars/want them to*
    Or ellys they bey the bargayn, that evyr they were so bold!   *buy (pay for)*
    I am Kyng of Marcylle, talys to be told—
Thus I wold it were knowyn ferre and nere!   *want it known*
940   [W]Ho sey contraly, I cast heym in carys cold,   *contrary/cold comfort*
And he shall bey the bargayn wondyr dere!   *make a very expensive purchase*

I have a favorows fode and fresse as the fakown,   *pleasing wife/ fresh/falcon*
    She is full fayur in hyr femynyte;
Whan I loke on this lady, I am losty as the lyon   *lusty*
945   In my syth;   *sight*
       Of delycyte most delycyows,   *sensual delight*
       Of felachyp most felecyows,   *companionship/happy*
       Of alle fodys most favarows—   *wives/pleasing*
       A, my blysse in beuteus brygth!   *bright beauty*

950　QUEEN. O of condycyons, and most onorabyll!　　*all these circumstances*
　　　Lowly I thank yow for this recummendacyon—　　*Humbly/commendation*
　　　The bovnteest and the boldest ondyr baner bryth,　　*most generous/bright*
　　　No creatur so coroscant to my consolacyon!　　*so shines*
　　　Whan the regent be resydent, itt is my refeccyon.　　*King/home/pleasure*
955　Yower dilectabyll dedys devydytt me from dyversyte.　　*keep/inconstancy*
　　　In my person I privyde to put me from polucyon—　　*take care*
　　　To be plesant to yower person, itt is my prosperyte!　　*own pleasure*

　　　KING. Now, Godamercy, berel brytest of bewte!　　*beryl brightest*
　　　Godamercy, ruby rody as the rose!　　*ruddy*
960　Ye be so ple[s]avnt to my pay, ye put me from peyn.　　*liking*
　　　Now, comly knygthys, loke that ye forth dresse　　*bring forth*
　　　Both spycys and wyn here in hast!

　　　Here shall the knygtys gete spycys and wynne, and
　　　here shall entyr a dylle in [h]orebyll aray, thus seyyng:　　*devil*

　　　SATAN. Owt, owt, harrow! I may crye and yelle,
　　　For lost is all ower labor, wherfor I sey alas!
965　For of all holddys that evyr hort, non so as hell!　　*confinements/hurt/so great*
　　　Owur barrys of iron ar all to-brost, stronge gatys of brasse!*　　*burst apart*
　　　The Kyng of Joy entyryd in therat, as bryth as fyrys blase!　　*bright as fires blaze*
　　　For fray of hys ferfull banere, ower felashep　　*battle promised by/fellowship*
　　　fled asondyr!
　　　Whan he towcheyd it wyth hys toukkyng, they brast as ony glase,　　*touching/burst*
970　And rofe asondyr, as it byn wyth thondore!　　*split/as it*

　　　Now ar we thrall that frest wher fre[e],　　*captive/once*
　　　Be the passyon of hys manhede.
　　　O[n] a crosce on hye hangyd was he,
　　　Whych hath dystroyd ower labor and alle ower dede!　　*deeds*
975　He hath lytynnyd lymbo, and to paradyse yede!　　*lightened, emptied/gone*
　　　That wondyrfull worke werkytt us wrake!　　*wrecked us*
　　　Adam and Abram and alle hyre kynred,　　*their*
　　　Owt of ower preson to joy were they take!　　*taken*

　　　All this hath byn wrowth syn Freyday at none!　　*done since/noon*
980　Brostyn do[w]n ower gatys that hangyd were full hye!　　*Broke*
　　　Now is he resyn, hys resurreccyon is don,　　*risen*
　　　And is procedyd into Galelye!
　　　Wyth many a temtacyon we tochyd hym to atrey,　　*enticed/try*
　　　To know whether he was God ore non.
985　Ye[t] for all ower besynes, bleryd is ower eye,　　*business/bleared*

·966. See Psalm 24:7-10.

	For wyth hys wyld werke he hath wonne hem everychon!	*them*
	Now for the tyme to come,	*all time*
	Ther shall non falle to ower chanse,	*to our lot*
	But at hys deleverans,	*Except/release*
990	And weyyd be rythfull balans,	*weighed in the scales of truth*
	And yowyn be rythfull domme.	*judged by righteous judgment*
	I telle yow alle in sum, to helle wyll I gonne!	*in conclusion*

*Here shall entyr the thre Mariis arayyd as chast
women, wyth sygnis of the passyon pryntyd
ypon ther brest, thus seyyng Mawdleyn:*

	MARY. Alas, alas, for that ryall bem!	*royal beam, cross*
	A, this percytt my hartt worst of all!	*pierces*
995	For here he turnyd ayen to the woman of Jerusalem,	*again*
	And for wherynesse lett the crosse falle!	*weariness*
	MARIA JACOBI. Thys sorow is beytterare than ony galle,	*more bitter*
	For here the Jevys spornyd hym to make hym goo,	*struck*
	And they dysspyttyd ther Kyng ryall.	*insulted/royal*
1000	That clyvytt[h] myn hart, and makett me woo.	*cleaves/woeful*

	MARIA SALOME. Yt ys intollerabyll to se or to tell,	
	For ony creature, that stronkg tormentry!	
	O Lord, thou haddyst a mervelows mell!	*amazing strife*
	Yt is to[o] hedyows to dyscry!	*describe*

Al the Maryys wyth one woyce sey this folowyng.

	THREE MARIES. Heylle, gloryows crosse! Thou baryst that Lord on hye,	
1005	Whych be thi mygth deddyst lowly bowe doun,	*might did*
	Mannys sowle from all thraldam to bye,	*captivity/redeem*
	That euyrmore in peyne shold a be [boun],	*would have been bound*
	Be record of Davyt, wyth myld stevyn:	*According to/voice*
1010	*Domine inclina celos tuos, et dessende!**	
	MARY. Now to the monument lett us gon,	*go*
	Wheras ower Lord and Savyower layd was,	*where*
	To anoynt hym, body and bone,	
	To make amendys for ower trespas.	

	MARIA JACOBI. [W]Ho shall putt doun the led of the monument,	*lid*
1015	Thatt we may anoy[n]tt hys gracyus woundys,	
	Wyth hartt and my[n]d to do ower intentt,	
	Wyth precyus bamys, this same stounddys?	*balms/hour*
	MARIA SALOME. Thatt blyssyd body wythin this boundys	

1010. Lord, bow down your heavens, and descend. [Psalms 144:5]

1020 Here was layd wyth rufull monys.
    Nevyr creature was borne upon gronddys   *the ground*
    That mygth sofere so hediows a peyne at onys!   *suffer*

Here shall apere t[w]o angelys in whyte at the grave.

ANGEL 1. Ye women presentt, dredytt yow ryth nowth!   *fear not*
    Jhesus is resun, and is natt here!   *risen*
1025 Loo, here is the place that he was in browth!   *brought into*
    Go, sey to hys dysypyllys and to Petur he shall apere.
ANGEL 2. In Galelye, wythowtyn ony wyre,   *doubt*
    Ther shall ye se hym, lyke as he sayd
    Goo yower way, and take comfortt and chyr,   *cheer*
1030 For that he sayd shall natt be delayyd.

Here shall the Maryys mete wyth Petyr and Jhon.

MARY. O, Petyr and Jhon! We be begylyd!   *have been tricked*
    Ower Lordys body is borne away!
    I am aferd itt is dyffylyd!
    I am so carefull, I wott natt whatt to saye.   *know not*
1035   PETER. Of thes[e] tydynggys gretly I dysmay!   *worry*
    I woll me thethere hye wyth all my myth!   *go/might*
    Now, Lord defend us as he best may!
    Of the sepulture we woll have a syth.   *sight*

JOHN. A, myn inward sowle stondyng in dystresse—
1040   The weche of my body xuld have a gyde—   *which/as a guide*
    For my Lord stondyng in hevynesse,
    Whan I remembyr hys wovndys wyde!

PETER. The sorow and peyne that he ded drye   *pain/did suffer*
    For ower offens and abomynacyon!
1045 And also I forsoke hym in hys turmentry—
    I toke no hede to hys techeyng and exortacyon!

Here Petyr and Jhon go to the sepulcur and the
Maryys folowyng.

PETER. A, now I se and know the sothe!   *truth*
    But, gracyus Lord, be ower protexcyon!—
    Here is nothyng left butt a sudare cloth,   *shroud*
1050   That of thi beryyng shuld make mencyon!   *testify*
    JOHN. I am aferd of wykkytt opressyon!
    Where he is becum, it can natt be devysyd,   *has gone*
    But he seyd aftyr the thrid day he shuld have resurrexyon.

Long beforn, thys was promysyd.
1055 MARY. Alas, I may no lengar abyde,
For dolour and dyssese that in my hartt doth dwell.   *sorrow and sadness*

[Mary goes aside.]

ANGEL 1. Woman, woman, wy wepest thou?
W[h]om sekest thou wyth dolare thus?
MARY. A, Fayn wold I wete, and I wyst how,
1060   W[h]o hath born away my Lord Jhesus!

Hic aparuit Jhesus.   *Here Jesus appears [dressed as a gardener]*

JESUS. Woman, woman, w[h]y syest thow?   *sigh*
W[h]om sekest thou? Tell me this.
MARY. A, good syr, tell me now
Yf thou have born awey my Lord Jhesus,

1065 For I have porposyd in eche degre   *tried in every way*
To have hym wyth me, verely,
The w[h]yche my specyall Lord hath be,   *been*
And I hys lovyr and cause wyll phy.   *undertake*

JESUS. O, O, Mari!

1070 MARY. A! Gracyus Mastyr and Lord, yow it is that I seke!
Lett me anoynt yow wyth this bamys sote!   *sweet balms*
Lord, long hast thou hyd the[e] from my spece,   *spice (balms)*
Butt now wyll I kesse thou for my hartys bote!   *remedy*

JESUS. Towche me natt, Mary! I ded natt asend   *not yet ascent*
1075   To my Father in Deyyte, and onto yowers!   *Deity*
Butt go sey to my brotheryn I wyll pretende   *venture*
To stey to my Father in hev[n]ly towyrs.   *ascend*

MARY. Whan I sye yow fyrst, Lord, verely   *saw*
I wentt ye had byn Symou[n]d the gardener.   *thought*
1080 JESUS. So I am, forsothe, Mary!
Mannys hartt is my gardyn here.
Therin I sow sedys of vertu all the yere.   *seeds*
The fowle wedys and vycys I reynd up be the rote!   *tear up*
Whan that gardyn is watteryd wyth terys clere,
1085 Than spryng vertuus, and smelle full sote.   *Then spring virtues/sweet*

MARY. O, thou dereworthy Emperowere, thou hye devyne!
To me this is a joyfull tydyng,

And onto all pepull that aftyr us shall reyngne,   *live*
Thys knowlege of thi deyyte,
1090 To all pepull that shall obteyne,
And know this be posybyl[y]te.
JESUS. I woll shew to synnars as I do to the[e],   *appear*
Yf they woll wyth vervens of love me seke.   *fervency/seek*
Be stedfast, and I shall evyr wyth the[e] be,
1095 And wyth all tho that to me byn meke!   *those/meek*

Here avoydyt[h] Jhesus sodenly, thus seyyng Mary Magdleyn   *exits*

MARY. O, systyrs, thus the hey and nobyll influentt grace   *high/flowing*
Of my most blessyd Lord Jhesus, Jhesus, Jhesus!
He aperyd onto me at the sepulcur ther I was!   *where*
That hath relevyd my woo, and moryd my blysche!   *woe/established my bliss*
1100 Itt is innumerabyll to expresse,   *too great*
Or for ony tong for to tell,   *tongue*
Of my joye how myche itt is,   *much*
So myche my peynnys itt doth excelle!   *greatly/pains*

MARIA SALOME. Now lett us go to the sette, to ower Lady dere,   *city*
1105 Hyr to shew of hys wellfare,   *tell*
And also to dyssypyllys, that we have syn here—   *what we have seen*
The more yt shall rejoyse them from care!

MARIA JACOBI. Now, systyr Magdleyn, wyth glad chyr!   *cheer*
So wold that good Lord we myth wyth hym mete!   *desires/might*

[Jhesus appears again]

1110 JESUS. To shew desyrows hartys I am full nere,
Women, I apere to yow and sey, *"Ave te!"*   *"Hail to you"*

MARIA SALOME. Now, gracyus Lord, of yowur nymyos charyte—   *great*
Wyth hombyll hartys to thi presens complayne—
Gravntt us thi blyssyng of thi hye deyte,   *high deity*
1115 Gostly ower sowlys for to sosteynne.   *Spiritually*
JESUS. Alle tho byn blyssyd that   *those are blessed who*
sore refreynne.   *endure sorrow*
We blysch yow—Father, and Son, and Holy Gost—   *bless*
All sorow and care to constryne,*   *counter (comfort)*
Be ower powyr of mytys most,

1118. See Matthew 5:3-12, "Blessed are they that mourn, for they shall be comforted" (5:5), and
"Blessed are they that suffer persecution for justice's sake" (5:10), as interpreted in the *Glossa
Ordinaria:* "The peaceful are those who quieten all motions of the soul and subdue them to reason."

1120   *In nomine Patrys ett Felii et Spiritus Sancti, amen!**

Goo ye to my brethryn, and sey to hem ther,   *say*
   That they procede and go into Gallelye,
And ther shall they se me, as I seyd before,
   Bodyly, wyth here carnall yye.   *their bodily eyes*

   Here Jhesus devoydytt[h] ayen.   *exits again*

1125 MARY. O thou gloryus Lord of heven regyon,
   Now blyssyd be thi hye devynyte,
Thatt evyr thow tokest incarnacyon,
   Thus for to vesyte thi pore servantys thre.   *visit*
Thi wyll, gracyows Lord, fulfyllyd shall be
1130 As thou commaundyst us in all thyng.
   Ower gracyows brethryn we woll go se,
Wyth hem to seyn all ower lekeyng.   *tell them our pleasure*

   Here devoyd all the thre Maryys, and the Kyng of Marcyll   *exit*
   shall begynne a sacryfyce.

KING. Now, lorddys and ladyys of grett aprise,   *worth*
   A mater to meve yow is in my memoryall,   *move*
1135 This day to do a sacryfyce
   Wyth multetude of myrth before ower goddys all,   *all our gods*

Wyth preors in aspecyall before hys presens,   *prayers*

Eche creature wyth hartt demure.

QUEEN. To that lord curteys and keynd,
1140 Mahond, that is so mykyll of myth,   *Mohammet/great of might*
Wyth mynstrelly and myrth in mynd,   *music*
   Lett us gon ofer in that hye kyngis syth.   *go offer/sight*

   [Heathen Temple Stage]

   Here shall entyr an hethen prest and hys boye.

PRESBYTER. Now, my clerke Hawkyn, for love of me,
   Loke fast myn awter were arayd!   *make sure my altar*
1145 Goo ryng a bell, t[w]o or thre!
   Lythly, chyld, it be natt delayd   *Quickly/that it*
For here shall be a grett solemnyte.

1120. In the name of the Father and of the Son and of the Holy Ghost, Amen.

Loke, boy, thou do it wyth a brayd!   *haste*
BOY. Whatt, mastyr! Woldyst thou have thi lemman to thi beddys syde?   *wench*
1150   Thow shall abyde tyll my servyse is sayd!

PRESBYTER. Boy! I sey, be Sentt Coppyn,   *by*
        No swyche wordys to the[e] I spake!
BOY. Wether thou ded or natt, the fryst jorny shall be myn,   *did/trip*
        For, be my feyth, thou beryst Wattys pakke!   *Wat's pack (fat)*

1155   But syr, my mastyr, grett Morell,
        Ye have so fellyd yower bylly wyth growell,   *filled/belly/gruel*
        That it growit grett as the dywll of hell   *devil!*
            Onshaply thou art to see!
        Whan women comme to here thi sermon,
1160   Pratyly wyth hem I can houkkyn,   *Prettily*
        Wyth Kyrchon and fayer Maryon—
            They love me bettyr than the[e]!

        I dare sey, and thou shulddys ryde,   *if/ride (sexual)*
        Thi body is so grett and wyde,
1165   That nevyr horse may the[e] abyde,
            Exseptt thou breke hys bakk asovndyre!   *But that*
        PRESBYTER. A, thou lyyst, boy, be the dyvll of hell!
        I pray God, Mahond mott the quell!   *May Mohammet crush you*
        I shall whyp the[e] tyll thi ars shall belle!   *peal*
1170   On thi ars com mych wondyre!

        BOY. A fartt, mastyr, and kysse my grenne!   *groin*
        The dyvll of hell was thi emme!   *thy uncle*
        Loo, mastyrs, of swyche a stokke he cam!
            This kenred is asprongyn late!   *family/widespread lately*
1175   PRESBYTER. Mahovndys blod, precyows knave!   *arrant*
        Stryppys on thi ars thou shall have,   *stripes*
            And rappys on thi pate!   *raps*

        Bete hym. Rex dicitt.   *The King says*

        KING. Now, prystys and clerkys, of this tempyll cler,
            Yower servyse to sey, lett me se.   *watch*
1180   PRESBYTER. A, soveryn lord, we shall don ower devyr.   *duty*
        Boy, a boke anon thou bryng me!
        Now, boy, to my awter I wyll me dresse—   *altar*
            On shall my vestment and myn aray.
        BOY. Now than, the lesson I woll expresse,
1185   Lyke as longytt[h] for the servyse of this day: *As belongs to*

Leccyo mahowndys, viri fortissimi sarasenorum:
Glabriosum ad glvmandum glvmardinorum,
Gormondorum alocorum, stampatinantum cursorum,
Cownthtys fulcatum, congrvryandum tersorum,
1190 *Mursum malgorum, mararayorum,*
Skartum sialporum, fartum cardiculorum,
Slavndri strovmppum, corbolcorum,
Snyguer snagoer werwolfforum
Standgardum lamba beffettorum,
1195 *Strowtum stardy strangolcorum,*
Rygour dagour flapporum,
Castratum raty rybaldorum, *
    Howndys and hoggys, in heggys and hellys,
    Snakys and toddys mott be yower bellys!
1200   Ragnell and Roffyn, and other in the wavys,
    Gravntt yow grace to dye on the galows!

PRESBYTER. Now, lordys and ladyys, lesse and more,   *lower and higher rank*
    Knele all don wyth good devocyon.
Yonge and old, rych and pore,
1205   Do yower oferyng to Sentt Mahownde,
    And ye shall have grett pardon,
    That longytt[h] to this holy place,   *belongs to*
    And receyve ye shall my benesown,   *benison*
And stond in Mahowndys grace.

    Rex dicitt.   *The King says*

1210 KING. Mahownd, thou art of mytys most,   *most mighty*
    In my syth a gloryus gost—   *sight/spirit*
    Thou comfortyst me both in contre and cost,   *inland/coast*
      Wyth thi wesdom and thi wytt,
    For truly, lord, in the[e] is my trost.
1215 Good lord, lett natt my sowle be lost!
    All my cownsell well thou wotst,   *you know*
      Here in thi presens as I sett.

    Thys besawnt of gold, rych and rownd,   *besant, gold coin*
      I ofer ytt for my lady and me,
1220 That thou mayst be ower counfortys in this stownd.   *hour*
    Sweth Mahovnd, remembyr me!   *Sweet*

PRESBYTER. Now, boy, I pray the[e], lett us have a song!
    Ower servyse be note, lett us syng, I say!   *by*

1186-97. Latin gibberish.

Cowff up thi brest, stond natt to long,   *Cough, puff*
1225   Begynne the offyse of this day.
BOY. I home and I hast, I do that I may,   *hum/what*
Wyth mery tune the trebyll to syng.

Syng both.

PRESBYTER. Hold up! The dyvll mote the afray,   *May the devil beat you*
For all owt of rule thou dost me bryng!   *out of tune*

1230 Butt now, syr kyng, quene, and knyth,   *Knight*
Be mery in hartt everychon!   *everyone*
For here may ye se relykys brygth—   *bright*
Mahowndys own nekke bon!   *neckbone*
And ye shall se or ever ye gon,   *see before you go*
1235   Whattsomewer yow betyde,   *whatever happens*
And ye shall kesse all this holy bon,
Mahowndys own yeelyd!   *eyelid*
Ye may have of this grett store;   *value*
And ye knew the cause wherfor,   *If*
1240   Ytt woll make yow blynd for ewyrmore,   *It would*
This same holy bede!

Lorddys and ladyys, old and ynge,   *young*
Golyas so good, to blysse may yow bryng,   *May Goliath*
Mahownd the [holy] and Dragon the dere,   *Holy Mohammet/beloved Dragon*
1245 Wyth Belyall in blysse evyrlastyng,
That ye may ther in joy syng
Before that comly kyng
That is ower god in fere.   *god of all, god of fear*

[Pilate's Court, Jerusalem]

PILATE. Now, ye serjauntys semly, qwat sey ye?   *what say*
1250   Ye be full wetty men in the law.   *wise*
Of the dethe of Jhesu I woll awysyd be—   *advised*
Ower soferyn Sesar the soth must nedys know.   *Caesar must know the truth*

Thys Jhesu was a man of grett vertu,
And many wondyrs in hys tyme he wrowth;   *wrought*
1255 He was put to dethe be cawsys ontru,   *for causes untrue*
Wheche matyr stekytt in my thowth;   *thought*
And ye know well how he was to the erth browth,   *brought*
Wacchyd wyth knygths of grett aray.   *Guarded/knights/display*

	He is resyn agayn, as before he tawth,	*risen/taught*
1260	And Joseph of Baramathye he hath takyn awey.*	*Arimathea/Jesus has taken*

	SARGEANT 1. Soferyn juge, all this is soth that ye sey,	*true*
	But all this must be curyd be sotylte,	*by subtlety*
	And sey how hys dysypyllys stollyn hym away—	
	And this shall be the answer, be the asentt of me!	
1265	SARGEANT 2. So it is most lylly for to be!	*likely*
	Yower covncell is good and commendabyll;	
	So wryte hym a pystyll of specyallte,*	*special letter*
	And that for us shall be most prophytabyll.	

	PILATE. Now, masengyr, in hast hether thou com!	*messenger*
1270	On masage thou mvst, wyth ower wrytyng,	*on a message trip*
	To the soferyn emperower of Rome.	
	But fryst thou shall go to Herodes the kyng,	*first*
	And sey how that I send hym knowyng	*knowledge*
	Of Crystys deth, how it hath byn wrowth.	*wrought*
1275	I charge the[e] make no lettyng,	*delay*
	Tyll this lettyr to the emperower be browth!	*brought*

	NUNCIUS. My lord, in hast yower masage to spede	
	Onto tho lordys of ryall renown,	*royal*
	Dowth ye nat, my lord, it shall be don indede!	*Doubt*
1280	Now hens woll I fast owt of this town!	*hence*

[Herod's Court]

Her[e] goth the masengyr to Herodes.

	NUNCIUS. Heyll, soferyn kyng ondyr crown!	
	The prynsys of the law recummende to yower heynesse,	*commend themselves*
	And sendytt[h] yow tydyngys of Crystys passyon,	
	As in this wrytyng doth expresse.	

	HEROD. A, be my trowth, now am I full of blys!	
1285	Thes[e] be mery tydyngys that they have thus don!	
	Now certys I am glad of this,	
	For now ar we frendys that afore wher fon.	*were foes*
	Hold a reward, masengyr, that thow were gon,	*Take/gone*
1290	And recummend me to my soferens grace.	*commend/sovereign's*

1260. Another of Pilate's "wondyrs." In the Gospel of Nicodemus (Chapter 15) Jesus appears to Joseph after the resurrection and takes him to see the empty tomb; afterwards he instructs him to remain in his home for forty days.

1267. For the special epistle see the Gospel of Nicodemus (Chapter 28).

Shew hym I woll be as stedfast as ston,
Ferr and nere, and in every place!

[Emporer Tiberius Caesar's Court, Rome]

Here goth the masengyr to the emperower.

NUNCIUS. Heyll be yow, sofereyn, settyng in solas! *comfort*
Heyll, worthy wythowtyn pere! *peer*
1295 Heyll, goodly to grauntt all grace!
Heyll, emperower of the word, ferr and nere!

Soferyn, and it plese yower hye empyre, *if/highness*
I have browth yow wrytyng of grett aprise, *brought/worth*
Wyche shall be pleseyng to yower desyre,
1300 From Pylatt, yower hye justyce.
He sentt yow word wyth lowly intentt; *humble*
In ewery place he kepytt[h] yower cummaundement, *(That) in every place*
As he is bovnd be hys ofyce.

IMPERATOR. A, welcum, mesengyr of grett pleseauns!
1305 Thi wrytyng anon lett me se!
My juggys, anon gyffe atendans, *judges, now attend*
To ondyrstond whatt this wrytyng may be,
Wethyr it be good, are ony deversyte, *or something else*
Or ellys natt for myn awayll— *good*
1310 Declare me this in all the hast!

PROVOST. Syr, the sentens we woll dyscus, *meaning*
And it plese yower hye exseleyns; *If*
The intentt of this pystull is thus: *letter*
Pylatt recummendytt[h] to yower presens, *commends himself*
1315 And of a prophett is the sentens, writing
Whos name was callyd Jhesus.
He is putt to dethe wyth vyolens,
For he chalyngyd to be kyng of Jewys. *claimed*

Therfor he was crucyfyed to ded,
1320 And syn was beryyd, as they thowth reson. *since then/thought right*
Also, he cleymyd hymsylf Son of the Godhed!
The therd nygth he was stollyn away wyth treson,
Wyth hys desypyllys that to hym had dyleccyon, *By/devotion*
So wyth hym away they yode. *went*
1325 I merveyll how they ded wyth the bodyys corupcyon— *did (it)*
I trow they wer fed wyth a froward fode! *imagine/perverse food*

IMPERATOR. Crafty was ther connyng, the soth for to seyn!

Thys pystyll I wyll kepe wyth me yff I can,   *letter*
Also I wyll have cronekyllyd the yere and the reynne,   *chronicled*
1330   That nevyr shall be forgott, whoso loke theron.

Masengyre, owt of this town wyth a rage!   *haste*
Hold this gold to thi wage,   *Take*
       Mery for to make!
NUNCIUS. Farewell, my lord of grett renown,
1335   For owt of town my way I take.

[Central Playing Place]

Her[e] entyr Mawdleyn wyth hyr dysypyll, thus seyyng:

MARY. A, now I remembyr my Lord that put was to ded
       Wyth the Jewys, wythowttyn gyltt or treson!   *By*
The therd nygth he ros be the myth of hys Godhed;   *night*
       Vpon the Sonday had hys gloryus resurrexcyon,
1340   And now is the tyme past of hys gloryus asencyon;
       He steyyd to hevyn, and ther he is kyng.   *rose*
       A! Hys grett kendnesse may natt fro my mencyon!   *does not leave my memory*
       Of alle maner tonggys he yaf us knowyng,   *tongues, languages*

For to undyrstond every langwage.
1345 Now have the dysypyllys take ther passage   *taken*
       To dyvers contreys her[e] and yondyr,
       To prech and teche of hys hye damage—   *injury, Passion*
       Full ferr ar my brothyrn departyd asondyr.

Her[e] shall hevyn opyn, and Jhesus shall shew [hymself].

JESUS. O, the onclypsyd sonne, tempyll of Salamon!   *uneclipsed sun (Mary)*
1350   In the mone I restyd, that nevyr chonggyd goodnesse!   *moon/changed*
       In the shep of Noee, fles of Judeon,   *ship/Noah, fleece of Gideon*
       She was my tapyrnakyll of grett nobyllnesse,   *tabernacle*
       She was the paleys of Phebus brygthnesse,   *palace/Phoebus'*
       She was the wessell of puere clennesse,
1355 Wher my Godhed yaff my manhod myth;   *gave/might*

My blyssyd mother, of demvre femynyte,
       For mankynd, the feynddys defens,   *defense against fiends*
       Quewne of Jherusalem, that hevenly cete,   *city*
       Empresse of hell, to make resystens.   *resistance against hell*
1360   She is the precyus pyn[e], full of ensens,   *incense*
       The precyus synamvyr, the body thorow to seche.   *cinnabar/purify*
       She is the muske ayens the hertys of vyolens,   *medicine against spasms*

The jentyll jelopher ayens the cardyakyllys wrech. *gillyflower against heart pain*

The goodnesse of my mothere no tong can expresse,   *tongue*
1365 Nere no clerke of hyre, hyre joyys can wryth. *Nor can a clerk write of*
   Butt now of my servantt I remembyr the kendnesse; *servant (Magdalene)*
    Wyth hevenly masage I cast me to vesyte;   *intend to*
    Raphaell, myn angell in my syte,
   To Mary Mavdleyn decende in a whyle,
1370 Byd here passe the se be my myth,   *cross the sea/might*
   And sey she shall converte the land of Marcyll.   *Marseilles*

ANGEL. O gloryus Lord, I woll resortt   *go*
   To shew your servant of yower grace.
   She shall labor for that londys comfortt,
1375 From hevynesse them to porchasse.   *show/redeem*

   Tunc decendet angelus.   *Then the Angel descends*

   Abasse the[e] noutt, Mary, in this place!   *Be not abashed*
   Ower Lordys preceptt thou must fullfyll.
    To passe the see in shortt space,   *time*
   Onto the lond of Marcyll.

1380 Kyng and quene converte shall ye,
    And byn amyttyd as an holy apostylesse.   *be admitted*
   Alle the lond shall be techyd alonly be the[e],
    Goddys lawys onto hem ye shall expresse.
    Therfore hast yow forth wyth gladnesse,   *go forth*
1385 Goddys commau[n]ddement for to fullfylle.

MARY. He that from my person seven dewllys mad[e] to fle,
   Be vertu of hym alle thyng was wrowth;   *everything was made*
   To seke thoys pepyll I woll rydy be.   *ready*
   As thou hast commaunddytt, in vertu they shall be browth.   *brought*

1390 Wyth thi grace, good Lord in Deite,
   Now to the see I wyll me hy,   *hie*
   Sum sheppyng to asspy.
   Now spede me, Lord in eternall glory!
   Now be my spede, allmyty Trenite!

   Here shall entyre a shyp wyth a mery song.

1395 SHIPMAN. Stryke! Stryke! Lett fall an ankyr to grownd!
   Her[e] is a fayer haven to se!
   Connyngly in, loke that ye sownd!   *sound the depth*

I hope good harbarow have shal wee! *harbor*

Loke that we have drynke, boy thou!
1400 BOY. I may natt, for slep, I make God a vow! *for I'm sleepy*

Thou shall abyde ytte, and thou were my syere! *wait even if the/father*
SHIPMAN. Why, boy, we are rydy to go to dynere!
    Shall we no mete have?
BOY. Natt for me, be of good chyr,
1405   Thowe ye be forhongord tyll ye rave, *Though/so hungry*
        I tell yow plenly beforn!
      For swyche a cramp on me sett is, *such/has beset*
      I am a poynt to fare the worse. *at a point*
      I ly and wryng tyll I pysse, *hurt*
1410   And am a poyntt to be forlorn! *at a point*

SHIPMAN. Now, boy, whatt woll the[e] this seyll? *what do you want?*
BOY. Nothyng butt a fayer damsell!
    She shold help me, I know it well,
      Ar ellys I may rue the tyme that I was born! *Or*
1415 SHIPMAN. Be my trowth, syr boye, ye shal be sped! *helped*
    I wyll hyr bryng onto yower bed!
    Now shall thou lern a damsell to wed— *a whip*
      She wyll nat kysse the[e] on skorn! *in scorn*

Bete hym.

BOY. A skorn! No, no, I fynd it hernest! *earnest*
1420 The dewlle of hell motte the[e] brest, *devil/might burst you*
    For all my corage is now cast!
      Alasse! I am forlorn!
MARY. Mastyr of the shepe, a word wyth the[e]! *ship*
SHIPMAN. All redy, fayer woman! Whatt wol ye?
1425 MARY. Of whense is thys shep? Tell ye me,
      And yf ye seyle wythin a whyle.
SHIPMAN. We woll seyle this same day,
    Yf the wynd be to ower pay.
    This shep that I of sey, *speak of*
1430   Is of the lond of Marcyll. *bound for*

MARY. Syr, may I natt wyth yow sayle?
    And ye shall have for yower awayle. *shall be paid*
SHIPMAN. Of sheppyng ye shall natt faylle,
    For us the wynd is good and saffe.

[Ship sails.]

1435	Yond ther is the lond of Tork[y]e	*Turkey*
	I wher full loth for to lye!	*would be*
	Yendyr is the lond of Satyllye—	*Attalia (Asia Minor)*
	Of this cors we thar nat abaffe.	*On this course/do not go*

Now shall the shepmen syng.

	SHIPMEN. Stryk! Beware of sond!	*sand*
1440	Cast a led and in us gyde!	
	Of Marcyll this is the kynggys lond.	
	Go a lond, thow fayer woman, this tyde,	*land/time*
	To the kynggys place. Yondyr may ye se.	

[Mary goes ashore.]

	BOY. Sett of[f]! Sett of[f] from lond!
1445	All redy, mastyr, at thyn hand!

Her[e] goth the shep owt of the place.

[King of Marseilles' Palace]

	MARY. O Jhesu, thi mellyfluos name	
	Mott be worcheppyd wyth reverens!	*Should*
	Lord, gravnt me vyctore ayens the fyndys flame,	*against/fiend's*
	And yn thi lawys gyf this pepyll credens!	*these people faith*
1450	I wyll resortt be grett convenyens;	*go with speed*
	On hys presens I wyll draw nere, his (King's)	
	Of my Lordys lawys to she[w] the sentens,	*meaning*
	Bothe of hys Godhed and of hys powere.	

Here shall Mary entyr before the kyng.

	MARY. Now, the hye Kyng Crist, mannys redempcyon,	
1455	Mote save yow, syr kyng, regnyng in equite,	*May he*
	And mote gydde yow the [way] toward sauasyon.	*may he guide/salvation*
	Jhesu, the Son of the mythty Trenite,	*mighty*
	That was, and is, and evyr shall be,	
	For mannys sowle the reformacyon,	
1460	In hys name, lord, I beseche the[e],	
	Wythin thi lond to have my mancyon.	

	KING. Jhesu? Jhesu? Qwat deylle is hym that?	*What devil*
	I defye the[e] and thyn apenyon!	*opinion*
	Thow false lordeyn, I shal fell the[e] flatt!	*scoundrel*

1465   Who made the[e] so hardy to make swych rebon?   *such reply*
    MARY. Syr, I com natt to the[e] for no decepcyon,
    But that good Lord Crist hether me compassyd.   *brought*
        To receyve hys name, itt is yower refeccyon,   *(spiritual) refreshment*
    And thi forme of mysbele[f] be hym may be losyd!   *banished*

1470 KING. And whatt is that lord that thow speke of her[e]?
    MARY. *Id est Salvator*, yf thow wyll lere,   *It is the Saviour/learn*
    The Secunde Person, that hell ded conquare,   *did conquer*

    And the Son of the Father in Trenyte!
    KING. And of whatt powyr is that God that ye reherse to me?
1475 MARY. He mad[e] hevyn and erth, lond and see,
    And all this he mad[e] of nowthe!
    KING. Woman, I pray the[e], answer me!
    Whatt mad God at the fyrst begynnyng?
    Thys processe ondyrstond wol we,
1480 That wold I lerne; itt is my plesyng!

    MARY. Syr, I wyll declare al and sum,
    What from God fryst ded procede.
    He seyd, '*In principio erat verbum*',   *In the beginning was the Word*
    And wyth that he provyd hys grett Godhed!
1485 He mad[e] heven for ower spede,   *aid*
    Wheras he sytth in tronys hyee;   *high thrones*
    Hys mynystyrs next, as he sawe nede,
    Hys angelus and archangyllys all the compeny.

    Upon the fryst day God mad[e] all this,
1490 As it was plesyng to hys intent.
    On the Munday, he wold natt mys
        To make sonne, mone, and sterrys, and the fyrmament,
    The sonne to begynne hys cors in the oryent,   *course/east*
    And evyr labor wythowtyn werynesse,   *ever to work*
1495 And kepytt[h] hys cours into the occedentt.   *west*

    The Twysday, as I ondyrstond this,
        Grett grace for us he gan to incresse.
    That day he satt upon watyris,
        As was lykyng to hys goodnesse,   *pleasing*
1500 As holy wrytt berytt[h] wettnesse.
    That tyme he made both see and lond,
        All that werke of grett nobyllnesse,
    As it was plesyng to hys gracyus sond.   *dispensation*

    On the Weddysday, ower Lord of mythe   *might*

1505   Made more at hys plesyng:
      Fysche in flod, and fowle in flyth—
      And all this was for ower hellpyng.
      On the Thorsday, that nobyll Kyng
      Mad[e] dyverse bestys, grett and smale.
1510   He yaff hem erth to ther fedyng,   *gave the earth to them*
      And bad hem cressyn be hylle and dale.   *increase*

      And on the Fryday God mad[e] man,
      As it plesett hys hynesse most,
      Aftyr hys own semelytude than,   *In his own likeness*
1515   And yaf hem lyfe of the Holy Gost.   *by means of*

      O[n] the Satyrday, as I tell can,
      All hys werkys he gan to blysse.
      He bad them multyply and incresse than,
      As it was plesyng to hys worthynesse.

1520 And on the Sonday, he gan rest take,
      As skryptur declarytt pleyn,
      That al shold reverens make
        To hyr Makar that hem doth susteyn   *their/who sustains them*
          Upon the Sonday to leven in hys servyse,   *believe*
1525   And hym alonly to serve, I tell yow pleyn.

      KING. Herke, woman, thow hast many resonnys grett!
      I thyngk, onto my goddys aperteynyng they beth!   *they pertain*
      But thou make me answer so[o]n, I shall the[e] frett,   *Unless/torture*
      And cut the tong owt of thi hed!

1530 MARY. Syr, yf I seyd amys, I woll retur[n] agayn.   *repeat*
      Leve yower encomberowns of perturbacyon,   *Leave the source of your troubles*
      And lett me know what yower goddys byn,   *be*
      And how they may save us from trevbelacyon.   *tribulation*

      KING. Hens to the tempyll that we ware,   *Hence/go*
1535   And ther shall thow se a solom syth.   *sight*
      Com on all, both lesse and more,   *low and high rank*
      Thys day to se my goddys myth!   *might*

      [Temple Stage]

      Here goth the kyng wyth all hys atendavnt to the tempyll.

KING. Loke now, qwatt seyyst thow be this syth? *What/sight*
How pleseavnttly they stond, se thow how?
1540 Lord, I besech thi grett myth, *might*
Speke to this Chrisetyn that here sestt thou! *you see*
Speke, god lord, speke! Se how I do bow!
Herke, thou pryst! Qwat menytt all this? *priest/What means*
What? Speke, good lord, speke! What eylytt[h] the[e] now? *ails*
1545 Speke, as thow artt bote of all blysse! *boot (aid to)*

PRESBYTER. Lord, he woll natt speke whyle Chriseten here is!
MARY. Syr kyng, and it plese yower gentyllnesse, *if*
Gyff me lycens my prayors to make
Onto my God in heven blysch, *heaven's bliss*
1550 Sum merakyll to shewyn for yower sake!
KING. Pray thi fylle tyll then knees ake! *until*

MARY. *Dominus, illuminacio mea, quem timebo?*
Dominus, protecctor vite mee, a quo trepedabo?[*]

Here shal the mament tremyll and quake. *Mohammet*

MARY. Now, Lord of lordys, to thi blyssyd name sanctificatt, *sanctified*
1555 Most mekely my feyth I recummend. *entrust*
Pott do[w]n the pryd of mamentys violatt! *Destroy/profane idols*
Lord, to thi lovyr thi goodnesse descend! *send down*
Lett natt ther pryd to thi poste pretend, *them not pretend to your power*
Wheras is rehersyd thi hye name Jhesus! *Wherever*
1560 Good Lord, my preor I feythfully send! *prayer*
Lord, thi rythwysnesse here dyscus! *righteousness/reveal*

Here shall comme a clowd from heven, and sett the
tempyl on afyer, and the pryst and the cler[k] shall synke,
and the kyng gothe hom, thus seyyng:

KING. A! Owt! For angur I am thus deludyd!
I wyll bewreke my cruell tene! *avenge/injury*
Alas, wythin mysylfe I am concludytt! *at wit's end*
1565 Thou woman, comme hether and wete whatt I mene! *learn*
My wyff and I together many yerys have byn,
And nevyr myth be conceyvyd wyth chyld; *might*
Yf thou for this canst fynd a mene, *means*
I wyll abey thi God, and to hym be meke and myld.

1552-53. The Lord is my light [and my salvation]; whom shall I fear? The Lord is the protector of my life; of whom shall I be afraid? [Psalms 27:1]

1570 MARY. Now, syr, syn thou seyst so,   *since*
          To my Lord I pr[a]ye wyth reythfull bone.   *rightful prayer*
          Beleve in hym, and in no mo,   *others*
          And I hope she shall be conceyvyd sone.
          KING. Awoyd, awoyd! I wax all seke!   *sick*
1575   I wyll to bed this same tyde!   *right away*
          I am so vexyd wyth yen sueke,   *illness*
          That hath nere to deth me dyth!   *nearly done*

          Here the kyng goth to bed in hast, and Mary goth
          into an old logge wythowt the gate, thus seyyng: *lodge, hut/outside*

          [The Old Lodge Stage]

          MARY. Now, Cryst, my creatur, me conserve and kepe,   *creator/save*
          That I be natt confunddyd wyth this reddure!   *ordeal*
1580   For hungore and thurst, to the[e] I wepe!
          Lord, demene me wyth mesuer!   *treat/moderately*
          As thou savydyst Daniell from the lyounys rigur,*   *lions'*
          Be Abacuk thi masengyre, relevyd wyth sustynovns,   *By Habakkuk/relieved*
          Good Lord, so hellpe me and sokore,   *succour me*
1585   Lord, as itt is thi hye pleseawns!   *pleasure*

          JESUS. My grace shall grow, and do[w]n decend
          To Mary my lovyr, that to me doth call,
          Hyr ass[t]att for to amend.   *state (condition)*
          She shall be relevyd wyth sustinons corporall.
1590   Now, awngelys, dyssend to hyr in especyall,
          And lede hyr to the prynssys chambyr ryth.   *right*
          Bed hyre axke of hys good be weyys pacyfycal.
          And goo yow before hyr wyth reverent lyth!   *light*

          ANGEL 1. Blyssyd Lord, in thi syth   *sight*
1595   We dyssend onto Mary.
          ANGEL 2. We dyssend from yower blysse bryth—   *bright*
          Onto yower cummaundement we aplye.

          Tunc dissenditt angelus. Primus dyxit.   *Then the angels descend; the first says:*

          ANGEL 1. Mary, ower Lord wyll comfortt yow send!
          He bad[e], to the kyng ye shuld take the waye,
1600   Hym to asay, yf he woll condesend,   *To test him/assent*
          As he is slepyng, hem to asaye.
          ANGEL 2. Byd hym releve yow, to Goddys pay,   *help/to offer to God*

1582. See Daniel 14:32-38 (Vulgate), an apocryphal addition to the book of Daniel.

And we shal go before yow wyth solem lyth;   *light*
 In a mentyll of whyte shall be ower araye.   *mantle/dress*
1605 The dorys shall opyn ayens us be ryth.

MARY. O gracyus God, now I undyrstond!
 Thys clothyng of whyte is tokenyng of mekenesse.
 Now, gracyus Lord, I woll natt wond,   *refuse*
 Yower preseptt to obbey wyth lowlynesse.   *humility*

 Here goth Mary, wyth the angelys before hyre, to
 he kynggys bed, wyth lythys beryng, thus seyyng Mary: *bearing lights*

 [King of Marseilles Palace]

1610 MARY. Thow froward kyng, trobelows and wood, *uncivil/troublous/mad*
 That hast at thi wyll all wor[l]ddys wele,   *wealth*
 Departe wyth me wyth sum of thi good, *give me/goods (wealth)*
 That am in hongor, threst, and chelle;   *cold*
 God hath the[e] sent warnyngys felle!   *many*
1615 I rede the[e], torne, and amend thi mood!   *turn (convert)*
 Beware of thi lewdnesse, for thi own hele! *sinfulness/health*
 And thow, qwen, turne from thi good!   *goods*

 Here Mari voydyt[h], and the angyll and Mary chongg *exits/change*
 hyr clotheyng, thus seyyng the kyng:

KING. A, this day is com! I am mery and glad!
 The son is up and shynyth bryth!   *brightly*
1620 A mervelows shewyng in my slep I had,   *appearance*
 That sore me trobelyd this same nyth—   *night*
 A fayer woman I saw in my syth,   *sight*
 All in whyte was she cladd;
 Led she was wyth an angyll bryth,   *by/bright*
1625 To me she spake wyth wordys sad.

QUEEN. I trow from Good that they were sentt!
 In ower hartys we may have dowte.
 I wentt ower chambyr sholld a brentt, *thought/have burned*
 For the lyth that ther was all abowth!   *light*
1630 To us she spake wordys of dred,   *warning*
 That we shuld help them that have nede,
 Wyth ower godys, so God ded byd,   *did bid*
 I tell yow wythowtyn dowthe.   *doubt*

KING. Now, semely wyff, ye sey ryth well.   *right*
1635 A knyth, anon, wythowtyn delay!

Now, as thou hast byn trew as stylle,   *steel*
  Goo fett that woman before me this daye!   *fetch*
MILES 1. My sovereyn lord, I take the waye!
She shall com at [y]ower pleseawns.   *pleasure*
1640   Yower soveryn wyll I wyll goo saye—   *Kingly wish/announce*
Itt is almesse hyr to awawns!   *alms (charity)/advance*

Thunc transit miles ad Mariam.   Then the soldier crosses to Mary

[Mary's Arbor]

MILES 1. Spe[e]d well, good woman! I am to the[e] sentt,
  Yow for to speke wyth the kyng.   *For you to*
MARY. Gladly, syr, at hys intentt,
1645   I comme at hys own pleseyng!

Tunc transytt Maria ad regem.   Then Mary crosses to the King

[King of Marseilles Palace]

MARY. The mythe and the powyre of the heye Trenyte,   *might*
  The wysdom of the Son, mott governe yow in ryth!   *may they/the right*
The Holy Gost mott wyth yow be!   *May*
What is yowre wyll? Sey me in sythe!   *straightaway*
1650 KING. Thow fayer woman, itt is my delyth,   *delight*
The[e] to refresch is myn intentt,
  Wyth mete and mony, and clothys for the nyth,   *food/night*
And wyth swych grace as God hathe me lentt.   *such*

MARY. Than fullfylle ye Goddys cummaundement,
1655   Pore folk in mysch[ef] them to susteyn!   *trouble*
KING. Now, blyssyd woman, reherse here presentt,   *recite*
  The joyys of yower Lord in heven.

MARY. A, blyssyd the ower, and blyssyd be the tyme,   *hour*
  That to Goddys lawys ye wyll gyff credens!
1660 To yowerselfe ye make a glad pryme   *beginning*
  Ayens the fenddys malycyows violens!   *Against the fiends'*
From God above comit[h] the influens,
Be the Holy Gost into thi brest sentt down,
  For to restore thi offens,   *make amends for*
1665 Thi sowle to bryng to evyrlastyng salvacyon.
Thy wyffe, she is grett wyth chyld!
Lyke as thou desyerst, thou hast thi bone!   *prayer is answered*

QUEEN. A, ye! I fel ytt ster in my wombe up and down!
    I am glad I have the[e] in presens!
1670 O blyssyd womman, rote of ower savacyon,   *root/salvation*
    Thi God woll I worshep wyth dew reverens!
KING. Now, fayer womman, sey me the sentens,   *tell*
    I beseche the, whatt is thi name?
MARY. Syr, ayens that I make no resystens!
1675 Mary Maudleyn, wythowtyn blame.

KING. O blyssyd Mary, ryth well is me,
    That ever I have abedyn this daye!   *lived until*
Now thanke I thi God, and specyally the[e],
    And so shall I do whyle I leve may.   *may live*
1680 MARY. Ye shall thankytt Petyr, my mastyr, wythowt delay!
He is thi frend, stedfast and cler.
    To allmythy God he halp me pray,   *helped*
And he shall crestyn yow from the fynddys powyr,   *fiends'*

In the syth of God an hye!   *sight/high*

1685 KING. Now, suerly ye answer me to my pay.   *surely/repaid my gifts*
    I am ryth glad of this tyddyngys!
Butt, Mary, in all my goodys I sese yow this day,   *give you*
    For to byn at yower gydyng,   *be*
    And them to rewlyn at yower pleseyng   *And rule them*
1690 Tyll that I comme hom agayn!
    I wyll axke of yow neythyr lond nore rekynyng,
But I here delevyr yow powere pleyn!   *full power*

QUEEN. Now, worshepfull lord, of a bone I yow pray,   *a favor*
    And it be pleseyng to yower hye dygnite.   *If*
1695 KING. Madam, yower dysyere onto me say.
    What bone is that ye desyere of me?
QUEEN. Now, worshepfull sovereyn, in eche degre,   *favor*
That I may wyth yow goo,   *every way*
    A Crestyn womman made to be.
1700   Gracyus lord, it may be soo.

KING. Alas! The wyttys of wommen, how they byn wylld!
    And therof fallytt many a chanse!   *they seize upon many situations*
Why desyer it yow, and ar wyth chyld?

QUEEN. A, my sovereyn, I am knett in care,   *bound up by*
1705   But ye consedyr now that I crave,   *Unless/that which*
For all the lovys that ever ware,   *were*
    Behynd yow that ye me nat leve!   *Don't leave me behind*

KING. Wyff, syn that ye woll take this wey of pryse,   *put it that way*
    Therto can I no more seyn.
1710 Now Jhesu be ower gyd, that is hye justyce,
    And this blyssyd womman, Mary Maugleyn!

MARY. Syth ye ar consentyd to that dede,   *Since*
    The blyssyng of God gyff to yow wyll I.
    He shall save yow from all dred,
1715   *In nomine Patrys, et Filij, et Spiritus Sancti. Amen!**

    Ett tunc navis venit in placeam, et navta dicit:*

    [The Boat Pageant]

SHIPMAN. Loke forth, Grobbe, my knave,
    And tell me qwat tydyngys thou have,   *what*
    And yf thou aspye ony lond.
BOY. Into the shrowdys I woll me hye!   *rigging/hasten*
1720 Be my fythe, a castell I aspye,   *faith*
    And as I ondyrstond!
SHIPMAN. Sett therwyth, yf we mown,   *Set the course/if we can*
    For I wott itt is a havyn town   *know/harbor*
    That stondyt[h] upon a strond.   *shore*

    Ett tuncc transitt rex ad navem, et dicit rex:*

1725 KING. How, good man, of whens is that shep?
    I pray the[e], syr, tell thou me.
SHIPMAN. Syr, as for that, I take no kepe!   *pay no attention*
    For qwat cause enquire ye?   *what*
KING. For causys of nede, seyle wold we,   *we want to sail*
1730 Ryth fayn we wold ovyr byn!   *Gladly would we be across*
SHIPMAN. Yee, butt me thynkytt[h], so mote I the[e],   *if I might say*
    So hastely to passe, yower spendyng is thyn!   *quickly to take passage*

    I trow, be my lyfe,   *might suspect*
    Thou hast stollyn sum mannys wyffe!
1735   Thou woldyst lede hyr owt of lond!
    Neveretheles, so God me save,
    Lett se whatt I shall have,   *show me*
    Or ellys I woll nat wend!   *go*

KING. Ten marke I wyll the[e] gyff,

1715. In the name of the Father and the Son and the Holy Spirit. Amen.
1715 s.d. And then the ship comes into the place and the sailor says:
1724 s.d. And then the King crosses to the ship, and the King says:

1740 Yf thou wylt set me up at the cleyff — *let me off at the headland*

In the Holy Lond!
SHIPMAN. Set of[f], boy, into the flod! — *sea*
BOY. I shall, mastyr! The wynd is good—
Hens that we were! — *Hence (Let's go)*

Lamentando regina. — *The Queen lamenting*

1745 QUEEN. A, lady, hellp in this nede,
That in this flod we drench natt! — *drown*
Mary, Mary, flowyr of wommanned!
O blyssyd lady, foryete me nowth! — *not*

KING. A, my dere wyffe, no dred ye have, — *have no fear*
1750 Butt trost in Mary Maudleyn,
And she from perellys shall us save! — *perils*
To God for us she woll prayyn. — *pray*

QUEEN. A, dere hosbond, thynk on me,
And save yowersylfe as long as ye may,
1755 For trewly itt wyll no otherwyse be!
Full sor my hart it makytt[h] this day. — *my heart mourns*
A, the chyld that betwyx my sydys lay, — *lies*
The wyche was conseyvyd on me be ryth— — *by right*
Alas, that wommannys help is away! — *that the midwives'*
1760 An hevy departyng is betwyx us in syth,
Fore now departe wee!
For defawte of wommen here in my nede, — *lack of women*
Deth my body makyth to sprede. — *spreads over*
Now, Mary Mavdleyn, my sowle lede! — *guide*
1765 *In manus tuas, Domine!* — *Into your hands, Lord!*

KING. Alas, my wyff is ded!
Alas, this is a carrfull chans! — *sorrowful accident*
So shall my chyld, I am adred, — *I fear*
And for defawth of sustynons. — *lack*
1770 Good Lord, thi grace graunte to me!
A chyld betwen us of increse, — *of us two*
An it is motherles!
Help me, my sorow for to relesse, — *release*
Yf thi wyl it be!

1775 SHIPMAN. *Benedicite, benedicite!* — *Bless us!*
Qwat wethyr may this be? — *What*
Ower mast woll all asondyr! — *break asunder*

BOY. Mastyr, I therto ley myn ere,   *I bet my ear*
  It is for this ded body that we bere!   *because of*
1780 Cast hyr owt, or ellys we synke ond[yr]!   *under*

  Make redy for to cast hyr owt.

KING. Nay, for Goddys sake, do natt so!
  And ye wyll hyr into the se cast,   *If*
  Gyntyll serys, for my love, do—   *for love of me*
  Yendyr is a roch in the west—   *yonder/rock*
1785 As ley hyr theron all above,   *to lay*
    And my chyld hyr by.
SHIPMAN. As therto I asent well.
    And she were owt of the vessell,
    All we shuld stond the more in hele,   *health*
1790   I sey yow, verely!

  Tunc remiga[n]t ad montem et dicit rex: *

KING. Ly here, wyff, and chyld the[e] by.
  Blyssyd Mavdleyn be hyr rede!   *guide*
  Wyth terys wepyng, and grett cause why, *and with good cause*
  I kysse yow both in this sted.
1795 Now woll I pray to Mary myld
    To be ther gyde here.

  Tunc remiga[n]t a monte, et navta dicit: *

[SHIPMAN]. Pay now, syr, and goo to lond,
  For here is the portt Yaf, I ondyrstond;   *given port*
  Ley down my pay in my hond,
1800 And belyve go me fro!

KING. I graunt the[e], syr, so God me save!
  Lo, here is all thi connownt,   *account*
  All redy thou shall it have,
  And a marke more than thi graunt!   *your due*

1805 And thou, page, for thi good obedyentt,   *obedience*
  I gyff yow, besyde yower styntt,   *amount*
    Eche of yow a marke for yower wage!
SHIPMAN. Now he that mad bothe day and nyth, *night*
  He sped yow in yower ryth,   *May He speed/right*

1790 s.d. Then they row to the mound, and the King says:
1796 s.d. Then they row to the mound, and the shipman says:

1810   Well to go on yower passage!

    [In Jerusalem The ship remains at the coast]

    PETER. Now all creaturs upon mold,   *earth*
        That byn of Crystys creacyon,   *are*
    To worchep Jhesu they are behold,   *beholden*
    Nore nevyr ayens hym to make varyacyon.   *against/complaint*

1815 KING. Syr, feythfully I beseche yow this daye:
        Wher Petyr the apostull is, wete wold I!   *that I would know*
    PETER. Itt is I, syr, wythowt delay!
        Of yower askyng, tell me qwy.   *why*

    KING. Syr, the soth I shall yow seyn,   *truth/tell*
1820   And tell yow myn intentt wythin a whyle.
    Ther is a woman, hyth Mary Mavdleyn,   *called*
        That hether hath laberyd me owt of Marcyll—   *hither/brought me*
        Onto the wyche woman I thynk no gyle—   *Of/suspect no guile*
    And this pylgramage causyd me to take.
1825   I woll tell yow more of the[e] stylle,   *what she said of thee*
    For to crestyn me from wo and wrake.   *christianize/harm*

    PETER. O, blyssyd be the tyme that ye are falle to grace,   *have fallen (come)*
        And ye wyll kepe yower beleve aftyr my techeyng,   *If/belief according to*
    And alle-only forsake the fynd Saternas,   *completely/fiend Satan*
1830   The commaundme[n]ttys of God to have in kepyng!
    KING. Forsoth, I beleve in the Father, that is of all wyldyng,   *power*
    And in the Son, Jhesu Cryst,
        Also in the Holy Gost, hys grace to us spredyng!
    I beleve in Crystys deth, and hys uprysyng!   *resurrection*

1835 PETER. Syr, than whatt axke ye?   *ask*
    KING. Holy father, baptym, for charyte,   *Baptism*
    Me to save in eche degre   *in every way*
        From the fyndys bond!   *fiends' bondage*
    PETER. In the name of the Trenite,
1840 Wyth this watyr I baptysse the[e],
    That thou mayst strong be,
        Ayen the fynd to stond.

    Tunc aspargit illum cum aqua.   *Then he sprinkles him with water*

    KING. A, holy fathyr, how my hart wyll be sor
        Of cummav[n]ddementt, and ye declare nat the sentens!   *if/meaning*
1845 PETER. Syr, dayly ye shall lobor more and more,   *labor*

Tyll that ye have very experyens.
Wyth me shall ye wall to have more eloquens,   *hope*
And goo vesyte the stacyons, by and by;
To Nazareth and Bedlem, goo wyth delygens,   *Bethlehem*
1850 And be yower own inspeccyon, yower feyth to edyfy.

KING. Now, holy father, dereworthy and dere,   *worthy*
     Myn intent now know ye.
Itt is gon full t[w]o yere   *Two years have passed*
     That I cam to yow overe the se,   *Since*
1855   Crystys servont, and yower to be,
And the lawe of hym evyr to fulfyll.
Now woll I hom into my contre.   *would I go*
Yower puere blyssynd gravnt us tylle—   *pure blessing*
     That, feythfully, I crave!
1860 PETER. Now in the name of Jhesu,
     Cum Patre et Sancto Speritu,   *With the Father and the Holy Spirit*
     He kepe the[e] and save!

*Et tunc rex transit ad navem, et dicit rex:**

[KING]. Hold ner, shepman, hold, hold!   *Come near*
BOY. Syr, yendyr is on[e] callyd aftyr cold!   *yonder*
1865 SHIPMAN. A, syr! I ken yow of old!   *know*
     Be my trowth, ye be welcum to me!

KING. Now, gentyll marranere, I the pray,   *mariner*
Whatsoewer that I pay,   *I must pay*
In all the hast that ye may,
1870   Help me owyr the se!

SHIPMAN. In good soth we byn atenddawntt!   *will be of service*
Gladly ye shall have yower graunt,   *request*
Wythowtyn ony connownt.   *charge*
     Comme in, in Goddys name!
1875 Grobbe, boy! The wynd is nor-west!
Fast abowth the seyle cast!   *come about*
Rere up the seyll in all the hast,
     As well as thou can!

*Et tunc navis venit adcirca placeam. Rex dicit:**

[KING]. Mastyr of the shyp, cast forth yower yee!   *eye*

1862 s.d. And then the King crosses to the ship, and the King says:
1878 s.d. And then the ship goes around the Place. The King says:

1880 Me thynkyt the rokke I gyn to aspye! *begin*
    Gentyll mastyr thether us gye— *guide us thither*
     I shall qwyt yower mede. *give you reward*
    SHIPMAN. I[n] feyth, it is the same ston
    That yower wyff lyeth upon!
1885 Ye shall be ther even anon, *right away*
    Verely, indede!

    KING. O thou myty Lord of heven region,
    Yendyr is my babe of myn own nature, *Yonder*
    Preservyd and keptt from all corrupcyon!
1890 Blyssyd be that Lord that the[e] dothe socure, *succours you*
    And my wyff lyeth here, fayer and puer!
    Fayere and clere is hur colour to se!
    A, good Lord, yower grace wyth us indure, *may your grace endure*

    My wyvys lyfe for to illumyn. *For illumining my wife's life*
1895 A, blyssyd be that puer vergyn!
    From grevos slepe she gynnyt revyve! *begins to*
    A, the sonne of grace on us doth shynne!
    Now blyssyd be God, I se my wyff alyve!

    QUEEN. *O virgo salutata*, for ower savacyon! *O Virgin pure*
1900 *O pulcra et casta, cum* of nobyll alyavns! *beautiful and chaste, and/kinship*
    O almyty Maydyn, ower sowlys confortacyon!
    O demvr Mavdlyn, my bodyys sustynavns!
    Thou hast wr[a]ppyd us in wele from all varyawns, *well-being/danger*
    And led me wyth my lord i[n]to the Holy Lond!
1905 I am baptysyd, as ye are, be Maryvs gyddauns,
    Of Sent Petyrys holy hand. *By*

    I sye the blyssyd crosse that Cryst shed on hys precyus blod; *saw*
    Hys blyssyd sepulcur also se I. *saw*
    Whe[r]for, good hosbond, be mery in mode, *heart*
1910 For I have gon the stacyounys, by and by! *stations (holy places)*
    KING. I thanke it Jhesu, wyth hart on hye! *high*
    Now have I my wyf and my chyld both!
    I thank ytt Mavdleyn and Ower Lady, *for it*
    And evyr shall do, wythowtyn othe. *oath*

    Et tunc remigant a monte, et navta dicit: *

1914 s.d. And then they row to the mound, and the shipman says:

1915 SHIPMAN. Now ar ye past all perelle—   *peril*
    Her[e] is the lond of Marcylle!
    Now goo a lond, syr, whan ye wyll,
        I pr[a]ye yow for my sake!
    KING. Godamercy, jentyll marraner!
1920 Here is ten poundys of nobyllys cler,   *gold coins*
    And ever thi frynd both ferre and nere,   *friend*
        Cryst save the[e] from wo and wrake!

[The Palace at Marseilles]

Here goth the shep owt of the place, and Mavd[leyn] seyth:

    MARY. O dere fryndys, be in hart stabyll!
        And [thynk] how dere Cryst hathe yow bowth!   *dearly/bought (redeemed)*
1925 Ayens God, be nothyng vereabyll—   *inconstant*
        Thynk how he mad all thyng of nowth!   *nothing*
        Thow yow in poverte sumtyme be browth,   *brought*
        [Y]itte be in charyte both nyth and day,   *night*
        For they byn blyssyd that so byn sowth,   *are blessed that be so*
1930 For *paupertas est donum Dei*.   *poverty is God's house*

    God blyssyt alle tho that byn meke and good,   *those who are*
        And he blyssyd all tho that wepe for synne.
    They be blyssyd that the hungor and the thorsty gyff fode;   *to the hungry/food*
    They be blyssyd that byn mercyfull ayen wrecched men;   *towards the wretched*
1935   They byn blyssyd that byn dysstroccyon of synne—   *are the destruction*
    Thes[e] byn callyd the chyldyren of lyfe,   *are*
        Onto the wyche blysse bryng both yow and me   *such blessings*
    That for us dyyd on the rode tre! Amen.   *Those for which He*

Here shall the kyng and the quvene knele doun. Rex dicit: *The King says:*

    KING. Heyll be thou, Mary! Ower Lord is wyth the[e]!
1940   The helth of ower sowllys, and repast contemplatyff!   *holy feast*
    Heyll, tabyrnakyll of the blyssyd Trenité!
        Heyll, counfortabyll sokore for man and wyff!

    QUEEN. Heyll, thou chosyn and chast of wommen alon!
        It passyt my wett to tell thi nobyllnesse!
1945 Thou relevyst me and my chyld on the rokke of ston,
        And also savyd us be thi hye holynesse.

    MARY. Welcum hom, prynse and prynsses bothe!   *princess*
        Welcum hom, yong prynsse of dew and ryth!   *prince*
    Welcum hom to your own erytage wythowt othe,   *heritage/oath*

1950	And to alle yower pepyll present in syth!	*sight*
	Now ar ye becum Goddys own knygth,	*Knight*
	For sowle helth salve ded ye seche,	*(your) soul's health/travel*
	In hom the Holy Gost hath take resedens,	*your heart (also, Jerusalem)*
	And drevyn asyde all the desepcyon of wrech.	*banished/self-deception of wretches*
1955	And now have ye a knowle[ge] of the sentens,	*inner way*
	How ye shall com onto grace!	
	But now in yower godys ayen I do yow sese.	*goods again/grant possession*
	I trost I have governyd them to yower hertys ese.	*content*
	Now woll I labor forth, God to plese,	
1960	More gostly strenkth me to purchase!	*spiritual strength/acquire*

KING. O blyssyd Mary, to comprehend
Ower swete sokor, on us have pete! *succour/pity*
QUEEN. To departe from us, why should ye pretende? *venture*
O blyssyd lady, putt us nat to that poverte! *loss*

1965 MARY. Of yow and yowers I wyll have rememberauns,
And dayly [y]ower bede woman for to be, *prayerful servant*
That alle wyckydnesse from yow may have deleverans, *be taken away*
In quiet and rest that leve may ye! *you might live*

KING. Now thanne, yower puere blyssyng gravnt us tylle. *pure/to last*
1970 MARY. The blyssyn of God mott yow fulfyll!

*Ille vos benedicatt, qui s[i]ne fine vivit et regnat!**

Her[e] goth Mary into the wyldyrnesse, thus seyyng Rex: *The King*

KING. A! We may syyn and wepyn also, *sigh*
That we have forgon this lady fre— *lost/noble*
It brynggytt my hart in care and woo— *woe*
1975 The whech ower gyde and governor should a be! *who/have been*
QUEEN. That doth perswade all my ble, *(Her leaving) makes me pale*
That swete sypresse, that she wold so. *Cypress (aromatic root)*
In me restytt[h] neyther game nor gle *delight nor joy*
That she wold from owere presens goo.

1980 KING. Now of hyr goyng I am nothyng glad!
But my londdys to gyddyn I must aplye, *to rule my kingdom*
Lyke as Sancte Peter me badde,
Chyrchys in cetyys I woll edyfye; *cities/build*
And whoso ayens ower feyth woll replye, *argue*
1985 I woll ponysch [s]wych personnys wyth perplyxcyon! *punish such/entanglement*

1971. May He who lives and reigns without end bless you!

Mahond and hys lawys I defye! *Mohammet*
A, hys pryde owt of my love shall have polucyon, *trouble*
And [w]holle onto Jhesu I me betake!

Mari in herimo. *Mary in the wilderness*

MARY. In this deserte abydyn wyll wee,
1990   My sowle from synne for to save;
I wyll evyr abyte me wyth humelyte,
And put me in pacyens, my Lord for to love.
In charyte my werkys I woll grave, *will set myself*
And in abstynens, all dayys of my lyfe.
1995   Thus my concyens of me doth crave; *call*
Than why shold I wyth my consyens st[r]yffe? *strive*
And ferdarmore, I wyll leven in charyte, *furthermore/live*
At the reverens of Ower Blyssyd Lady,
In goodnesse to be lyberall, my sowle to edyfye. *generous/instruct*
2000   Of wor[l]dly fodys I wyll leve all refeccyon; *foods/leave off/partaking*
Be the fode that commyt[h] from heven on hye, *(I will live) By*
Thatt God wyll me send, be contemplatyff. *(and) be contemplative*

JESUS. O, the swettnesse of prayors sent onto me
Fro my wel-belovyd frynd wythowt varyovns! *From/unfaithfulness*
2005 Wyth gostly fode relevyd shall she be. *spiritual*
Angellys! Into the clowdys ye do hyr hauns, *raise her up*
Ther fede wyth manna to hyr systynovns. *sustenance*
Wyth joy of angyllys, this lett hur receyve.
Byd hur injoye wyth all hur afyawns, *all her kind*
2010 For fynddys frawd shall hur non deseyve. *fiendish fraud*

ANGEL 1. O thou redulent rose, that of a vergyn sprong!
O thou precyus palme of vytory! *victory*
O thou osanna, angellys song! *hosanna*
O precyus gemme, born of Ower Lady!
2015 Lord, thi commav[n]ddement we obbey lowly! *humbly*
To thi servant that thou hast grauntyd blysse,
We angellys all obeyyn devowtly.
We woll desend to yen wyldyrnesse. *yon*

Here shall to angyllys desend into wyldyrnesse, and
other to shall bryng an oble, opynly aperyng aloft in *mass wafer*
the clowddys; the t[w]o benethyn shall bryng Mari, and
she shall receyve the bred, and than go ayen into wyldyrnesse. *go again*

ANGEL 2. Mari, God gretyt the[e] wyth hevenly influens! *grace*
2020 He hath sent the[e] grace wyth hevenly synys. *signs*

Thou shall byn onoryd wyth joye and reverens,
   Inhansyd in heven above vergynnys!
   Thou hast byggyd the[e] here among spynys—   *dwelt/thorns*
God woll send the[e] fode be revelacyon.
2025   Thou shall be receyvyd into the clowddys,
Gostly fode to reseyve to thi sa[l]vacyon.

MARY. *Fiat voluntas tua* in heven and erth!   *Your will be done*
   Now am I full of joye and blysse!
Laud and preyse to that blyssyd byrth!   *Praise/birth*
2030   I am redy, as hys blyssyd wyll isse.   *is*

   Her[e] shall she be halsyd wyth angellys wyth reverent song.   *hauled up*
   Asumpta est Maria in nubibus. Celi gavdent, angeli lavdantes
   felium Dei, et dicit Mari: *

MARY. O thou Lord of lorddys, of hye domenacyon!   *dominion*
   In hewen and erth worsheppyd be thi name.
How thou devydyst me from houngure and vexacyon!   *you keep me from*
   O gloryus Lord, in the[e] is no frauddys nor no defame!   *infamy*
2035   But I shuld serve my Lord, I were to blame,   *Unless*
Wych fullfyllyt me wyth so gret felicete,   *Who/happiness*
   Wyth melody of angyllys shewit me gle and game,   *joy and delight*
And have fed me wyth fode of most delycyte!

   Her[e] shall speke an holy prest in the same wyldyrnesse,
   thus seyyng the prest:

HERMIT. O Lord of lorddys! What may this be?
2040   So gret mesteryys shewyd from heven,   *mysteries*
Wyth grett myrth and melody
   Wyth angyllys brygth as the lewyn!   *bright/lightning*
Lord Jhesu, for thi namys sevynne,   *seven*
As graunt me grace that person to se!

   Her[e] he shal go in the wyldyrnesse and spye Mari in
   hyr devocyon, thus seyyng the prest:

2045 HERMIT. Heyl, creature, Crystys delecceon!
   Heyl, swetter than sugur or cypresse!   *cypress (aromatic root)*
Mary is thi name be angyllys relacyon;   *by the angel's account*
   Grett art thou wyth God for thi perfythnesse!   *Greatly beloved*
The joye of Jherusallem shewyd the[e] expresse,   *expressly*

2030 s.d. Mary taken up into the clouds, the Heavens rejoice, the Angels praising the son of God, and Mary says:

2050 The wych I nevyr sawe this thirty wyntyr and more!   *which rejoicing*
    Wherfor I know well thou art of gret perfy[t]nesse,
    I woll pray yow hartely to she[w] me of yower Lord!   *a revelation*

MARY. Be the grace of my Lord Jhesus
    This thirty wyntyr this hath byn my selle,   *These/cell*
2055 And thryys on the day enhansyd thus   *thrice each day raised up*
    Wyth more joy than ony tong can telle   *tongue*
    Nevyr creature cam ther I dwelle,   *where*
    Tyme nor tyde, day nore nyth,   *night*
    That I can wyth spece telle,   *mention*
2060 But alonly wyth Goddys angyllys brygth.   *bright*
    But thou art wolcum onto my syth,   *welcome in my sight*
    Yf thou be of good conversacyon.   *holy*
    As I thynk in my delyth,   *ecstasy*
    Thow sholddyst be a man of devocyon.

2065 HERMIT. In Crystys law I am sacryed a pryst,   *consecrated*
    Mynystryyd be angelys at my masse.   *Assisted by*
    I sakor the body of ower Lord Jhesu Cryst,   *consecrate*
    And be that holy manna I leve in sowthfastnesse.   *live*
MARY. Now I rejoyse of yower goodnesse,
2070 But tyme is comme that I shall asende.
HERMIT. I recummend me wyth all umbylnesse;
    Onto my sell I woll pretend.   *Unto/cell/intend to go*

    Her[e] shall the prest go to hys selle, thus seyyng Jhesus:

JESUS. Now shall Mary have possessyon,
    Be ryth enirytawns a crown to bere.   *true inheritance/bear*
2075 She shall be fett to evyrlastyng savacyon,   *brought*
    In joye to dwell wythowtyn fere.
    Now, angelys, lythly that ye were ther!   *quickly*
    Onto the prystys sell apere this tyde.   *Unto/cell*
    My body in forme of bred that he bere,
2080 Hur for to hossell, byd hym provyde.   *To administer to her*

ANGEL 1. O blyssyd Lord, we be redy,
    Yower massage to do wythowtyn treson!   *disobedience*
ANGEL 2. To hyr I wyll goo and make reportur,   *report*
    How she shall com to yower habytacyon.

    Here shall t[w]o angellys go to Mary and to the prest,
    thus seyyng the angellys to the prest:

2085 ANGELS 1 AND 2. Syr pryst, God cummau[n]dytt[h] from heven region
    Ye shall go hosyll hys servont expresse,   *minister to/right away*
    And we wyth yow shall take mynystracyon   *serve*
    To bere lyth before hys body of worthynesse.   *light (candles)*
HERMIT. Angyllys, wyth all umbyllnesse,   *humility*
2090 In a vestment I wyll me aray,
    To mynystyr my Lord of gret hynesse;   *highness*
    Straytt therto I take the way!

    In herimo.   *In the wilderness*

ANGEL 2. Mary, be glad, and in hart strong
    To reseyve the palme of grett vytory!   *victory*
2095 This day ye shall be reseyvyd wyth angellys song!
    Yower sowle shall departe from yower body.

MARY. A, good Lord, I thank the wythowt veryawns!   *wavering*
    This day I am groundyd all in goodnesse,   *fixed*
    Wyth hart and body concludyd in substawns.   *bodily form ended*
2100   I thanke the[e], Lord, wyth speryt of perfythnesse!

    Hic aparuit angelus et presbiter cum corpus domenicum. [*]

HERMIT. Thou blyssyd woman, inure in mekenesse,   *set*
    I have browth the the bred of lyf to thi syth,   *brought/thy sight*
    To make the[e] suere from all dystresse,   *safe*
    Thi sowle to bryng to evyrlastyng lyth.   *light*

2105 MARY. O thou mythty Lord of hye mageste,
    This celestyall bred for to determyn,   *(Thanks for) this heavenly bread*
    Thys tyme to reseyve it in me,   *(For) this time*
    My sowle therwyth to illumyn.

    Her[e] she reseyvyt[h] it.

MARY. I thank the[e], Lord of ardent love!
2110   Now I know well I shall nat opprese.   *be overwhelmed*
    Lord, lett me se thi joyys above!
    I recummend my sowle onto thi blysse!
    Lord, opyn thi blyssyd gatys!
    Thys erth at thys tyme fervenly I kysse!   *I fervently kiss goodbye*
2115 *In manus tuas, Domine!*   *Into your hands, Lord*
    Lord, wyth thi grace me wysse!   *guide*

2100 s.d. Here appears the angel and the priest with a host.

Commendo spiritum meum! Redemisti me,   *I commend my spirit. You have*
 Domine Devs veritatis!   *redeemed me, Lord God of truth.*

ANGEL 1. Now reseyve we this sowle, as reson is,
2120 In heven to dwelle us among.
ANGEL 2. Wythowtyn end to be in blysse!
 Now lett us syng a mery song!

 Gaudent in celis.   *They rejoice in heaven*

HERMIT. O good God, grett is thi grace!
 O Jhesu, Jhesu! Blessyd be thi name!
2125 Mary, Mary! Mych is thi solas,
  In heven blysse wyth gle and game!   *joy and delight*
 Thi body wyl I cure from alle manyr blame,
 And I wyll passe to the bosshop of the sete   *Bishop/city*
 Thys body of Mary to berye be name,
2130 Wyth alle reverens and solemnyte.

Sufferens of this processe, thus enddyt[h] the sentens
 That we have playyd in yower syth.   *sight*
Allemythty God, most of magnyfycens,
 Mote bryng yow to hys blysse so brygth,   *May He/bright*
2135   In presens of that Kyng!
 Now, frendys, thus endyt[h] thys matere—
 To blysse bryng tho that byn here!   *those who are*
 Now, clerkys, wyth voycys cler,
  "Te Deum lavdamus" lett us syng! *"We praise you, O Lord" (a hymn)*

 Explycit oreginale de Sancta Maria Magdalena. *

2140 Yff ony thyng amysse be,
 Blame connyng, and nat me!   *lack of cleverness*
 I desyer the redars to be my frynd,
 Yff ther be ony amysse, that to amend.

2139 s.d. Here ends the original of the play of Saint Mary Magdalene.

The Digby *Killing of the Children*

The Digby *Killing of the Children* (or, as it is entitled in the manuscript, *Candlemes Day and the Kyllyng of the Children of Israelle*) is preserved at Oxford in Bodleian Library MS. Digby 133 (fols. 146^r-157^v), the manuscript compilation briefly described in the introduction to the Digby *Conversion of St. Paul.* The play is dated 1512 (in three places); its language is East Midland, with a mix of East Anglian characteristics and some identifiable Norfolk vocabulary forms. Manuscript evidence indicates that the main scribe of *The Killing of the Children* may also have had some hand in its composition, for he makes emendations and rearranges the material freely in the Digby text. Whether this was the "Jhon Parfre" who, it is claimed at the end of the manuscript, "ded wryte thys booke" is not at all clear. In any case, the main scribe of this play has been identified as the same scribe who copied the Digby *Wisdom,* which (like the Digby *Mary Magdalene* and *The Conversion of St. Paul*) was later owned by Myles Blomefylde. Whether the theatrical career of *The Killing of the Children* extended into Chelmsford, Essex, during the third quarter of the sixteenth century, as seems to have been the case with the other Digby plays, remains an intriguing possibility.

Whenever and wherever the play was performed, it seems originally to have been written as part of an annual series, as Poeta's Prologue and Epilogue indicate. In the Prologue, Poeta refers to another play that "last yeere we shewid you in this place" (1. 25), a play depicting the adoration of the shepherds and the coming of the magi. And at the end of the *Killing of the Children*, Poeta proposes to show a play of the doctors in the temple "next yeer." Like the character of the same name in *The Conversion of St. Paul,* Poeta serves as a combination of master of ceremonies, interpreter, and apologist. Strangely, in the Prologue he gives the two main episodes in reverse order of appearance in the play, specifying that Mary's purification in the temple will be followed by the massacre of the innocents. These references to a yearly sequence of plays and the changed order of episodes are only two of several details in the play indicating a confused textual history and a widely ranging performance history under a variety of circumstances. At the end of the massacre episode, for example, occurs the stage direction *"vacat ab hinc"* ("omit from here on") (l. 388 s.d.), clearly suggesting that in at least one instance the purification episode was left out altogether. At some point, too, the number of dancing "virgyns" was changed from five to one, making the number of "pleyers" total seventeen, while in the text the virgins number "as many as a man wylle."

This slow annual procession of Biblical plays that included *The Killing of the Children* was evidently performed, one play per year, on St. Anne's day (26 July). The mode of performance contrasts with that of the cycle plays, which customarily put all the pageants on in one festive occasion. It might be noted that in the cycle play tradition the scope and sweep of Biblical history can hardly be missed; indeed, the interpenetration of past, present and future is one of the large themes consciously played out on the streets of the sponsoring towns. In the non-cycle mode, however, with isolated episodes, the emphasis falls more immediately and locally on the meaning of the action or on one of the characters in the play. In the case of *The Killing of the Children* it falls naturally on Watkyn, the pusillanimous soldier eager for advancement in Herod's troops. The play dramatizes one of the most grisly stories in the Bible: Herod's learning of Christ's birth and Kingly stature, and his slaughter of all children under two, but it introduces the darkly humorous extra-Biblical figure of Watkyn, who begins in the text as a "Messanger." Watkyn takes Herod's instructions well, despite his cowardly misgivings about being beaten with distaffs—which is, of course, exactly what happens as he and the other soldiers slaughter the children before their mothers' eyes. The dramatic effect of humor, pathos, and terrible violence joined together so wrenchingly in this play has yet to be explored adequately.

In the Digby text, the story of the killing is followed by Mary's purification in the temple, far away in Jerusalem, which perhaps provides distance too for the audience to contemplate the savage horror that it has just witnessed, and which Mary, Joseph and the baby Jesus have escaped.

Except for three rhyme-royal stanzas, the entire Digby *Killing of the Children* is written in unvarying double quatrains rhyming *ababbcbc*. The basic metrical form is a four-stress line, sometimes alliterating. A curious feature of the play is the passage from lines 97-104, which corresponds completely with the sense of lines 217-24 in the Digby *Mary Magdalene*.

The *Killing of the Children* was first edited by Thomas Sharp in *Ancient Mysteries from the Digby Manuscripts* (1835). The standard scholarly edition of the play, edited by Donald C. Baker, John L. Murphy, and Louis B. Hall, Jr., appears in the EETS *The Late Medieval Religious Plays of Bodleian MSS. Digby 133 and E Museo 160* (1982); a facsimile of the manuscript, edited by Donald C. Baker and John L. Murphy, appears in *The Digby Plays: Facsimiles of the Plays in Bodley MSS Digby 133 and e Museo 160* 1976). A discussion of the history of the text can be found in Donald C. Baker and John L. Murphy, "The Late Medieval Plays of MS Digby 133: Scribes, Dates and Early History," *RORD*, x (1967); the Digby Plays' connection with Chelmsford is explored by John C. Coldewey in "The Digby Plays and the Chelmsford Records," *RORD*, xviii (1975); the theatrical histories of the plays (including the Digby *Killing of the Children*), as evidenced by their texts, appears in Donald C. Baker's "When is a Text a Play" in Briscoe and Coldewey, *Contexts for Early English Drama* (see Suggestions for Further Reading).

THE DIGBY *KILLING OF THE CHILDREN*

[DRAMATIS PERSONAE:]*

THE NAMYS OF THE PLEYERS (SUMMA 17)

THE POETE
KYNG HEROWDE
   FIRSTE KNYGHT [MILES 1]
   THE SECUNDE KNYGHT [MILES 2]
   THIRDE KNYGHT [MILES 3]
   FOURTH KNYGHT [MILES 4]
   WATKYN, MESSANGER
SYMEON THE BYSSHOPE
JOSEPH
MARIA

ANNA PROPHETISSA*	*Anne the Prophetess*
A VIRGYN *["FIVE" VIRGINS DELETED IN MS]*	*Dancing maidens*
ANGELUS	*An Angel*
PRIMA MULIER [MULIER 1]	*First Mother*
SECUNDA MULIER [MULIER 2]	*Second Mother*
TERCIA MULIER [MULIER 3]	*Third Mother*
QUARTA MULIER [MULIER 4]	*Fourth Mother*

MDXII   Anno Domini 1512

POETA. This solenne fest to be had in remembraunce	*feast day*
Of blissed Seynt Anne,* modere to Oure Lady,	*mother*
Whos right discent was fro kynges alyaunce—	*rightful*

DRAMATIS PERSONAE: the following list appears in the manuscript at the end of the play.
ANNA PROPHETISSA: Anna, the prophetess, not Anne, Mother of Mary. [See Luke 2:36]
2. St. Anne's day, 26 July.

Of Davyd and Salamon, witnesseth the story.*   *according to*
5   Hir blissid doughtere, that callid is Mary,
By Goddes provision an husbond shuld have,
Callid Joseph, of nature old and drye,
And she, moder unto Crist, that alle the world shalle save.   *mother*

This glorious maiden doughter unto Anna,
10   In whos worshippe this fest we honoure,
And by resemblaunce likenyd unto manna,*
       Wiche is in tast celestialle of savoure,   *of heavenly flavor*
       And of Jerico the sote rose floure,*   *sweet*
       Gold Ebryson callid in picture,*   *pure gold/image*
15   Chosyn for to bere mankyndes Savyoure,
       With a prerogative above eche creature!

These grett thynges remembred, after oure entent,
Is for to worshippe Oure Ladye and Seynt Anne.
We be comen hedere as servauntes diligent,   *hither*
20   Oure processe to shewe you, as we can.   *play*
       Wherfor of benevolens we pray every man   *forbearance*
To have us execused that we no better do—
       Another tyme to emende it if we can,
Be the grace of God, if oure cunnyng be thertoo.   *By/learning/capable*

25   The last yeere we shewid you in this place
       How the shepherdes of Cristes birthe made letificacion,   *joy*
     And thre kynges that come fro ther cuntrees be grace   *by God's grace*
       To worshippe Jhesu with enteere devocion.   *complete*
       And now we purpose with hoolle affeccion   *intend*
30   To procede in oure matere as we can,
       And to shew you of Oure Ladies purificacion*
That she made in the temple, as the usage was than.

And after that shalle Herowde have tydynges*
       How the thre kynges be goon hoom another way,   *went home*
35   That were with Jhesu and made ther offrynges,   *Who*
       And promysed Kyng Herowde without delay
       To come ageyn by hym—this is no nay;   *to him/without doubt*
       And whan he wist that thei were goon,   *learned*

---

4. See Matthew 1:1-20; Luke 1:27.
11. Manna. [See Exodus 16:4-35]
13. The rose of Jericho. [See Ecclesiasticus 24:14]
14. Gold Ebryson: "aurum obrizum" or pure gold. [See Job 28:15]
31. Our Lady's purification, celebrated on the feast of Candlemas (2 February). [See Luke 2:22; Leviticus 12:6]
33. The order of the episodes in the play is the opposite of what Poeta declares here.

Like as a wodman he gan to fray,   *madman/began to rage*
40   And commaundid his knyghtes for to go anoon   *immediately*

Into Israelle, to serche every town and cite
For alle the children that thei coude ther fynde
Of too yeeres age and within, sparyng neither bonde nor free,   *servant nor master*
But sle them alle, either for foo or frende—   *to slay/whether friend or foe*
45   Thus he commaundid in his furious wynde,   *wild manner*
Thought that Jhesu shuld have be oon.   *Thinking/one*
And yitt he failed of his froward mynde,   *cruel intent*
For by Goodes purviaunce, Oure Lady was into Egipte gon!   *provision*

Frendes, this processe we purpose to pley, as we can,   *story (procession of events)*
50   Before you alle here in youre presens,
To the honor of God, Oure Lady, and Seynt Anne,
Besechyng you to geve us peseable audiens!   *quiet attention*
And ye menstrallis, doth youre diligens!   *strike up!*
And ye virgynes, shewe summe sport and plesure,   *young women*
55   These people to solas, and to do God reverens!   *bring pleasure*
As ye be appoynted, doth your besy cure!   *Have been instructed/careful duty*

  Et tripident.   *And they dance*

  [Jerusalem: Herod's Palace]

HERODES. Above alle kynges under the clowdys cristalle,   *on earth*
Royally I reigne in welthe without woo!   *woe*
Of plesaunt prosperyte I lakke non at alle!
60   Fortune, I fynde that she is not my foo!   *foe*
I am Kyng Herowdes! I wille it be knowen soo!   *proclaim*
Most strong and myghty in feld for to fyght,
And to venquysshe my enemyes that ageynst me do!   *set themselves against*
I am most bedred, with my bronde bright!   *dreaded/shining sword*

65   My grett goddes I gloryfye with gladnesse,
And to honoure them I knele upon my knee,
For thei have sett me in solas from alle sadnesse,   *comfort*
That no conqueroure nor knyght is comparid to me!
Alle tho that rebelle ageyns me, ther bane I wille be,   *those/their scourge*
70   Or grudge ageyns my goddes on hylle or hethe!   *Or those who complain against/heath*
Alle suche rebellers I shalle make for to flee,
And with hard punysshementes putt them to dethe!

What erthely wretches, with pompe and pride,   *Whatever villains*
Do ageyns my lawes, or withstonde myn entent,   *transgress/oppose my will*
75   Thei shalle suffre woo and peyne thurgh bak and syde!   *woe*

With a very myschaunce ther flesshe shalbe alle torent,		*misfortune/flayed*
And alle my foes shalle have suche commaundement,		*endure*
That they shalbe glad to do my byddyng ay!		*forever*
Or elles thei shalbe in woo and myscheff permanent,		*woo*
80 That thei shalle fere me nyght and day!*		

HERODES. I do perceyve, though I be here in my cheff cite,	*city*
Callid Jerusalem, my riche royalle town,	
I am falsly disceyvid by straunge kynges three!	*deceived/foreign*
Therfor, my knyghtes, I warne you, without delacion,	*delay*
85 That ye make serche thurghout alle my region—	*throughout*
Withoute ony tarieng, my wille may be seen—	*any tarrying*
And sle alle tho children, without excepcion,	*slay all those*
Of t[w]o yeeres of age that within Israelle bene!	*who live*

For within myself thus I have concluded,	*decided*
90 For to avoide awey alle interrupcion,	*always/insurrection*
Sythen they thre kynges have me thus falsly deluded,	*Since these*
As in maner by froward collusion,	*villainous*
And ageyn resortid hom into ther region—	*returned home*
But yitt, maugre ther hertes, I shalle avengid be!	*yet, despite*

---

80. Between lines 80 and 81 the following lines are cancelled in the MS. and incorporated in the next speeches:

HERODES. My messangere, at my commaundement come heder to me,		*hither*
And take he[e]d what I shalle to the[e] say!		*heed*
I charge the loke abought thurgh alle my cuntre,		*throughout*
To aspye if ony rebelles do ageynst oure lay,		*find/act/law*
5 And if ony suche come in thy way,		
Brynge hem into oure high presens,		
And we shalle se them correctid or thei go hens!		*ere*

WATKYN. My lord, your commaundement I have fulfilled,		
Evyn to the uttermest of my pore powere,		
10 And I wold shew you more, so ye wold be contentid,		*If*
But I dare not, lest ye wold take it in angere!		
For if it liked you not, I am sure my deth were nere,		
And therfor, my lord, I wole hold my peas!		*keep still*
HERODES. I warne the[e], thu traytour, that thu not seas		*cease*

15 To shewe every thyng thu knowist ageyns oure reverence!		*all plots against me*
WATKYN. My lord, if ye have it in youre remembraunce,		
Ther were thre straungere kynges but late in your presence,		*foreign*
That went to Bedlem to offre with due observaunce,		*Bethlehem*
And promysed to come ageyn by you, without variaunce;		*back to/without fail*
20 But by thes bonys ten, thei be to you untrue,		*fingers/these hands*
For homward another wey thei doo sue!		*go*

HERODES. Now, be my grett goddes that be so fulle of myght,		*by*
I wille be avengid upon Israelle if thi tale be true!		
WATKYN. That it is, my lord, my trouth I you plight,		*pledge*
25 For ye founde me never false syn ye me knewe!		*since*

95   Bothe in Bedlem and my provynces everychone,   *Bethlehem/all*
      Sle alle the children, to kepe my liberte!   *Slay*

      MILES 1.   My lord, ye may be sure that I shalle not spare,   *spare (them)*
         For to fulfille your noble commaundement,
      With sharpe sword to perse them alle bare,   *pierce/naked*
100   In alle cuntrees that be to you adiacent!
         MILES 2.   And for your sake, to observe your commaundement!
         MILES 3.   Not on of them alle oure handes shalle astert!   *one/escape*
           MILES 4.   For we wole cruelly execute youre judgement,
      With swerde and spere to perse them thurgh the hert!   *pierce*

105   HERODES.   I thanke you, my knyghtes, but loke ye make no tarieng!   *delay*
        Do arme yourself in stele shynyng bright,   *steel armor*
      And conceyve in your myndes that I am your kyng,   *understand*
        Gevyng you charge that with alle your myght,
        In conservacion of my tytelle of right,   *saving my rightful lineage*
110   That ye go and loke for myn advauntage,
        And sle alle the children that come in your sight,   *slay*
      Wiche ben within too yeere of age!   *under two*

      Now beware that my byddyng ye truly obey,
        For non but I shalle reigne with equyte!   *rightfully*
115   Make alle the children on your swordes to dey!   *run through*
        I charge you, spare not oon for mercy nor pyte!   *one/pity*
        Am not I lord and kyng of the cuntre?
      The crowne of alle Jerusalem longith to me of right!   *belongs/by right*
        Whosoever sey nay, of high or lowe degre,
120   I charge you sle alle suche that come in your sight!   *slay*

      MILES 1.   My lord, be ye sure accordyng to your wille,
        Like as ye charge us be streigt commaundement,   *Just/direct command*
      Alle the children of Israelle doughtles we shalle kylle,
        Within to yeere of age—this is oure entent!   *under two*
125   MILES 2.   My lord, of alle Jurerye we hold you for chef regent,   *Jewry/chief*
      By titelle of enheritaunce, as your auncetours beforn;   *ancestors*
        He that seith the contrary, be Mahound, shalbe shent,   *by Mohammed/destroyed*
      And curse the tyme that ever [he] was borne!

130   HERODES.   I thanke you, my knyghtes, with hoolle affeccion,   *whole*
        And whan ye come ageyn I shalle you avaunce.   *promote*
      Therfor, quyte you wele in feld and town,   *conduct yourselves*
      And of alle tho fondlynges make a delyveraunce!   *from/those foundlings*

      Here the knyghtes shalle departe from Herodes to Israelle,
      and Watkyn shalle abyde, seyng thus to Herodes:

WATKYN. Now, my lord, I beseche you to here my dalyaunce!　　*hear why I delay*
I wold aske you a bone, if I durst aright,　　*boon/dare*
135　But I were loth ye shuld take ony displesaunce—
Now, for Mahoundes sake, make me a knyght!　　*Mohammed's*

For oon thyng I promyse you: I wille manly fight,　　*strongly*
And for to avenge your quarelle I dare undertake;
Though I sey it myself, I am a man of myght,
140　And dare live and deye in this quarelle for your sake!
For whan I com amonge them, for fere thei shalle quake!
And though thei sharme and crye, I care not a myght,　　*scream*
But with my sharpe sworde ther ribbes I shalle shake,
Evyn thurgh the guttes, for anger and despight!　　*through/contempt*

145　HERODES. Be thi trouthe, Watkyn, woldest thu be made a knyght?　　*By thy word*
Thu hast be my servaunt and messangere many a day,　　*You have been*
But thu were never provid in bataile nor in fight,　　*proved in battle*
And therfor to avaunce the[e] so sodeynly I ne may.　　*may not*
But oon thyng to the[e] I shalle say,
150　Because I fynde the[e] true in thyn entent:
Forth with my knyghtes thu shalt take the way,
And quyte the[e] wele, and thu shalt it not repent!　　*conduct yourself*

WATKYN. Now, a largeys, my lord! I am right wele apaid!　　*largess*
If I do not wele, ley my hed upon a stokke!　　*stock*
155　I shalle go shew your knyghtes how ye have seid,
And arme myself manly, and go forth on the flokke　　*flock*
And if I fynde a yong child, I shalle choppe it on a blokke!
Though the moder be angry, the child shalbe slayn!
But yitt I drede no thyng more thanne a woman with a rokke!　　*distaff*
160　For if I se ony suche, be my feith, I come ageyn!　　*I see/will return*

HERODES. What! Shalle a woman with a rokke drive the[e] away?　　*distaff*
Fye on the[e], traitour! Now I tremble for tene!　　*anger*
I have trosted the[e] long and many a day—
A bold man, and an hardy, I went thu haddist ben!　　*I thought*
165　WATKYN. So am I, my lord, and that shalbe seen,
That I am a bold man, and best dare abyde!　　*that remains*
And ther come an hundred women, I wole not fleen,　　*If/flee*
But fro morowe tylle nyght, with them I dare chide!　　*dawn till dusk/abuse*

And therfor, my lord, ye may trust unto me,
170　For alle the children of Israelle your knyghtes and I shalle kylle!
I wylle not spare on, but dede thei shalbe—　　*one*
If the fader and moder wille lete me have my wille!
HERODES. Thu lurdeyn! Take hede what I sey the[e] tylle,　　*wretch*

	And high the[e] to my knyghtes as fast as thu can!	*hie*
175	Say, I warne them in ony wyse ther blood that thei spille,	
	Abought in every cuntre, and lette for no man!	*delay*

	WATKYN. Nay, nay, my lord! We wylle let for no man,	*delay*
	Though ther come a thousand on a rought,	*in a mob*
	For your knyghtes and I wille kylle them alle, if we can!	
180	But for the wyves, that is alle my dought,	*Except*
	And if I se ony walkyng abought,	
	I wille take good hede tylle she be goon,	
	And as sone as I aspye that she is oute,	*out of doors*
	By my feith, into the hous I wille go anon!	*immediately*

185	And this I promyse you, that I shalle never slepe,	
	But evermore wayte to fynde the children alone,	
	And if the moder come in, under the benche I wille crepe,	
	And lye stille ther tylle she be goon!	
	Than manly I shalle come out and hir children sloon!	*slay*
190	And whan I have don, I shalle renne fast away!	
	If she founde hir child dede, and toke me ther alone,	*discovered*
	Be my feith, I am sure we shuld make a fray!	*have a fight*

	HERODES. Nay, harlott! Abyde stylle with my knyghtes,	*scoundrel/Stay*
	I warne the[e],	
	Tylle the children be slayn, alle the hoolle rought!	*group*
195	And whan thu comyst home ageyn, I shalle avaunce the[e],	*promote*
	If thu quyte the[e] like a man whille thu art ought!	*conduct yourself/out*
	And if thu pley the coward, I put the[e] owt of dought,	*But*
	Of me thu shalt neyther have fee nor advauntage!	*payment nor promotion*
	Therfor, I charge you, the contre be weelle sought,	*searched*
200	And whan thu comyst home, shalt have thi wage!	

	WATKYN. Yis, syre, be my trouthe, ye shalle wele knowe	
	Whille I am oute, how I shalle aquyte me,	*conduct myself*
	For I purpos to spare neither high nor lowe—	
	If ther be no man wole smyte me!	*who will*
205	The most I fere, the wyves wille bete me!	
	Yitt shalle I take good hert to me, and loke wele abought,	
	And loke that your knyghtes be not ferre fro me,	*see to it/far*
	For if I be alone, I may sone get a clought!	*blow*

	HERODES. I say, hye the[e] hens! That thu were goon!	*get thee/(I wish) that*
210	And unto my knyghtes, loke ye, take the way,	
	And sey, I charge them that my commaundement be don	
	In alle hast possible, without more delay!	*haste*
	And if ther be ony that wille sey you nay,	*refuse*

Redde hym of his lyff out of hand, anon!   *Deprive*
215   And if thu quyte the[e] weelle unto my pay,   *conduct yourself*
    I shalle make the[e] a knyght aventururos whan thu comyst home!

    Et exeat.   *And let him leave*

WATKYN. Syr knyghtes, I must go forth with you!
    Thus my lord commaunded me for to don,
    And if I quyte me weelle whille I am amonge you,   *conduct myself*
220   I shalbe made a knyght aventures whan I come home!
    For oon thyng I promyse you, I wille fight anon—
    If my hert faile not whan I shal begynne!
    The most I fere is to come amonge women,
    For thei fight like develles with ther rokkes whan thei spynne!   *distaffs/spin*

225   MILES 1. Watkyn, I love the[e], for thu art ever a man!
    If thu quyte the[e] weelle in this grett viage,   *conduct yourself/journey*
    I shalle speke to my lord for the[e] that I can,   *however I can*
    That thu shalt no more be neither grome nor page!   *groom*
    MILES 2. I wylle speke for the[e], that thu shalt have better wage,
230   If thu quyte the[e] manly amonge the wyves,
    For thei be as fers as a lyon in a cage,   *fierce*
    Whan thei are broken ought, to reve men of ther lives!   *deprive*

    Here the knyghtes and Watkyn walke abought the place
    tylle Mary and Joseph be conveid into Egipt.

    Dixit angelus: *The Angel speaks*

ANGEL. O Joseph, ryse up, and loke thu tary nought!
    Take Mary with the[e], and into Egipt flee!
235   For Jhesu, thi sone, pursuyd is and sought,
    By Kyng Herowdes, the wiche of gret inyquyte   *who through*
    Commaundid hath thurgh Bedlem cite,   *Bethlehem*
    In his cruelle and furyous rage,
    To sle alle the children that be in that cuntre   *slay*
240   That may be founde within to yeere of age!   *under two*

    Ther shalle he shewe in that region   *i.e., Jesus*
    Diverse myracles of his high regalye—   *royal divinity*
    In alle ther temples the mawmentes shalle falle down,*   *idols*
    To shew a tokyn towardes the partie!   *people*
245   This child hath lordship, as prophetes do specifie,
    And at his comyng, thurgh his myghty hond,

---

243. The mohammeds (idols) shall fall down. [See Isaiah 19:1; Hosea 10:2]

In despight of alle idolatrie,   *contempt*
Every oon shalle falle, whan he comyth into the lond!

JOSEPH.   O good Lord, of thi gracious ordenaunce,
250   Like as thu list for oure jorney provide   *Just as you want*
In this viage with humble attendaunce,   *journey*
    As God disposeth, and list to be oure gyde.   *ordains/consents*
    Therfor, upon them bothe mekely I shalle abide,
    Praying to that Lord to thynk upon us three,
255   Us to preserve, wheder we go or ryde   *walk or ride*
Towardes Egipte, from alle advercite.

MARIA.   Now, husbond, in alle hast I pray you, go we hens   *haste*
    For drede of Herowdes, that cruelle knyght.
Gentylle spouse, now do youre diligens,   *act quickly*
260   And bryng your asse, I pray you, anon right,   *right away*
    And from hens let us passe with alle oure myght,
    Thankyng that Lord so for us doth provide
    That we may go from Herowdes, that cursid wight,   *man*
    Wiche wille us devoure if that we abide!   *Who/destroy/stay here*

265   JOSEPH.   Mary, you to do plesaunce without ony lett,   *to please you/delay*
    I shalle brynge forth your asse without more delay.
Ful sone, Mary, theron ye shalbe sett,   *Very soon*
    And this litelle child that in your wombe lay;
    Take hym in your armys, Mary, I you pray,
270   And of your swete mylke lete hym sowke inowe,   *Milk/suck/enough*
    Mawgere Herowdes and his grett fray,   *In spite of/rage*
    And as your spouse, Mary, I shalle go with you.

This ferdelle of gere I ley up my bakke—   *bundle*
Now I am redy to go from this cuntre.
275   Alle my smale instrumentes is putt in my pakke;   *tools*
    Now go we hens, Mary, it wille no better be!

    Et exeant.   *And let them leave*

JOSEPH.   For drede of Herowdes apaas I wylle high me!   *quickly/go*
Lo, now is oure geere trussid, both more and lesse.   *bundled up*
    Mary, for to plese you, with alle humylite,
280   I shalle go before, and lede forth youre asse.

*Here Mary and Joseph shalle go out of the place, and the goddes shalle falle,
and than shalle come in the women of Israel, with young children in ther
armys, and than the knyghtes shalle go to them, sayng as foluyth:*

MILES 1. Herke ye, wyffys! We be come your housholdes to visite,   *have come to*
  Though ye be never so wroth nor wood,   *Even though/angry/mad*
  With sharpe swerdes that redely wille byte,   *readily*
  Alle your children within to yeere age in oure cruelle mood,   *under two*
285   Thurgheout alle Bethleem to kylle and shed ther yong blood,
  As we be bound be the commaundement of the kyng!   *required/command*
    Who that seith nay, we shalle make a flood   *resists*
  To renne in the stretis, by ther blood shedyng!   *bloodshed*

MILES 2. Therfor, unto us ye make a delyveraunce
290   Of youre yong children, and that anone!   *right away*
  Or elles, be Mahounde, we shalle geve you a myschaunce!   *trouble*
    Oure sharpe swerdes thurgh your bodies shalle goon!
  WATKYN. Therfor beware, for we wille not leve oon   *one*
  In alle this cuntre that shalle us escape!
295   I shalle rather slee them everychoon,   *gladly*
  And make them to lye and mowe like an ape!   *moan*

MULIER 1. Fye on you traitours of cruelle tormentrye,
  Wiche with your swerdes of mortalle violens   *Brought on*
MULIER 2. Oure yong children, that can no socoure but crie,   *not help*
300   Wylle slee and devoure in ther innocens!   *destroy*
  MULIER 3. Ye false traitours! Unto God ye do grett offens,
  To sle and mordere yong children that in ther cradelle slumber!
  MULIER 4. But we women shalle make ageyns you resistens,
  After oure powere, youre malice to encomber!

305 WATKYN. Peas, you folysshe quenys! Wha shuld you defende   *women/How*
  Ageyns us armyd men in this apparaile?
  We be bold men, and the kyng us ded sende
  Hedyr into this cuntre to hold with you bataile!   *Hither/battle against you*
  MULIER 1. Fye upon the[e], coward! Of the[e] I wille not faile
310   To dubbe the[e] knyght with my rokke rounde!   *distaff*
  Women be ferse when thei list to assaile   *fierce/want to attack*
  Suche prowde boyes, to caste to the grounde!

WATKYN. Avaunt ye, skowtys! I defye you everychone!   *Out, shrews!*
  For I wole bete you alle, myself alone!

  Hic occident pueros.   *Here they slaughter the boys*

315 MULIER 1. Alas, alasse, good gossyppes! This is a sorowfulle peyn,   *god-sisters*
  To se oure dere children that be so yong
  With these caytyves thus sodeynly to be slayn!   *villains*
  A vengeaunce I aske on them alle for this grett wrong!

MULIER 2. And a very myscheff mut come them amonge,   *may great misfortune*
320 Whersoever thei be come or goon,   *wherever they go*
　　　For thei have kylled my yong sone John!

MULIER 3. Gossippis, a shamefulle deth I aske upon Herowde our kyng,
　　　That thus rygorously oure children hath slayn!   *cruelly*
MULIER 4. I pray God bryng hym to an ille endyng,
325 And in helle pytte to dwelle ever in peyn!
WATKYN. What, ye harlottes! I have aspied certeyn   *scoundrels/indeed*
　　　That ye be traytours to my lord the kyng,
　　　And therfor I am sure ye shalle have an ille endyng!

MULIER 1. If ye abide, Watkyn, you and I shalle game   *play*
330 With my distaff that is so rounde!
MULIER 2. And if I seas, thanne have I shame,   *cease*
　　　Tylle thu be fellid down to the grounde!
MULIER 3. And I may gete the[e] within my bounde,   *reach*
　　　With this staff I shalle make the[e] lame!
335 WATKYN. Yee, I come no more ther, be Seynt Mahounde!
　　　For if I do, me thynketh I shalle be made tame!   *It seems to me/brought down*

MULIER 1. Abyde, Watkyn! I shalle make the[e] a knyght!   *Stay*
WATKYN. Thu make me a knyght? That were on the newe!   *a new one*
　　　But for shame—my trouthe I you plight—
340 I shuld bete you bak and side tylle it were blewe!
　　　But be my god Mahounde that is so true,   *by*
　　　My hert begynne to fayle and waxeth feynt,
　　　Or elles, be Mahoundes blood, ye shuld it rue!   *by*
　　　But ye shalle lose your goodes as traitours atteynt!   *condemned*

345 MULIER 1. What, thu javelle! Canst not have do?   *knave/be done*
　　　Thu and thi cumpany shalle not depart
　　　Tylle of oure distavys ye have take part!   *distaffs/tasted*
　　　Therfor, ley on, gossippes, with a mery hart,
　　　And lett them not from us goo!

　　　*Here thei shalle bete Watkyn, and the knyghtes shalle come
　　　to rescue hym, and than thei go to Herowdes, thus sayng:*

350 MILES 1. Honorable prynce of grett apparayle,
　　　Thurgh Jerusalem and Jude your wylle we have wrought;   *Judea*
　　　Fulle suerly harneysed in armour of plate and maile,   *safely*
　　　The children of Israelle unto deth we have brought!
MILES 2. Syr, to werke your commaundement we lettid nought,   *kept back nothing*
355 In the stretes of the children to make a flood!

We sparid neithere for care nor thought   *sentiment*
Thurgh Bethlem to shede alle the yong blood!

WATKYN. In feyth, my lord, alle the children be dede,
    And alle the men out of the cuntre be goon!
360 Ther be but women, and thei crie in every stede: *place*
    "A vengeaunce take Kyng Herode, for he hath our children sloon!"   *slain*
    And bidde "A myscheff take hym!" both evyn and morn;   *misfortune/evening*
    For kyllyng of ther children on you thei crie oute,
    And thus goth your name alle the cuntre abought!

365 HERODES. Oute! I am madde! My wyttes be ner goon!
    I am wo for the wrokyng of this werke wylde!   *wreaking*
    For as wele I have slayn my frendes as my foon!   *foes*
    Wherfor, I fere, deth hath me begyled!   *tricked*
    Notwithstondyng syn thei be alle defyled,   *since/killed*
370 And on the yong blood of Bethlem wrought wo and wrake,   *destruction*
    Yitt I am in no certeyn of that yong child!   *not sure*
    Now for woo myn herte gynneth to quake!   *begins*

Alas! I am so sorowfulle and sett in sadnes!
    I chille and chevere for this orrible chaunce!   *shiver/horrible happening*
375 I commaunde you alle, as ye wole stond in my grace,   *would stand*
    After this yong kyng to make good enqueraunce!   *inquiry*
    And he that bryngeth me tydynges, I shalle hym avaunce.   *news/promote*
    Now, unto my chambere I purpose me this tyde,   *intend to go/time*
    And I charge you to my preceptes geve attendaunce,
380 In ony place where ye goo or ryde!

What! Out, out! Allas! I wene I shalle dey this day!   *believe/die*
    My hert tremelith and quakith for feere!   *trembles*
    My robys I rende ato, for I am on a fray,   *tear apart/in a rage*
    That my hert wille brest asundere evyn heere!   *burst asunder*
385 My lord Mahound, I pray the[e] with hert enteere,   *whole heart*
    Take my soule into thy holy hande,
    For I fele be my hert I shalle dey evyn heere,
    For my legges faltere, I may no lengere stande!

*Here dieth Herowde, and Symeon shalle sey as foluyth:**

[Jerusalem: The Temple]

---

388 s.d. *Vacat ab hinc:* "Omitted from here on" is written in the MS in a later hand, which may indicate that the rest of the play was not performed on one or more occasions.

SIMEON. Now, God, that art both lok and keye   *lock*
390   Of alle goodnesse and goostly governaunce,   *Spiritual guidance*
So yeve us grace thi lawys to obeye,   *give*
   That we unto the[e] do no displesaunce;   *displeasure*
   Lett thi grace of mercifulle haboundaunce   *abundance*
Upon me shyne, that callid am Symeon,
395   So that I may without ony variaunce
Teche thi people thi lawis everychon.   *all thy laws*

From the sterrid hevyn, Lord, thu list come down   *starry/You deigned to*
   Into the closett of a pure virgyn,   *womb*
Oure kynde to take for mannys salvacion!   *humanity to assume*
400   Thi grett mercy thu lowe lyst enclyne,   *You wished to bring down*
   Lyke as prophetys by grace that is divyne   *Just as*
Have prophecied of the[e] sythe longe afforn.   *since long ago*
   It is fulfilled, I knowe be ther doctryne,   *by*
And of a chast maide I wote wele thu art born. *chaste/know well*

405   Now, good Lord, hertly I the[e] pray,
   Here my requeste, grounded upon right!   *Hear*
Most blissed Lord, lett me never dey
   Tylle that I of the[e] may have a sight!
   Thu art so gloryous, so blissed, and so bright,
410   That thi presence to me shuld be gret solas!   *comfort*
   I shalle not reste, but pray bothe day and nyght,
Tylle I may behold, o Lord, thi swete face!

Here shalle Oure Lady come forth, holdyng Jhesu in
hir armys, and sey this language foluyng to Joseph:

MARIA. Joseph, my spouse, tyme it is we goo
Unto the temple to make an offrynge
415   Of oure swete son—the lawe commaundith so—
   And too yonge dovys with us for to bryng   *doves*
Into a prestes handes, withoute tarieng;   *delay*
I shalle presente for an observaunce
Oure babe so blissed wiche is but yonge.
420   With me to go, I pray you, make purviaunce.   *provision*

JOSEPH. Most blissed spouse, me list not to feyne—   *I wish/hesitate*
Fayn wold I plese you with hoolle affeccion.   *Gladly*
Behold now, wyff, her are dovys tweyne,   *here*
Of wiche ye shulle make an oblacion   *shall/offering*
425   With oure child, of fulle grett devocion.
Goth forth aforn, hertly I you pray,   *ahead*

And I shalle folue, voide of presumpcion,   *follow*
With true entent, as an old man may.

Here Maria and Joseph go toward the temple with Jhesu
and too doves, and Oure Lady seith unto Symeon: *two*

MARIA. Heylle, holy Symeon, fulle of grett vertu!   *Hail*
430   To make an offryng I gan myself purveye   *have provided myself*
Of my sovereigne sone, that callid is Jhesu,   *For the sake of*
With too yonge doves, the lawe to obeye.   *doves*
Toward this temple grace list me conveye,   *the wish for grace brought me*
Of Goddes sone to make a presentacion.
435   Wherfore, Symeon, hertly I you pray,
Into your handes take myn oblacion!   *offering*

Her shalle Symeon receyve of Maria Jhesu and too dovis, and holde
Jhesu in his armys, expownyng "Nunc dimittis," et cetera, * seyng thus:*

SIMEON. Wolcome, Lord, excellent of powere!
And wolcome, Maria, with youre sone sovereigne!
Your oblacion, of hoolle herte and enteere,   *whole and complete*
440   I receyve with these dovys tweyn.   *two doves*
Wolcome, babe! For joye what may I seyn?
Atwen myn armys now shalle I the[e] enbrace!   *Between*
My prayer, Lord, was not made in veyn,
For now I se thy celestialle face!

Here declare "Nunc dimittis."

445   SIMEON. O blissed Lord, after thi langage,
In parfight peas, now lett thy servaunt reste,
Forwhy myn eyen have seyn thi visage,   *Because/eyes*
And eke thyn helthe, thurgh my meke request.   *also/salvation*
Of the derk dungeon let the gates brest   *burst*
450   Before the face of thyn people alle!
Thu hast brought triacle and bawme of the best,*   *treacle*
With souereigne sugere geyn alle bitter galle!   *against*

I mene thiself, Lord, gracious and benigne,
That woldest come down from thyn high glorye,
455   Poyson to repelle. Thi mercy doth now shyne
To chaunge thynges that are transitory.

·436 s.d. See Luke 2:28-32. *Nunc dimittis servum tuum, Domine, secundum verbum tuum in pace.*
Used after the Gradual of the mass for the Feast of the Purification of the Blessed Virgin, or Candlemas
(2 February).
451. Treacle and balm: medieval restoratives.

Thu art the light and the hevynly skye!
To the relevyng of folk most cruelle,   *For the relief/most tortured*
Thu hast brought gladnesse to oure oratorye,
460   And enlumyned thy people of Israelle.

Here shalle Anna Prophetissa sey thus to the virgynes:

ANNA. Ye pure virgynes, in that ye may or can,
With tapers of wex, loke ye come forth here,
And worship this child, very God and man,
Offrid in this temple be his moder dere.

Her virgynes, as many as a man wylle, shalle holde
tapers in ther handes, and the first seyth:

465   VIRGO 1. As ye comaunde we shal do oure devere,   *duty*
That Lord to plese, echon for oure partye.   *each one*
He makyth vn[to] us so comfortable chere,   *mood*
That we must nedes this babe magnifie!   *glorify*
SIMEON. Now, Mary, I shalle telle you how I am purposed.   *what I intend*
470   To worshippe this Lord I wil go procession,   *in procession*
For I se Anna with virgynes disposed,
Mekly as nowe to youre sonys laudacion.   *praise*
MARIA. Blissed Symeon, with hertly affeccion,
As ye han seyd, I concent therto.   *have said*
475   JOSEPH. In worshippe of oure child with gret devossion,
Abought the tempille in ordire let us go.

SIMEON. Ye virgynes alle, with feythfulle intent
Dispose youresilf a song for to synge,   *Prepare*
To worshippe this childe that is here present,
480   Whiche to mankende gladnes list bryng.   *loves to bring*
In tokyn, oure hertes withe joye doth spryng!   *as a sign*
Betwyn myn armys this babe shalbe born.   *carried*
Now, ye virgynis, to this Lordes preysyng
Syngyth *Nunc dimittis* of whiche I spak afforn.   *spoke before*

Here shal Symeon bere Jhesu in his armys, goyng a procession
rounde aboute the tempille, and al this wyle the virgynis synge
"Nunc dimittis" and whan that is don, Symeon seyth:

485   SIMEON. O Jhesu, chef cause of oure welfare,
In yone tapire ther be thyng thre: *candle*
Wax, week, and light, whiche I shalle declare   *wick*
To the[e] apporpride by moralite—   *according to*
Lord, wax betoknyth thyn humanyte,

490   And week betoknyth thy soule most swete;   *wick*
       Yone lyght I lykene to the Godhed of the[e],
       Brightere than Phebus, for al his fervent hete.*   *the Sun*

       Pes and mercy han set in the[e] here swete,   *have*
       To slake the sharpnes, o Lord, of rigoure;
495   Very God and man gun togedire mete   *Truly/together have met*
       In the tabirnacle of thy modrys bowere.   *bower (and womb)*
       Now shalt thou exile wo and alle langoure,   *woe/sorrow*
       And of mankende t'appese infernalle stryf;
       Record of prophetes, thou shalt be redemptoure,
500   And singulere repast of everlastyng lyf.   *unique sustenance*

       My spretes joyen, thou art so amyable,   *spirits*
       I am nat wery to loke on thi face.   *do not tire*
       Oure trewe entent, let it be acceptable
       To the honor of the[e], shewyd in this place.
505   For thy seruauntes, a dwellyng thou shalt purchase,
       Brighter than beralle outhere clere cristalle.   *beryl or clear crystal*
       The[e] to worshippe as chef welle of grace,   *well, or font*
       On both my knees now doun knele I shalle.

       MARIA. Now Semyon, take me my childe that is so bright,   *give*
510   Chef lodesterre of my felicyte,   *lodestar*
       And alle that longyth to the lawe of right   *belongs*
       I shalle obeye, as it lyth in me.   *as the power lies*
       SIMEON. This Lord, I take you knelyng on my kne,
       Whiche shalle to blisse folk ageyn restore,
515   And eke be called tonne of tranquylyte,   *also/vessel*
       To yeve hem drynke that han thrustyd sore.   *give them/have thirsted*

       Here she receyveth hire sone, thus seyng:

       MARIA. Now is myn offryng to an ende conveyed,   *brought*
       Wherfore, Symeon, hens I wole wende.   *hence*
       SIMEON. The lawes, Mary, ful welle ye han obbeyed   *have*
520   In this tempille, with hert and mende.   *mind*
       Nowe ferwelle, Lord, comfort to alle mankende!   *farewell*
       Farwelle, Maria and Josephe on you waytyng.   *attending*
       JOSEPH. Selestialle socoure oure sone mot you sende,   *Celestial/may our son*
       And for his high mercy, yeve you his blissyng.   *give*

486-92. This explanation of the significance of the wax, wick, and light derives from *The Golden Legend,* where it is also associated with Candlemas.

Here Maria and Josephe goyng from the tempille seyng:

525   MARIA. Husbond, I thanke you of youre gentilnes   *for*
       That ye han shewed onto me this day;
       With oure child most gracious of godenes,
         Let us go hens, hertly I you pray!
       JOSEPH. Go forthe afforn, my oune wyf, I sey,   *ahead*
530   And I shalle come aftire, stil upon this ground.
       Ye shal me fynde plesaunt at every assaye;   *test*
       To cherysshe you, wyf, gretly am I bounde.

       SIMEON. Nowe may I be glad in myn inward mende,   *my soul*
        For I have seyn Jhesu with my bodely eye,
535   Wiche on a cros shalle bey al menkende,   *redeem*
        Slayn by Jwes at the Mount of Calvery;   *Jews*
       And throwe devyn grace here I wille provysye   *prophecy*
        Of blissed Mary howe she shalle suffre peyn,
        Whan hire swete sone shalle on a rood deye—   *cross*
540   A sharpe sward of sorowe shalle cleve hire hert atweyn.

       Anna Prophetissa, hertly I prey you nowe,
        Doth youre devire and youre diligent laboure,   *duty*
       And take these virgynis everychon with you,
        And teche hem to plese God, of most honoure.
545   ANNA. Lyke as ye say, I wille do this houre.
       Ye chast virgynis, with alle humylite,
        Worshippe we Jhesu, that shalbe oure savyoure—
       Alle at ones, come on, and folowe me.

       And shewe ye summe plesure as ye can,
550   In the worshippe of Jhesu, Oure Lady, and Seynt Anne!

Anna Prophetissa et [virgynes] tripident.   Anne the Prophetess and the virgins dance

       POETA. Honorable souereignes, thus we conclude
        Oure matere that we have shewid here in your presens,
       And though oure eloquens be but rude,
        We beseche you alle, of youre paciens,
555   To pardon us of oure offens,
       For after the sympylle cunnyng that we can,
        This matere we have shewid to your audiens,
       In the worshippe of Oure Lady and hir moder Seynt Anne.

       Now of this pore processe we make an ende,   *play*
560   Thankyng you alle of your good attendaunce,
       And the next yeer, as we be purposid in oure mynde,

The disputacion of the doctours to shew in your presens.
Wherfor now, ye virgynes, er we go hens,   *ere*
With alle your cumpany, you goodly avaunce!   *step forward*
565   Also, ye menstralles, doth your diligens;
Afore oure departyng, geve us a daunce!

Finis
Anno domini millione 1512
Jhon Parfre ded wryte thys booke

The Croxton *Play of the Sacrament*

The text of the Croxton *Play of the Sacrament* survives in folios 338^r-356^r of Trinity College, Dublin, MS. F.4.20 (Catalogue No. 652), a manuscript compilation of various works once belonging to John Madden (d. 1703), the late seventeenth-century President of the Royal College of Physicians of Ireland. The worn condition of the outer leaves of the play indicates that it originally existed independent of the Trinity collection, and the quires containing the play are now kept unbound and separate from the rest of the manuscript. Judging from its handwriting and watermarks, this copy of the play appears to have been made in the mid-sixteenth century, although the date of composition was probably late in the fifteenth century, certainly after 1461, the date given at the close of the play as the time when the enacted events were supposed to have taken place in Heraclea. Despite the location of the manuscript in Ireland, the play's language—East Midland, with some Norfolk forms—and the place-names mentioned in it suggest an East Anglian origin. The Croxton mentioned in the banns of the play might conceivably refer to any of several Croxtons in England, but most of them are in East Anglia, and the one nearest Babwell Mill (referred to in the Doctor episode), itself only a mile from Bury St. Edmunds in Suffolk, is located very close to Thetford, Norfolk.

The *Play of the Sacrament* is a unique representative in England of a true miracle play in the sense that it depicts a miraculous event, but its real form as it has come down to us in the manuscript is a hybrid of legend, conversion play, and folk play. Some liturgical elements can be discerned as well, in the parody of the consecration of the mass and in the explicit references to the events of Christ's passion that the mass commemorates. The story of Jews gaining possession of a consecrated host, testing it by torture, and having the host come to life as convincing proof of transubstantiation offers tremendous opportunity for dramatic effect. But to this plot is added an episode at almost the precise center of the play, featuring a quack folk doctor, Master Brundiche of Brabant. The episode—almost certainly interpolated, as it is not mentioned

274

in the banns—is introduced by the irreverent servant Colle. Brundiche ("Brown ditch") boasts that he can heal the hand of Jonathas the Jew, pulled off in the previous frantic scene; the doctor's failure contrasts with the successful ministrations of Jesus, who appears next in the most spectacular fashion out of an exploding oven.

The interpolated episode clearly derives from the English folk play tradition, in particular those mummers plays in which a boastful doctor repairs a fallen figure (the exotic and grotesque "Big Head," for example, the "Turkish Knight" or the "Turkey Snipe"), who has lost his head or otherwise been slain in a fight. The energy and vitality of that tradition inform the *Play of the Sacrament,* not only in the exuberance of the Doctor episode, but in the slapdash characterization of the bargaining, skeptical Jews, in the clownish treatment of the host, and particularly in the loss of the hand of Jonathas. All the howling antics lead to the Jews' conversion and baptism, rather than to their slaughter (as happens in a contemporary French analogue, *Le jeu et mystere de la sainte hostie par personnages),* so that by the end of the play its tone shifts easily to one of thanksgiving and praise. Indeed, the play concludes with the hymn of praise *Te Deum Laudamus*.

The banns of the *Play of the Sacrament* which advertise its action, along with the assertion in the manuscript that "Nine may play yt at ease," suggests that the play enjoyed a stage career on the road as part of an itinerant playing company's repertoire, or perhaps as a travelling script. With doubling, nine actors could manage the play handily, including the Brundiche and Colle episode. How the role of Jesus might have been played by a speaking "image" (ll. 716 s.d., 825 s.d.) remains open to conjecture.

The predominant stanzaic form in the Croxton *Play of the Sacrament* is double quatrains rhyming *ababbcbc,* though a good many single quatrains (*abab*) occur as well. Most lines have four stresses. The interpolated Doctor episode is composed mainly in tail-rhyme stanzas (*aaabcccb*), which are rarely found in the rest of the play. But a variety of other stanza forms do appear, often registering significant moments in the action. One notable feature is the heavy use of alphabetical alliteration by Jonathas in his opening boastful speech (ll. 95-114); he reverts to alliteration again in the description of his jewels (ll. 161-72), and the other Jews echo his alliterative habit as they make plans to steal the host (ll. 209-22).

The Croxton *Play of the Sacrament* was first edited by Whitley Stokes in an Appendix to *Transactions of the Philological Society* (1860-61), pp. 101-52. The standard scholarly edition, by Norman Davis, appears in the EETS *Non-Cycle Plays and Fragments*; a facsimile of the manuscript, also edited by Davis, appears in *Non-Cycle Plays and the Winchester Dialogues*. For more on the Doctor in folk plays see E.K. Chambers, *The English Folk-Play*. For recent critical explorations, see Sarah Beckwith, "Ritual, Church and Theatre:

Medieval Dramas of the Sacramental Body" in David Aers, *Culture and History 1350-1600* (see Suggestions for Further Reading).

THE CROXTON *PLAY OF THE SACRAMENT*

[*DRAMATIS PERSONAE:**]

THE NAMYS AND NUMBERE OF THE PLAYERS:

[VEXILLATOR 1]	*Banner Bearer 1*
[VEXILLATOR 2]	*Banner Bearer 2*
JH[ES]US	
EPISCOPUS	*The Bishop*
ARISTORIUS, Christianus mercator	*A Christian Merchant*
[PRESBYTER, Isoder]	*A Priest (Aristory's Chaplain Isoder)*
CLERICUS [Peter Paul]	*Clerk*
JONATHAS, Judeus primus Magister	*The first Jew, Master*
JASON, Judeus secundus	*The second Jew*
JASDON, Judeus tertius	*The third Jew*
MASPHAT, Judeus quartus	*The fourth Jew*
MALCHUS, Judeus quintus	*The fifth Jew*
MAGISTER PHISICUS [BRUNDYCHE]	*The Physician (Brundiche of Brabant)*
COLL[E], SERVUS	*Colle, his servant*

NINE MAY PLAY YT AT EASE

[*THE BANNS*]

VEXILLATOR 1. Now the Father and the Sune and the Holy Goste,
    That all this wyde worlde hat wrowght,   *Who has made*
Save all thes semely, bothe leste and moste,   *these worthy people of every degree*
    And bryn[g]e yow to the blysse that he hath yow to bowght!
5   We be ful purposed with hart and with thowght
Off our mater to tell the entent,
    Off the marvellys that wer wondursely wrowght
Off the holi and blyssyd Sacrament.   *By*

DRAMATIS PERSONAE: The following list appears in the manuscript at the end of the play.

VEXILLATOR 2. S[o]vereyns, and yt lyke yow to here   *Masters, if/hear*
            the purpoos of this play
10   That [ys] representyd now in yower syght,
    Whych in Aragon was doon, the sothe to saye,   *occurred/truth*
      In Eraclea, that famous cyté, aryght—   *truly*
      Therin wonneth a merchaunte off mekyll myght,   *dwells/great*
    Syr Arystorye was callyd hys name,
15   Kend full fere with mani a wyght,   *Known/far/man*
    Full fer in the worlde sprong hys fame.   *far*

VEXILLATOR 1. Anon to hym ther cam a Jewe,
      With grete rychesse for the nonys,
    And wonneth in the cyté of Surrey—this full trewe—   *dwells/Syria*
20   The wyche hade gret plenté off precyous stonys.   *Who*

Off this Cristen merchaunte he freyned sore,   *bargained hard*
    W[h]ane he wolde have had hys entente.   *At the point that/wish*
Twenti pownd and merchaundyse mor[e]
He proferyd for the Holy Sacrament.

25 VEXILLATOR 2.   But the Cristen marchaunte theroff sed nay,
    Because hys profer was of so lityll valewe;   *offer*
An hundder pownd but he wolde pay   *unless*
    No lenger theron he shuld pursewe.

But mor[e] off ther purpos they gunne speke,   *began to*
30   The Holi Sacramente for to bey;
And all for the wo[r]lde be wreke,   *to be avenged*
    A gret sume off gold begune down ley.
VEXILLATOR 1.   Thys Crysten merchante consentyd, the sothe to sey,
    And in the nyght affter made hym delyveraunce.   *made delivery*
35   Thes Jewes all grete joye made they;
But off thys betyde a straunger chaunce: *from this occurred*

They grevid our Lord gretly on grownd,   *tortured/on earth*
    And put hym to a new passyoun;   *through a new Passion*
With daggers goven hym many a greuyos wound;   *gave*
40   Nayled hym to a pyller, with pynsons plukked hym doune.   *pincers*

VEXILLATOR 2. And sythe thay toke that blysed brede so sownde   *then/good*
    And in a cawdron they ded hym boyle.   *cauldron/did*
In a clothe full just they yt wounde,   *tight*
    And so they ded hym sethe in oyle;   *did/boil/oil*

45   And than thay putt hym to a new turmentry,   *then/torment*
    In an hoote ovyn speryd hym fast.   *hot oven/thrust*

There he appyred with woundys blody;
  The ovyn rofe asondre and all tobrast.   *split/burst*
VEXILLATOR 1.   Thus in our lawe they wer made stedfast;
50 The Holy Sacrament sheuyd them grette favour;   *showed*
  In contrycyon thyr hertys wer cast
And went and shewyd ther lyves to a confesour.

Thus be maracle off the Kyng of Hevyn,   *miracle*
  And by myght and power govyn to the prestys mowthe,   *given/mouth*
55 In an howshold wer convertyd iwys elevyn.   *certainly*
  At Rome this myracle ys knowen welle kowthe.   *well-known*

VEXILLATOR 2.   Thys marycle at Rome was presented, forsothe,   *miracle*
  Yn the yere of our Lord, a thowsand four hundder sixty and on[e],   *1461*
  That the Jewes with Holy Sa[c]rament dyd woth,   *injury*
60 In the forest seyd of Aragon.   *aforesaid*

Loo, thus God at a tyme showyd hym there,   *himself*
  Thorwhe hys mercy and hys mekyll myght;   *Through/great*
Unto the Jewes he gan appere   *appeared*
  That thei shuld nat lesse hys hevenly lyght.   *So that/lose*
65 VEXILLATOR 1.   Therfor, frendys, with all your myght
Unto youer gostly father shewe your synne;   *spiritual*
  Beth in no wanhope daye nor nyght.   *Be/despair*
No maner off dowghtys that Lord put in.   *doubts*

For that the dowghtys the Jewys than in stode—   *Because/stood in*
70 As ye shall se pleyd, both more and lesse—   *see acted*
Was yff the Sacrament were flesshe and blode;   *whether*
  Therfor they put yt to suche dystresse.   *Thus*
VEXILLATOR 2.   And yt place yow, thys gaderyng that here ys,   *please/group*
At Croxston on Monday yt shall be sen;   *seen*
75 To see the conclusyon of this lytell processe   *story*
Hertely welcum shall yow bene.

Now Jhesu yow save from trey and tene,   *pain and suffering*
  To send us hys hyhe ioyes of hevyne;   *exalted*
There myght ys withouton mynd to mene.   *Where might is beyond description*
80 Now, mynstrell, blow up with a mery stevyn.   *song*

EXPLICIT

Hereafter foloweth the Play of the Conversion of Ser Jonathas the Jew
by Myracle of the Blyssed Sacrament

ARISTORIUS. Now Cryst, that ys our Creatour, from shame he cure us;
    He maynteyn us with myrth that meve upon the mold;   *moves/earth*
    Unto hys en [d] elesse joye myghtly he restore us,   *mightily may he*
    All tho that in hys name in peas well them hold;   *those*
85 For of a merchante most myght therof my tale ys told,   *most powerful*
    In Eraclea ys non suche, w[h]oso wyll understond,
        For off all Aragon I am most myghty of sylver and of gold—
    For and yt wer a countre to by, now wold I nat wond.   *For if/country/buy/hesitate*

    Syr Arystory ys my name,
90   A merchaunte myghty of a royall araye;
    Ful wyde in this worlde spryngyth my fame,
        Fere kend and knowen, the sothe for to saye,   *Known far*
        In all maner of londys, without ony naye,   *surely*
    My merchaundyse renneth, the sothe for to tell;   *travels*
95   In Gene and in Jenyse and in Genewaye,   *Genoa/Geneva*
    In Surrey and in Saby and in Salern I sell;   *Syria/Saba/Salerno*

    In Antyoche and in Almayn moch ys my myght,   *Germany*
        In Braban and in Brytayn I am full bold,   *Brabant*
    In Calabre and in Coleyn ther rynge I full ryght,   *Calabria/Cologne/reign*
100   In Dordrede and in Denmark be the clyffys cold;   *Dordrecht*
    In Alysander I have abundaw[n]se in the wyde world.   *Alexandria*
    In France and in Farre fresshe be my flower [ys],   *Faeroe (?)*
        In Gyldre and in Galys have I bowght and sold,   *Guelderland/Galacia*
    In Hamborowhe and in Holond moch merchantdyse ys owrys;   *Hamburg/ours*

105 In Jerusalem and in Jherico among the Jewes jentle,
        Amo[n]g the Caldeys and Cattlyngys kend   *Chaldees/Catalans/known*
                            ys my komyng;
    In Raynes and in Rome to Seynt Petyrs temple,   *Rheims*
        I am knowen certenly for bying and sellyng;

    In Mayn and in Melan full mery have I be;   *Maine/Milan/been*
110   Owt of Navern to Naples moch good ys that I bryng;   *Navarre/great wealth*
    In Pondere and in Portyngale moche ys my gle;   *Portugal/happiness*
        In Spayne and in Spruce moche ys my spedyng;   *Prussia/flourishing*
        In Lombardy and in Lachborn there ledde ys my lykyng;   *Luxembourg*
    In Taryse and in Turkey there told ys my tale;   *Tharsia*
115   And in the dukedom of Oryon moche have I in weldyng: *Orleans(?)/wielding*
    And thus thorowght all this world sett ys my sale.   *sail*

No man in thys world may weld more rychesse;   *wield*
   All I thank God of hys grace, for he that me sent;
   And as a lordys pere thus lyve I in worthynesse.   *lord's equal*
120 My curat wayteth upon me to knowe myn entent,
   And men at my weldyng, and all ys me lent   *command/granted*
   My well for to worke in thys world so wyde.   *will*
   Me dare they not dysplese by no condescent.   *by any means*
   And who so doth, he ys not able to abyde.

125 PRESBYTER. No man shall you tary ne t[r]owble thys tyde,   *hinder nor trouble/time*
   But every man delygently shall do yow plesance;
   And I unto my connyng to the best shall hem guyde
   Unto Godys plesyng to serue yow to attrueaunce.   *in attendance*

   For ye be worthy and notable in substance of good,   *wealth*
130 Off merchauntys of Aragon ye have no pere—   *equal*
   And therof thank God that dyed on the roode,   *cross*
   That was your makere and hath yow dere.   *holds you dear*

   ARISTORIUS. Forsoth, syr pryst, yower talkyng ys good;
   And therfor affter your talkyng I wyll atteyn   *attempt*
135 To wourshyppe my God that dyed on the roode,
   Never, whyll that I lyve, ageyn that wyll I seyn.   *against/speak*
   But, Petyr Powle, my clark, I praye the[e] goo wele pleyn   *completely*
   Thorowght all Eraclea, that thow ne wonde,   *do not delay*
   And wytte yff ony merchaunte be come to this reyn   *learn/kingdom*
140 Of Surrey or of Sabe or of Shelysdown.   *Syria/Saba/Chalidonia*

   CLERICUS. At your wyll for to walke I wyl not say nay,   *As you wish*
   Smertly to go serche at the waterys syde;   *Immediately*
   Yff ony plesaunt bargyn be to your paye,   *profit*
   As swyftly as I can I shall hym to yow guyde.
145 Now wyll I walke by thes pathes wyde,
   And seke the haven both up and down,   *harbor*
   To wette yff ony onkowth shyppes therin do ryde   *To learn/foreign*
   Of Surrey or of Saby [or] of Shelysdown.

   Now shall the merchantys man withdrawe hym
   and the Jewe Jonathas shall make hys bost.

   JONATHAS. Now, almyghty Machomet, marke in thi magesté,
150 Whose lawes tendrely I have to fulfyll,   *closely*
   After my dethe bryng me to thy hyhe see,   *high seat*
   My sowle for to save yff yt be thy wyll;
   For myn entent ys for to fulfyll,
   As my gloryus God the[e] to honer,

155   To do agen thy entent yt shuld grve me yll,   *against/grieve*
        Or agen thyn lawe for to reporte.   *speak*
        For I thanke the[e] hayly that hast me sent   *greatly*
          Gold, syluer, and presyous stonys,
        And abu[n]ddaunce of spycys thou hast me lent,   *granted*
160   A[s] I shall reherse before yow onys: *once*
        I have amatystys, ryche for the nonys,   *amethysts*
        And baryllys that be bryght of ble;   *beryls/aspect*
          And saphyre semely, I may show yow attonys,   *at once*
        And crystalys clere for to se;

165   I have dyamantys derewourthy to dresse,   *precious diamonds to set*
        And emerawdys, ryche I trow they be,
        Onyx and achatys both more and lesse,   *agates large and small*
          Topazyouns, smaragdys of grete degré,   *topazes, emeralds*
          Perlys precyous grete plenté;
170   Of rubes ryche I have grete renown;
          Crepwadys and calcedonyes semely to se,   *Toadstones*
        A[nd] curyous carbunclys here ye fynd mown;   *can you find*

        Spycys I hawe both grete and smale
          In my shyppes, the sothe for to saye,
175   Gyngere, lycoresse and cannyngalle,   *galingale*
          And fygys fatte to plese yow to paye;
        Peper and saffyron and spycys smale,
          And datys wole dulcett for to dresse,   *all sweet/use*
        Almundys and rys, full every male,   *rice/every sack full*
180   And reysones both more and lesse: *raisins*

        Clowys, greynis, and gynger grene,   *grains of paradise*
          Mace, mastyk that myght ys,   *mastic/strong*
        Synymone, suger, as yow may sene,
          Long peper and Indas lycorys;   *Indian*
185   Orengys a[nd] apples of grete apryce,   *value*
          Pungarnetys and many other spycys,—   *Pomegranates*
        To tell yow all I have now, iwyse,
        And moche other merchandyse of sondry spycys.

        Jew Jonathas ys my name,
190   Jazon and Jazdon thei waytyn on my wyll,
        Masfat and Malchus they do the same,
          As ye may knowe yt ys bothe rycht and skyll.   *right and proper*
          I tell yow all, bi dal and by hylle,   *by dale*
        In Eraclea ys noon so moche of myght.
195   Werfor ye owe tenderli to tende me tyll,   *listen to me attentively*
        For I am chefe merchaunte of Jewes, I tell yow be ryght.

But Jazon and Jazdon, a mater wollde I mene—   *mention*
Mervelously yt ys ment in mynde—
The beleve of thes cristen men ys false, as I wene;
200   For the[y] beleve on a cake—me thynk yt ys onkynd.   *unnatural*
And all they seye how the prest dothe yt bynd,   *they all/consecrate*
And be the myght of hys word make yt flessh and blode—
And thus be a conceyte the wo[r]lde make us blynd—   *by a trick*
And how that yt shuld be he that deyed upon the rode.   *died/cross*

205   JASON. Yea, yea, master, a strawe for talis!   *such tales*
That ma not fale in my beleve;
But myt we yt gete onys within our pales,   *if we might/grasp*
I trowe we shuld sone affter putt yt in a preve.   *to the test*
JAZDON.   Now, be Machomete so myghty,
that ye doon of meve,   *that which you propose*
210   I wold I wyste how that we myght yt gete;   *I wish I knew*
I swer be my grete god, and ellys mote I nat cheve   *may/thrive*
But wyghtly the[r]on wold I be wreke.   *quickly/revenged*

MASPHAT. Yea, I dare sey feythfulli that ther feyth [ys fals]:
That was never he that on Calvery was kyld,
215   Or in bred for to be blode yt ys ontrewe als;   *also*
But yet with ther wyles thei wold we were wyld.   *want us fooled*
MALCHUS.   Yea, I am myghty Malchus, that boldly am byld;   *built*
That brede for to bete byggly am I bent.   *beat much/inclined*
Onys out of ther handys and yt myght be exyled,   *if it/taken*
220   To helpe castyn yt in care wold I counsent.   *torment*

JONATHAS. Well, syrse, than kype cunsel, I cummande yow all,   *keep*
And no word of all thys be wyst.   *made known*
But let us walke to see Arystories hall,
And affterward more counsell among us shall caste.   *we'll advise each other*
225   With hym to bey and to sel I am of powere prest: *buy/ready*
A bargyn with hym to make I wyll assaye;   *try*
For gold and sylver I am nothyng agast   *I have no doubt*
But that we shall get that cake to ower paye.   *for our pleasure*

Her[e] shall Ser Ysodyr the prest speke ont[o] Ser Arystori,
seyng on thys wyse to hym; and Jonatas goo don of[f] his stage.

PRESBYTER. Syr, be yowr leve, I may [no] lengere dwell;   *stay*
230   Yt ys fer paste none, yt ys tyme to go to cherche,   *far past noon*
There to saye myn evynsong, forsothe as I yow tell,
And syth coume home ageyne, as I am wont to werche.   *then/used to doing*

ARISTORIUS. Sir Isydor, I praye yow wallke at yowr wyll,
    For to serfe God yt ys well doune,
235 And syt[h] com agen and ye shall suppe your fyll,
    And walke than to your chamber as ye are wont to doon.

Her[e] shall the marchant men mete with the Jewes.

JONATHAS. A, Petre Powle, good daye and wele imett!   *well met*
    Wer ys thy master, as I the[e] pray?
CLERICUS. Lon[g] from hym have I not lett   *tarried*
240   Syt[h] I cam from hym, the sothe for to saye.   *Since*
    Wat tidyng with yow, ser, I yow praye,   *What news*
    Affter my master that ye doo frayne?   *ask*
    Have ye ony bargen that wer to hys paye?   *would be/profit*
    Let me have knowlech; I shall wete hym to seyn.   *shall know what to tell him*

245 JONATHAS. I have bargenes royall and ry[c]h
    For a marchaunt with to bye and sell;
    In all thys lond is ther non lyke
    Off aboundaunce of good, as I will tell.   *goods*

Her[e] shall the clerk goon to Ser Aristori, saluting him thus:

CLERICUS. All hayll, master, and wel mot yow be!   *may*
250   Now tydyngys can I yow tell:
    The grettest marchaunte in all Surré   *Syria*
    Ys come with yow to bey and sell:
      This tal ryght wele he me told.   *This conversation*
    Sir Jonatas ys hys nam,
255   A marchant of ryght gret fame;
    He wolld sell yow, without blame,   *trouble*
    P[l]enté of clothe of golde.

ARISTORIUS. Petre Powle, I can the[e] thanke!
    I prey the[e] rychely araye myn hall
260 As owyth for a marchant of the banke;   *befits*
    Lete non defawte be fownd at all.   *no defect*
CLERICUS.   Sekyrly, master, no m[o]re ther shall!   *certainly*
    Styffly about I thynke to stere,   *Smartly/stir*
    Hasterli to hange your parlowr with pall,   *Hastily/rich cloth*
265 As longeth for a lordis pere.   *As is proper*

Here shall the Jewe merchaunt and his men come to the Cristen merchaunte.

JONATHAS. All haylle, Syr Aristorye, semelé to se,   *seemly*
    The myghtyest merchaunte off Arigon!

Off yower welfare fayn wet wold we,   *gladly would we learn*
And to bargeyn with you this day am I boun.   *determined*

270   ARISTORIUS.   Sir Jonathas, ye be wellcum unto myn hall!
     I pray yow come up and sit bi me,
     And tell me wat good ye have to sell,   *goods*
     And yf ony bargeny mad[e] may be.

JONATHAS.   I have clothe of gold, precyous stons and spycys plente.
275   Wyth yow a bargen wold I make—
     I wold bartre wyth yow in pryvyté   *privacy*
     On lytell thyng, [that] ye wyll me yt take   *For a*
     Prevely in this stownd;   *secretly/place*
     And I woll sure yow be thys lyght,   *assure*
280   Never dystre[n] yow daye nor nyght,   *to constrain*
     But be sworn to yow full ryght   *completely*
     And geve yow twenti pownd.

ARISTORIUS.   Sir Jonathas, sey me for my sake,   *tell me*
     What man[er] of marchandis ys that ye mene?
285   JONATHAS.   Yowr God, that ys full mytheti, in a cake,   *mighty*
     And thys good anoon shall yow seen.
     [ARISTORIUS.]   Nay, in feyth, that shall not bene.
     I woll not for an hundder pownd
     To stond in fere my Lord to tene;   *offend*
290   And for so lytell a valew in conscyen[c]e to stond bownd.   *small a price*

JONATHAS.   Sir, the entent ys, if I myght knowe or undertake   *so that/understand*
     Yf that he were God allmyght,
     Off all my mys I woll amende make,   *misdeeds/would*
     And doon hym wourshepe bothe day and nyght.

295   ARISTORIUS.   Jonathas, trowth I shall the[e] tell:
     I stond in gret dowght to do that dede,   *fear*
     To yow that dere all for to sell   *who sells everything dear*
     I fere me that I shuld stond in drede;   *danger*
     For and I unto the chyrche yede,   *if/went*
300   And preste or clerke myght me aspye,
     To the bysshope thei wolde go tell that dede
     And apeche me of eresye.   *accuse/heresy*

JONATHAS.   Sir, as for that, good shyffte may ye make,   *strategy*
     And, for a vaylle, to walkyn on a nyght   *concealment*
305   Wan prest and clerk to rest ben take;   *When/have gone*
     Than shall ye be spyde of no wyght.   *by no one*
     ARISTORIUS.   Now sey me, Jonathas, be this lyght!   *tell me*

Wat payment therfor wollde yow me make?   *What*
JONATHAS.   Forty pownd, and pay yt ful ryght,   *right away*
310 Evyn for that Lorde sake.   *Lord's*

ARISTORIUS. Nay, nay, Jonathas, there-ageyn   *once more*
    I w[o]ld not for an hundder pownd.
JONATHAS. Sir, hir ys [yo]wr askyng toolde pleyn,   *paid in full*
    I shall yt tell in this stownd.   *count/place*

315 Here is an hundder pownd, neyther mor nor lasse,
    Of dokettys good, I dar well saye;   *ducats*
Tell yt ere yow from me passe;   *Count*
    Me thynketh yt a royall araye.   *kingly display (of wealth)*

But fyrst, I pray yow, tell me thys:
320   Off thys thyng whan shall I hafe delyverance?
ARISTORIUS. To-morowe betymes; I shall not myse;   *early*
    This nyght therfor I shall make purveaunce.   *arrangement*

Syr Isodyr he ys now at chyrch,
    There seyng hys evynsong,
325 As yt ys worshepe for to werche;   *pious to do*
    He shall sone cum home, he wyll nat be long,
        Hys sopere for to eate;
    And when he ys buskyd to hys bedde,   *is gone to*
    Ryght sone hereafter he shalbe spedd.   *his business shall be done*
330 No speche among yow there be spredd;
    To kepe yowr toungys ye nott lett.   *do not fail*

JONATHAS. Syr, almyghty Machomyght be with yow!   *Mohammed*
    And I shall cum agayn ryght sone.
ARISTORIUS. Jonathas, ye wott what I have sayd, and how *know*
335 I shall walke for that we have to doun.   *that which/do*

Here goeth the Jewys away and the preste commyth home.

PRESBYTER. Syr, Almyghty God mott be yowr gyde   *may*
    And glad yow wheresoo ye rest!   *gladden*
ARISTORIUS. Syr, ye be welcom home thys tyde.   *time*
    Now, Peter, gett us wyne of the best.

340 CLERICUS. Syr, here ys a drawte of Romney red,
    Ther ys no better in Aragon,
And a lofe of lyght bred—
    Yt ys holesom as sayeth the fesycyon.   *physician*

ARISTORIUS. Drynke of[f], Ser Isoder, and be of good chere!
345   Thys Romney ys good to goo with to reste;
    Ther ys no precyouser fer nor nere,   *none more precious, far or near*
    For all wykkyd metys yt wyll degest.   *unpalatable foods*

PRESBYTER. Syr, thys wyne ys good at a taste,
    And therof have I drunke ryght well.
350 To bed to gone thus have I cast,   *decided*
    Evyn strayt after thys mery mele.

    Now, Ser, I pray to God send yow good nyght.
    For to my chambere now wyll I gonne.
    ARISTORIUS. Ser, with yow be God almyght,
355   And sheld yow ever from yowr fone.   *foes*

Here shall Aristorius call hys clarke to hys presens.

ARISTORIUS. Howe, Peter! In the[e] ys all my trust,
    In especyall to kepe my counsell: *secrets*
    For a lytyl waye walkyn I must.
    I wyll not be long; trust as I the[e] tell.

360 Now prevely wyll I preve my pace,   *secretly/set/steps*
    My bargayn thys nyght for to fulfyll.
    Ser Isoder shall nott know of thys case,
    For he hath oftyn sacred as yt ys skyll.   *consecrated*
    The chyrche key ys at my wyll;
365 Ther ys no thyng that me shall tary,   *hinder*
    I wyll nott abyde by dale nor hyll   *dally*
    Tyll yt be wrowght, by Saynt Mary!   *be done*

Here shal he enter the chyrche and take the Hoost.

ARISTORIUS. Ah! now have I all myn entent;
    Unto Jonathas now wyll I fare;
370 To fullfyll my bargayn have I ment,   *intended*
    For that mony wyll amend my fare,   *state*
        As thynkyth me.
    But now wyll I passe by thes pathes playne;
    To mete with Jonathas I wold fayne.   *will gladly*
375 Ah! yonder he commytht in certayn;
    Me thynkyth I hym see.

    Welcom, Jonathas, gentyll and trew,
    For well and truly thou kepyst thyn howre;

Here ys the Host, sacred newe,   *newly consecrated*
380   Now wyll I home to halle and bowre.   *house and home*

JONATHAS. And I shall kepe thys trusty treasure
    As I wold doo my gold and fee.
Now in thys clothe I shall the[e] cure   *cover*
    That no wyght shall the[e] see.

Here shall Arystory goo hys waye and Jonathas
and hys seruantys shall goo to the tabyll thus sayng:

385   JONATHAS. Now, Jason and Jasdon, ye be Jewys jentyll,
    Masfatt and Malchus, that myghty arn in mynd,
Thys merchant from the Crysten temple
    Hathe gett us thys bred that make us thus blynd.   *blinded, hoodwinked*
    Now, Jason, as jentyll as ever was the lynde,   *linden tree*
390   Into the forsayd parlowr prevely take thy pase;   *secretly/steps*
    Sprede a clothe on the tabyll that ye shall ther fynd,
And we shall folow after to carpe of thys case.   *talk*

Now the Jewys goon and lay the Ost on the tabyll, sayng:

JONATHAS. Syrys, I praye yow all, harkyn to my sawe!   *speech*
    Thes Cryten men carpyn of a mervelows case;   *talk*
395   They say that this ys Jhesu that was attayntyd in owr lawe   *condemned*
    And that thys ys he that crucyfyed was.

On thes wordys ther law growndyd hath he
    That he sayd on Shere Thursday at hys sopere: *Holy Thursday*
He brake the brede and sayd *Accipite*,   *Take*
400   And gave hys dyscyplys them for to chere.   *to cheer them*
    And more he sayd to them there,
Whyle they were all togethere and sum,   *gathered*
    Syttyng at the table soo clere,   *so beautiful*
Comedite Corpus Meum.   *Eat my body*

405   And thys powre he gave to Peter to proclame,
    And how the same shuld be suffycyent to all prechors;
The bysshoppys and curatys saye the same,
    And soo, as I vnderstond, do all hys progenytors.

JASON. Yea, sum men in that law reherse another:
410   They say of a maydyn borne was hee,
And how Joachyms dowghter shuld be hys mother,   *(Mary)*
    And how Gabrell apperyd and sayd *"Ave;"*   *"Hail"*
    And with that worde she shuld conceyvyd be,

And that in hyr shuld lyght the Holy Gost.   *alight*
415 Ageyns owr law thys ys false heresy,
And yett they saye he ys of myghtys most.   *most powerful*

JAZDON. They saye that Jhesu to be owr kyng,   *declare*
But I wene he bowght that full dere.   *believe he paid dearly*
But they make a royall aray of hys uprysyng;   *big affair*
420 And that in every place ys prechyd farre and nere.
And how he to hys dyscyples agayn dyd appere,
To Thomas and to Mary Mawdelen,   *Magdalene*
And syth how he styed by hys own power;   *then/ascended*
And thys, ye know well, ys heresy full playn.   *open*

425 MASPHAT. Yea, and also they say he sent them wytt and wysdom
For to understond every language;
When the Holy Gost to them come,
They faryd as dronk men of pymente or vernage;   *spiced or sweet wine*
And sythen how that he lykenyd hymself a lord of parage,   *then/high birth*
430 On hys fatherys ryght hond he hym sett.
They hold hym wyser than ever was Syble sage,   *Sibyl*
And strenger than Alexander, that all the wor[l]de ded gett.

MALCHUS. Yea, yet they saye as fals, I dare laye my hedde,   *bet*
How they that be ded shall com agayn to Judgement,
435 And owr dredfull Judge shalbe thys same brede,   *bread*
And how lyfe everlastyng them shuld be lent.   *given*
And thus they hold, all at on[e] consent,   *maintain/with*
Because that Phylyppe sayd for a lytyll g[l]osse—   *comment*
To turne us from owr beleve ys ther entent—   *belief*
440 For that he sayd, "*Judecare viuos et mortuos.*"   *To judge the living and the dead*

JONATHAS. Now, serys, ye have rehersyd the substance of ther lawe,
But thys bred I wold myght be put in a prefe   *to a test*
Whether this be he that in Bosra of us had awe.   *Bozrah*
Ther staynyd were hys clothys, this may we belefe;
445 Thys may we know, ther had he grefe,
For owr old bookys veryfy thus.
Theron he was jugett to be hangyd as a thefe—
*Tinctis Bosra vestibus**

JASON. Yff that thys be he that on Caluery was mad red,
450 Onto my mynd, I shall kenne yow a conceyt good: *teach/trick*
Surely with owr daggars we shall ses on thys bredde,   *seize*
And so with clowtys we shall know yf he have eny blood.   *blows*

---

448. With dyed garments from Bozrah. [See Isaiah 63:1]

JAZDON.   Now, by Machomyth so myghty,   *Mohammed*
                    that mevyth in my mode!   *moves/mind*
Thys ys masterly ment, thys matter thus to meve: *put/move*
455   And with owr strokys we shall fray hym as he was on the rood,   *torture*
That he was on don with grett repreve.   *undone/reproof*

MASPHAT.   Yea, I pray yow, smyte ye in the myddys of the cake,   *middle*
And so shall we smyte theron woundys fyve.
We wyll not spare to wyrke yt wrake,   *harm*
460   To prove in thys brede yf ther be eny lyfe.

MALCHUS.   Yea, goowe to, than, and take owr space,   *take our places*
And looke owr daggarys be sharpe and kene:
And when eche man a stroke smytte hase,   *has struck*
In the mydyll part thereof owr master shall bene.   *shall be, appear*
465 JONATHAS.   When ye have all smytyn, my stroke shalbe sene;
With this same dagger that ys so styf and strong,   *hard*
In the myddys of thys prynt I thynke for to prene;   *middle/design/prick*
On[e] lashe I shall hyme lende or yt be long.   *give/before long*

Here shall the four Jewys pryk ther daggerys
in [the] four quarters, thus sayng: *corners*

JASON.   Have at yt! have at yt, with all my myght!
470   Thys syde I hope for to sese!   *pierce*
JAZDON.   And I shall with thys blade so bryght
Thys other syde freshely afeze!   *strike*
MASPHAT.   And I yow plyght I shall hym not please,   *promise*
For with thys punche I shall hym pryke!   *this jab*
475 MALCHUS.   And with thys augur I shall hym not ease,
Another buffett shall he lykke!   *blow shall he take*

JONATHAS.   Now am I bold with batayle hym to bleyke,   *make pale*
The mydle part alle for to prene;   *prick*
A stowte stroke also for to stryke—
480   In the myddys yt shalbe sene!

Here the Ost must blede.

Ah! owt! owt! harrow! what deuyll ys thys?
Of thys wyrk I am in were;   *fear*
Yt bledyth as yt were woode, iwys;   *as if/mad*
But yf ye helpe, I shall dyspayre.   *Unless*

485 JASON.   A fyre! a fyre! and that in hast!
Anoon a cawdron full of oyle!   *Quickly*

JAZDON. And I shalle helpe yt were in cast,   *cast in*
    All the thre howrys fo[r] to boyle.

MASPHAT. Ye, here is a furneys stowte and strong,
490 And a cawdron therin dothe hong.
    Malcus, wher art thow so long,
      To helpe thys dede were dyght?   *done*
MALCHUS. Loo, here ys fowr galouns off oyle clere.   *gallons*
    Have doon fast! blowe up the fere!   *fire*
495 Syr, bryng that ylke cake nere,   *same*
    Manly, with all yowre my[g]the.   *Manfully*

JONATHAS. And I shall bryng that ylke cak[e]
    And throwe yt in, I undertake.
    Out! Out! yt werketh me w[r]ake!   *harm*
500 I may not avoyd yt owt of my hond.   *get it off*
    I wylle goo drenche me in a lake.   *drown*
    And in woodnesse I gynne to wake!   *begin to go mad*
    I renne, I lepe ouer this lond.   *run*

    Her[e] he renneth wood, with the Ost in hys hond.   *goes berserk*

JASON. Renne, felawes, renne, for Cokkys peyn,   *God's*
505 Fast we had owr mayster ageyne!   *Quickly to have*
    Hold prestly on thys pleyn   *Hold him (the host) fast to the ground*
      And faste bynd hyme to a poste.
JAZDON. Here is an hamer and naylys thre, I s[e]ye;
    Lyffte up hys armys, felawe, on hey,   *Jonathas's/high*
510 Whyll I dryue thes nayles, I yow praye,
      With strong strokys fast.

MASPHAT. Now set on, felouse, with mayne and myght,   *fellows*
    And pluke hys armes awey in fyght!
    Wat yfe he twycche, felowse, aryght!   *So what if*
515 Alas, balys breweth ryght badde!   *evils*

    Here shall thay pluke the arme, and the hond shall hang
    styll wyth the Sacrament.

MALCHUS. Alas, alas, what devyll ys thys?
    Now hat[h] he but oon hand iwyse!
    Forsothe, mayster, ryght woo me is   *woe*
    That ye this harme have hadde.

520 JONATHAS. Ther ys no more; I must enduer!
    Now hastely to owr chamber lete us gon;   *go*

Tyll I may get me sum recuer;   *remedy*
And therfor charge yow everychoon   *order/everyone*
That yt be counsell that we have doon.   *secret*

Here shall the lechys man come into the place sayng: *physician's man*

525 COLLE. Aha! here ys a fayer felawshyyppe,
Thewh I be nat sh[a]pyn, I lyst to sleppe.   *Though/well-formed/long/escape*
I have a master I wolld he had the pyppe,   *a disease*
I tell yow in counsel.   *secret*
He ys a man off all syence,   *learning*
530 But off thryffte—I may with yow dyspence!   *Except for finances*
He syttyth with sum tapstere in the spence: *barmaid/wine cellar*
Hys hoode there wyll he sell.   *His very hood*

Mayster Brendyche of Braban,   *Brabant*
I tell yow he ys that same man,
535 Called the most famous phesy[cy]an
That ever sawe uryne.   *ever made a diagnosis*
He seeth as wele at noone as at nyght,
And sumtyme by a candelleyt   *candlelight*
Can gyff a judgyment aryght—   *diagnosis*
540 As he that hathe noon eyn.   *Like one who has no eyes*

He ys allso a boone-setter;   *surgeon (and dice-player)*
I knowe no man go the better;   *better (and a bettor)*
In every tauerne he ys detter;   *a debtor*
That ys a good tokenyng.   *sign (or use of bet markers)*
545 But ever I wonder he ys so long;   *always/takes so long*
I fere ther gooth [sumthyng] awrong,
For he hath dysa[rv]yde to be hong—   *deserved/hanged*
God send never wurse tydyng!   *news*

He had a lady late in cure;   *in his care*
550 I wot be this she ys full sure;   *take care of*
There shall never Cristen creature   *Thus*
Here hyr tell no tale.
And I stode here tyll mydnyght,   *If*
I cowde not declare aryght
555 My masteris cunyng insyght—
That he hat[h] in good ale.

But what dvyll ayleth hym, so long to tare!   *tarry*
A seek man myght soone myscary.   *sick/have trouble*
Now alle the devyllys of hell hym wari;   *beset*
560   God grante me my boon!

I trowe best, we mak a crye: *think it/make a proclamation*
Yf any man can hym aspye
Led hym to the pylleri.   *Lead/pillory*
    In fayth, yt shall be don.

Here shall he stond up and make proclamacion, seyng thys:

565 COLLE. Yff ther be eyther man or woman
That sawe Master Brundyche of Braban,
Or owyht of hym tel can,   *anything*
    Shall wele be quit hys med;   *be well-rewarded*
He hath a cut berd and a flatte noose,   *split/nose*
570 A therde-bare gowne and a rent hoose;   *torn*
He spekyt[h] never good matere nor purpoose;
    To the pyllere ye hym led!   *pillory*

BRUNDYCHE. What, thu boye, what janglest here?   *do you babble*
COLLE. A! master, master, but to your reverence!   *only praises of you*
575 I wend never to a seen yowr goodly chere,   *thought never to see/face*
    Ye tared hens so long.   *tarried hence*
BRUNDYCHE. What hast thow sayd in my absense?
COLLE. Nothyng, master, but to yowr reverence
I have told all this audiense—
580   And some lyes among.   *Along with*

But, master, I pray yow, how dothe yowr pa[c]yent
That ye had last under medycament?
BRUNDYCHE. I waraunt she never fele anoyment.   *guarantee/felt any pain*
COLLE.   Why, ys she in hyr grave?
585 BRUNDYCHE. I have gyven hyr a drynke made full well
Wyth scamoly and with oxennell,   *scammony/oxymell (medicinal herbs)*
Letwyce, sawge and pympernelle.   *sage*
    COLLE.   Nay, than she ys full save,   *saved*

For, now ye ar cum, I dare well saye
590 Betuyn Dovyr and Calyce the ryght wey   *Dover and Calais*
Dwellth non so cunnyng, be my fey,   *faith*
    In my judgyment.
BRUNDYCHE. Cunnyng? Yea, yea, and with pratt[y]ffe;   *practice*
I have savid many a mannys lyfe.
595 COLLE. On wydowes, maydese and wyfe
    Yowr connyng yow have nyhe spent.   *nearly*

BRUNDYCHE. Were ys [my] bowg[e]tt with drynk profytable?   *bag*
    COLLE.   Here master, master, ware how ye tugg.   *beware/drink*

The devyll I trowe within shrugge,   *dwells within*
600   For yt gooth rebyll rable.   *goes "gurgle"*

BRUNDYCHE. Here ys a grete congregacyon,
And all be not hole, without negacyon;   *healthy*
I wold have certyfycacyon:
Stond up and make a proclamacion.
605   Have do faste, and make no pausa[c]yon,   *Do it*
But wyghtly mak a declaracion   *quickly*
    To all people that helpe w[o]lde have.

    Hic interim proclamacionem faciet.   *Here for a while he will make proclamation*

COLLE. All manar off men that have any syknes,
    To Master Brentberecly loke that yow redresse.   *address yourselves*
610   What dysease or syknesse that ever ye have,   *Whatever*
He wyll never leve yow tyll ye be in yow[r] grave.
Who hat[h] the canker, the collyke, or the laxe,   *Whoever/diarrhea*
The tercyan, the quartan, or the brynny[n]g axs—   *three or four day fevers/pains*
For wormys, for gnawyng, g[r]yndy[n]g in the wombe
                            or in the boldyro—   *penis (?)*
615   All maner red eyn, bleryd eyn, and the myegrym also, *inflamed/migraine*
For hedache, bonache, and therto the tothache—
The colt-evyll, and the brostyn men he wyll undertak,   *swollen genitals/burst*
All tho that [have] the poose, the sneke, or the tyseke— *catarrh/cold/asthma*
Thowh a man w[e]re ryght heyle, he cowd soone make hym sek. *healthy*
620   Inquyre to the colkote, for ther ys hys loggyng,   *coal shed/lodging*
A lytyll besyde Babwell Myll,* yf ye wyll have und[er]stondyn[g].

BRUNDYCHE. Now, yff ther be ether man or woman
That nedethe helpe of a phesyscian—
COLLE. Mary, master, that I tell can,
625   And ye wyll understond.
BRUNDYCHE. Knoest any abut this plase?
COLLE. Ye, that I do, mastre, so have [I] grase;   *grace*
Here ys a Jewe, hyght Jonathas,   *called*
    Hath lost hys ryght hond.   *Who has*

630   BRUNDYCHE. Fast to hym I wold inquere.   *Quickly*
COLLE. For God, master, the gate ys hyre.   *Before/door*
BRUNDYCHE. Than to hym I wyll go nere.
    My master, wele mot yow be!   *well may*
JONATHAS. What doost here, felawe? what woldest thu hanne? *have*
635   BRUNDYCHE. Syr, yf yow nede ony surgeon or physycyan,

---

621. Babwell Mill: near Bury St. Edmunds (Suffolk).

Off yow[r] dyse[se] help yow welle I cane,   *can*
    What hurtys or hermes so-ever they be.   *harms*

JONATHAS. Syr, thu art ontawght to come in thus homly,   *untutored/simply*
    Or to pere in my presence thus malepertly.   *appear/badly*
640 Voydoth from my syght, and that wyghtly,   *quickly*
    For ye be mysse-avysed.
    COLLE. Syr, the hurt of yowr hand ys knowen full ryfe,   *commonly*
    And my maste[r] have sauyd many a manes lyfe.
    JONATHAS. I trowe ye be cum to make sum stryfe.
645 Hens fast, lest that ye be chastysed.

    COLLE. Syr, ye know well yt can nott mysse;
    Men that be masters of scyens be profytable.
    In a pott yf yt please yow to pysse,
    He can tell yf yow be curable.
650 [JONATHAS.]   Avoyde, fealows, I love not yowr bable!
    Brushe them hens bothe and that anon!
    Gyff them ther reward that they were gone!   *Reward them so that*

Here shall the four Jewys bett away the leche and hys man.

    JONATHAS. Now have don, felawys, and that anon,   *cease*
    For dowte of drede what after befall!   *fear of*
655 I am nere masyd, my wytte ys gon;   *dazed*
    Therfor of helpe I pray yow all.

    And take yowre pynsonys that ar so sure,   *pincers*
    And pluck owt the naylys won and won;   *one by one*
    Also in a clothe ye yt cure   *cover*
660 And throw yt in the cawdron, and that anon.

Here shall Jason pluck owt the naylys and shake the hond into the cawdron.

    JASON.   And I shall rape me redely anon   *hasten at once*
    To plucke owt the naylys that stond so fast,
    And beare thys bred and also thys bone
    And into the cawdron I wyll yt cast.

665 JAZDON. And I shall with thys dagger so stowte   *strong*
    Putt yt down that yt myght plawe,   *Push/boil*
    And steare the clothe rounde abowte   *stir*
    That nothyng therof shalbe rawe.   *uncooked*

    MASPHAT. And I shall manly, with all my myght,   *manfully*
670 Make the fyre to blase and brynne,   *burn*

And sett therunder suche a lyght
That yt shall make yt ryght thynne.   *cook it away*

Here shall the cawdron b[o]yle, apperyng to be as blood.

MALCHUS.   Owt and harow! what deuyll ys herein?
All thys oyle waxyth redde as blood,
675   And owt of the cawdron yt begynnyth to rin.   *run*
I am so aferd I am nere woode.   *nearly mad*

Here shall Jason and hys compeny goo to Ser Jonathas sayng:

JASON. Ah! master, master, what chere ys with yow?   *how are you*
I can nott see owr werke wyll avayle;   *be effective*
I beseche yow avance yow now   *come forward*
680   Sumwhatt with yowr counsayle.

JONATHAS. The best counsayle that I now wott,   *know*
That I can deme, farre and nere,   *judge*
Ys to make an ovyn as redd hott
As ever yt can be made with fere;   *fire*
685   And when ye see yt soo hott appere,
Then throw yt into the ovyn fast—   *it (the host)*
Sone shall he stanche hys bledyng chere.   *bleeding appearance*
When ye have donne, stoppe yt—be not agast!   *plug the oven/afraid*

JAZDON. Be my fayth, yt shalbe wrowgh[t],   *done*
690   And that anon, in gret hast.
Bryng on fyryng, serys, here ye nowght?   *Start the fire/hear*
To hete thys ovyn be nott agast.   *afraid*

MASPHAT. Here ys straw and thornys kene:
Com on, Malchas, and bryng on fere,   *fire*
695   For that shall hete yt well, I wene;   *I think*

Here thei kyndyll the fyre.

MASPHAT.   Blow on fast, that done yt were!
MALCHUS.   Ah, how thys fyre gynnyth to brenne clere!
Thys ovyn ryght hotte I thynk to make.
Now, Jason, to the cawdron that ye stere   *stir*
700   And fast fetche hether that ylke cake.   *same*

*Here shall Jason goo to the cawdron and take owt the
Ost with hys pynsonys and cast yt into the ovyn.*   *pincers*

JASON. I shall with thes pynsonys withowt dowt,
 Shake thys cake owt of thys clothe,
 And to the ovyn I shall yt rowte   *throw*
 And stoppe hym there, thow he be loth.   *plug it*
705 The cake I have cawght here in good sothe— *in truth*
 The hand ys soden, the fleshe from the bonys— *boiled*
 Now into the ovyn I wyll therwith.
 Stoppe yt, Jasdon, for the nonys!   *Plug*

JAZDON. I stoppe thys ovyn, wythowtyn dowte,
710 With clay I clome yt uppe ryght fast,   *plaster*
 That non heat shall cum owtte.
 I trow there shall he hete and drye in hast! *quickly*

 Here the ovvyn must ryve asunder and blede owt at the
 cranys, and an image appere owt with woundys bledyng. *corners*

MASPHAT. Owt! owt! here ys a grete wondere!
 Thys ovyn b[l]edyth owt on every syde!
715 MALCHUS. Yea, the ovyn on peacys gynnyth to ryve asundre; *burst*
 Thys ys a mervelows case thys tyde.   *time*

 Here shall the image speke to the Juys sayng thus:

JESUS. *O mirabiles Judei, attendite et videte*
 Si est dolor sicut dolor meus.[*]
 Oh, ye merveylows Jewys,
720 Why ar ye to yowr kyng onkynd,
 And [I] so bytterly bowt yow to my blysse? *paid to deliver*
 Why fare ye thus fule with yowre frende? *act/foully*
 Why peyne yow me and straytly me pynde, *torture and confine*
 And I yowr love so derely have bowght? *Although*
725 Why ar ye so vnstedfast in yowr mynde?
 Why wrath ye me? I greve yow nowght. *do you anger me*
 Why wyll ye nott beleve that I have tawght, *that which*
 And forsake yowr fowle neclygence,
 And kepe my commandementys in yowr thowght,
730 And unto my godhed to take credence?

 Why blaspheme yow me? Why do ye thus?
 Why put yow me to a newe tormentry,
 And I dyed for yow on the crosse?
 Why consyder not yow what I dyd crye?
735 Whyle that I was with yow, ye ded me velanye. *villainy*

---

718. O Jews of wonder, behold and see if any sorrow is like my sorrow. [See Lamentations 1:12]

     Why remember ye nott my bytter chaunce,   *fortune*
       How yowr kynne dyd me awance   *help*
       For claymyng of myn enherytaunce?
       I shew yow the streytnesse of my greavance,   *difficulty*
740   And all to meve yow to my mercy.   *move*

JONATHAS. *Tu es protector vite mee; a quo trepidabo?**
       O thu, Lord, whyche art my defendowr,
       For dred of the[e] I trymble and quake.
       Of thy gret mercy lett us receyve the showre;
745   And mekely I aske mercy, amendys to make.

     Here shall they knele down all on ther kneys, sayng:

JASON. Ah! Lord, with sorow and care and grete wepyng
       All we felawys lett us saye thus,
     With condolent harte and grete sorowyng: *sympathetic*
     *Lacrimis nostris conscienciam nostram baptizemus!**

750   JAZDON. Oh thow blyssyd Lord of mykyll myght,   *great power*
       Of thy gret mercy, thou hast shewyd us the path,
     Lord, owt of grevous slepe and owt of dyrknes to lyght,
     *Ne gravis sompnus irruat.**

MASPHAT. Oh Lord, I was very cursyd, for I wold know thi crede.   *secrets*
755   I can no menys make but crye to the[e] thus:
     O gracyows Lorde, forgyfe me my mysdede!
     With lamentable hart: *miserere mei, Deus!*   *Have mercy on me, O God*

MALCHUS. Lord, I have offendyd the[e] in many a sundry vyse,
       That styckyth at my hart as hard as a core.
760   Lord, by the water of contrycion lett me aryse:
     *Asparges me, Domine, ysopo, et mundabor**

JESUS. All ye that desyryn my serauntys for to be
       And to fullfyll the preceptys of my lawys,
     The intent of my commandement knowe ye:
765   *Ite et ostendite vos sacerdotibus meis**

    To all yow that desyre in eny wyse
       To aske mercy, to graunt yt redy I am.

---

741. You are the protector of my life; of whom should I be afraid? [See Psalms 27:1]
749. With our tears may we baptize our conscience.
753. May grievous sleep not hold [us].
761. Sprinkle me, Lord, with hyssop, and I will be cleansed. [See Psalms 51:7]
765. Go and present yourselves to my priests.

Remember and lett yowr wyttys suffyce,
*Et tunc non auertam a vobis faciem meam**

770 No, Jonathas, on thyn hand thow art but lame,
And [it] ys thorow thyn own cruelnesse.
For thyn hurt thou mayest thiselfe blame,
Thow woldyst preve thy powre me to oppresse;   *prove*
But now I consydre thy necesse;   *necessity*
775 Thow wasshest thyn hart with grete contrycion;
Go to the cawdron—thi care shalbe the lesse—
And towche thyn hand to thy salvacion.

Here shall Ser Jonathas put hand into the cawdron,
and it shalbe [w]hole agayn; and then say as fo[lo]wyth:

JONATHAS. Oh thow my Lord God and Sauyowr, osanna!
Thow Kyng of Jewys and of Jerusalem!
780 O thow myghty, strong Lyon of Juda,
Blyssyd be the tyme that thou were in Bedlem!   *Bethlehem*
Oh thou myghty, strong, gloryows, and gracyows oyle streme,
Thow myghty conquerrowr of infernall tene,   *harm*
I am quyt of moche combrance thorowgh thy meane,   *relieved/great burdens*
785 That ever blyssyd mott thou bene!   *So/may*

Alas, that ever I dyd agaynst thy wyll,
In my wytt to be soo wood   *mad*
That I so ongoodly wyrk shuld soo gryll!   *should work so evilly and cruelly*
Ayens my mysgouernaunce thow gladdyst me with good: *In response to/gladden*
790 I was soo prowde to prove the[e] on the Roode,   *so proud as to test*
And thou haste sent me lyghtyng that late was lame;   *relief who lately*
To bete the[e] and boyle the[e] I was myghty in moode,   *was determined*
And now thou hast put me from duresse and dysfame.   *hardship/ignominy*

But, Lord, I take my leve at thy hygh presens,
795 And put me in thy myghty mercy;
The bysshoppe wyll I goo fetche to se[e] owr offens,
And onto hym shew owr lyfe, how that we be gylty.

Here shall the Jew goo to the byshopp and hys men knele styll.

JONATHAS. Hayle, father of grace! I knele upon my knee,
Hertely besechyng yow and interely,   *entirely*
800 A swemfull syght all for to see   *sorrowful*
In my howse apperyng verely:

---

769. And then I shall not turn my face away from you. [See Psalms 27:9, 88:14, 143:7]

The holy Sacrament, the whyche we have done tormentry,   *hurt*
And ther we have putt hym to a newe passyon,
A chyld apperyng with wondys blody:
805 A swemfull syght yt ys to looke upon.   *sorrowful*

.EPISCOPUS. Oh Jhesu, Lord, full of goodnesse!
With the[e] wyll I walke with all my myght.
Now, all my pepull, with me ye dresse   *prepare*
For to goo see that swymfull syght.   *sorrowful*

810 Now, all ye peple that here are,
I commande yow, every man,
On yowr feet for to goo bare,
In the devoutest wyse that ye can.

Here shall the bysshope entere into the Jewys howse and say:

EPISCOPUS. *O Jhesu fili Dei,*   *O Jesus, Son of God*
815 How thys paynfull passyon rancheth myn hart!   *wrenches*
Lord, I crye to the[e], *miserere mei,*   *have mercy on me*
From thys rufull syght thou wylt reverte.   *change back*
Lord, we all with sorowys smert,
For thys unlefull work we lyve in langowr;   *unlawful*
820 Now, good Lord, in thy grace let us be gert,   *clothed*
And of thy soverreyn marcy send us thy socowr;   *succour*
And for thy holy grace forgyfe us owr errowr.
Now lett thy pete spryng and sprede;   *pity*
Thowgh we have be unrych[t]full, forgyf us owr rygore,   *obstinance*
825 And of owr lamentable hartys, good Lord, take hed[e].

Here shall the im[a]ge change agayn into brede.

EPISCOPUS. Oh thu largyfluent Lord, most of lyghtnesse,   *generous/most radiant*
Onto owr prayers thow hast applyed: *listened*
Thu hast receyvyd them with grett swettnesse,
For all owr dredfull dedys thou hast not us denyed.   *repudiated*
830 Full mykyll owte thy name for to be magnyfyed   *greatly ought*
With mansuete myrth and gret swettnes,   *gentle joy*
And as owr gracyows God for to be gloryfyed,
For thu shewyst us gret gladnes.

Now wyll I take thys Holy Sacrament
835 With humble hart and gret devocion,
And all we wyll gon with on[e] consent
And beare yt to chyrche with sole[m]pne processyon;

Now folow me, all and summe,   *many*
And all tho that bene here, both more and lesse,   *rich and poor*
840   Thys holy song, *O sacrum Convivium,**   *O sacred feast*
Lett us syng all with grett swetnesse.

Here shall the pryst, Ser Isoder, aske hys master what this menyth.

[PRESBYTER.] Ser Arystory, I pray yow, what menyth all thys?
Sum myracle, I hope, ys wrowght be Goddys myght;   *by*
The bysshope commyth processyon with a gret meny of Jewys;   *comes in*
845   I hope sum myracle ys shewyd to hys syght.
To chyrche in hast wyll I rune full ryght,
For thether, me thynk, he begynnyth to take hys pace.   *direct his steps*
The Sacrament so semly ys borne in syght,
I hope that God hath shewyd of hys grace.

850   ARISTORIUS. To tell yow the trowth I wyll nott lett: *stint*
Alas that ever thys dede was dyght!   *done*
An onlefull bargayn [I] began for to beat;   *unlawful/arrange*
I sold yon same Jewys owr Lord full ryght
For covytyse of good, as a cursyd wyght.   *goods*
855   Woo the whyle that baragyn I dyd ever make!   *woe*
But yow be my defensour in owr dyocesans syght,   *Unless/bishop's*
For an heretyke I feare he wyll me take.

PRESBYTER. For sothe, nothyng well-avysed was yowr wytt;   *not/mind*
Wondrely was yt wrowght of a man of dyscrescion   *Strangely/good sense*
860   In suche perayle yowr solle for to pytt;   *peril/put*
But I wyll labor for yowr absolucyon.
Lett us hye us fast that we were hens,
And beseche hym of hys benygne grace
That he wyll shew us hys benyvolens
865   To make a menys for yowr trespas.   *amends*

Here shall the merchant and hys prest go to the chyrche and the bysshop
shall entre the chyrche and lay the Ost on the auter, sayng thus: *altar*

EPISCOPUS. *Estote fortes in bello et pugnate cum antico serpente,*
*Et accipite regnum eternum, et cetera**
My chyldern, ye be strong in batayll gostly   *spiritual*
For to fyght agayn the fell serpent,   *against*
870   That nyght and day ys ever besy;

---

840. "O Sacrum Convivium," a hymn to the Blessed Sacrament, originally the part of the Vespers on the Feast of Corpus Christi.
866-67. Be strong in battle and fight with the old serpent, and receive the eternal kingdom, etc. [See Revelations 20:2]

To dystroy owr sollys ys hys intent.
Look ye be not slow nor neclygent
To arme yow in the vertues sevyn;
Of synnys fo[r]gotyn take good avysement,   *consideration*
875   And knowlege them to yowr confessor full evyn;   *acknowledge/fully*

For that serpent, the devyll, ys full strong,
Mervelows myschevos for man to mene;   *Amazingly treacherous/understand*
But that the Passyon of Cryst ys meynt us among,   *Except/is given out*
And that ys in dyspyte of hys infernall tene.   *his (devil's)/injury*
880   Beseche owr Lord and Savyowr so kene
To put doun that serpent, cumberer of man,   *ensnarer*
To withdraw hys furyous froward doctryn bydene,   *perverse/completely*
Fulfyllyd of the fend callyd Levyathan.   *by the fiend*

Gyff lawrell to that Lord of myght   *laurel (praise)*
885   That he may bryng us to the joyows fruycion,
Form us to put the fend to flyght,
That never he dystroy us by hys temptacion.

PRESBYTER. My father under God, I knele unto yowr kne,
In yowr myhty mysericord to tak us in remembrance;   *mercy*
890   As ye be materyall to owr degre,   *Since/essential/status (holiness)*
We put us in yowr moderat ordynaunce,   *under your gentle governance*
Yff yt lyke yowr hyghnes to here owr grevaunce: *If it please*
We have offenddyd sorowfully in a syn mortall,
Wherfor we fere us owr Lord wyll take vengaunce
895   For owr synnes both grete and small.

EPISCOPUS. And in fatherhed that longyth to my dygnyte,   *belongs*
Unto yowr grefe I wyll gyf credens.
Say what ye wyll, in the name of the Trynyté,
Agayn[s]t God yf ye have wroght eny inconvenyens.   *impropriety*

900   ARISTORIUS. Holy father, I knele to yow under benedycité.   *blessing*
I have offendyd in the syn of covytys:
I sold owr Lordys body for lucre of mony
And delyueryd to the wyckyd with cursyd advyce.   *damnable*
And for that pres[u]mpcion gretly I agryse   *shudder with dread*
905   That I presumed to go to the autere   *altar*
There to handyll the holy sacryfyce—
I were worthy to be putt in brennyng fere.   *should/burning*

But, gracyous lord, I can no more,   *can (do)*
But put me to Goddys mercy and to yowr grace:

910 My cursyd werkys for to restore,   *to atone for*
      I aske penaunce now in thys place.

      EPISCOPUS. Now for thys offence that thou hast donne
        Ayens the Kyng of Hevyn and Emperowr of Hell,   *Against*
      Ever whyll thou lyvest good dedys for to done
915   And nevermore for to bye nor sell:
        Chastys thy body as I shall the[e] tell,
      With fastyng and prayng and other good wyrk,
        To withstond the temtacyon of fendys of hell;
      And to call to God for grace looke thou never be irke.   *tired*

920 Also, thou preste, for thy neclygens,
        That thou were no wyser in thyn office,   *Because*
      Thou art worthy inpresu[n]ment for thyn offence;   *deserve*
        But beware ever herafter and be more wyse.

      And all yow creaturys and curatys that here be,
925   Off thys dede yow may take example
      How that yowr pyxys lockyd ye shuld see,   *holy containers*
        And be ware of the key of Goddys temple.

      JONATHAS. And I aske Crystendom with great devocion,
        With repentant hart in all degrees,
930   I aske for us all a generall absolucion.

      Here the Juys must knele al down.

      For that we knele all upon owr knees;   *that (absolution)*
      For we have grevyd owr Lord on ground   *Because/earth*
        And put hym to a new paynfull passioun:
      With daggars styckyd hym with grevos wo[u]nde,
935   New naylyd hym to a post and with pynsonys pluckyd hym down.   *pincers*

      JASON. And syth we toke that blyssyd bred so sownd   *then*
        And in a cawdron we dyd hym boyle,
      In a clothe full just we hym wounde   *full tightly*
        And so dyd we seth hym in oyle.   *boil*

940 JAZDON. And for that we myght not overcom hym with tormentry,   *And because*
        In an hott ovyn we speryd hym fast,   *thrust*
      There he apperyd with wondys all bloody:
        The ovyn rave asunder and all tobrast.   *split/burst*
      MASPHAT.   In hys law to make us stedfast,
945   There spake he to us woordys of grete favore;

In contrycyon owr hartys he cast
And [bad] take us to a confessore.   *bade us go*

MALCHUS. And, therfor, all we with on[e] consent
    Knele onto yowr hygh sovereynte,
950 For to be crystenyd ys owr intent;
    Now all owr dedys to yow shewyd have we.

Here shall the bysshoppe crysten the Jewys with gret solempnyte.

EPISCOPUS. Now the Holy Gost at thys tyme mot yow blysse   *may*
    As ye knele all now in hys name,
And with the water of baptyme I shall yow blysse
955   To save yow all from the fendys blame.   *fiend's guilt*
    Now, that fendys powre for to make lame,   *fiend's*
In the name of the Father, the Son and the Holy Gost,
    To saue yow from the devyllys flame,
I crysten yow all, both lest and most.   *lowest and highest*

960 JONATHAS. Now owr father and byshoppe that we well knaw,
    We thank yow interly, both lest and most.   *entirely*
Now ar we bownd to kepe Crystys lawe   *obliged*
    And to serve the Father, the Son and the Holy Gost.
Now wyll we walke by contre and cost,   *coast*
965 Owr wyckyd lyvyng for to restore: *atone*
    And trust in God, of myghtys most,
Never to offend as we have don befor.

Now we take owr lea[v]e at lesse and mare—
    Forward on owr vyage we wyll us dresse;   *press*
970 God send yow all as good welfare
    As hart can thynke or towyng expresse.   *tongue*

ARISTORIUS. Into my contre now wyll I fare
    For to amende myn wyckyd lyfe,
And to kep the people owt of care
975   I wyll teache thys lesson to man and wyfe.

Now take I my leave in thys place,
    I wyll go walke my penaunce to fullfyll;
Now, God, ayens whom I have done thys trespas,   *against*
    Graunt me forgyfnesse yf yt be thy wyll!

980 PRESBYTER. For joy of thys me thynke my hart do wepe,
    That yow have gyvyn yow all Crystys servauntys to be,   *given yourselves*

And hym for to serve with hart full meke—
God, full of pacyens and humylyté—

And the conversacion of all thes fayre men,	*And at the testimony*
985 With hartys stedfastly knett in on[e],	
Goddys lawys to kepe and hym to serve bydene,	*completely*
As faythfull Crystyanys evermore for to gone.	*go*

EPISCOPUS. God Omnypotent evermore looke ye serve	*look that you serve*
With devocion and prayre whyll that ye may;	
990 Dowt yt not he wyll yow preserve	
For eche good prayer that ye sey to hys pay;	*devotion*
And therfor in every dew tyme loke ye nat delay	*due*
For to serve the Holy Trynyté,	
And also Mary, that swete may,	*maid*
995 And kepe yow in perfyte love and charyté.	

Crystys commandementys ten there bee;	
Kepe well them; doo as I yow tell.	
Almyght God shall yow please in every degre,	
And so shall ye saue yowr sollys from hell.	*And thus/souls*
1000 For there ys payn and sorow cruell,	
And in hevyn ther ys both joy and blysse,	
More then eny towyng can tell,	*tongue*
There angellys syng with grett swetnesse;	

To the whyche blysse he bryng us	*may he bring*
1005 Whoys name ys callyd Jhesus,	*Whose*
And in wyrshyppe of thys name gloryows	
To syng to hys honore *Te Deum Laudamus*.	*We praise you, O Lord*

Finis

*Thus endyth the Play of the Blyssyd Sacrament, which myracle was don
in the forest of Aragon, in the famous cité Eraclea, the yere of our Lord
God 1461, to whom be honour, Amen.*

Appendix:
Pageants from the Cycle Plays

The mystery (from the French *mystere,* "craft") cycle plays portray the cycle of Christian history from the creation of the world until the Last Judgment. This long history was broken into short pageants, dramatized episodes based on Biblical and apocryphal sources. Cycle plays flourished from the last quarter of the fourteenth century to the third quarter of the sixteenth, and four virtually complete English cycles have survived: those of York, Wakefield, Chester, and N-Town. Together they preserve a total of nearly one hundred and fifty pageants. In addition, a few individual pageants have survived independently of their cycles.

This substantial body of dramatic material has attracted the lion's share of whatever scholarly or critical attention has been paid to the late medieval drama, in part because of its sheer bulk. But it is also fair to say that many scholarly and critical issues must be negotiated in order to "unpack" the cycle plays. Vexed matters of textual transmission, of interaction between cycles and pageants, of voluminous civic and ecclesiastical records pertinent to performance histories, of political, doctrinal, ideological, economic and aesthetic concerns, all call for attention in order that the plays might be understood properly.

The general circumstances of cycle play performance can be sketched out fairly easily. Individual pageants were the responsibility of craft or trade guilds to put on, usually with the oversight and coordination of civic authorities. That is, the town council ordinarily would decide on a venue, and then each guild had to arrange for the financing of its pageant, assemble the cast, secure props and costumes, erect and decorate stages or pageant wagons (carts with decorated superstructures to accommodate the action), arrange for rehearsals, and, finally, mount the play. Few towns put their cycles on annually, but they were performed often enough for the guilds to establish routines. Sometimes, as at York and Chester, pageant wagons followed a set course through the town, stopping at several stations to perform; in other places the pageants were apparently mounted in a single location, sometimes after a procession through main streets. Songs are a common feature of many pageants, and town musicians frequently accompanied the performances. An entire cycle might take a whole day to perform, and sometimes two or three, especially if it were part of larger civic festival. In one way or another a sizeable segment of the community participated in the productions, as managers, actors, supporting cast, or stage crew.

The audience, too, was large and diverse, made up of virtually every level of provincial society in towns and villages within travelling distance of the sponsoring community. Practically speaking, it would have been very difficult for any single spectator to see an entire cycle in any given year, but over the course of a lifetime the repeated exposure to a cycle might well familiarize one with all its episodes. The urge to instruct as well as delight is readily apparent in these plays, a fact that acts as both the obvious strength and the main weakness of the cycles.

Meanwhile, the manner of performance and the intention of the cycles have important critical consequences. Because individual pageants were performed by separate guilds, each can to some degree be approached as an independent dramatic entity. This critical strategy has in the past singled out pageants like the Wakefield *Second Shepherds' Play* or the Wakefield *Noah* (both included here) as having excellent literary merit, revealing the influence and genius of the anonymous "Wakefield Master." It has pointed to the York *Crucifixion* (also included here) as a definitive work of the "York Realist" (also anonymous). But in conception and in performance the cycle plays were constructed to be a single process, an organically unified sequence of episodes whose pious intent dictated form and content and mode of production. Not only characters, but motifs and themes carry from pageant to pageant, establishing for each cycle a unique character, but freighting it with shared ideological resonance as well. The ideological core was of course Catholic, ineradicably so, and it finally worked against them during the Reformation, when they were thoroughly suppressed.

It should be remarked that instructional impulse and the sponsorship of the cycle plays by cities had theatrical consequences too. The conditions and methods of performance provided neither a means nor a reason to emphasize spectacle within the cycle plays—nothing, that is, beyond the traditional flamboyance of the characters deriving from the Biblical or apocryphal sources. Unlike the non-cycle plays, their success and survival did not depend upon their performance so much as upon the traditions and community machinery in which they played a part.

The four pageants chosen for this appendix thus speak with more complex voices than is apparent when they are separated, as is the case here, from their cycles. And at the same time they are, as it were, genetically determined to be less theatrical than the non-cycle plays. Two of them—The Wakefield *Second Shepherds' Play* and the York *Crucifixion*—are perhaps the most widely known and accomplished of all the cycle play pageants. The Wakefield *Noah* is generally considered to offer the most spirited version of this popular episode. The Chester *Abraham and Isaac* is included here as an "ordinary" pageant, but one which shares a close textual relationship with the Brome *Abraham and Isaac*. How effectively each of the plays exploits the theatricality, the tension, and the pathos of the Biblical episode will highlight how the different missions and sensibilities of cycle and non-cycle plays affect technique.

The Wakefield cycle (also known as the Towneley Cycle) manuscript is preserved at the Huntington Library (MS HM 1); the standard scholarly edition, by George England and Alfred W. Pollard, appears in EETS, Extra Series, 71 (1897); the facsimile of the manuscript has been edited by A. C. Cawley and Martin Stevens. The Chester cycle has survived more or less intact in five manuscripts, none dating from before 1591; three copies are located in the British Library, one at the Bodleian Library at Oxford, and one at the Huntington Library. This cycle has recently been edited for EETS by R. M. Lumiansky and David Mills, and the manuscripts are available in facsimiles; the records of drama in Chester before 1642 have been collected and edited for REED (Records of Early English Drama) by Lawrence Clopper. The York plays are still available in the EETS edition of 1885 by Lucy Toulmin Smith, and in a more modern version by Richard Beadle. The facsimile has been edited by Richard Beadle and Peter Meredith (1983). Records of the drama in York before 1642 have been collected and edited for REED by Alexandra Johnston and Margaret Dorrell. Those mavericks of the English cycle play tradition, the N-Town Plays (or Play), have recently been edited for EETS by Stephen Spector; the manuscript facsimile was edited by Peter Meredith and Stanley J. Kahrl.

NOAH
(from The Wakefield Cycle)

[DRAMATIS PERSONAE:

NOAH
DEUS
WIFE
THEIR THREE SONS:
  CAM (Cain)
  SEM (Shem)
  JAPHET (Japheth)
THEIR THREE SONS' WIVES:
  WIFE 1
  WIFE 2
  WIFE 3]

NOAH. Myghtfull God veray, maker of all that is,		*true*
Thre persons withoutten nay, oone God in endles blis,		*without doubt*
Thou maide both nyght and day, beest, fowle, and fysh;		
All creatures that lif may wroght thou at thi wish,		*that live, you made*
5 As thou wel myght.		
The son, the moyne, verament,		*moon/truly*
Thou maide; the firmament;		*earth*
The sternes also full fervent,		*stars/burning*
To shyne thou maide ful bright.		
10 Angels thou maide ful even, all orders that is,		*equal in bliss*
To have the blis in heven: this did thou more and les,		*in every detail*
Full mervelus to neven. Yit was ther unkyndnes		*name*
More bi foldys seven then I can well expres,		*seven times*
Forwhi		*Because*
15 Of all angels in brightnes		

God gaf Lucifer most lightnes,
Yit prowdly he flyt his des,   *fled his throne (dais)*
    And set hym even Hym by.   *even with God*

He thoght hymself as worthi as hym that Hym made,   *God who made him*
20   In brightnes, in bewty; therfor He hym degrade,   *God put him down*
Put hym in a low degré soyn after, in a brade,   *soon/moment*
Hym and all his menye, wher he may be unglad   *group*
    For ever.
Shall thay never wyn away   *never escape*
25   Hence unto domysday,   *doomsday*
Bot burn in bayle for ay;   *torment/forever*
    Shall thay never dyssever.   *never undo that*

Soyne after, that gracyous Lord to his liknes maide man,   *in his likeness*
That place to be restord, even as he began;   *The (angels) place/reoccupied/as planned*
30   Of the Trinité bi accord, Adam, and Eve that woman,
To multiplie without discord, in Paradise put he thaym,
    And sithen to both   *afterwards*
Gaf in commaundement   *Gave*
On the tre of life to lay no hend.   *hand*
35   Bot yit the fals feynd   *yet*
    Made hym with man wroth,

Entysyd man to glotony, styrd him to syn in pride.
Bot in Paradise, securly, myght no syn abide;   *indeed*
And therfor man full hastely was put out in that tyde,   *time*
40   In wo and wandreth for to be, in paynes full unrid   *woe/to be homeless/severe*
    To knowe:
Fyrst in erth, and sythen in hell   *afterwards*
With feyndys for to dwell,
Bot he his mercy mell   *Unless (God)/declare*
45   To those that will hym trawe.   *believe in*

Oyle of mercy he hus hight, as I have hard red,   *promised us/heard told*
To every lifyng wight that wold luf hym and dred;   *love and fear Him*
Bot now before his sight every liffyng leyde,   *person*
Most party day and nyght, syn in word and dede   *For the most part*
50   Full bold:
Som in pride, ire, and envy,
Som in covetous and glotyny,
Som in sloth and lechery,
    And other wise manyfold.

55   Therfor I drede lest God on us will take venjance,   *fear*
For syn is now alod, without any repentance.   *common*

Sex hundreth yeris and od have I, without distance,   *exaggeration*
In erth, as any sod, liffyd with grete grevance
   Allway;
60 And now I wax old,
Seke, sory, and cold;
As muk apon mold   *dung upon the earth*
   I widder away.   *wither*

Bot yit will I cry for mercy and call:
65 Noe, thi servant, am I, Lord over all!
Therfor me, and my fry shal with me fall,   *and if my children*
Save from velany, and bryng to thi hall
   In heven;
And kepe me from syn
70 This warld within.
Comly kyng of mankyn,   *mankind*
   I pray the[e] here my stevyn!   *voice*

DEUS. Syn I have maide all thyng that is liffand,   *living*
Duke, emperour, and kyng, with myne awne hand,   *own*
75 For to have thare likyng bi see and bi sand,   *love*
Every man to my bydyng shuld be bowand   *bidding/be bowing*
   Full fervent,   *eagerly*
That maide man sich a creatoure,   *to me who/such*
Farest of favoure;   *fairest*
80 Man must luf me paramoure   *passionately*
   By reson, and repent.

Me thoght I shewed man luf when I made hym to be
All angels abuf, like to the Trynyté;
And now in grete reprufe full low ligys he,   *shame/lies*
85 In erth hymself to stuf with syn that displeasse me   *sins*
   Most of all.
Venjance will I take
In erth for syn sake;   *because of sin*
My grame thus will I wake   *anger*
90   Both of grete and small.   *regarding every creature*

I repente full sore that ever maide I man;
Bi me he settys no store, and I am his soferan.   *sovereign*
I will distroy therfor both beest, man, and woman:
All shall perish, les and more. That bargan may thay ban   *curse*
95   That ill has done.   *who have sinned*
In erth I se right noght   *nothing*
   Bot syn that is unsoght;   *gratuitous*

    Of those that well has wroght   *who acted well*
      Fynd I bot a fone.   *a few*

100 Therfor shall I fordo all this medill-erd   *do in/world*
    With floodys that shal flo and ryn with hidous rerd.   *run/hideous roar*
    I have good cause therto; for me no man is ferd.   *fears me*
    As I say shal I do, of venjance draw my swerd,
      And make end
105 Of all that beris life,   *bears*
    Sayf Noe and his wife,   *Except*
    For thay wold never stryfe
      With me then me offend.   *nor*

    Hym to mekill wyn, hastly will I go   *To his great profit*
110 To Noe my servand, or I blyn, to warn hym of his wo.   *ere I stop*
    In erth I se bot syn reynand to and fro   *see only sin running*
    Emang both more and myn, ichon other fo   *Among/less/each one other's*
      With all thare entent.
    All shall I fordo   *destroy*
115 With floodys that shall floo;
    Wirk shall I thaym wo   *do them harm*
      That will not repent.   *Who will not repent*

    Noe, my freend, I the[e] commaund, from cares the[e] to keyle,   *keep*
    A ship that thou ordand of nayle and bord ful wele.   *build/solid*
120 Thou was alway well-wirkand, to me trew as stele,   *doing good*
    To my bydyng obediand; frendship shal thou fele   *bidding*
      To mede.   *As reward*
    Of lennthe thi ship be
    Thre hundreth cubettys, warn I the[e];
125 Of heght even thirté;
      Of fyfty als in brede.   *also in breadth*

    Anoynt thi ship with pik and tar without and als within,   *pitch*
    The water out to spar: this is a noble gyn.   *shut/device*
    Look no man the[e] mar. Thre chese chambres begyn;   *tiers of rooms*
130 Thou must spend many a spar, this wark or thou wyn   *use/beam/ere you complete*
      To end fully.
    Make in thi ship also
    Parloures oone or two,
    And houses of offyce mo   *more stables*
135   For beestys that ther must be.

    Oone cubite on hight a wyndo shal thou make;
    On the syde a doore, with slyght, beneyth shal thou take.   *skill/make*
    With the[e] shal no man fyght, nor do the[e] no kyn wrake.   *kind of harm*

When all is doyne thus right, thi wife, that is thi make, *who/mate*
140 Take in to the[e];
Thi sonnes of good fame,
Sem, Iaphet, and Came, *Shem/Cain*
Take in also thame, *them too*
  Thare wifys also thre. *and their three wives*

145 For all shal be fordone that lif in land, bot ye, *destroyed*
With floodys that from abone shal fall, and that plenté. *above*
It shall begyn full sone to rayn uncessantlé,
After dayes seven be done, and induyr dayes fourty, *and last for*
  Withoutten fayll.
150 Take to thi ship also
Of ich kynd beestys two,
Mayll and femayll, bot no mo,
  Or thou pull up thi sayll; *Ere*

For thay may the[e] avayll when al this thyng is wroght. *come to thee*
155 Stuf thi ship with vitayll, for hungre that ye perish noght. *so that for*
Of beestys, foull, and catayll for thaym have thou in thoght. *keep in mind*
For thaym is my counsayll that som socour be soght *comfort*
  In hast;
Thay must have corn and hay
160 And oder mete alway. *other feed*
Do now as I the[e] say,
  In the name of the Holy Gast. *Ghost*

NOAH. A, benedicite! what art thou that thus *bless me*
Tellys afore that shall be? Thou art full mervelus! *tells the future*
165 Tell me, for charité, thi name so gracius.
DEUS. My name is of dignyté, and also full glorius
  To knowe:
I am God most myghty,
Oone God in Trynyty,
170 Made the[e] and ich man to be; *Who made/each*
  To luf me well thou awe. *ought*

NOAH. I thank the[e], Lord so dere, that wold vowchsayf
Thus low to appere to a symple knafe.
Blis us, Lord, here, for charité I hit crafe; *crave it*
175 The better may we stere the ship that we shall hafe, *have*
  Certayn.
DEUS. Noe, to the[e] and to thi fry
My blyssyng graunt I;
Ye shall wax and multiply
180 And fill the erth agane,

When all thise floodys ar past, and fully gone away.	
NOAH. Lord, homward will I hast as fast as that I may;	
My wife will I frast what she will say,	*ask*
And I am agast that we get som fray	*argument*
185 Betwixt us both,	
For she is full tethee,	*touchy*
For litill oft angré;	*over little things*
If any thyng wrang be,	
Soyne is she wroth.	*Soon*
Tunc perget ad uxorem	*Then he travels to his wife*
190 God spede, dere wife! How fayre ye?	
WIFE. Now, as ever myght I thryfe, the wars I the[e] see.	*worse now*
Do tell me belife, where has thou thus long be?	*quickly*
To dede may we dryfe, or lif, for the[e],	*we may live or die*
For want.	*Out of need*
195 When we swete or swynk,	*sweat or toil*
Thou dos what thou thynk,	*You do*
Yit of mete and of drynk	*Yet*
Have we veray skant.	
NOAH. Wife, we ar hard sted with tythyngys new.	*hard pressed*
200 WIFE. Bot thou were worthi be cled in Stafford blew,*	
For thou art alway adred, be it fals or trew.	*always fearful*
Bot God knowes I am led, and that may I rew,	*antagonized*
Full ill;	
For I dar be thi borow,	*I'll be bound*
205 From even unto morow	*evening*
Thou spekys ever of sorow;	
God send the[e] onys thi fill!	*once/fill (of sorrow)*
We women may wary all ill husbandys;	*curse of*
I have oone, bi Mary that lowsyd me of my bandys!	*delivered/bands (of childbirth)*
210 If he teyn, I must tary, howsoever it standys,	*vexed*
With seymland full sory, wryngand both my handys	*seeming*
For drede;	
Bot yit otherwhile,	*meanwhile*
What with gam and with gyle,	*trick*
215 I shall smyte and smyle,	
And qwite hym his mede.	*give him his reward*
NOAH. We! hold thi tong, ram-skyt, or I shall the[e] still.	*ram-shit*
WIFE. By my thryft, if thou smyte, I shal turne the[e] untill.	*on you*
NOAH. We shall assay as tyte, Have at the[e], Gill!	*try as quickly*

---

200. Should be beaten black and blue (?)

220 Apon the bone shal it byte. *[Strikes her]*
   WIFE.   A, so! Mary, thou smytys ill!
     Bot I suppose
   I shal not in thi det
   Flyt of this flett: *Fly up off this floor*
   Take the[e] ther a langett   *lace*
225 To tye up thi hose! *[Strikes him]*

   NOAH. A! wilt thou so? Mary, that is myne! *[Strikes her]*
   WIFE. Thou shal thre for two, I swere bi Godys pyne! *[Strikes]* *get three/pain*
   NOAH. And I shall qwyte the[e] tho, in fayth, or syne. *[Strikes]* *then/ere long*
   WIFE. Out apon the[e], ho! *[Strikes]*
   NOAH.   Thou can both byte and whyne
230   With a rerd;   *roar*
   For all if she stryke,   *for all of her blows*
   Yit fast will she skryke;   *quickly shriek*
   In fayth, I hold none slyke   *none like*
     In all medill-erd.

235 Bot I will kepe charyté, for I have at do.   *things to do*
   WIFE. Here shal no man tary the[e]; I pray the[e] go to! *hinder*
   Full well may we mys the[e], as ever have I ro. *ever/fight*
   To spyn will I dres me.   *prepare*
   NOAH.   We! fare well, lo;
     Bot, wife,
240 Pray for me beselé   *busily (diligently)*
   To eft I com unto the[e].   *Until again*
   WIFE. Even as thou prays for me,
     As ever myght I thrife.

   NOAH. I tary full lang fro my warke, I traw;   *think*
245 Now my gere will I fang, and thederward draw. *fetch/take thither*
   I may full ill gang, the soth for to knaw;   *fare*
   Bot if God help amang, I may sit downe daw *Unless/helps out/a fool*
     To ken.   *(be) known*
   Now assay will I   *try*
250 How I can of wrightry,   *carpentry*
   In nomine patris, et filii,   *In the name of the Father, and of the Son*
     Et spiritus sancti. Amen.   *And of the Holy Ghost. Amen*

   To begyn of this tree my bonys will I bend;   *with this wood*
   I traw from the Trynyté socoure will be send.   *trust/sent*
255 It fayres full fayre, thynk me, this wark to my hend; *fares well*
   Now blissid be he that this can amend.
   Lo, here the lenght,
   Thre hundreth cubettys evenly;

Of breed, lo, is it fyfty;
260   The heght is even thyrty
          Cubettys full strenght.

Now my gowne will I cast, and wyrk in my cote;   *cast off*
Make will I the mast or I flyt oone foote.   *ere I go a single step*
A, my bak, I traw, will brast! This is a sory note!   *I think/break*
265   Hit is wonder that I last, sich an old dote,   *dotard*
          All dold,   *done in*
      To begyn sich a wark.
      My bonys ar so stark: *stiff*
      No wonder if thay wark,   *are painful*
270   For I am full old.

The top and the sayll both will I make;
The helme and the castell also will I take;   *house*
To drife ich a nayll will I not forsake.
This gere may never fayll, that dar I undertake   *affirm*
275   Onone.   *At once*
      This is a nobull gyn: *device*
      Thise nayles so thay ryn   *run*
      Thoro more and myn,   *through thick and thin*
          Thise bordys ichon.

280   Wyndow and doore, even as he saide;
      Thre ches chambre, thay ar well maide;   *tiers of*
      Pyk and tar full sure therapon laide.   *pitch*
      This will ever endure, therof am I paide,   *last long/pleased*
          Forwhy   *Because*
285   It is better wroght
      Then I coude haif thoght.   *have*
      Hym that maide all of noght   *nothing*
          I thank oonly.

Now will I hy me, and nothyng be leder,   *hurry/not be slow*
290   My wife and my meneye to bryng even heder.   *family/hither*
      Tent hedir tydely, wife, and consider;   *Pay attention here*
      Hens must us fle, all sam togeder,   *flee*
          In hast.
      WIFE. Whi, syr, what alis you?
295   Who is that asalis you?   *assails*
      To fle it avalis you   *avails*
          And ye be agast.   *If*

NOAH. Ther is garn on the reyll other, my dame.* — *yarn/reel*

WIFE. Tell me that ich a deyll, els get ye blame. — *every bit*

300 NOAH. He that cares may keill, blissid be his name! — *who stops cares*

He has behete, for oure seyll, to sheld us fro shame; — *promised/our happiness*

And sayd

All this warld aboute

With floodys so stoute, — *heavy*

305 That shall ryn on a route, — *run in currents*

Shall be overlaide. — *covered*

He saide all shall be slayn, bot oonely we, — *except us*

Oure barnes that ar bayn, and thare wifys thre. — *children/obedient*

A ship he bad me ordayn, to safe us and oure fee; — *build/save/goods*

310 Therfor with all oure mayn thank we that fre, — *might/that generous (one)*

Beytter of bayll. — *healer of harm*

Hy us fast, go we thedir. — *Hurry*

WIFE. I wote never whedir; — *I don't know where*

I dase and I dedir — *am dazed and I tremble*

315 For ferd of that tayll. — *fear*

NOAH. Be not aferd. Have done; trus sam oure gere, — *gather together*

That we be ther or none, without more dere. — *So that/ere noon/harm*

CAM. It shall be done full sone. Brether, help to bere.

SEM. Full long shall I not hoyne to do my devere. — *delay/duty*

320 Brether, sam. — *do the same*

JAPHET. Without any yelp, — *complaint*

At my myght shall I help.

WIFE. Yit, for drede of a skelp, — *slap*

Help well thi dam! — *mother*

325 NOAH. Now ar we there as we shuld be.

Do get in oure gere, oure catall and fe, — *goods*

Into this vessell here, my chylder fre. — *noble*

WIFE. I was never bard ere, as ever myght I the[e], — *barred in/thrive*

In sich an oostré as this! — *such an inn*

330 In fath, I can not fynd

Which is before, which is behynd.

Bot shall we here be pynd, — *penned*

Noe, as have thou blis?

NOAH. Dame, as it is skill, here must us abide grace; — *reasonable*

335 Therfor, wife, with good will com into this place.

WIFE. Sir, for Jak nor for Gill will I turne my face,

Till I have on this hill spon a space — *spun a while*

---

298. *i.e.,* I have other things to do.

On my rok.
Well were he myght get me!   *where*
340   Now will I downe set me;
Yit reede I no man let me,   *advise/to hinder*
      For drede of a knok.

NOAH. Behold to the heven! The cateractes all,
Thai ar open full even, grete and small,   *completely*
345   And the planettys seven left has thare stall.   *stations*
Thise thoners and levyn downe gar fall   *thunders and lightning/cause*
      Full stout   *heavily*
Both halles and bowers,
Castels and towres.
350   Full sharp ar thise showers
      That renys aboute.

Therfor, wife, have done; com into ship fast.   *safe*
WIFE. Yei, Noe, go cloute thi shone! The better will thai last. *mend/shoes*
WIFE 1. Good moder, com in sone, for all is overcast,   *soon*
355   Both the son and the mone.
WIFE 2.   And many wynd-blast
      Full sharp.
Thise floodys so thay ryn;   *run*
Therfor, moder, com in.
WIFE. In fayth, yit will I spyn;
360   All in vayn ye carp.   *cry out*

WIFE 3. If ye like ye may spyn, moder, in the ship.
NOAH. Now is this twyys com in, dame, on my frenship. *for the second time/love*
WIFE. Wheder I lose or I wyn, in fayth, thi felowship,
      Set I not at a pyn. This spyndill will I slip   *empty*
365   Apon this hill
Or I styr oone fote.   *Ere/stir a step*
NOAH. Peter! I traw we dote.   *think/act foolishly*
Without any more note,   *business*
      Com in if ye will.

370   WIFE. Yei, water nyghys so nere that I sit not dry;   *approaches*
Into ship with a byr, therfor, will I hy   *rush/hasten*
For drede that I drone here.   *drown*
NOAH.   Dame, securly,   *certainly*
It bees boght full dere ye abode so long by   *will cost dearly*
      Out of ship.
375   WIFE. I will not, for thi bydyng,   *bidding*
Go from doore to mydyng.   *dung heap*

NOAH. In fayth, and for youre long taryyng
    Ye shal lik on the whyp.   *taste*

WIFE. Spare me not, I pray the[e], bot even as thou thynk;
380 Thise grete wordys shall not flay me.
NOAH.   Abide, dame, and drynk,
For betyn shall thou be with this staf to thou stynk.   *beaten/until*
Ar strokys good? say me.   *tell me*
WIFE.   What say ye, Wat Wynk?   *(A derisive name)*
NOAH. Speke!
Cry me mercy, I say!
385 WIFE. Therto say I nay.
NOAH. Bot thou do, bi this day,
    Thi hede shall I breke!

    [To Audience]
WIFE. Lord, I were at ese, and hertely full hoylle,   *healthy of heart*
Might I onys have a measse of wedows coyll.   *once/dish/widow's food*
390 For thi saull, without lese, shuld I dele penny doyll;   *your soul/lies/I'd give pennies*
So wold mo, no frese, that I se on this sole   *others, no question/in this place*
    Of wifys that ar here,
For the life that thay leyd,   *Because of*
Wold thare husbandys were dede;   *Wish/dead*
395 For, as ever ete I brede,
    So wold I oure syre were!

    [To Audience]
NOAH. Yee men that has wifys, whyls thay ar yong,
If ye luf youre lifys, chastice thare tong.
Me thynk my hert ryfys, both levyr and long,   *splits/liver and lung*
400 To se sich stryfys, wedmen emong.   *among husbands*
    Bot I,
As have I blys,   *hope to be saved*
Shall chastyse this.
WIFE. Yit may ye mys,
405 Nicholl Nedy!   *(A derisive name)*

NOAH. I shall make the[e] still as stone, begynnar of blunder!   *trouble*
I shall bete the[e] bak and bone, and breke all in sonder.   *[They fight]*
WIFE. Out, alas, I am gone! Oute apon the[e], mans wonder!
NOAH. Se how she can grone, and I lig under!   *with me underneath*
410   Bot, wife,
In this hast let us ho,   *business/halt*
For my bak is nere in two.
WIFE. And I am bet so blo   *beaten/blue*
    That I may not thryfe.   *get better*

415	CAM. A! whi fare ye thus, fader and moder both?	
	SEM. Ye shuld not be so spitus, standyng in sich a woth.	*spiteful/such/danger*
	JAPHET. Thise weders ar so hidus, with many a cold coth.	*weather/hideous/disease*
	NOAH. We will do as ye bid us; we will no more be wroth,	
	Dere barnes.	*children*
420	Now to the helme will I hent,	*take the helm*
	And to my ship tent.	*attend*
	WIFE. I se on the firmament,	
	Me thynk, the seven starnes.	*planets*

	NOAH. This is a grete flood, wife, take hede.	
425	WIFE. So me thoght, as I stode. We ar in grete drede;	*danger*
	Thise wawghes ar so wode.	*waves/wild*
	NOAH. Help, God, in this nede!	
	As thou art stere-man good, and best, as I rede,	*best pilot/think*
	Of all,	
	Thou rewle us in this rase,	*rush*
430	As thou me behete hase.	*had promised*
	WIFE. This is a perlous case.	
	Help, God, when we call!	

	NOAH. Wife, tent the stere-tre, and I shall asay	*take the tiller*
	The depnes of the see that we bere, if I may.	*bears us*
435	WIFE. That shall I do ful wysely. Now go thi way,	
	For apon this flood have we flett many day	*floated*
	With pyne.	*suffering*
	NOAH. Now the water will I fownd:	*measure*
	A, it is far to the grownd.	
440	This travell I expownd	*labor/explained*
	Had I to tyne.	*wasted*

	Aboue all hillys bedeyn the water is rysen late	*together/lately*
	Cubettys fifteen. Bot in a highter state	
	It may not be, I weyn, for this well I wate:	*believe/will wait*
445	This fourty dayes has rayn beyn; it will therfor abate	
	Full lele.	*truly*
	This water in hast	
	Eft will I tast;	*Again/test*
	Now am I agast,	*amazed*
450	It is wanyd a grete dele!	

	Now ar the weders cest, and cateractes knyt,	*bad weather ceased/stopped*
	Both the most and the leest.	
	WIFE. Me thynk, bi my wit,	
	The son shynes in the eest. Lo, is not yond it?	
	We shuld have a good feest, were thise floodys flyt	*gone*

455   So spytus.   *cruel*
        NOAH. We have been here, all we,
        Three hundred dayes and fyfty.
        WIFE. Yei, now wanys the see;   *drops*
          Lord, well is us!

460   NOAH. The thryd tyme will I prufe what depnes we bere.   *test*
        WIFE. How long shall thou hufe? Lay in thy lyne there.   *heave*
        NOAH. I may towch with my lufe the grownd evyn here.   *hand*
        WIFE. Then begynnys to grufe to us mery chere.   *grow*
          Bot, husband,
465   What grownd may this be?
        NOAH. The hyllys of Armonye.   *Armenia*
        WIFE. Now blissid be he
          That thus for us ordand!   *Who/provided*

        NOAH. I see toppys of hyllys he, many at a syght;   *high*
470   Nothyng to let me, the wedir is so bright.   *hinder*
        WIFE. Thise ar of mercy tokyns full right.
        NOAH. Dame, thi counsell me what fowll best myght   *bird might best*
          And cowth   *know how*
          With flight of wyng   *For*
475   Bryng, without taryyng,.
          Of mercy som tokynyng,
            Ayther bi north or southe.   *Either*

        For this is the fyrst day of the tent moyne.   *tenth month*
        WIFE. The ravyn, durst I lay, will com agane sone.   *I wager*
480   As fast as thou may, cast hym furth, have done!
        He may happyn to-day com agane or none   *ere noon*
          With grath.   *speed*
        NOAH. I will cast out also
          Dowfys oone or two.   *doves*
485   Go youre way, go;
          God send you som wathe!   *hunting*

        Now ar thise fowles flone into seyr countré.   *barren*
        Pray we fast ichon, kneland on oure kne,   *each of us, kneeling*
        To hym that is alone, worthiest of degré,
490   That he wold send anone oure fowles som fee   *sign*
          To glad us.
        WIFE. Thai may not fayll of land,   *to find*
        The water is so wanand.   *ebbing so*
        NOAH. Thank we God all-weldand,   *all-ruling*
495   That Lord that made us!

It is a wonder thyng, me thynk, sothlé,   *truly*
Thai ar so long taryyng, the fowles that we
Cast out in the mornyng.
WIFE.   Syr, it may be
Thai tary to thay bryng.   *until/bring back something*
NOAH.   The ravyn is a-hungrye
500   Allway.
He is without any reson;
And he fynd any caryon,   *If*
As peraventure may be fon,   *found*
    He will not away.   *leave it*

505 The dowfe is more gentill: her trust I untew,   *I trust her*
Like unto the turtill, for she is ay trew.   *turtle-dove/ever*
WIFE. Hence bot a litill she commys, lew, lew!   *little ways off*
She bryngys in her bill som novels new.   *new news*
    Behald!
510 It is of an olif-tre
A branch, thynkys me.
NOAH. It is soth, perdé;   *by God*
    Right so is it cald.

Doufe, byrd full blist, fayre myght the[e] befall!   *good luck*
515 Thou art trew for to trist as ston in the wall;   *trust*
Full well I it wist thou wold com to thi hall.   *I know well*
WIFE. A trew tokyn ist we shall be savyd all,   *it is*
    Forwhi   *Because*
The water, syn she com,   *since/returned*
520 Of depnes plom
Is fallen a fathom
    And more, hardely.

CAM. Thise floodys ar gone, fader, behold!
SEM. Ther is left right none, and that be ye bold.   *sure*
525 JAPHET. As still as a stone oure ship is stold.   *stopped*
NOAH. Apon land here anone that we were, fayn I wold.   *fondly I wish*
    My childer dere,
Sem, Iaphet and Cam,
With gle and with gam,
530 Com go we all sam;   *all together*
    We will no longer abide here.

WIFE. Here have we beyn, Noy, long enogh
With tray and with teyn, and dreed mekill wogh.   *misery/suffering/great many woes*
NOAH. Behald on this greyn! Nowder cart ne plogh
535 Is left, as I weyn, nowder tre then bogh,   *I think/tree nor bough*

Ne other thyng,
Bot all is away;
Many castels, I say,
Grete townes of aray,
540   Flitt has this flowyng.   *Swept away*

WIFE. Thise floodys not afright all this warld so wide   *undeterred*
Has mevid with myght on se and bi side.   *swept all away/shore*
NOAH. To dede ar thai dyght, prowdist of pryde,   *put to death*
Everich a wyght that ever was spyde   *every man/seen*
545   With syn:
All ar thai slayn,
And put unto payn.
WIFE. From thens agayn
May thai never wyn?   *escape*

550 NOAH. Wyn? No, iwis, bot he that myght hase   *truly, unless/has power*
Wold myn of thare mys, and admytte thaym to grace.   *be mindful of their need*
As he in bayll is blis, I pray hym in this space,   *joy in sorrow*
In heven hye with his to purvaye us a place,   *prepare*
That we,
555   With his santys in sight,   *saints in our vision*
And his angels bright,
May com to his light.
Amen, for charité.

Explicit processus Noe   *Thus ends the pageant of Noah*
Sequitur Abraham   *Abraham follows*

ABRAHAM AND ISAAC
(from The Chester Cycle)

[DRAMATIS PERSONAE:

MESSENGER (ARMIGER)
ABRAHAM
LOTH (LOT)
MELCHISADECK, REX SALEM (KING OF SALEM)
DEUS
ISAAC
ANGELUS
EXPOSITOR (A DOCTOR)]

PLAY IV: THE BARBERS PLAYE

*Incipit Quarta Pagina qualiter reversus est a cede quatuor regum.
Occurrit rex Salim etc. equitando et Lothe; et dicat Abraham.* *

Preco dicat:		*The Messenger speaks*

[MESSENGER]

1	All peace, lordinges that bine presente,	*be here*
	and herken mee with good intente,	*listen to*
	howe Noe awaye from us hee went	
	and all his companye;	
5	and Abraham through Godes grace,	
	he is commen into this place,	
	and yee will geeve us rowme and space	*if*
	to tell you thys storye.	

Headnote: The fourth pageant begins where he has returned from the slaughter of the four kings [See Genesis 17:22]. In it appears the king of Salem [Melchisadech] and others, mounted on horses, and Lot; and Abraham speaks.

	2 This playe, forsothe, begynne shall hee	*truly*
10	in worshippe of the Trynitie	
	that yee may all here and see	*hear*
	that shalbe donne todaye.	*what*
	My name is Goobett-on-the-Greene.*	
	With you I may no longer beene.	*stay*
15	Farewell, my lordinges, all bydene	*quickly*
	for lettynge of [your] playe.	*so as not to hinder*
	Et exit	*And he leaves*

*Abraham, having restored his brother Loth into his owne place, doth
firste of all begine the play and sayth:*

ABRAHAM

	3 Ah, thou high God, graunter of grace,	
	that endinge ne begininge hase,	*who ending nor*
	I thanke thee, lorde, that thou hase	
20	todaye give mee the victorye.	*given*
	Lothe, my brother, that taken was,	
	I have restored him in this case	
	and brought him home in this place	
	through thy might and masterye.	

25	4 To worshippe thee I will now wonne,	*now begin*
	that four kynges of uncouth landes	*because of what*
	todaye hath sent into my hand,	
	and ryches with greate araye.	*along with treasures of*
	Therefore of all that I have wone	*because/received*
30	to give thee teath I will begynne,	*a tithe*
	the cyttee sonne when I come in,	*when I arrive*
	and parte with thee my praye.	*share with*

	5 Melchysedech, that here kinge is	
	and Goddes preyste allsoe iwisse,	*truly*
35	the teathe I will give him of this,	*tithe*
	as skyll is that I doe.	*reason*
	Godd that hase sende mee the vyctorye	
	of four kynges gracyously,	
	with him I praye parte will I,	*divide (the goods)*
40	the cyttie when I come to.	

Here Lothe, torninge him to his brother Abraham, doth saye:

---

13. This call for quiet by a figure named Gobett on the Green links the opening to the folk play tradition.

LOTH

6	Abraham, brother, I thanke thee	
	that this daye haste delyvered mee	
	of enimyes handes and ther postee,	*out of/power*
	and saved mee from woo.	*woe*
45	Therefore I will give teathinge	*tithes*
	of my good whille I am livinge;	*goods*
	and nowe alsoe of his sendinge	*message*
	the teath I will give alsoe.	*tithe*

*Tune venit Armiger Melchysedech ad ipsum et gratulando dicit Armiger
(Here the Messenger doth come to Melchysedech, kinge of Salem, and
rejoysinge greatly doth saye):*

KNIGHT

7	My lorde the kinge, tydinges on right	*certain tidings*
50	your hart to glade and to light—	*gladden/lighten*
	Abraham hath slayne in fight	
	four kinges since hee went.	
	Here hee will bee this ylke night,	*this very*
	and ryches enough with him dight.	*arrayed*
55	I harde him thanke God almight	
	of grace hee had him sente.	*for*

*Here Melchysedech, lookinge up to heaven, doth thanke God for
Abrahams victorye, and doth prepare himselfe to goe present Abraham.* *

MELCHYSEDECH, REX SALEM

8	Ah, blessed bee God that is but one.	
	Agaynste Abraham will I gonne	*along with*
	worshipfullye and that anonne,	*right away*
60	myne office to fulfill,	
	and presente him with bread and wyne,	
	for grace of God is him within.	
	Spede for love myne,	*Hurry*
	for this is Godes will.	

KNIGHT (cum pocula)   *with a chalice*

---

56 s.d. The Huntington ms. offers an additional stage direction: *Melchis extendens manus ad coelum*
[Melchisadech raising his hands towards heaven]. What follows echoes the consecration and
communion service in the mass.

Here the Messenger, offeringe to Melchysedeck a standinge-cuppe and bread alsoe, dothe saye:

65	9	Sir, here is wyne, withowten were,	*without doubt*
		and therto bred white and cleare	
		to present him with good chere,	
		that soe us holpenn hasse.	*who/helped*

Here Melchysedeck answeringe sayth:

MELCHISADECK

	To God I wott hee is full deare,	*know*
70	for of all thinges in his prayer	
	hee hath withowten dangere,	*reserve*
	and speciallye his grace.	

Melchysedeck, comminge unto Abraham, doth offer to him a cuppe full of wynne and bred, and sayth unto him:

	10	Abraham, welcome moste thou bee—	*greatly*
		Godes grace is fullye in thee.	
75		Blessed ever muste thou bee	
		that enimyes soe can meeke.	*humble*
		Here is bred and wyne for thy degree;	*rank*
		I have brought as thou maye see.	
		Receyve this present nowe at mee,	*from me*
80		and that I thee beeseche.	

Here Abraham, receyvinge the offeringe of Melchysedeck, dothe saye:

ABRAHAM

	11	Syr Kynge, welcome in good faye;	*faith*
		thy presente is welcome to my paye.	
		God that hath holpen mee todaye,	*helped*
		unworthye though I were,	
85		ye shall have parte of my praye	*my gain*
		that I wan sinse I wente awaye.	*have received*
		Therefore to thee that take it maye,	
		the teathe I offer here.	*tithe*

Here Abraham offereth to Melchysedeck an horse that is laden. Melchysedeck, receivinge the horse of Abraham verey gladly, doth saye:

MELCHISADECH

12 And your present, syr, take I
90   and honoure hit devoutlye,
     for much good it may signifye
     in tyme that is commynge.
     Therefore horse, harnesse, and petrye,   *jewels, ornaments*
     as falles for your dignitye,   *befits*
95   the teathe of hit takes of mee   *tithe/from me*
     and receyve here my offeringe.

Here Loth doeth offer to Melchysedeck a goodly cuppe, and sayth:

LOTH

13 And I will offer with good intente
     of such goodes as God hath mee lente
     to Melchysedeck here presente,
100   as Gods will is to bee.
     Abraham, my brother, offered hasse,   *has offered*
     and soe will I through Godes grace.
     This royall cuppe before your face
     receyve yt nowe at mee.   *from me*

Here Melchysedeck receaveth the cuppe of Loth.

MELCHYSEDECK

105 14 Syr, your offeringe welcome ys;
     and well I wott, forsoth iwys,   *know/indeed*
     that fullye Godes will yt is
     that is nowe donne today.
     Goe wee together to my cyttie;
110   and God nowe hartely thanke wee   *heartily*
     that helps us aye through his postee,   *power*
     for soe wee full well maye.

*Here they doe goe together, and Abraham dothe take the bred and wyne,
and Melchisedech the laden horse.*

EXPOSITOR (equitando)   *(riding a horse)*

15 Lordinges, what may this signifye
     I will expound yt appertly—   *openly*
115   the unlearned standinge herebye

maye knowe what this may bee.
This present, I saye veramente, *truly*
signifieth the newe testamente
that nowe is used with good intente
120 throughout all Christianitye.

16 In the owld lawe, without leasinge, *lying*
when these too good men were livinge, *two*
of beastes were there offeringe
and eke there sacramente. *also*
125 But synce Christe dyed one roode-tree, *cross*
in bred and wyne his death remember wee;
and at his laste supper our mandee *Maundy*
was his commandemente.

17 But for this thinge used should bee
130 afterwardes, as nowe done wee, *we do*
in signification—as leeve you mee— *believe me*
Melchysedeck did soe.
And teathinges-makinge, as you seene here, *tithing/saw*
of Abraham begonnen were. *by Abraham*
135 Therefore to God hee was full deare,
and soe were both too. *of the two*

18 By Abraham understand I maye
the Father of heaven, in good faye; *faith*
Melchysedecke, a pryest to his paye *in his service*
140 to minister that sacramente
that Christe ordayned the foresayde daye
in bred and wyne to honour him aye. *forever*
This signifyeth, the sooth to saye,
Melchysedeck his presente.

Here God appeareth to Abraham and saythe:

DEUS

145 19 Abraham, my servante, I saye to thee
thy helpe and thy succour will I bee. *comfort*
For thy good deede myche pleaseth mee,
I tell thee witterly. *plainly*

Here Abraham, torninge to God, saythe:

ABRAHAM

	Lord, on thinge that wouldest see,	*one*
150	that I praye after with harte full free:	
	grante mee, lorde, through thy postee	*power*
	some fruite of my bodye.	

20	I have noe chylde, fowle ne fayre,	
	save my nurrye, to bee my hayre;	*foster-child*
155	that makes mee greatly to appeare.	*suffer shame*
	One mee, lord, have mercye.	*on*

DEUS

	Naye Abraham, frend, leeve thou mee—	*believe me*
	thy nurrye thine hayre hee shall not bee;	*foster-child*
	but one sonne I shall send thee,	
160	begotten of thy bodye.	

21	Abraham, doe as I thee saye—	
	looke and tell, yf thou maye,	*say how many*
	stares standinge one the[e] straye;	*may stars shine on*
	that unpossible were.	*seems impossible*
165	Noe more shalt thou, for noe neede,	
	number of thy bodye the seede	
	that thou shalt have withowten dreede;	
	thou arte to mee soe dere.	

22	Therfore Abraham, servante free,	
170	looke that thou bee trewe to mee;	
	and here a forwarde I make with thee	*hear/covenant*
	thy seede to multiplye.	
	Soe myche folke forther shalt thou bee,	*many/father*
	kinges of this seede men shall see;	
175	and one chylde of greate degree	
	all mankynde shall forbye.	*redeem*

23	I will hethen-forward alwaye	*command henceforth*
	eyche man-chylde one the eyght daye	*on the eighth*
	bee circumsysed, as I thee saye,	
180	and thou thyselfe full soone.	
	Whosoe cyrcumsyed not ys	
	forsaken shalbe with mee iwys,	*unredeemed*
	for unobedyent that man ys.	*disobedient*
	Looke that this bee done.	

ABRAHAM

185	24	Lord, all readye in good faye.	*faith*
		Blessed bee thou ever and aye,	*ever*
		for therby knowe thou maye	*thus*
		thy folke from other men.	
		Cyrcumsysed they shalbe all	
190		anon for ought that maye befall.	*soon/anything*
		I thanke thee, lorde, thyne one thrall,	*subject*
		kneelinge one my kneene.	

EXPOSITOR

	25	Lordinges all, takys intent	*meaning*
		what betokens this commandement:	
195		this was sometyme an sacrament	*was once*
		in the ould lawe truely tane.	*taken*
		As followeth nowe verament,	*truly*
		soe was this in the owld testamente.	
		But when Christe dyed away hit went,	
200		and then beganne baptysme.	

	26	Alsoe God a promise behett us here	*made*
		to Abraham, his servant dere:	
		soe mych seede that in noe manere	*many descendents*
		nombred yt may bee,	
205		and one seede mankinde for to bye.	*redeem*
		That was Christe Jesus wytterlye,	*plainly*
		for of his kynde was our ladye,	
		and soe alsoe was hee.	

DEUS

27 Abraham, my servante Abraham!

ABRAHAM

210   Loe, lord, alreadye here I am.

DEUS

Take Isaack, thy sonne by name
that thou lovest the best of all,
and in sacryfyce offer him to mee
upon that hyll there besydes thee.

215   Abraham, I will that yt soe bee   *decree*
       for ought that maye befall.   *anything*

ABRAHAM

28 My lord, to thee is myne intent
      ever to bee obedyent.
      That sonne that thou to mee haste sent
220   offer I will to thee,
      and fulfill thy commandement
      with hartye will, as I am kent.   *taught*
      High God, lorde omnipotent,
      thy biddinge, lorde, done shalbee.

225 29 My meanye and my chyldren eycheone   *company/everyone*
      lenges at home, both all and one,   *remains*
      save Isaack, my sonne, with mee shall gonne
      to an hyll here besyde.

Here Abraham, torninge him to his sonne Isaack, sayth:

      Make thee readye, my dere darlinge,
230   for we must doe a little thinge.
      This wood doe thou on thy backe bringe;
      wee may noe lenger byde.   *remain*

30 A sworde and fyer that I will take,
      for sacrifyce mee behoves to make.   *it behooves me*
235   Godes biddinge will I not forsake,
      but ever obedyent bee.

Abraham taketh a sworde and fyer.
Here Isaack speakes to his father, taketh the bundell of stickes, and beareth after his father.

ISAACK

      Father, I all readye
      to doe your byddinge moste meekely,
      and to beare this wood full beane am I,   *obedient*
240   as ye commande mee.

ABRAHAM

31 O Isaack, my darlinge deare,
      my blessinge nowe I give thee here.

Take up this fagott with good chere,   *bundle of sticks*
and on thy backe yt bringe.
245   And fyer with us I will take.

ISAACK

Your bydding I wyll not forsake;
father, I will never slake   *slacken*
to fulfill your byddinge.

ABRAHAM

32 Nowe Isaack, sonne, goe wee our waye
250   to yonder monte, yf that wee maye.

Here they goe both to the place to doe sacrafice.

ISAACK

My dere father, I will assaye   *try*
to follow you full fayne.   *gladly*

*Abraham, beinge minded to slea his sonne, lifte us his handes to heaven
and sayth:*

ABRAHAM

O my harte will breake in three!
To here thy wordes I have pittye.   *hear*
255   As thou wilte, lorde, soe muste yt bee:
to thee I will bee beane.   *obedient*

33 Laye downe thy fagott, my owne sonne.   *sticks*

ISAACK

All readye, father; loe yt here.   *here it is*
But why make yee soe heavye chere?   *such a sad face*
260   Are ye any thinge adread?
Father, yf yt bee your will,
where is the beaste that wee shall kyll?

ABRAHAM

Therof, sonne, is none upon the hill
that I see here upon this stedde.

Isaack, fearinge leste his father will slea him, sayth:

ISAACK

265 34 Father, I am full sore afrayde
        to see you beare that drawen sworde.
        I hope for all myddylarde   *all the world*
        you will not slaye your chylde.

Abraham, comfortinge his sonne, sayth:

ABRAHAM

        Dreade thee not, my chylde. I reade   *assure you*
270   our lorde will sende of his goodheade
        some manner of beast into this fyelde,
        eyther tame or wylde.

ISAACK

  35 Father, tell mee or I goe   *ere*
        whether I shall harme or noe.

ABRAHAM

275   Ah, deare, God, that mee ys woe!
        Thou breakeste my harte in sunder.

ISAACK

        Father, tell mee of this case;
        why you your sworde drawen hase,
        and beares yt naked in this place.
280   Therof I have greate wonder.

ABRAHAM

  36 Isaack, sonne, peace, I praye thee.
        Thou breakest my harte anon in three.

ISAACK

        I praye you, father, leane nothinge from mee;   *keep*
        but tell mee what you thinke.

ABRAHAM

285   Ah, Isaack, Isaack, I muste thee kyll.

ISAACK

Alas, father ys that your wyll,
your owne chylde for to spyll   *kill*
upon thys hilles bryncke?

37 If I have trespassed in any degree,
290   with a yarde you may beate mee.   *a rod*
Put up your sworde yf your wyll bee,
for I am but a chylde.

ABRAHAM

O my deare sonne, I am sorye
to doe to thee this great anoye.   *harm*
295   Godes commandement doe must I;
his workes are aye full mylde.   *ever/merciful*

ISAACK

38 Would God my mother were here with mee!
Shee would kneele downe upon her knee,
prayeinge you, father, if yt might bee,
300   for to save my liefe.

ABRAHAM

39 O comely creature, but I thee kyll   *unless*
I greeve my God, and that full yll.   *offend*
I may not worke agaynste his wyll
but ever obedyent bee.
305   O Isaack, sonne, to thee I saye
God hase commanded mee todaye
sacryfyce—this is noe naye—
to make of thy bodye.

ISAACK

40 Is yt Godes will I shalbe slayne?

ABRAHAM

310   Yea, sonne, yt is not for to leane;   *not blameful*
    to his byddinge I will bee beane,   *be obedient*
    ever to him pleasinge.
    But that I doe this deolfull deede,   *Unless/doleful*
    my lorde will not quite mee my meede.   *pay/reward*

ISAACK

315   Marye, father, God forbydde
    but you doe your offeringe.

41 Father, at home your sonnes you shall fynde
    that you muste love by course of kynde.   *of nature*
    Be I once out of your mynde,
320   your sorrowe may sonne cease.
    But yet you must doe Godes byddinge.
    Father, tell my mother for nothinge.

Here Abraham, wringinge his handes, sayth:

ABRAHAM

For sorrowe I maye my handes wringe;
thy mother I cannot please.

325 42 O Isaak, Isaack, blessed most thow bee!
    Almoste my wytt I loose for thee.   *mind*
    The blood of thy body soe free   *so noble*
    I am full loth to sheede.

ISAACK

Father, synce you muste needes doe soe,
330   lett yt passe lightly and over goe.
    Kneelinge upon my knees too,
    your blessinge one mee spreade.   *on me*

ABRAHAM

43 My blessinge, deare sonne, give I thee,
    and thy mothers with harte soe free.
335   The blessinge of the Trinitye,
    my deare sonne, one thee light.   *on*

ISAACK

Father, I praye you hyde my eyne
that I see not the sworde soe keene.
Your strooke, father, would I not seene
340   leste I agaynst yt gryll.   *tremble*

ABRAHAM

44 My deare sonne Isaack, speake noe moare;
     thy wordes make my harte full sore.

ISAACK

O deare father, wherfore, wherfore?
Sythenn I muste needes bee dead,
345   of one thinge I would you praye.
Sythen I must dye the death todaye,
as fewe strokes as yee well maye
when yee smyte of my head.   *cut off*

ABRAHAM

45 Thy meekenes, chylde, makes mee affraye.   *disturbed*
350   My songe maye bee "Wele-Awaye".

ISAACK

O deare father, doe away, doe away
your makinge of myche mone.   *great*
Now truely, father, this talkinge
doth but make longe taryinge.
355   I praye you come of and make endinge,   *off*
and lett mee hence bee gone.

ABRAHAM

46 Come hyther, my chylde; thow art soe sweete.
     Thow must be bounden hand and feete.

Here Isaack ryseth and cometh to his father, and hee taketh him and
byndeth him and layeth him one the alter for to sacrifyce him.

ISAACK

Father, we muste noe more meete   *see each other*

360   by ought that I cane see.   *anything*
        But doe with mee then as thou will;
        I muste obey, and that is skyll,   *a distinction*
        Godes commandement to fulfill,
        for needes soe must it bee.

365 47 Upon the purpose that you have sett you,
        forsooth, father, I wyll not lett you;
        but evermore to doe your vowe
        while that ever yee maye.
        Father, greete well my brethen yonge,
370   and praye my mother of hir blessinge;
        I come no more under her winge.
        Farewell, for ever and aye.

      48 But, father, I crye you mercye
        for all that ever I have trespased to thee;
375   forgiven, father, that hit may bee
        untill domesdaye.

        ABRAHAM

      49 My deare sonne, lett bee thy mones;   *cries*
        my chylde, thow greeves mee every ones.
        Blessed bee thow, body and bones,
380   and I forgive thee here.
        Nowe, my deare sonne, here shall thow lye.
        Unto my worke nowe must I hye.   *hasten*
        I had as leeve myselfe to dye   *rather*
        as thow, my darlinge deare.

        ISAACK

385 50 Father, if yee bee to mee kynde,
        about my head a carchaffe bynde   *kerchief*
        and lett mee lightly out of your mynde,
        and soone that I were speede.   *as soon as/killed*

        ABRAHAM

        Farewell, my sweete sonne of grace.

*Here kisse him and binde the carchaffe about his head, and lett him
kneele downe and speake.*

ISAACK

390   I praye you, father, turne downe my face
a little while, while you have space,
for I am full sore adreade.

ABRAHAM

51 To doe this deede I am sorye.

ISAACK

Yea, lorde, to thee I call and crye!
395   Of my soule thow have mercye,
hartely I thee praye.

ABRAHAM

Lord, I would fayne worke thy will.   *gladly*
This yonge innocent that lieth soe still,
full loth were mee him to kyll
400   by any manner of waye.

ISAACK

52 My deare father, I thee praye,
let mee take my clothes awaye,
for sheeding blood on them todaye
at my laste endinge.

ABRAHAM

405 53 Harte, yf thow would breake in three,
thou shall never mayster mee.
I will noe longer lett for thee;   *hold back*
my God I may not greeve.

ISAACK

A mercye, father, why tarrye yee soe?
410   Smite of my head and lett mee goe.   *off*
I praye you rydd mee of my woo,   *woe*
for nowe I take my leave.

ABRAHAM

54 My sonne, my harte will breake in three
     to here thee speake such wordes to mee.
415   Jesu, one mee thow have pyttye,   *on me*
     that I have moste of mynde.   *strength of purpose*

ISAACK

     Nowe, father, I see that I shall dye.
     Almighty God in majestie,
     my soule I offer unto thee.
420   Lorde, to yt bee kynde.

Here lett Abraham take and bynde his sonne Isaack upon the aulter, and leett him make a signe as though hee would cutt of his head with the sword. Then lett the Angell come and take the sworde by the end and staye yt, sayinge:

ANGELUS

55 Abraham, my servante deare!

ABRAHAM

     Loe, lord, I am all readye here.

ANGELUS

     Laye not thy sworde in noe manere
     one Isaack, thy deare darlinge;
425   and doe to him none anoye.   *harm*
     For thou dreades God, well wott I,   *know*
     that of thy sonne hasse noe mercye   *who*
     to fulfill his byddinge.

ANGELUS SECUNDUS

56 And for his byddinge thow doest aye,   *always*
430   and sparest neyther for feare nor faye   *faith*
     to doe thy sonne to death todaye,
     Isaack to thee full deare,
     therfore God hath sent by mee in faye   *faith*
     a lambe that is both good and gaye.   *lively*
435   Loe, have him right here.

ABRAHAM

57 Ah, lorde of heaven and kinge of blysse,
 thy byddinge shall be donne iwys.   *indeed*
 Sacrifyce here mee sent ys,
 and all, lorde, through thy grace.
440 An horned wether here I see;   *sheep*
 amonge these bryers tyed is hee
 To thee offered now shall hee bee,
 anonright in this place.   *right now*

Then lett Abraham take the lambe and kyll him, and lett God saye:

DEUS

58 Abraham, by my selfe I sweare:
445 for thou hast bine obedient ayere,   *because/always*
 and spared not thy sonne to teare   *harm*
 to fulfill my byddinge,
 thou shall bee blessed that pleased mee.   *who has*
 Thy seede shall I soe multiplye
450 as starres and sande, soe many highe I   *so many I promise*
 of thy bodye comminge.   *from*

59 Of enimyes thou shalte have power,
 and thy blood alsoe in feare.   *together*
 Thow haste beene meeke and bonere   *humble/obedient*
455 to doe [as] I thee bade.
 And of all natyons, leeve now mee,   *believe me now*
 blessed evermore shalbee
 through fruyte that shall come of thee,   *from*
 and saved through thy seede.

Here the Docter saythe

EXPOSITOR

460 60 Lordinges, this significatyon
 of this deede of devotyon—
 and yee will, yee wytt mon—   *if you wish/must know*
 may torne you to myche good.
 This deede yee seene done here in this place,
465 in example of Jesus done yt was,
 that for to wynne mankinde grace
 was sacrifyced one the roode.   *on*

61   By Abraham I may understand
       the Father of heaven that cann fonde   *did undertake*
470   with his Sonnes blood to breake that bonde
       that the dyvell had brought us to.
       By Isaack understande I maye
       Jesus that was obedyent aye,   *always*
       his Fathers will to worke alwaye
475   and death for to confounde.

Here lett the Docter kneele downe and saye:

62   Such obedyence grante us, O lord,
       ever to thy moste holye word;
       that in the same wee may accorde
       as this Abraham was beyne.   *was obedient*
480   And then altogether shall wee
       that worthye kinge in heaven see,
       and dwell with him in great glorye
       for ever and ever. Amen.

Here the Messenger maketh an ende:

63   Make rowme, lordings, and give us waye,
485   and lett Balack come in and playe,
       and Balaham that well can saye,
       to tell you of prophecye.
       That lord that dyed one Good Frydaye,   *on*
       the same you all, both night and daye.
490   Farewell, my lordings, I goe my waye;
       I may noe lenger abyde.

FINIS

THE SECOND SHEPHERDS' PLAY
(from The Wakefield Cycle)

[*DRAMATIS PERSONAE:*

PASTOR 1 (Shepherd 1, Coll)
PASTOR 2 (Shepherd 2, Gib)
PASTOR 3 (Shepherd 3, Daw)
MAK
GYLL (Mak's Wife)
ANGELUS
MARY]

Incipit Alia eorundem   *Here begins the other (shepherds' play)*

[*Enter Shepherd 1*]

PASTOR 1. Lord, what these weders ar cold! And I am yll happyd.   *weather/clothed*
I am nerehande dold, so long have I nappyd;   *almost numb*
My legys thay fold, my fyngers ar chappyd.   *collapse*
It is not as I wold, for I am al lappyd   *would like/wrapped*
5   In sorow.
In stormes and tempest,
Now in the eest, now in the west,
Wo is hym has never rest
   Mydday nor morow!

10   Bot we sely husbandys that walkys on the moore,   *simple farmhands*
In fayth we ar nerehandys outt of the doore.   *almost homeless*
No wonder, as it standys, if we be poore,
For the tylthe of oure landys lyys falow as the floore,   *cultivation/ground*
   As ye ken.   *know*
15   We ar so hamyd,   *hemmed in*
Fortaxed and ramyd,   *overtaxed/beaten down*

343

We ar mayde handtamyd   *submissive*
  With thyse gentlery-men.   *By/gentry*

Thus thay refe us oure rest, oure Lady theym wary!   *rob us of/curse*
20 These men that ar lord-fest, thay cause the ploghe tary.   *bound to a lord*
  That men say is for the best, we fynde it contrary.   *That which*
  Thus ar husbandys opprest, in ponte to myscary   *farmhands/almost to losing*
    On lyfe;   *their lives*
  Thus hold thay us hunder,   *under*
25 Thus thay bryng us in blonder;   *trouble*
  It were greatte wonder
    And ever shuld we thryfe.   *If*

For may he gett a paynt slefe or a broche now-on-dayes,   *livery/badge**
Wo is hym that hym grefe or onys agane says!   *Woe/bothers/once gainsays*
30 Dar noman hym reprefe, what mastry he mays;   *Dares reprove/whatever power/wields*
  And yit may noman lefe oone word that he says—   *believe*
  No letter.   *Not a*
  He can make purveance   *a requisition*
  With boste and bragance,   *bragging*
35 And all is thrugh mantenance*
    Of men that ar gretter.   *From*

Ther shall com a swane as prowde as a po;   *swain/peacock*
He must borow my wane, my ploghe also;   *wagon*
Then I am full fane to graunt or he go.   *must be/ere*
40 Thus lyf we in payne, anger, and wo,   *live*
    By nyght and day.
  He must have if he langyd,   *what he longs for*
  If I shuld forgang it;   *Even if/give it up*
  I were better be hangyd
45   Then oones say hym nay.   *once*

It dos me good, as I walk thus by myn oone,   *myself*
Of this warld for to talk in maner of mone.   *of complaint*
To my shepe wyll I stalk, and herkyn anone,   *go*
Ther abyde on a balk, or sytt on a stone   *stay on an unplowed strip of land*
50   Full soyne;   *soon*
  For I trowe, perdé,   *trust, by God*
  Trew men if thay be,
  We gett more compané
    Or it be noyne.   *Ere/noon*

---

28. Signs of authority.
35. Maintenance: lords supporting their vassals, sometimes with abitrary power for unlawful purposes.

[Enter Shepherd 2]

55 PASTOR 2. Bensté and Dominus, what may this bemeyne?   *Bless us/mean*
    Why fares this warld thus? Oft have we not sene.
    Lord, thyse weders ar spytus, and the wyndys full kene,   *weather/cruel/sharp*
    And the frostys so hydus thay water myn eeyne—   *hideous/eyes*
        No ly.
60 Now in dry, now in wete,
    Now in snaw, now in slete,
    When my shone freys to my fete   *shoes freeze*
        It is not all esy.

    Bot as far as I ken, or yit as I go,   *know*
65 We sely wedmen dre mekyll wo;   *simple husbands suffer great*
    We have sorow then and then; it fallys oft so.   *again and again/happens*
    Sely Copyle, oure hen, both to and fro   *Simple*
        She kakyls;
    Bot begyn she to crok,   *croak*
70 To groyne or to clok,   *cluck*
    Wo is hym is oure cok,   *Woe to him who is*
        For he is in the shakyls.

    These men that ar wed have not all thare wyll;
    When they ar full hard sted, thay sygh full styll.   *very hard put/greatly*
75 God wayte thay ar led full hard and full yll;   *knows/treated*
    In bowere nor in bed thay say noght thertyll.   *can say nothing*
        This tyde   *Now*
    My parte have I fun,   *found*
    I know my lesson:
80 Wo is hym that is bun,   *bound*
        For he must abyde.   *endure*

    Bot now late in oure lyfys—a meruell to me,
    That I thynk my hart ryfys sich wonders to see;   *breaks/such wonders*
    What that destany dryfys it shuld so be—   *Whatever destiny makes*
85 Som men wyll have two wyfys, and som men thre
        In store;
    Som ar wo that has any.   *woeful/none*
    Bot so far can I: *I know*
    Wo is hym that has many,
90   For he felys sore.   *pain*

    [To the audience]
    Bot, yong men, of wowyng, for God that you boght,   *in wooing/redeemed*
    Be well war of wedyng, and thynk in youre thoght: *wary/wedding*
    "Had-I-wyst" is a thyng that servys of noght.   *"Had I known..."*

Mekyll styll mowrnyng has wedyng home broght,	*Great continual unhappiness*
95 And grefys,	
With many a sharp showre;	*pang*
For thou may cach in an owre	*find*
That shall sow the[e] full sowre	*bring/great sorrow*
As long as thou lyffys.	

100 For, as ever rede I pystyll, I have oone to my fere	*Epistle/as companion*
As sharp as thystyll, as rugh as a brere;	*rough*
She is browyd lyke a brystyll, with a sowre-loten chere;	*sour face*
Had she oones wett hyr whystyll, she couth syng full clere	*Once she is drunk*
Hyr Paternoster.	*Her Our Father*
105 She is as greatt as a whall,	*a whale*
She has a galon of gall;	
By hym that dyed for us all,	
I wald I had ryn to I had lost hir!	*wish I had run until*

PASTOR 1. God looke over the raw! Full defly ye stand.	*bless/company/deafly*
110 PASTOR 2. Yee, the dewill in thi maw, so tariand!	*stomach//for tarrying so*
Sagh thou awre of Daw?	*Saw/anything*
PASTOR 1. Yee, on a ley-land	*pasture*
Hard I hym blaw. He commys here at hand,	*Heard/blow (his horn)*
Not far.	
Stand styll.	
PASTOR 2. Qwhy?	
115 PASTOR 1. For he commys, hope I.	*I think*
PASTOR 2. He wyll make us both a ly	*tell us/lies*
Bot if we be war.	*Unless/beware*

[Enter Shepherd 3]

PASTOR 3. Crystys crosse me spede, and Sant Nycholas!	*help me*
Therof had I nede; it is wars then it was.	*worse now than*
120 Whoso couthe take hede and lett the warld pas,	*Whoever could see/world*
It is ever in drede and brekyll as glas,	*fear/brittle*
And slythys.	*it slips away*
This warld fowre never so,	*never fared so*
With meruels mo and mo—	*more*
125 Now in weyll, now in wo,	*weal*
And all thyng wrythys.	*everything shifts*

Was never syn Noe floode sich floodys seyn,	*since Noah's*
Wyndys and ranys so rude, and stormes so keyn—	*rains so violent*
Som stamerd, som stod in dowte, as I weyn.	*staggered/think*
130 Now God turne all to good! I say as I mene,	
For ponder:	*consider*

These floodys so thay drowne,
Both in feyldys and in towne,
And berys all downe;   *sweeps all away*
135   And that is a wonder.

We that walk on the nyghtys, oure catell to kepe,   *stock/guard*
We se sodan syghtys when othere men slepe.   *see apparitions*
Yit me thynk my hart lyghtys; I se shrewys pepe.   *heat leaps/rascals peeping*
Ye ar two all-wyghtys—I wyll gyf my shepe   *ghosts*
140   A turne.   *a move to another pasture*
Bot full yll have I ment;   *been speaking*
As I walk on this bent,   *heath*
I may lyghtly repent,   *quickly*
My toes if I spurne.   *stumble*

[He recognizes his friends]

145   A, syr, God you save, and master myne!
A drynk fayn wold I have, and somwhat to dyne.   *gladly/something to eat*
PASTOR 1. Crystys curs, my knave, thou art a ledyr hyne!   *lazy servant*
PASTOR 2. What, the boy lyst rave! Abyde unto syne;   *does/Wait until later*
We have mayde it.   *eaten*
150   Yll thryft on thy pate!   *Bad luck/head*
Though the shrew cam late,   *rascal*
Yit is he in state   *ready*
To dyne—if he had it.

PASTOR 3. Sich seruandys as I, that swettys and swynkys,   *Such servants/work*
155   Etys oure brede full dry, and that me forthynkys.   *Eat/bothers me*
We ar oft weytt and wery when master-men wynkys;   *wet/sleep*
Yit commys full lately both dyners and drynkys.   *very slowly*
Bot nately   *thoroughly*
Both oure dame and oure syre,
160   When we have ryn in the myre,   *run*
Thay can nyp at oure hyre,   *cut our wages*
And pay us full lately.   *late*

Bot here my trouth, master: for the fayr that ye make,   *But hear/pledge/for your pay*
I shall do therafter—wyrk as I take.   *Will I work accordingly/as I receive*
165   I shall do a lytyll, syr, and emang ever lake,   *labor a little/in between play*
For yit lay my soper never on my stomake   *supper never bothered*
In feyldys.
Wherto shuld I threpe?   *haggle*
With my staf can I lepe;
170   And men say, "Lyght chepe   *"A cheap bargain*
Letherly foryeldys."   *repays badly."*

PASTOR 1. Thou were an yll lad to ryde on wowyng   *to go courting with*
With a man that had bot lytyll of spendyng.
PASTOR 2. Peasse, boy, I bad. No more janglyng,   *Quiet, I said*
175   Or I shall make the[e] full rad, by the hevens kyng!   *an example of*
    With thy gawdys—   *With all your tricks*
Where ar oure shepe, boy?—we skorne.   *are scornful*
PASTOR 3. Sir, this same day at morne
I thaym left in the corne,
180   When thay rang lawdys.   *lauds**

Thay have pasture good, thay can not go wrong.
PASTOR 1. That is right. By the roode, thyse nyghtys ar long!   *the cross*
Yit I wold, or we yode, oone gaf us a song.   *ere we went/(that) one would give*
PASTOR 2. So I thoght as I stode, to myrth us emong.   *to amuse meanwhile*
185   PASTOR 3.   I grauntt.   *agree*
PASTOR 1. Lett me syng the tenory.   *tenor*
PASTOR 2. And I the tryble so hye.   *treble*
PASTOR 3. Then the meyne fallys to me.   *middle*
    Lett se how ye chauntt.

        [They sing]

        Tunc intrat Mak, in clamide   *Then Mak enters with a cloak*
        se super togam vestitus   *draped over his tunic*

190   MAK. Now, Lord, for thy naymes seven,* that made
                both moyn and starnes   *moon/stars*
Well mo then I can neven, thi will, Lorde, of me tharnys.   *more/name/is lacking*
I am all uneven; that moves oft my harnes.   *upset/brains*
Now wold God I were in heven, for ther wepe no barnes   *children*
    So styll.   *all the time*
195   PASTOR 1. Who is that pypys so poore?   *squeaks so poorly*
MAK. Wold God ye wyst how I foore!   *knew/fared*
Lo, a man that walkys on the moore,   *I'm a man*
    And has not all his wyll.   *all he'd like*

PASTOR 2. Mak, where has thou gone? Tell us tythyng.   *news*
200   PASTOR 3. Is he commen? Then ylkon take hede   *everyone watch/*
               to his thyng.   *possessions*

        *Et accipit clamidem ab ipso**   *And he takes his cloak*

        MAK. What! ich be a yoman, I tell you, of the kyng,   *I am a yeoman*

---

180. Early morning canonical hour.
190. Seven names of God, as in the rabbinical tradition.
200 s.d. As a precaution against Mak hiding anything underneath it.

The self and the some, sond from a greatt lordyng,   *same/messenger from*
  And sich.   *such like*
Fy on you! Goyth hence   *Go*
205 Out of my presence!
I must have reverence.   *deserve*
  Why, who be ich?   *Who do you think I am*

PASTOR 1. Why make ye it so qwaynt?* Mak, ye do wrang.   *such odd speech*
PASTOR 2. Bot, Mak, lyst ye saynt? I trow   *would you be a saint?*
                   that ye lang.   *know you long to*
210 PASTOR 3. I trow the shrew can paynt, the dewyll myght hym hang! *can pretend*
MAK. Ich shall make complaynt, and make you all to thwang   *get a flogging*
  At a worde,
And tell evyn how ye doth.   *do*
PASTOR 1. Bot, Mak, is that sothe?   *true*
215 Now take outt that Sothren tothe,   *cut out/accent*
  And sett in a torde!   *put it*

PASTOR 2. Mak, the dewill in youre ee! A stroke wold I leyne you.   *eye/give*
PASTOR 3. Mak, know ye not me? By God, I couthe teyn you.   *could hurt*
    [Admitting he knows them]
MAK. God looke you all thre! Me thoght I had sene you.   *watch over*
220 Ye ar a fare compané.
PASTOR 1.   Can ye now mene you?   *be yourself*
PASTOR 2.   Shrew, pepe!   *Troublemaker, look out*
Thus late as thou goys,   *When you go out late this way*
What wyll men suppos?   *think*
And thou has an yll noys   *bad reputation*
225 Of stelyng of shepe.   *For*

MAK. And I am trew as steyll, all men waytt;   *steel/know*
Bot a sekenes I feyll that haldys me full haytt: *makes me full ofhot*
My belly farys not weyll; it is out of astate.   *fares/shape*
PASTOR 3. Seldom lyys the dewyll dede by the gate.   *dead/roadside*
230 MAK.   Therfor
Full sore am I and yll,   *in pain*
If I stande stone-styll.   *have to stand still*
I ete not an nedyll   *ate*
  Thys moneth and more.   *month*

235 PASTOR 1. How farys thi wyff? By thi hoode, how farys she?
MAK. Lyys walteryng—by the roode—by the fyere, lo!   *She lies lounging/cross*
And a howse full of brude. She drynkys well, to[o];   *children*
Yll spede othere good that she wyll do!   *Bad luck to her*

---

208 Mak is attempting a pretentious accent from the south—"goith," "ich," "doth," etc.

    Bot sho   *she*
240 Etys as fast as she can,
    And ilk yere that commys to man   *every*
    She bryngys furth a lakan—   *babe*
        And, som yeres, two.

    Bot were I now more gracyus and rychere be far,   *even if I were*
245 I were eten outt of howse and of harbar.   *I would be*
    Yit is she a fowll dowse, if ye com nar;   *foul slut/near*
    Ther is none that trowse nor knowys a war   *no one who knows a worse*
        Then ken I.   *Than I*
    Now wyll ye se what I profer?
250 To gyf all in my cofer   *money box*
    To-morne at next to offer   *at the next chance*
        Hyr hed-maspenny.   *For her funeral donation*

    PASTOR 2. I wote so forwakyd is none in this shyre;   *think/none so tired*
    I wold slepe, if I takyd les to my hyere.   *even if I earnèd*
255 PASTOR 3. I am cold and nakyd, and wold have a fyere.
    PASTOR 1. I am wery, forrakyd, and run in the myre—   *tired/muddy*
        Wake thou!   *You stay up!*
    PASTOR 2. Nay, I wyll lyg downe by,   *lie/nearby*
    For I must slepe, truly.
260 PASTOR 3. As good a mans son was I
     As any of you.

    Bot, Mak, com heder! Betwene shall thou lyg downe.
    MAK. Then myght I lett you bedene of that ye wold rowne, *hinder/perhaps/whisper*
        No drede.   *No doubt*
265 Fro my top to my too,   *head to toe*
    Manus tuas commendo,   *Into your hands I commend*
    Poncio Pilato;   *Pontius Pilate*
        Cryst-crosse me spede!   *Christ's cross*

    *Tunc surgit, pastoribus dormientibus, et dicit**

    Now were tyme for a man that lakkys what he wold   *who lacks/wants*
270 To stalk prevely than unto a fold,   *secretly into/sheepfold*
    And neemly to wyrk than, and be not to[o] bold,   *nimbly*
    For he myght aby the bargan, if it were told   *pay for*
        At the endyng.
    Now were tyme for to reyll;   *move quickly*
275 Bot he nedys good counsell
    That fayn wold fare weyll,   *who eagerly*

---

268 s.d. He rises while the shepherds are sleeping, and says

And has bot lytyll spendyng. *money*

Bot abowte you a serkyll, as rownde as a moyn, *circle/moon*
To I have done that I wyll, tyll that it be noyn, *until/noon*
280 That ye lyg stone-styll to that I have doyne; *until I am finished*
And I shall say thertyll of good wordys a foyne: *thereto/few*
"On hight, *high*
Over youre heydys, my hand I lyft.
Outt go youre een! Fordo youre syght!" *eyes/Perish*
285 Bot yit I must make better shyft *arrangement*
And it be right. *If/will be*

Lord, what thay slepe hard! That may ye all here.
Was I never a shepard, bot now wyll I lere. *I was/learn*
If the flok be skard, yit shall I nyp nere. *scared/come near*
290 How! drawes hederward! Now mendys oure chere *this way!/changes/mood*
From sorow
A fatt shepe, I dar say,
A good flese, dar I lay. *fleece/bet*
Eft-whyte when I may, *Pay back*
295 Bot this will I borow.

[Mak steals a sheep and brings it home]

How, Gyll, art thou in? Gett us som lyght.
GYLL. Who makys sich dyn this tyme of the nyght?
I am sett for to spyn; I hope not I myght *How can I*
Ryse a penny to wyn, I shrew them on hight! *earn a penny/curse/on high*
300 So farys *Thus fares*
A huswyff that has bene *who has been*
To be rasyd thus betwene. *interrupted like this*
Here may no note be sene *no notice is taken*
For sich small charys. *chores*

305 MAK. Good wyff, open the hek! Seys thou not what I bryng? *door/See you*
GYLL. I may thole the[e] dray the snek. A, com in, my swetyng! *let/draw/bolt*
MAK. Yee, thou thar not rek of my long standyng. *pay no attention to*
GYLL. By the nakyd nek art thou lyke for to hyng. *likely to hang*
MAK.   Do way! *Get away*
310 I am worthy my mete, *food*
For in a strate can I gett *fix*
More then thay that swynke and swette *work and sweat*
All the long day.

Thus it fell to my lott, Gyll; I had sich grace.   *luck*
315 GYLL. It were a fowll blott to be hanged for the case. *would be a bad thing*
 MAK. I have skapyd, Ielott, oft as hard a glase. *escaped/Gill/often/blow*
 GYLL. "Bot so long goys the pott to the water," men says, *So long the pot goes*
  "At last
 Comys it home broken."
320 MAK. Well knowe I the token,   *omen*
  Bot let it never be spoken!   *Don't say it*
   Bot com and help fast.

 I wold he were flayn; I lyst well ete.   *skinned/I want to*
 This twelmothe was I not so fayn of oone shepe-mete. *year/glad/sheep-meal*
325 GYLL. Com thay or he be slayn, and here the shepe blete— *If they come ere/bleat*
 MAK. Then myght I be tane. That were a cold swette! *be caught/sweat*
  Go spar   *fasten*
 The gaytt-doore.
 GYLL.   Yis, Mak,
 For and thay com at thy bak—
330 MAK. Then myght I by, for all the pak,   *If*
  The dewill of the war!   *get/from them all*
              a devil of a bad time

 GYLL. A good bowrde have I spied, syn thou can none: *jest/since/know*
 Here shall we hym hyde, to thay be gone,   *till*
 In my credyll. Abyde! Lett me alone,   *my cradle*
335 And I shall lyg besyde in chylbed, and grone.
 MAK. Thou red,   *get ready*
 And I shall say thou was lyght   *delivered*
 Of a knave-childe this nyght.   *boy*
 GYLL. Now well is me day bright   *happy days*
340 That ever was I bred!   *born*

 This is a good gyse and a far-cast;   *clever device*
 Yit a woman avyse helpys at the last.   *Thus/woman's advice*
 I wote never who spyse; agane go thou fast.   *don't know/watches/return*
 MAK. Bot I com or thay ryse, els blawes a cold blast! *Unless I return ere*
345 I wyll go slepe.
  [Mak returns to the circle of shepherds]
 Yit slepys all this meneye;   *Still/company*
 And I shall go stalk prevely,   *sneak secretly*
 As it had never bene I   *As though*
  That caryed thare shepe.

350   PASTOR 1. *Resurrex a mortuus* ! Have hold my hand.   *Rise from the dead*
         *Judas carnas dominus!** I may not well stand;
         My foytt slepys, by Iesus, and I water fastand.   *foot/need water*
         I thoght that we layd us full nere Yngland.   *dreamt*
         PASTOR 2.   A, ye?
355   Lord, what I have slept weyll!   *how well I have slept*
              As fresh as an eyll,   *eel*
              As lyght I me feyll
                   As leyfe on a tre.

         PASTOR 3. Bensté be herein! So me qwakys,   *Blessings*
360   My hart is outt of skyn, whatso it makys.   *whatever causes it*
         Who makys all this dyn? So my browes blakys,   *As my brows are black*
         To the dowore wyll I wyn. Harke, felows, wakys!   *door go/wake up!*
              We were fowre—
              Se ye awre of Mak now?   *See anything*
365   PASTOR 1. We were vp or thou.   *before*
         PASTOR 2. Man, I gyf God avowe,
              Yit yede he nawre.   *went/nowhere*

         PASTOR 3. Me thoght he was lapt in a wolfe-skyn.   *dressed in*
         PASTOR 1. So ar many hapt now, namely within.   *dressed/especially*
370   PASTOR 3. When we had long napt, me thoght with a gyn   *trap*
         A fatt shepe he trapt; bot he mayde no dyn.
         PASTOR 2.   Be styll!
         Thi dreme makys the[e] woode;   *mad*
         It is bot fantom, by the roode.   *phantasm/cross*
375   PASTOR 1. Now God turne all to good,
              If it be his wyll.

                                                                                    Macrobius

         PASTOR 2. Ryse, Mak, for shame! Thou lygys right lang.   *lies*
         MAK. Now Crystys holy name be us emang!
         What is this? For Sant Jame, I may not well gang!   *go well*
380   I trow I be the same. A! my nek has lygen wrang   *lain wrong*
              Enoghe.
         Mekill thank! Syn yister-even,
         Now by Sant Stevyn,
         I was flayd with a swevyn—   *tortured/dream*
385   My hart out of sloghe!   *(leaped out) of my skin*

         I thoght Gyll began to crok and travell full sad,   *moan and labor so hard*
         Wel-ner at the fyrst cok, of a yong lad
         For to mend oure flok. Then be I never glad;   *increase*

---

351. Literally "Judas flesh lord," perhaps a mistranscription (or a parody) of *Laudes canas domino,*
"Sing praises to the Lord."

I have tow on my rok more than ever I had.*

390   A, my heede!   *head*
A house full of yong tharmes,   *bellies*
The dewill knok outt thare harnes!   *brains*
Wo is hym has many barnes,   *Woe/children*
    And therto lytyll brede.   *bread*

395 I must go home, by youre lefe, to Gyll, as I thoght.
I pray you looke my slefe, that I steyll noght;   *check my sleeve*
I am loth you to grefe, or from you take oght.   *bother/anything*
    [Goes towards home]
PASTOR 3. Go furth, yll mygtht thou chefe! Now wold I we soght,   *I want to look*
    This morne,
400 That we had all oure store.   *If we have/livestock*
PASTOR 1. Bot I will go before;
Let us mete.
PASTOR 2.   Whore?   *Where*
PASTOR 3.   At the crokyd thorne.   *thorn tree*

[The Shepherds search for their sheep; Mak arrives at his home]

MAK. Undo this doore! Who is here? How long shall I stand?
405 GYLL. Who makys sich a bere? Now walk in the wenyand!   *din/waning (moon)**
MAK. A, Gyll, what chere? It is I, Mak, youre husbande.
GYLL. Then may we se here the dewill in a bande,   *noose (i.e., Mak hanged)*
    Syr Gyle!
Lo, he commys with a lote,   *noise*
410 As he were holden in the throte.   *gagging*
I may not syt at my note   *work*
    A handlang while.   *short*

MAK. Wyll ye here what fare she makys to gett hir a glose?   *hear/excuse*
And dos noght bot lakys, and clowse hir toose.   *lay about/scratch/toes*
415 GYLL. Why, who wanders, who wakys? Who commys, who gose?
Who brewys, who bakys? What makys me thus hose?   *hoarse*
    And than
It is rewthe to beholde—   *sad*
Now in hote, now in colde,
420 Full wofull is the householde
    That wantys a woman.   *lacks*

Bot what ende has thou mayde with the hyrdys, Mak?   *shepherds*
MAK. The last worde that thay sayde when I turnyd my bak,

---

389. "I have hemp on my distaff"—*i.e.*, trouble.
405. *i.e.*, in an unlucky time.

Thay wold looke that thay hade thare shepe, all the pak.

425 I hope thay wyll nott be well payde when thay thare shepe lak,   *pleased/their/miss*
   Perdé!   *By God*
Bot howso the gam gose,   *however*
To me thay wyll suppose,   *suspect*
And make a fowll noyse,
430   And cry outt apon me.

Bot thou must do as thou hyght.   *promised*
GYLL.   I accorde me thertyll;   *consent to that*
I shall swedyll hym right in my credyll.   *swaddle*
If it were a gretter slyght, yit couthe I help tyll.   *better trick/could*
I wyll lyg downe stright. Com hap me.   *lie/cover*
MAK.   I wyll.
435 GYLL.   Behynde!
Com Coll and his maroo,   *friend*
Thay will nyp us full naroo.   *trap/tightly*
MAK. Bot I may cry "out, haroo!"   *help!*
   The shepe if thay fynde.

440 GYLL. Harken ay when thay call; thay will com onone.   *anon*
Com and make redy all, and syng by thyn oone;   *alone*
Syng "lullay" thou shall, for I must grone,
And cry outt by the wall on Mary and Iohn,
   For sore.
445 Syng "lullay" on fast
When thou heris at the last;   *you hear them*
And bot I play a fals cast,   *If I don't play a trick*
   Trust me no more.

[The Shepherds meet]
PASTOR 3. A, Coll, goode morne! Why slepys thou nott?
450 PASTOR 1. Alas, that ever was I borne! We have a fowll blott—   *bad news*
A fat wedir have we lorne.   *wether/lost*
PASTOR 3.   Mary, Godys forbott!
PASTOR 2. Who shuld do us that skorne? That were a fowll spott.   *sin*
PASTOR 1.   Som shrewe.   *wretch*
I have soght with my dogys
455 All Horbery shrogys,*   *bushes*
And of fifteen hogys   *young sheep*
   Fond I bot oone ewe.

PASTOR 3. Now trow me, if ye will—by Sant Thomas of Kent,   *Canterbury*
Ayther Mak or Gyll was at that assent.   *a party to that*

---

455. Horbery: a town near Wakefield.

460   PASTOR 1. Peasse, man, be still! I sagh when he went.   *I saw*
       Thou sklanders hym yll; thou aght to repent   *slander*
         Goode spede.   *speedily*
       PASTOR 2. Now as ever myght I the,   *thrive*
       If I shuld evyn here de,   *die*
465   I wold say it were he
         That dyd that same dede.

       PASTOR 3. Go we theder, I rede, and ryn on oure feete.   *thither/advise/run*
       Shall I never ete brede, the sothe to I wytt.   *till I know the truth*
       PASTOR 1. Nor drynk in my heede, with hym tyll I mete.   *enter my mouth*
470   PASTOR 2. I wyll rest in no stede tyll that I hym grete,   *place*
         My brothere.
       Oone I will hight: *One thing I promise*
       Tyll I se hym in sight,
       Shall I never slepe one nyght
475   Ther I do anothere.   *In the same place*

[They approach Mak's house; Mak sings while Gyll moans as if in labor]

       PASTOR 3. Will ye here how thay hak? Oure syre lyst croyne.   *sing/likes crooning*
       PASTOR 1. Hard I never none crak so clere out of toyne.   *Heard/no one/tune*
       Call on hym.
       PASTOR 2.   Mak, undo youre doore soyne!   *soon*
       MAK. Who is that spak, as it were noyne,   *noon*
480   On loft?
       Who is that, I say?
       PASTOR 3. Goode felowse, were it day.   *I wish it were*
       MAK. As far as ye may,
         Good, spekys soft,

485   Over a seke womans heede that is at maylleasse;   *who is sick*
       I had lever be dede or she had any dyseasse.   *rather/than that*
       GYLL. Go to anothere stede! I may not well qweasse;   *place/breathe*
       Ich fote that ye trede goys thorow my nese   *Each/nose*
         So hee.   *high*
490   PASTOR 1. Tell us, Mak, if ye may,
       How fare ye, I say?
       MAK. Bot ar ye in this towne to-day?
         Now how fare ye?

       Ye have ryn in the myre, and ar weytt yit;   *run/still wet*
495   I shall make you a fyre, if ye will sytt.
       A nores wold I hyre. Thynk ye on yit?   *nurse/Remember?*
       Well qwytt is my hyre—my dreme, this is itt—   *my efforts are repaid*
         A seson.   *For a season*

	I have barnes, if ye knew,	
500	Well mo then enewe;	*enough*
	Bot we must drynk as we brew,	
	And that is bot reson.	

	I wold ye dynyd or ye yode. Me thynk that ye swette.	*ate ere you go*
	PASTOR 2. Nay, nawther mendys oure mode drynke nor mette.	
505	MAK. Why, syr, alys you oght bot goode?	*ails/anything but good*
	PASTOR 3. Yee, oure shepe that we gett	*tend*
	Ar stollyn as thay yode. Oure los is grette.	*wandered*
	MAK. Syrs, drynkys!	
	Had I bene thore,	
	Som shuld have boght it full sore.	*paid for it*
510	PASTOR 1. Mary, som men trowes that ye wore,	*believe*
	And that us forthynkys.	*displeases us*

	PASTOR 2. Mak, som men trowys that it shuld be ye.	*believe*
	PASTOR 3. Ayther ye or youre spouse, so say we.	
	MAK. Now if ye have suspowes to Gill or to me,	*suspicions of*
515	Com and rype oure howse, and then may ye se	*ransack*
	Who had hir.	*took the sheep*
	If I any shepe fott,	*stole*
	Ayther cow or stott—	*or livestock*
	And Gyll, my wyfe, rose nott	
520	Here syn she lade hir—	*since she lay down*

	As I am true and lele, to God here I pray	*honest*
	That this be the fyrst mele that I shall ete this day.	
	PASTOR 1. Mak, as have I ceyll, avyse the[e], I say:	*As I hope for salvation/consider*
	He lernyd tymely to steyll that couth not say nay.*	
525	GYLL. I swelt!	*swoon*
	Outt, thefys, fro my wonys!	*house*
	Ye com to rob us for the nonys.	*no purpose*
	MAK. Here ye not how she gronys?	
	Youre hartys shuld melt.	

530	GYLL. Outt, thefys, fro my barne! Negh hym not thor!	*Don't approach him*
	MAK. Wyst ye how she had farne, youre hartys	*If you knew how she labored*
	wold be sore.	
	Ye do wrang, I you warne, that thus commys before	*who*
	To a woman that has farne—bot I say no more.	*has given birth*
	GYLL. A, my medyll!	*middle*
535	I pray to God so mylde,	
	If ever I you begyld,	

---

524. A proverb: He who couldn't say no [to himself] learned to steal quickly.

That I ete this chylde
   That lygys in this credyll.

MAK. Peasse, woman, for Godys payn, and cry not so!
540 Thou spyllys thy brane, and makys me full wo.   *You destroy your brain*
PASTOR 2. I trow oure shepe be slayn. What fynde ye two?
PASTOR 3. All wyrk we in vayn; as well may we go.
   Bot hatters!   *Bother!*
I can fynde no flesh,
545 Hard nor nesh,   *Firm or soft*
Salt nor fresh—
   Bot two tome platers.   *Except/empty platers*

Whik catell bot this, tame nor wylde,   *No livestock but this (baby)*
None, as have I blys, as lowde as he smylde.   *(None) smelled so awful*
550 GYLL. No, so God me blys, and gyf me ioy of my chylde!
PASTOR 1. We have merkyd amys; I hold us begyld.   *made a mistake*
PASTOR 2.   Syr, don.   *absolutely*
Syr—oure Lady hym save!
Is youre chyld a knave?   *boy*
555 MAK. Any lord myght hym have,
   This chyld, to his son.   *as*

When he wakyns he kyppys, that ioy is to se.   *he grabs*
PASTOR 3. In good tyme to hys hyppys, and in celé!   *happiness*
Bot who was his gossyppys so sone redé?   *godparents/soon ready*
560 MAK. So fare fall thare lyppys!   *Only good can be said*
PASTOR 1.   Hark now, a le.   *lie*
MAK.   So God thaym thank,
Parkyn, and Gybon Waller, I say,
And gentill Iohn Horne,* in good fay—   *faith*
He made all the garray—   *commotion*
565   With the greatt shank.   *long legs*

PASTOR 2. Mak, freyndys will we be, for we ar all oone.   *in accord*
MAK. We? Now I hald for me, for mendys gett I none.   *apologies*
Fare well all thre! All glad were ye gone. *[The Shepherds leave]*
PASTOR 3. Fare wordys may ther be, bot luf is ther none
570   This yere.
PASTOR 1. Gaf ye the chyld any thyng?
PASTOR 2. I trow not oone farthyng.
PASTOR 3. Fast agane will I flyng;   *quickly dash back*
   Abyde ye me there.   *Wait*

---

563. In the Wakefield *First Shepherds' Play* John Horne quarrelled with Gib.

575 Mak, take it to no grefe if I come to thi barne.   *don't be offended/child*
       MAK. Nay, thou dos me greatt reprefe, and fowll has thou farne.   *reproof/done ill*
       PASTOR 3. The child will it not grefe, that lytyll day-starne.   *not mind/star*
       Mak, with youre leyfe, let me gyf youre barne   *permission*
          Bot six pence.
580 MAK. Nay, do way! He slepys.
       PASTOR 3. Me thynk he pepys.   *looks about*
       MAK. When he wakyns he wepys.   *cries aloud*
          I pray you go hence!

       PASTOR 3. Gyf me lefe hym to kys, and lyft up the clowtt.   *cloth*
585 What the dewill is this? He has a long snowte!
       PASTOR 1. He is merkyd amys. We wate ill abowte.   *deformed/do ill to pry*
       PASTOR 2. Ill-spon weft, iwys, ay commys foull owte.*
          Ay, so! *[He recognizes the sheep]*
       He is lyke to oure shepe!
590 PASTOR 3. How, Gyb, may I pepe?
       PASTOR 1. I trow kynde will crepe
          Where it may not go.*

       PASTOR 2. This was a qwantt gawde and a far-cast: *crafty prank/clever device*
       It was a hee frawde.   *high fraud*
       PASTOR 3.   Yee, syrs, wast.   *it was*
595 Lett bren this bawde and bynd hir fast.   *Let's burn*
       A fals skawde hang at the last;   *false scold will hang*
          So shall thou.
       Wyll ye se how thay swedyll   *bound up*
       His foure feytt in the medyll?   *together*
600 Sagh I never in a credyll   *Saw*
          A hornyd lad or now.   *ere*

       MAK. Peasse, byd I. What, lett be youre fare!   *stop your din*
       I am he that hym gatt, and yond woman hym bare.   *begat/bore*
       PASTOR 1. What dewill shall he hatt, Mak? Lo, God,   *the devil/be called*
                                          Makys ayre!   *heir*
605 PASTOR 2. Lett be all that! Now God gyf hym care,   *make him sorry*
          I sagh.   *saw (the sheep)*
       GYLL. A pratty child is he
       As syttys on a wamans kne;   *woman's*
       A dyllydowne, perdé,   *darling/by God*
610   To gar a man laghe.   *make*

---

587. A proverb: Ill-spun woof always comes out badly.
591-92. A proverb: Nature will creep along even when it might not walk—i.e., evil will out.

PASTOR 3. I know hym by the eere-marke; that is a good tokyn.
MAK. I tell you, syrs, hark! Hys noyse was brokyn.   *nose*
Sythen told me a clerk that he was forspokyn.   *Afterwards/spooked*
PASTOR 1. This is a fals wark; I wold fayn be wrokyn.   *lie/revenged*
615   Gett wepyn!   *a weapon*
GYLL. He was takyn with an elfe,   *by*
I saw it myself;
When the clok stroke twelf
     Was he forshapyn.   *transformed*

620 PASTOR 2. Ye two ar well feft sam in a stede.   *suited together/place*
PASTOR 1. Syn thay manteyn thare theft, let do thaym   *defend/let's*
                         to dede.   *kill them*
MAK. If I trespas eft, gyrd of[f] my heede.   *again/cut*
With you will I be left.   *On your mercy will I be left*
PASTOR 3.   Syrs, do my reede: *take my advice*
For this trespas
625 We will nawther ban ne flyte,   *curse nor quarrel*
Fyght nor chyte,   *chide*
Bot have done as tyte,   *finish quickly*
     And cast hym in canvas.

[They toss Mak in a canvas sheet]

PASTOR 1. Lord, what I am sore, in poynt for to bryst!   *ready/burst*
630 In fayth, I may no more; therfor wyll I ryst.   *rest*
PASTOR 2. As a shepe of seven skore he weyd in my fyst.   *weighed*
For to slepe aywhore me thynk that I lyst.   *anywhere/would like*
PASTOR 3.   Now I pray you
Lyg downe on this grene.   *lie*
635 PASTOR 1. On these thefys yit I mene.   *think*
PASTOR 3. Wherto shuld ye tene?   *why/be angry*
     Do as I say you.

[They sleep]
Angelus cantat "Gloria in exelsis,"   *An Angel sings "Glory to God in the highest,"*
postea dicat: *afterwards let him say*

ANGEL. Ryse, hyrd-men heynd, for now is he borne   *gentle shepherds*
That shall take fro the feynd that Adam had lorne;   *lost*
640 That warloo to sheynd, this nyght is he borne.   *warlock to destroy*
God is made youre freynd now at this morne,
     He behestys.   *promises*
At Bedlem go se   *Bethlehem*
Ther lygys that fre   *lies/noble one*

645 In a cryb full poorely,
  Betwyx two bestys.

  PASTOR 1. This was a qwant stevyn that ever yit I hard.   *the strangest voice*
  It is a mervell to nevyn, thus to be skard.   *tell of/scared*
  PASTOR 2. Of Godys son of heuyn he spak upward.   *from on high*
650 All the wod on a levyn me thoght that he gard   *woods in light/caused*
   Appere.
  PASTOR 3. He spake of a barne   *babe*
  In Bedlem, I you warne.   *Bethlehem*
  PASTOR 1. That betokyns yond starne;
655 Let us seke hym there.

  PASTOR 2. Say, what was his song? Hard ye not how he crakyd it,   *Heard/sang*
  Thre brefes to a long?   *short notes*
  PASTOR 3.   Yee, Mary, he hakt it: *trilled*
  Was no crochett wrong, nor nothyng that lakt it.   *note/it lacked nothing*
  PASTOR 1. For to syng us emong, right as he knakt it,   *together/sang*
660 I can.   *I know how*
  PASTOR 2. Let se how ye croyne!   *croon*
  Can ye bark at the mone?   *moon*
  PASTOR 3. Hold youre tonges! Have done!
  PASTOR 1. Hark after, than.   *Follow my lead*

   [They sing]

665 PASTOR 2. To Bedlem he bad that we shuld gang;   *go*
  I am full fard that we tary to[o] lang.   *afraid*
  PASTOR 3. Be mery and not sad—of myrth is oure sang!
  Euerlastyng glad to mede may we fang,   *joy as reward/get*
   Withoutt noyse.   *fuss*
670 PASTOR 1. Hy we theder forthy,   *thither, therefore*
  If we be wete and wery,
  To that chyld and that lady;
   We have it not to lose.   *nothing*

  PASTOR 2. We fynde by the prophecy—let be youre dyn!—
675 Of Dauid and Isay and mo then I myn—   *Isaiah/more/remember*
  Thay prophecyed by clergy—that in a vyrgyn   *learnedly*
  Shuld he lyght and ly, to slokyn oure syn,   *alight/quench*
   And slake it,   *ease*
  Oure kynde, from wo;   *race*
680 For Isay sayd so:
  Ecce virgo   *Behold the virgin*
   Concipiet a chylde that is nakyd.   *will conceive*

PASTOR 3. Full glad may we be, and abyde that day   *wait for*
That lufly to se, that all myghtys may.   *lovely (one)/can do all*
685 Lord, well were me for ones and for ay,   *better/once and forever*
Myght I knele on my kne, som word for to say
    To that chylde.
Bot the angell sayd
In a cryb was he layde;
690 He was poorly arayd,
    Both mener and mylde.   *very poor*

PASTOR 1. Patryarkes that has bene, and prophetys beforne,   *earlier*
Thay desyryd to have sene this chylde that is borne.
Thay ar gone full clene; that have thay lorne.   *died/lost*
695 We shall se hym, I weyn, or it be morne,   *believe/ere*
    To tokyn.   *As a sign*
When I se hym and fele,   *touch him*
Then wote I full weyll   *well I know*
It is true as steyll   *as steel*
700   That prophetys have spokyn: *What the*

To so poore as we ar that he wold appere,   *such poor people*
Fyrst fynd, and declare by his messyngere.   *First to find (us), and then*
PASTOR 2. Go we now, let us fare; the place is us nere.
PASTOR 3. I am redy and yare; go we in fere   *eager/together*
705   To that bright.   *bright one*
Lord, if thi wylles be—
We ar lewde all thre—   *simple*
Thou grauntt us somkyns gle   *something joyful*
    To comforth thi wight.   *child*

710 PASTOR 1. Hayll, comly and clene! Hayll, yong child!   *pure*
Hayll, maker, as I meyne, of a madyn so mylde!
Thou has waryd, I weyne, the warlo so wylde: *curse/believe/warlock*
The fals gyler of teyn, now goys he begylde.   *evil beguiler of harm/goes*
    Lo, he merys,   *smiles*
715 Lo, he laghys, my swetyng!
A wel fare metyng!   *happy*
I have holden my hetyng: *kept my promise*
    Have a bob of cherys.*

PASTOR 2. Hayll, sufferan savyoure, for thou has us soght!
720 Hayll, frely foyde and floure, that all thyng has wroght!   *noble child*
Hayll, full of favoure, that made all of noght!

718-36. The gifts are symbolic. Cherries in winter=miraculous rebirth (and future suffering); the
bird=Holy Ghost (and future resurrection); the ball=earthly humanity (and future kingly orb).

Hayll! I kneyll and I cowre. A byrd have I broght
   To my barne.   *babe*
Hayll, lytyll tyne mop!   *tiny moppet*
725 Of oure crede thou art crop;   *faith/head*
   I wold drynk on thy cop,   *from your cup*
   Lytyll day-starne.

PASTOR 3. Hayll, derlyng dere, full of Godhede!
   I pray the[e] be nere when that I have nede.
730 Hayll, swete is thy chere! My hart wold blede   *face*
   To se the[e] sytt here in so poore wede,   *such shabby clothes*
     With no pennys.
   Hayll! Put furth thy dall!   *hand*
   I bryng the[e] bot a ball:
735 Have and play the[e] withall,
     And go to the tenys.   *to the lawn*

MARY. The fader of heven, God omnypotent,
   That sett all on seven, his son has he sent.   *made all/seven (days)*
   My name couth he neven, and lyght or he went.   *did he name/and he alighted ere*
740 I conceyuyd hym full even thrugh myght, as he ment;   *(God's) power/willed*
     And now is he borne.
   He kepe you fro wo!
   I shall pray hym so.
   Tell furth as ye go,   *Spread the tidings*
745   And myn on this morne.   *remember*

PASTOR 1. Fare well, lady, so fare to beholde,
With thy childe on thi kne.
PASTOR 2.   Bot he lygys full cold.
Lord, well is me! Now we go, thou behold.
PASTOR 3. Forsothe, allredy it semys to be told   *i.e., this story seems familiar*
750   Full oft.
PASTOR 1. What grace we have fun!   *found*
PASTOR 2. Com furth; now ar we won!   *redeemed*
PASTOR 3. To syng ar we bun—   *bound*
   Let take on loft!   *Let's begin on a high note (loudly)*

[They exit, singing]

Explicit pagina Pastorum   *The end of the Shepherds' play*

THE CRUCIFIXION OF CHRIST
(from The York Cycle)

[DRAMATIS PERSONAE:

JESUS
FOUR SOLDIERS (MILES 1-4)]

THE PINNERES* AND PAINTERS
Crucifixio Christi.

[Calvary]

	MILES 1. Sir knightis, take heede hydir in hie!	*now pay attention quickly*
	This dede on-dergh we may noght drawe.	*negligently/do*
	Yee wootte youreselffe als wele as I	*know/as well*
	Howe lordis and leders of owre lawe	
5	Has geven dome that this doote schall die.	*judgment/fool*
	MILES 2. Sir, alle thare counsaile wele we knawe.	
	Sen we are comen to Calvarie,	*Since*
	Latte ilke man helpe nowe as him awe.	*each/he ought*
	MILES 3. We are alle redy, loo,	
10	That forward to fullfille.	*agreement*
	MILES 4. Late here howe we schall doo,	*Let's hear what*
	And go we tyte thertille.	*quickly to it*
	MILES 1. It may nog[h]t helpe her[e] for to hone	*delay*
	If we schall any worshippe winne	*honor*
15	MILES 2. He muste be dede nedelingis by none.	*necessarily by noon*
	MILES 3. Thanne is goode time that we beginne.	*Then it's*
	MILES 4. Late dinge him doune! Than is he done;	*Let's knock/Then*
	He schall nought dere us with his dinne.	*not bother/cries*
	MILES 1. He schall be sette and lerned sone—	*put down/taught a lesson*

PINNERES: Makers of pins, nails, and pegs to fasten boards.

20   With care to him and all his kinne!   *sorrow*
      MILES 2. The foulest dede of all   *death*
      Shalle he die for his dedis.   *deeds*
      MILES 3. That menes, crosse him we schall.   *crucify him*
      MILES 4. Behalde, so right he redis.   *he counsels*

25   MILES 1. Thanne to this werke us muste take heede,
      So that oure wirking be noght wronge.
      MILES 2. None othir noote to neven is nede,   *business need be mentioned*
      But latte us haste him for to hange.   *let/crucify*
      MILES 3. And I have gone for gere, goode speede;   *quickly*
30   Bothe hammeres and nailes, large and lange.
      MILES 4. Thanne may we boldely do this dede.
      Commes on, late kille this traitoure strange.   *let's/arrant traitor*
      MILES 1. Faire might ye falle in feere,   *Good Luck to all*
      That has wrought on this wise!   *in this way*
35   MILES 2. Us nedis nought for to lere   *we need/learn*
      Suche faitoures to chastise.   *deceivers*

      MILES 3. Sen ilke a thing es right arrayed,   *Since every/is*
      The wiselier nowe wirke may we.
      MILES 4. The crosse on grounde is goodely graied,   *prepared*
40   And boorede even as it awith to be.   *bored/ought*
      MILES 1. Lokis that the ladde on lenghe be laide   *See to it*
      And made me thane unto this tree.*
      MILES 2. For alle his fare, he schalle be flaied: *boasting/tortured*
      That on assaye sone schalle ye see.   *by trial soon*
45   MILES 3 *[to Jesus]*. Come forthe, thou cursed knave!
      Thy comforte sone schall kele.   *soon/grow cold*
      MILES 4. Thine hire here schall thou have.   *wages*
      MILES 1. Walkes oon! Now wirke we wele.   *Walk on*

      JHESUS. Almighty God, my Fadir free,   *noble*
50   Late this[e] materes be made in minde: *Let these/kept*
      Thou badde that I schulde buxsome be   *willing*
      For Adam plight for to be pined.   *Adam's/tortured*
      Here to dede I obblisshe me   *death/submit myself*
      Fro that sinne for to save mankinde,   *From sin to redeem*
55   And soverainely beseke I the[e]   *above all I beseech*
      That thay for me may favoure finde;   *on my account*
      And fro the fende thame fende,   *from the fiend/defend*
      So that ther saules be saffe
      In welthe withouten ende.   *happiness*
60   I kepe nought ellis to crave.   *I desire nothing else*

---

42. An ethical dative construction: "And then fastened before me onto this cross."

MILES 1. We! Herke, sir knightis, for Mahoundis bloode! *by Mohammed's*
Of Adam-kinde is allhis thoght. *Adam's race*
MILES 2. The warlowe waxis werre than woode! *warlock/acts worse than mad*
This doulfull dede ne dredith he noght. *painful/he dreads not*
65 MILES 3. Thou schulde have minde, with maine and moode, *remember/with might*
Of wikkid werkis that thou haste wrought.
MILES 4. I hope that he hadde bene as goode *I think he'd be better*
Have sesed of sawes that he uppe sought. *to have ceased/sayings/thought*
MILES 1. Thoo sawes schall rewe him sore, *Those sayings*
70 For all his sauntering, sone! *Despite/babbling/soon*
MILES 2. Ille spede thame that him spare *Bad luck to those who*
Tille he to dede be done! *death*

MILES 3. Have done belive, boy, and make the[e] boune, *Finish quickly/obedient*
And bende thy bakke unto this tree.
75 MILES 4. Bihalde, himselffe has laide him doune,
In lenghe and breede as he schulde bee! *breadth*
MILES 1. This traitoure, here teynted of tresoune, *convicted*
Gose faste and fette him than, ye thre. *Go/fetter*
And sen he claimeth kingdome with croune, *since/crown*
80 Even as a king here have schall hee. *have (his crown)*
[The soldiers station themselves at the four ends of the cross]
MILES 2. Nowe, certis, I schall nog[h]t feyne *certainly/stop*
Or his right hande be feste. *ere/fastened*
MILES 3. The lefte hande thanne is mine.
Late see who beres him beste. *Let's/bears himself*

85 MILES 4. His limmys on lenghe than schalle I lede, *limbs/stretch*
And even unto the bore thame bringe. *bored hole bring them*
MILES 1. Unto his heede I schall take hede,
And with mine hande helpe him to hing. *hang*
MILES 2. Nowe, sen we foure schall do this dede,
90 And medill with this unthrifty thing, *meddle*
Late no man spare for special spede *Let/fail to hurry*
Tille that we have made ending.
MILES 3. This forward may not faile. *agreement must not fail*
Nowe are we right arraiede. *set*
95 MILES 4. This boy here in oure baile *knave/custody*
Shall bide full bittir brayde. *endure/torment*

[They begin to stretch Christ's limbs to the bored holes]

MILES 1. Sir knightis, saye, howe wirke we nowe?
MILES 2. Yis, certis, I hope I holde this hande. *certainly/think*
MILES 3. And to the boore I have it brought, *bored hole*
100 Full boxumly, withouten bande. *obediently, readily/without cord*

MILES 1. Strike on than, harde, for Him the[e] boght!   *Hammer on/who redeemed you*
MILES 2. Yis, here is a stubbe will stiffely stande!   *stob, or peg*[*]
Thurgth bones and senous it schall be soght.   *sinews/be struck*
This werke is wele, I will warande.   *goes well/warrant*
105   MILES 3. Saye, sir, howe do we thore?   *there*
This bargaine may not blinne.   *business/cease*
MILES 1. It failis a foote and more!   *It is short*
The senous are so gone inne.   *sinews/shrunken*

MILES 4. I hope that marke amisse be bored.   *I think/wrongly*
110   MILES 2. Than muste he bide in bittir bale.   *endure/torment*
MILES 3. In faith, it was overe-skantely scored;   *too lightly marked*
That makis it fouly for to faile.   *to fall short*
MILES 1. Why carpe ye so? Faste on a corde   *talk/Hold*
And tugge him to, by toppe and taile.   *stretch him/head and foot*
115   MILES 3. Ya, thou comaundis lightly as a lorde!   *as readily*
Come helpe to haale, with ille haile!   *haul/with bad luck to you*
MILES 1. Nowe certis, that schall I doo—   *certainly*
Full suerly as a snaile.   *surely*
MILES 3. And I schall tacche him too   *nail*
120   Full nemely with a naile.   *nimbly*

This werke will holde, that dar I heete,   *I dare promise*
For nowe are feste faste both his handis.   *fastened securely*
MILES 4. Go we all foure, thanne, to his feete;
So schall oure space be spedely spende.   *our time/best spent*
125   MILES 2. Latte see what bourde his bale might beete!   *jest/sorrow/mend*
Tharto my bakke nowe wolde I bende.
MILES 4. Owe! This werke is all unmeete.   *badly measured*
This boring muste all be amende.   *redone*
MILES 1. A, pees, man, for Mahounde!
130   Latte no man wotte that wondir;[*]   *know about/strangeness*
A roope schall rugge him doune   *yank*
If all his sinuous go asoundre.   *Even if/sinews*

MILES 2. That corde full kindely can I knitte,   *firmly/tie*
The comforte of this karle to kele.   *churl/to cool*
135   MILES 1. Feste on, thanne, faste that all be fitte.   *Hold/quickly/fit*
It is no force howe felle he feele.   *no matter how cruelly*
MILES 2. Lugge on, ye both, a litill yitt!   *Pull*
MILES 3. I schalle nought sese, as I have seele!   *cease/bliss*
MILES 4. And I schall fonde him for to hitte.   *try*
140   MILES 2. Owe, haille!   *haul*

---

102. See Psalm 22 and commentary, where Christ stretched on the cross is likened to a harp that can be "played" by Christians. Turning the peg increases the tension.
130. Such oddness—the holes all out of position.

MILES 4.   Hoo nowe! I halde it wele.   *Whoa/I think that did it*
MILES 1. Have done! Drive in that naile,   *Enough*
So that no faute be foune.   *fault be found*
MILES 4. This wirking wolde nog[h]t faile
If foure bullis here were boune.   *Even if/bound*

145   MILES 1. Ther cordis have evill encressed his paines,   *These/sorely*
Or he wer tille the booringis brought.   *Ere/to the borings (holes)*
MILES 2. Yaa, assoundir are bothe sinuous and veinis   *sinews*
On ilke a side, so have we soughte.   *each/gouged*
MILES 3. Nowe all his gaudis nothing him gaines.   *tricks gain him nothing*
150   His sauntering schall with bale be bought.   *ramblings/suffering*
MILES 4. I wille goo saye to oure soveraines
Of all this werkis howe we have wrought.   *How well we've done*
MILES 1. Nay, sirs, anothir thing
Fallis firste to you [and] me:
155   They badde we schulde him hing   *commanded/hang*
On heghte that men might see.   *high*

MILES 2. We woote wele so ther wordes wore,   *know/were*
But sir, that dede will do us dere!   *harm*
MILES 1. It may not mende for to moote more;   *It won't help to argue*
160   This harlotte muste be hanged here.   *rascal*
MILES 2. The mortaise is made fitte therfore.
MILES 3. Feste on youre fingeres than, in feere.   *Grasp with/together*
MILES 4. I wene it wolle nevere come thore!   *believe/fit there*
We foure raise it nog[h]t right, to-yere.   *won't raise it/this year*
165   MILES 1. Say, man, why carpis thou soo?   *complain*
Thy lifting was but light.   *feeble*
MILES 2. He menes, ther muste be moo   *more*
To heve him uppe on hight.   *heave/high*

MILES 3. Now certis, I hope it schall noght nede   *we don't need*
170   To calle to us more companye.
Methinke we foure schulde do this dede
And bere him to yone hille on high.
MILES 1. It muste be done, withouten drede.   *doubt*
No more, but loke ye be redy;
175   And this parte schalle I lifte, and leede.   *part (the head)/lead*
On lenghe he schalle no lenger lie.   *Prone*
Therfore nowe makis you boune: *make yourselves ready*
Late bere him to yone hill.   *Let's*
MILES 4. Thanne will I bere here doune,   *down (at the foot)*
180   And tente his tase untill.   *attend to his toes*

MILES 2. We twoo schall see tille aythir side,   *to either side (of the cross)*
For ellis this werke wille wrye all wrang.   *go awry*
MILES 3. We are redy. In Gode, sirs, abide,   *In God's name*
And late me first his fete up fang.   *let/take up*
185 MILES 2. Why tente ye so to tales this tide?   *attend/stories/time*
MILES 1. Lifte uppe!
MILES 4.   Latte see!   *Look out!*
MILES 2.   Owe! Lifte alang!   *lengthwise*
MILES 3. Fro all this harme he schulde him hide,   *protect himself*
And he war God.   *If he were*
MILES 4.   The devill him hang!
MILES 1. For grete harme have I hente: *received*
190 My schuldir is in soundre!   *has come apart*
MILES 2. And sertis I am nere schente,   *certainly/ruined*
So lange have I borne undir.   *lifted up*

MILES 3. This crosse and I in twoo muste twinne.   *part*
Ellis brekis my bakke in sondre son!   *Or else breaks/in two*
195 MILES 4. Laye downe againe, and leve youre dinne!   *leave, stop*
This dede for us will nevere be done.
MILES 1. Assaye, sirs: latte se if any ginne   *Try/let's see/device*
May helpe him uppe, withouten hone;   *delay*
For here schulde wight men worschippe winne,   *valiant men win honor*
200 And noght with gaudis al day to gone!   *tricks/play*
MILES 2. More wighter men than we   *valiant*
Full fewe, I hope, ye finde.   *Very few I think*
MILES 3. This bargaine will noght bee,   *This business won't get finished*
For certis me wantis winde.   *I am short of breath*

205 MILES 4. So wille of werke nevere we wore!   *bewildered at work/were*
I hope this carle some cautellis caste.   *I think/churl has cast a spell*
MILES 2. My bourdeyne satte me wondir soore!   *burden distressed me*
Unto the hill I might noght laste.   *I can't hold out*
MILES 1. Lifte uppe, an sone he schall be thore.   *there*
210 Therfore, feste on youre fingeres faste.   *grasp/firmly*
MILES 3. Owe, lifte!
MILES 1.   We, loo!
MILES 4.   A litill more.
MILES 2. Holde, thanne!
MILES 1.   Howe nowe?
MILES 2.   The werste is paste   *past*
MILES 3. He weyes a wikkid weght.   *weighs*
MILES 2. So may we all foure saye,
215 Or he was heved on heght   *Ere he was heaved up*
And raised in this array.   *manner*

MILES 4. He made us stande as any stones, *stand still*
So boustous was he for to bere. *bulky*
MILES 1. Nowe, raise him nemely for the nonys, *nimbly/nonce*
220 And sette him by this mortas heere, *mortice (slot to hold cross)*
And latte him falle in alle at ones; *let the cross*
For certis that paine schall have no pere. *equal*
MILES 3. Heve uppe!
MILES 4.   Latte doune so all his bones *Let (it) down*
Are asoundre, nowe on sides seere! *asunder/on all sides (at once)*
225 MILES 1. This falling was more felle *cruel*
Than all the harmes he hadde!
Nowe may a man wele telle *easily count*
The leste lith of this ladde. *smallest joint*/fellow*

MILES 3. Me thinkith this crosse will noght abide *hold firm*
230 Ne stande stille in this mo[r]teyse, yitt.
MILES 4. Att the firste time was it made overe-wide;
That makis it wave, thou may wele witte. *it loose/well know*
MILES 1. Itt schall be sette on ilke a side *wedged/every*
So that it schall no forther flite. *move*
235 Goode wegges schall we take this tide, *wedges/time*
And feste the foote; thanne is all fitte. *fasten*
MILES 2. Here are wegges arrayed *prepared*
For that, both grete and smale.
MILES 3. Where are oure hameres laide
240 That we schulde wirke withall?

MILES 4. We have them here, even atte oure hande.
MILES 2. Giffe me this wegge. I schall it in drive. *wedge*
MILES 4. Here is anodir yitt ordande. *yet another ready*
MILES 3. Do, take it me hidir belyve. *bring/hither quickly*
245 MILES 1. Laye on thanne, faste.
MILES 3.   Yis, I warrande.
I thring thame same, so motte I thrive! *knock them together*
Nowe will this crosse full stabely stande;
All if he rave, they will noght rive. *Even if he raves/won't come out*
MILES 1. [*to Jesus*]. Say, sir, howe likis thou nowe
250 This werke that we have wrought?
MILES 4. We praye youe, says us howe *tell us*
Ye fele, or fainte ye ought? *or if you're at all faint*

JESUS. Al men that walkis, by waye or strete, *walk*
Takes tente ye schalle no travaile tine! *Take heed/no labor lose*
255 Biholdes min[e] heede, min[e] handis, and my feete, *Behold*

---

228. Or, as in Psalm 22, Christ's smallest bones.

And fully feele nowe, or ye fine, *reflect/ere you finish*
If any mourning may be meete *matched with*
Or mischeve mesured unto mine. *misfortune compared*
My Fadir, that alle bales may bete, *sorrows/remedy*
260 Forgiffis thes men that dois me pine. *Forgive/cause me pain*
What thay wirke wotte they noght. *They know not what they do*
Therfore, my Fadir, I crave,
Latte nevere ther sinnys be sought, *Let/their/examined*
But see ther saules to save. *see that you save*

265 MILES 1. We, harke! He jangelis like a jay. *chatters*
MILES 2. Me thinke he pratis liek a py. *prates/magpie*
MILES 3. He has ben doand all this day, *doing this*
And made grete meving of mercy. *movings to*
MILES 4. Es this the same that gune us say *Is/who did say to us*
270 That he was Goddis sone almighty?
MILES 1. Therfore he felis full felle affraye, *Because of that/very cruel torment*
And demyd this day for to die. *(is) condemned*
MILES 2. *Vah! qui destruis templum . . .* *
MILES 3. His sawes wer so, certaine. *sayings/like that*
275 MILES 4. And, sirs, he saide to some
He might raise it againe.

MILES 1. To mustir that he hadde no might, *manage that*
For all the kautelles that he couthe kaste; *Despite/tricks/could devise*
All if he wer in worde so wight, *Even if/strong*
280 For all his force, nowe is he feste. *fast bound*
Als Pilate demed, is done and dight; *As/decreed/dealt with*
Therfore I rede that we go reste. *counsel*
MILES 2. This race mon be rehersed right, *action must be reported*
Thurgh the worlde, both este and weste.
285 MILES 3. Yaa, late him hinge here stille, *let him hang*
And make mowes on the mone. *faces at the moon*
MILES 4. Thanne may we wende at wille. *Thus we can go*
MILES 1. Nay, goode sirs, noght so sone. *not*

For certis us nedis anodir note: *one more thing*
290 This kirtill wolde I of you crave. *cloak*
MILES 2. Nay, nay, sir, we will loke by lotte *we'll see by lottery*
Whilke of us foure fallis it to have. *Which/it falls to*
MILES 3. I rede we drawe cutte for this coote— *advise/lots/coat*
Loo, se howe sone—alle sidis to save. *everyone is pleased*
295 MILES 4. The schorte cute schall winne, that wele ye woote, *well/know*

---

273. *Hah! You who would destroy the temple. . .* [See Mark 15:29 and Matthew 27:40: "Ah, thou that destroyest the temple, and buildest it in three days, save thyself, and come down from the cross."]

Whedir itt falle to knight or knave.   *Whether*
MILES 1. Felowes, ye thar noght flyte,   *need not quarrel*
For this mantell is mine.
MILES 2. Goo we thanne hense, tyte.   *quickly*
300   This travaile here we tine.   *labor/lose*

      [Exeunt]

Suggestions for Further Reading

ANTHOLOGIES:

Chief Pre-Shakespearean Dramas, ed. by Joseph Q. Adams. Boston: Houghton Mifflin, 1924.

Medieval Drama, ed. by David Bevington. Boston: Houghton Mifflin, 1975.

Everyman and Medieval Miracle Plays, ed. by Arthur C. Cawley. London: J.M. Dent & Sons, 1956 (rev. 1974).

EDITIONS

The Chester Mystery Cycle, 2 Vols., ed. by R.M. Lumiansky and David Mills. Vol. 1, EETS, Supplementary Series 3. London: Oxford University Press, 1974; vol. II, EETS, Supplementary Series 9. London: Oxford University Press, 1986.

The Late Medieval Religious Plays of Bodleian MSS. Digby 133 and E Museo 160, intro. by Donald C. Baker, John L. Murphy, and Louis B. Hall, Jr. Oxford: EETS, Extra Series 283. London: Oxford University Press, 1982.

The Macro Plays, ed. by Mark Eccles. EETS, Original Series 262. London: Oxford University Press, 1969.

The Mirror of Everyman's Salvation: A Prose Translation of the Original Everyman, trans by John Conley, Guido deBaere, H.J.C. Schaap, and W.H. Toppen. Atlantic Highlands, New Jersey: Humanities Press, 1985.

The N-Town Play, 2 Vols., ed. by Stephen Spector. EETS, Supplementary Series 11 and 12. Oxford: Oxford University Press, 1991.

373

Non-Cycle Plays and Fragments, ed. by Norman Davis. EETS, Supplementary Text 1. London: Oxford University Press, 1970.

The Summoning of Everyman, ed. by Geoffrey Cooper and Christopher Wortham. Nedlands, Western Australia: University of Western Australia Press, 1980.

The Towneley Plays, ed. by. George England and Alfred W. Pollard. EETS, Extra Series 71. London: Oxford University Press, 1897.

The Wakefield Pageants in the Townley Cycle, ed. by A.C. Cawley. Manchester: Manchester University Press, 1958 (repr. 1971).

The Play of Wisdom, ed. by Milla Riggio. New York: AMS Press, 1992.

York Plays, ed. by Lucy Toulmin Smith. Oxford: Clarendon Press, 1885.

The York Plays, ed. by Richard Beadle. York: York Medieval Texts, 1982.

FACSIMILES

The Chester Mystery Cycle: A Facsimile of British Library MS Harley 2124, intro. by David Mills. Leeds Texts and Monographs, *Medieval Drama Facsimiles VIII,* gen. eds. Stanley Ellis and Peter Meredith. Leeds: The University of Leeds School of English, 1984.

The Chester Mystery Cycle: A Facsimile of MS Bodley 175, intro. by R.M. Lumiansky and David Mills. Leeds Texts and Monographs, *Medieval Drama Facsimiles I,* gen. ed. A.C. Cawley. Leeds: The University of Leeds School of English, 1973.

The Chester Mystery Cycle: A Reduced Facsimile of Huntington Library MS 2, intro. by R.M. Lumiansky and David Mills. Leeds Texts and Monographs, *Medieval Drama Facsimiles VI,* gen. eds. A.C. Cawley and Stanley Ellis. Leeds: The University of Leeds School of English, 1980.

The Digby Plays: Facsimiles of the Plays in Bodley MSS Digby 133 and e Museo 160, intro. D.C. Baker and John L. Murphy. Leeds Texts and Monographs, *Medieval Drama Facsimiles III,* gen. eds. A.C. Cawley and Stanley Ellis. Leeds: The University of Leeds School of English, 1976.

The Macro Plays: The Castle of Perseverance, Wisdom, Mankind, A Facsimile Edition with Facing Transcriptions, ed. by David Bevington. The Folger Facsimiles Manuscript Series, 1. Washington D.C.: The Folger Shakespeare Library, 1972.

The N-Town Plays, ed. by Peter Meredith and Stanley J. Kahrl. Leeds: Leeds Texts and Monographs, 1977.

Non-Cycle Plays and The Winchester Dialogues: Facsimiles of Plays and Dramatic Fragments in Various Manuscripts and the Dialogues in Winchester College MS 33, intro. by Norman Davis. Leeds Texts and Monographs, *Medieval Drama Facsimiles V,* gen. eds. A.C. Cawley and Stanley Ellis. Leeds: The University of Leeds School of English, 1979.

The Towneley Cycle: A Facsimile of Huntington MS HM 1, ed. by A.C. Cawley and Martin Stevens. San Marino, California: The Huntington Library, 1976.

The York Play: A Facsimile of British Library MS Additional 35290, ed. by Richard Beadle and Peter Meredith, and a note on the music by Richard Rastall. Leeds: The University of Leeds School of English, 1983.

BIBLIOGRAPHIES

Berger, Sidney E. *Medieval English Drama: An Annotated Bibliography of Recent Criticism* (Garland Medieval Bibliographies, Vol. 2; Garland Reference Library, Vol. 956). New York: Garland Publishing, 1990.

Blackstone, Mary. "A Survey and Annotated Bibliography of Records Research and Performance History Relating to Early British Drama and Minstrelsy for 1984-8." *Records of Early English Drama Newsletter,* Vol. 15, Nos. 1 and 2 (1990).

Lancashire, Ian. *Dramatic Texts and Records of Britain: A Chronological Topography to 1558.* Toronto: University of Toronto Press, 1984. See also his bibliographical articles appearing in *Records of Early English Drama Newsletter,* 1976-84.

Stratman, Carl J. *Bibliography of Medieval Drama,* 2 Vols., 2nd. ed. New York: Frederick Ungar, 1972.

White, D. Jerry. *Early English Drama, Everyman to 1580: A Reference Guide.* New York: G.K. Hall, 1986.

RECORDS OF EARLY ENGLISH DRAMA

Records of Early English Drama: Cambridge, 2 Vols., ed. by Alan Nelson. Toronto: Records of Early English Drama, University of Toronto Press, 1989.

Records of Early English Drama: Chester, ed. by Lawrence M. Clopper. Toronto: Records of Early English Drama, University of Toronto Press, 1979.

Records of Early English Drama: Norwich 1540-1642, ed. by David Galloway. Toronto: Records of Early English Drama, University of Toronto Press, 1984.

Records of Early English Drama: York, 2 Vols., ed. by Alexandra Johnston and Margaret Rogerson. Toronto: Records of Early English Drama, University of Toronto Press, 1978.

CRITICAL STUDIES

Axton, Richard. *European Drama of the Early Middle Ages*. London: Hutchinson University Library, 1974.

Baker, Donald C. "The Drama: Learning and Unlearning," in *Fifteenth-Century Studies: Recent Essays,* 189-214. Ed. by Robert F. Yeager. Hamden, Conn.: Archon Books, 1984.

_____. "The Date of *Mankind,*" *Philological Quarterly,* vol. 42 (1963), 90-91.

_____. "When is a Text a Play?" in *Contexts for Early English Drama,* 20-40. Ed. by Marianne G. Briscoe and John C. Coldewey. Bloomington, Indiana: Indiana University Press, 1989.

Beckwith, Sarah. "Ritual, Church and Theatre: Medieval Dramas of the Sacramental Body" in *Culture and History 1350-1600,* 65-89. Ed. by David Aers. Detroit: Wayne State University Press, 1992.

Bevington, David. *From Mankind to Marlowe*. Cambridge, Mass.: Harvard University Press, 1962.

_____. *Tudor Drama and Politics*. Cambridge, Mass.: Harvard University Press, 1968

Boas, F.S. *University Drama in the Tudor Age*. London: Oxford University Press, 1914.

Briscoe, Marianne G. and John C. Coldewey, eds. *Contexts for Early English Drama*. Bloomington, Indiana: Indiana University Press, 1989.

Brody, Alan. *The English Mummers and Their Plays*. Philadelphia: University of Pennsylvania Press, 1970.

Cawley, Arthur C. *The Wakefield Pageants in the Towneley Cycle*. Manchester, Manchester University Press, 1958.

Chambers, E.K. *The Elizabethan Stage*. 4 Vols. Oxford: Oxford University Press, 1923.

_____. *The English Folk-Play*. London: Oxford University Press, 1933.

_____. *The Mediaeval Stage*. 2 Vols. London: Oxford University Press, 1903.

Clopper, Lawrence. *"Miracula* and the *Treatise of Miraclis Pleyinge,"* Speculum: A *Journal of Medieval Studies,* vol. 65.4 (1990), 878-905.

Coldewey, John C. "The Digby Plays and the Chelmsford Records," *Research Opportunities in Renaissance Drama,* vol. 18 (1975), 103-21.

_____. "Some Economic Aspects of the Late Medieval Drama," in *Contexts for Early English Drama,* 77-102. Ed. by Marianne G. Briscoe and John C. Coldewey. Bloomington, Indiana: Indiana University Press, 1989.

Craig, Hardin. *English Religious Drama of the Middle Ages*. London: Oxford University Press, 1955.

Craik, T.W. *The Tudor Interlude*. Leicester: Leicester University Press, 1967.

Davenport, W.A. *Fifteenth Century English Drama: The Early Moral Plays and Their Literary Relations*. Cambridge: D.S. Brewer, 1982.

Diller, Hans Jürgen. *The Middle English Mystery Play: A Study in Dramatic Speech and Form*. Cambridge: Cambridge University Press, 1992.

Enders, Jody. *Rhetoric and the Origins of Medieval Drama*. Cornell University Press, 1992.

Fifield, Merle. "The Use of Doubling and Extras in *Wisdom,"* Ball State University *Forum,* vol. 6 (1965), 65-8.

Flannigan, C. Clifford. "The Roman Rite and the Origins of the Liturgical Drama," *University of Toronto Quarterly,* vol. XLIII.3 (1974), 263-83.

Gardiner, Harold C. *Mysteries End: An Investigation of the Last Days of the Medieval Religious Stage*. New Haven: Yale University Press, 1947.

Gash, Anthony. "Carnival against Lent: The Ambivalence of Medieval Drama," in *Medieval Literature: Criticism, Ideology and History,* 74-98. Ed. by David Aers. New York: St. Martin's Press, 1986.

Gibson, Gail Macmurray. "Bury St. Edmunds, Lydgate, and the *N-Town Cycle,"* in *Speculum: A Journal of Medieval Studies,* vol. 56.1 (1981), 56-90.

_____. *The Theater of Devotion: East Anglian Drama and Society in the Late Middle Ages*. Chicago: University of Chicago Press, 1989.

Hardison, O.B. *Christian Rite and Christian Drama in the Middle Ages*. Baltimore, MD: Johns Hopkins University Press, 1965.

Hummelen, W.M.H. "The Drama of the Dutch Rhetoricians," in Donald Gilman, ed., *Everyman and Company: Essays on the Theme and Structure of the European Moral Play*. New York: AMS Press, 1989.

James, Mervyn. "Ritual, Drama and Social Body in the Late Medieval English Town," in *Society, Politics and Culture: Studies in Early Modern England*, 16-47. Cambridge: Cambridge University Press, 1986.

Kahrl, Stanley J. *Traditions of Medieval English Drama*. London: Hutchinson University Library, 1974.

King, Pamela. "Spacial Semantics and the Medieval Theatre," *The Theatrical Space*. (Themes in Drama, Vol. 9). Cambridge: Cambridge University Press, 1987, 45-58.

Kolve, V.A. *The Play Called Corpus Christi*. Stanford, California: Stanford University Press, 1966.

Lumianski, R.M., and David Mills. *The Chester Mystery Cycle: Essays and Documents*. Chapel Hill and London: University of North Carolina Press, 1983.

Nelson, Alan. *The Medieval English Stage: Corpus Christi Pageants and Plays*. Chicago: University of Chicago Press, 1974.

_____, and Jerome Taylor, eds. *Medieval English Drama*. Chicago: University of Chicago Press, 1972.

Neuss, Paula, ed. *Aspects of Early English Drama*. Cambridge: D.S. Brewer, 1983.

Potter, Robert. *The English Morality Play*. London: Routledge and Kegan Paul, 1975.

Prosser, Eleanor. *Drama and Religion in the English Mystery Plays*. Palo Alto, CA: Stanford University Press, 1961.

Richardson, Christine, and Jackie Johnston. *Medieval Drama*. New York: St. Martin's Press, 1991.

Riggio, Milla. *The Wisdom Symposium*. New York: AMS Press, 1986.

Righter, Anne. *Shakespeare and the Idea of the Play*. London: Chatto and Windus, 1962.

Smart, W.K. *Some English and Latin Sources and Parallels for the Morality of Wisdom*. Menasha, Wisconsin: G. Banta Publishing, 1912.

Southern, Richard. *The Medieval Theatre in the Round: A Study of the Staging of the Castle of Perseverance, and Related Matters*. London: Faber and Faber, 1957.

Stevens, Martin. *Four Middle English Mystery Cycles*. Princeton: Princeton University Press, 1988.

Streitman, Elsa. "The Middle Dutch *Elckerlijc* and the English *Everyman*," *Medium Aevum* 52.1 (1983), 111-14.

Travis, Peter. "Affective Criticism, the Pilgrimage of Reading, and Medieval English Literature," in *Medieval Texts and Contemporary Readers*, 201-15. Ed. by Laurie Finke and Martin Shichtman. Ithaca, NY: Cornell University Press, 1987.

_____. *Dramatic Design in the Chester Cycle*. Chicago: University of Chicago Press, 1982.

Tydeman, William. *The Theatre in the Middle Ages*. Cambridge: Cambridge University Press, 1978.

Wickham, Glynne. *Early English Stages*. 2 Vols. in 3. London: Oxford University Press, 1959-72.

_____. *The Medieval Theatre*. London: Weidenfeld and Nicolson, 1974.

Womack, Peter. "Imagining Communities: Theatres and the English Nation in the Sixteenth Century," in *Culture and History 1350-1600*, 91-145. Ed. by David Aers. Detroit: Wayne State University Press, 1992.

Woolf, Rosemary. *The English Mystery Plays*. Berkeley: California University Press, 1972.

Young, Karl. *The Drama of the Medieval Church*. 2 Vols. London: Oxford University Press, 1933.